Mindfull Ideograms

What do you see?

The Crone-Beauty Illusion
Depending on which feature you take to be the eye, you will see the profile of a toothless old woman, or a girl with a choker, her face almost averted.

Mindfull Ideograms

*Crazy Times . . .
    Crazy Ideas*

David Beebe

Introduction by Bruce Ario

 Lily Pad Publishing

Edina, Minnesota

MINDFULL IDEOGRAMS: CRAZY TIMES ... CRAZY IDEAS © copyright 2009 by David Beebe. All rights reserved. No part of this book may be reproduced in any form whatsoever, by photography or xerography or by any other means, by broadcast or transmission, by translation into any kind of language, nor by recording electronically or otherwise, without permission in writing from the author, except by a reviewer, who may quote brief passages in critical articles or reviews.

ISBN 10: 1-59298-278-6
ISBN 13: 978-1-59298-278-3

Printed in the United States of America
First Printing: April 2009
13 12 11 10 09   6 5 4 3 2 1

Cover and interior design by Clay Schotzko

 Lily Pad Publishing

Lily Pad Publishing is an imprint of
Beaver's Pond Press
7104 Ohms Lane
Edina, MN 55439-2129
(952) 829-8818

Dedicated to

Mom and Dad and Brother
Donna and Dana
Annie Herring and Sheila Walsh
The Tasks Unlimited Training Center
and
The Coffee Gallery

EPIGRAPH

Suppose one of you has a friend and goes to him in the middle of the night to say, 'My friend, lend me three loaves, because a friend of mine on his travels has just arrived at my house and I have nothing to offer him'; and the man answers from inside the house, 'Do not bother me. The door is bolted now, and my children and I are in bed; I cannot get up to give it you.' I tell you, if the man does not get up and give it him for friendship's sake, persistence will be enough to make him get up and give his friend all he wants.

There was a judge in a certain town who had neither fear of God nor respect for man. In the same town there was a widow who kept on coming to him and saying, 'I want justice from you against my enemy!' For a long time he refused, but at last he said to himself, 'Maybe I have neither fear of God nor respect for man, but since she keeps pestering me I must give this widow her just rights, or she will persist in coming and worry me to death.'

FACE OF GOD

As I pressed my way upon the road, I noticed the night was coming.

I would walk all night. I knew that.

As I walked I felt a presence, then a pressure, finally the weight of a great force bearing down upon me. I staggered, but I pressed on.

The force became concretized into a great rock upon my back. Again I staggered, but I pressed on into the night.

The sky of the night came alive with thunder and flashes of lightning. Hammer blows rained down upon the rock upon my back. Receiving the blows I lurched, but I carried on.

When morning came, when the sky was blue and the sun shone again, I shifted the burden from my back. Placing the rock on the ground and looking to where the hammer blows had fallen, I saw before me the sculpted, face of God.

TABLE OF CONTENTS

PREFACE xiii

INTRODUCTION xv

I. STORIES 1

  ✓ 1. RANSOM IN TELLUS 2

  2. OLD POSSUM'S PRACTICAL CAT 19

  3. MENTAL SUICIDE 39

  ✓ 4. CRYSTALL, AND CLEAR 54

  5. OH-PUN THE BUY-BULL 57

  6. THE DESCENT OF THE GODS 63

  7. GODOT 69

  ✓ 8. THE WIND BARRIER 76

  9. ...THE SHADOW KNOWS 79

  10. MURDER! 84

  11. DEATH 90

  12. RAGING BULL 100

  13. RESIGNATION 104

  14. DECKED OUT AND DECKED 110

  15. A FAILURE, IN TWO PARTS 120

  16. RACCOON TO KING FOUR 125

  17. SKIT SEE ACT ONE: SEEIN' TWO .. 132

  18. SHADOW 138

  19. ONCE WHEN I WAS UNHAPPY 140

20. STILL LIFE: A GLIMPSE OF
    MANY APPLES. 143
21. INCARNATIONS 146
22. LIGHT 147
23. TWENTY-FOUR HOUR RESTAURANT . 148
24. MINI-FEST-OH!. 149

II. ESSAYS 151
   1. REFLECTIONS ON ACUTE PSYCHOSIS 152
   2. THERE AND BACK AGAIN
      ANOTHER HOBBIT TAKES A TRIP. 157
   3. SHAMANISM AND PSYCHOSIS. 160
   4. ONE DAY, ON MY WAY TO JAIL 168
   5. A MORE REFLECTIVE PEACE NOW 173
   6. SCHIZOPHRENIA DANGER AND
      OPPORTUNITY 181
   ✓ 7. NOTES ON PSYCHOSIS. 193
   – 8. THE STRUGGLE FOR "EXISTENCE" 218
   9. A "SECULAR" SOCIETY? 224
   – 10. – FOR FLOYD – GAMBLING ON GOD . . 230
   11. SYMBOLIC CONSCIOUSNESS 235
   12. MEMORY AND MEANING 238
   13. "I" AND "IT". 242
   14. THREE LETTERS ON DEATH. 245
   15. MYSTERY RELIGION 259

(handwritten margin note: "homilies" / "sermons")

16. AUTOBIOGRAPHICAL SKETCH UPON
    EMBARKING ON CAREER AS
    MADMAN/ARTIST 266

III. POEMS 271
   1. CHRISTPOEM 272
   2. LOVE 273
   3. LOVE AND DEATH 275
   4. FUNERAL HOUSE 276
   5. HORROR SHOW 278
   6. THE MAN WAS SPEEDING 279
   7. COSMIC MAN 280
   8. (EGGS ARE FOR EASTER) 281
   9. 5/24/77 282
  10. 6/2/77 283

PREFACE

The first half of this book is short stories exhibiting psychosis. These documents are far simpler than the experience but they are authentic.

We have a text.

The second half of this book is essays which seek to understand psychosis. I create intellectual frameworks for understanding psychosis.

We have an interpretation.

∼

Psychosis is only one part of schizophrenia. Psychosis represents the "positive" symptoms—hallucinations, delusions, and major thought disorder. Schizophrenia also has "negative" symptoms—anhedonia, anergy, amotivation, and isolation. When people living with schizophrenia are "well" (free of positive symptoms), they are usually still experiencing negative symptoms. Psychosis "burns one out"—leaving the person devastated. There are whole lives one no longer needs to live. It takes a long time to rebuild the personality. One can begin again, but it takes time.

∼

Nothing in this book is to be construed as an argument for not taking your pills. Pills are effective and psychosis should be avoided at all costs. But if—despite your best efforts—psychosis does happen, one can learn from it. This book is about learning from psychosis.

In order to learn from psychosis one must be sane. Only after psychosis is over can one look back and learn. While actively psychotic one has no insight. With the exception of

"Ransom in Tellus" (a manic monologue) all short stories in this book were written while perfectly sane.

Anti-psychotic medication creates new possibilities in mental health. I am convinced that without Lithium and Navane, and then Clozaril and Zyprexa, I would be lost on the farther shore. But medication makes the return trip possible. I can then effectively communicate what I saw on the farther shore. Not only myself, but thousands of others, are recovering and can tell their stories.

—David Beebe
January 1, 2009

INTRODUCTION

Ever wonder what that uncle who spent time on the psych ward was really thinking? Read *Mindful Ideograms* and get an idea. David tells us what it's like to be that uncle when the author gives a rare candid insight into psychosis.

"The fundamental conflict in human development," the character Peter says, "is the struggle between the conscious and the unconscious." The book is an attempt to define the two. Of course David had different names for it, including the cognitive versus the conditioned, but there are always two sides to the coin. While characters in what David calls his "crazy stories" spend their time in their unconscious mind, they are always being confronted by those from the conscious world. Whether it's a doctor or a fellow student or a police officer, the main character is constantly running into opposing forces. We half wonder if the conflict is really necessary and why these characters are being opposed. Instead, why people won't listen to them.

David's characters skillfully eave one foot in reality and the other foot out in the fantasies of the unconscious mind. The characters make sense, albeit not in the sense the straight world is looking for, and they are undaunted when shown conflicting truths. Ransom or Peter, the two main characters, turn sessions with the mental health teams upside down. There's method in the madness. This is not to say his mental breaks are half-blown. They are full breaks from reality. His characters face the illness head-on, almost welcoming the challenge of it. There are flirtations with the law, numerous dialogues with psychiatrists, and critical moments with fellow students all of which could stop the character; however, they don't. The author creates the perfect psychotic world. The reader can forget it's psychosis and not a very alluring creation by David. His characters shirk straight life struggles during the illness, refusing to budge on their craziness.

There are many attempts by those outside the illness to alleviate the psychosis of the characters, but the characters will not have any of it. They will take their meds, but that only slows them down a little. The characters are on a journey they can't get off of, and perhaps don't want to get off of. They seem to be totally absorbed in their experiences.

When Ransom or Peter are up against the wall, they use double talk or crazy babble to confuse the medical team. Harvard becomes Half-Yard or sparrow becomes Spare-O. It's as though they use the language to throw up their own walls in the face of the doctor or others. Psycho-babble is very effective at pitting a psychotic mind against any intruding forces. It's like saying, "I can still joke. I'm O.K." or "I can still belittle your knowledge with my word play." Words are a powerful weapon, and what are often used by the more successful psychotics. The less successful can turn violent.

David's characters remain likeable. They're fairly innocuous, and highly intelligent. They've pitted their minds against the world if not creating a new one, and "a new one" can mean both their minds and the world. They will take you on a journey, and you will really feel you're going somewhere. Whether they're taking off their clothes to be close to God, or sculpturing toiletries, they are making a statement about the human condition. Maybe they have a key to a new way, and the doctors have it all wrong. Whatever it is, it's powerful.

David's characters are searching but not for traditional things like security or wealth. It's more a search for their next thought which always seems one step out of their reach.

There's an attachment to the illness that causes them to fly high, making them not even want to have the next thought which could be defeat for them. For now they're on a mental rampage because they have insight that others don't, or it might be those brown eyes of Ransom that others can't penetrate.

Always present is the nod and wink as to what the main character is up to as if we already know, but we don't, so the author tells us. His stories are descriptions of the characters' activities which shed light on the characters' mental state of mind. In the background we have Harvard College and psych wards, but always the idiosyncratic activities of the main characters front and center.

When a reader is reading about mental illness, he's always trying to understand it through his own lens. David ties in the psychotic episodes with the physical landscape. His characters seem bound to the reality of the material world—they haven't escaped everything. David renders descriptions of the weather, the buildings, and other people as if there is no question of their reality. The psychosis comes in how his characters try to manipulate or interpret reality, and his characters always prevail. In their world, they are the winners.

"You see, I am disturbed that there are not real scientists left anymore, persons prepared to truly experiment, with their own lives if necessary." David's characters are doing just that—experimenting—at a high cost to their health. There's something they're after and it's elusive, but possibly not impossible. They've entered the world of the unconscious mind and left no bread crumbs to find their way back to reality. They will return to reality when they've accomplished their mission.

"The other world need not be an end in itself. Rather it may be a means to an end. The journey to the center of the mind need not be for the purpose of making a permanent home there. The journey to the center of the mind may be for the purpose of securing some required object, attaining some missing experience, solving some perplexing problem, bearing fully in mind that one will return home with the prize."

David's short stories describe psychosis; his essays explain it.

"One 'de-realizes' the present and enters the purely potential. The 'purely potential' is the realm of death." "Death is the final unknowable." David's pull towards death is equal to his pull towards psychosis. Aware of the power of both, he stands up to defend them. He is a voice in the wilderness pointing out; "Meaning cannot be sold in the market place and is thus neglected."

"I am suggesting that the psychotic is not even attempting to speak 'rational-empirical-materialism,' he has adopted a different cognitive mode and is pursuing another kind of knowledge altogether."

David views psychosis like a kite that's been cut loose and is flying wildly through the sky. Free of the string, the kite can really do what it's been meant to do all along.

David is a shaman. "The individual may not wish to become a shaman and may resist the call but the community belief is that such resistance can only lead to misfortune or death. The individual must eventually present himself to a practicing shaman for teaching, training, and ceremonial initiation—whether the individual likes it or not. The decision does not belong to the individual—the gods have decided."

David has found advantage in his illness. "Yet I feel I have been well rewarded by my illness." He made a decision to shun the life of an elitist as offered up to him at Harvard. Instead he chose the road of a psychotic traveler (even though it's never perfectly clear that it was a choice, and more like an acceptance). Now he must defend himself.

Mindful Ideograms is a book that anyone who has been psychotic would be proud to have written. It's similar to a young man who has gone into battle. It's not really his choice, but as long as he's in war, he will fight. David defends the experience to the point of showing its necessity for happening.

The human mind is a miraculous thing. David shows us how miraculous it can be. Einstein said we only use about 10% of our brain. David is trying to dip into the other 90%. It's not only in David's head though. He can explain it to others, as he does in the book, and he shows us the path to what he's learned.

The uncle we had, the one with psychosis, really couldn't or wouldn't talk to us about it. We wondered what he was thinking. What motivated him? After reading *Mindful Ideograms* we will have a better idea.

David has written a wondrous work on mental illness. He explains schizophrenia as only a person who has experienced it could. In his stories, essays, and poems, we can get to know and like a character like one of which David has created. It's not an illness to bear; it's a free opportunity to go to the other side. *Mindful Ideograms* stands next to great works in literature in which authors told their story.

—Bruce Ario

STORIES

You will listen and listen again, but not understand, see and see again, but not perceive.

For the heart of this nation has grown coarse.

Who has believed our report?

RANSOM IN TELLUS

Second Beginnings

My name *is* Elwin Ransom: Granted I am an impatient—oh so impatient—at a mental institution, but my only complaint is that they don't have an obstetrics division at *this* kind of hospital. I have headaches which are labor pains. I want to be delivered, I want to deliver—a new mind. I want to give birth to a new mode of consciousness.

I've come to see my keeper, as a friend. I tell him bits and pieces from my life, and he thinks he understands, devising a diagnostic category. But his eyes are that shade of blue that can never see through a brown-eyed type like me.

I have something to tell him now, which is *my* only secret. You see, he wants to know my number, so that he can place it on my forehead or in the palm of my hand or write the number in my chart. But my only secret is that what he wishes most, can never be done. My name is written on a white stone and what that name is—only God and I know.

But my name is Ransom, and I have paid the price.

Ransom, tell-us, where have you been?

I am a nonstudent at a noncollege, nongraduating in non-June. I half been attending Half-Yard University but I dwell at the Radical Cliff. This is my non-thesis. But my Commencement is indeed taking place.

I take the lone ranger approach to human existence. I have a traveling fellowship in life, where three months stay in one place is too long. I come in, I do what I can, absorb what I can, contribute what I can, and then I leave. But now I am in one place for more than a short while. I have found a hospital and a home. And thus the Deep See diver is about to surface, but first he must decompress, I am decompressing the density of my head. Ideas are compacted in me—condensed, pressed together: I am decompressing the density of my head.

I even caught a case of the bends the other day, while decompressing. I reacted physically to my medication and I could not straighten up to walk. I walked with my limbs twisted in various contorted positions, I caught a case of the bends while decompressing.

My cigarettes tell the story as well as any arbitrary set of cymbals I might use for sounding off with. I began by smoking Tarry-tons because I was waiting my fate, weighting my fate. When the work of weighting, waiting, was finished, when my fate was heavy but I was waitless, I smoked Done-hills.

Then I got tired of waiting for Godot so I went off to find him. And this is what I found: a search. It was fun so I began smoking Larks.

Eves were the most difficult cigarette to smoke—a guaranteed negative reaction every time I asked for them. I needed Eves for the eve-ning, the balancing out of internal male and female, but people in business think that I am what I want, they identify me with what I'm asking for. When I ask to buy Eves everyone thinks I'm a cigarette, everyone thinks I'm a fag. But that's only what I asked for.

Besides, I was only eves-dropping on certain conversations persons regularly have with themselves, but that bugs the hell out of most people.

When I need a rest, from the search for Godot, I go back, way back to smoke those old Old Golds. Kools are good (there are many souls on ice), but now I enjoy a New-port (for the Deep See diver, decompressing).

This paper, my non-thesis, is in fact an open letter to Professor Quoin, a marvelously good logician. Quoin keys lock the type into a letter press. Logic locks communication into place. But what logic will serve my purpose now? Nonetheless, communication is set free by the discipline and control it maintains. I will make a new logic.

The content of my cortex is multivalent. I am decompressing the density of my head. My head is compacted, intense, tense: I have been in the past, tense, I am in the present, tense, but I do not wish to be in the future, tense. So I will tell you what I can.

Ransom, tell-us, where have you been?

First Beginnings
When I was small I learned to read reading mythology. Edict Hamilton's *Mythology* issued to me the laws of being. Now that I'm tall, or almost, I am learning to write writing mythology. But while I read Collective Myth while small, now tall I write personal myth, or rather, personalized myth. I have made a myth my own myth.

I have gone to that place in my mind where there is no distinguishing myth and reality so that the myth I write is as real to me as the rocks and trees which I might otherwise describe. On the other hand I have memories and perceptions of ordinary physical objects, real things, that are more mysterious to me than the myths I know. I have seen the world afresh and crystal clear, luminous and radiant, as it was at the Beginning, is now, if I could only see, and ever shall be—for those granted Vision.

My own personal myth is that of Pursue-us and Medusa's head.

Ransom, tell-us, where have you been?

I first wanted to be a philosopher and not a mythologizer. I wanted to be a philosopher with great yearning but I did not know what philosophers thought about. I did not know what the questions were, to the extent that in August of my fourteenth year I spent eight days and seven nights reading *A History of Western Philosophy*. I read those eight days in order to find out what a philosopher thought constituted a question. But their questions were not my questions, they had been talking to each other and to nobody else for too long. I thought of my own questions. The Guns of August.

It took time, however. Still two years later I met Ino Choyce, a very nice girl from New York City who seemed to spend far too much of her time looking enormously contemplative. I would watch her and ask, "Ino, Ino, what are you thinking about?" And Ino would look up surprised and ask, "David, don't you know?" But I didn't know.

That same summer I got into T.S. Cooccoon and entered terrible darkness. I learned that the world may be divided into perceptual and conceptual realities. We do not see what we think is there (the categories, the mental constructs), we only think we see what we think is there. Our models of reality, our frameworks, our maps and schematics, do not exist in the same way a chair does. Thus we do not see atoms not because they are too small but because they are too abstract. While some things may not be seen at a given time , some things, intrinsically, can never be seen. The loss of faith in the scientific method was shattering enough to a would-be physicist, but my whole universe collapsed when I realized it was of my making and not an unshakable given.

I began to read *The Waste Land*.

Freshman Year

As a freshman I began a pattern, continued to this day. I work mindlessly for a semester, but at the end of that semester

I spend my time drawing all the loose ends from four months mindless effort into a pattern.

The other part of the pattern may not seem happy but it is fruitful as well. After three semesters in school, I spend one in the hospital. The intellectual integration at the end of a semester is not wholly sufficient. I need total psychic integration, where thought becomes experience which is lived. A psychosis pulls the lines of personal impact from three semesters effort into place.

As a freshman in college I read D.H. Lawrence on sons and lovers, sons and mothers. New women entered my life and they were different and I developed the theory of the Maternal Presence which was with me and supported me and perhaps surrounded me.

I discovered the receptive and the feminine inside in Lao Tzu. I explored "actionless activity" in a 55 page paper on Taoism. Discovering my true feelings and flowing with them was The Way, while a freshman.

However, I encountered obstacles and I disintegrated during the second semester of freshman year. I could not decide whether I wanted good grades or a good education from four years of college. I had always been a gladiatorial Achiever. School had taught me only competition ,without quarter, struggling to be the biggest bit of ferment in the culture dish. I wanted now to learn not what would win me a prize but what would prepare me to meet the world competently.

But "value-free" education was ruled by the dollar and prestige and prizes and I was confused and disappointed so I flew kites down by the Child's River and watched the water go by.

I might have flunked out, seeking desperately to leave without knowing how, but my freshman year ended abortively when the "whole world" stopped, or, rather, the Students *struck* the University. A reality reacted to its own abstraction.

Sophomore Year

As a sophomore I thought about many things.

I discovered the third "I" of wisdom. I learned that "I am that I am." And ye shall be as gods. And the truth shall set you free.

In social psychology I was taught that I am me, I am myself as a Social Psychological Identity. But how could "I" be an SPI? I have choice, I have options, I am that I am. I need no pictures of myself to live up to. I need no mirrors with which to prove to myself that I'm here.

My picture of me is not a gull free over the ocean. It is no picture at all.

And I thought about motivation. Everyone tells me that there are things that I need and that that is what keeps me going. Everyone tells me that we have cars in order to go to the gas station with them. Sure, there are different kinds of gas stations: one where I buy food, and one where I buy sex, and one where I buy affiliation, and one where I buy power and one where I buy achievement. There are many different kinds of gas. But its all only gas, and supposedly I own a car in order to go to a gas station.

I discovered that *acting is its own justification*, done for its own sake. There was no alternative: as I examined each "reason" for acting, individually, I found each one, individually, insufficient for so much as getting out of bed in the morning. There was nothing I wanted to do so much as I wanted to do something.

And I examined time and found it not three but one. Not a past, a present, and a future, but an ever expanding present, a growing memory. Time passing by is the startling realization that one can remember more now than one did before.

The present is indeed a gift. I have analyzed the present as the interplay of fields of color and fields of depth, each field insufficient by itself, but the two working together to create visual image.

I have broken down the motion picture of my mind and looked at my experience frame by tiny frame, in order to see what reel-ly is, and the present stops at mysterious borders, and is indeed a gift.

I questioned my fear of death as a sophomore, and I realized that my fear was a fear and an idea. *I* was not afraid to die, *me* was afraid to die, me, the picture, that horrible portrait that it is so tempting to struggle to preserve.

The First Death

Finally, early in the second semester of my sophomore year, I met and slew my Medusa. I approached her while me was invisible, while me was flying backwards, while me looked back over my shoulder using the mirror which was the inside of my shield. I cut off her head, that ugly head that no one can face directly, with vipers for her hair. I glimpsed in a mirror, in a glass darkly, what cannot be seen face to face. I severed the head which turns all before it into stone. I have kept it as my trophy and have learned to use it. I went Deep See diving for the first time, as a novice, and I found a sunken treasure.

As I sink down my fate, my psyche, becomes weighted and appears before me. Remember: "Fate and temperament are two words for one and the same concept." At these times the contents of my psyche are turned to stone, my fate appears before me in the form of material objects. These material objects are the symbolic, yet physical, representations of the ideas and feelings within me. They come pouring out of me as I turn Medusa's head within my soul, and I then practice magic, I manipulate these symbol-objects as they appear in order to control my descent and subsequent ascent.

At the First Death I went to my own Funeral. I sought to humiliate myself totally, to completely destroy my false dignity. I lay myself down naked in my dormitory lounge and became Catatonic. All those attending my Funeral came to present to me the Reasons for Living. They talked, and they coaxed, and much that was said was reassuring. But I was determined to complete my own Funeral.

One man told me I was lying in a fine meadow, that the trees were trembling in a gentle wind, and that the grass was growing tall around me. He told me that I was lying (in a fine meadow) but I knew that he was lying (about a fine meadow).

A policeman came to speak directly: "Look, son, what have you been doing, drugs or something? Wake up, boy, I'm tough, you're tough." But I didn't "wake up."

The doctor at the University Health Service was astounded, for never in his professional career had he seen a Classical Catatonic! He raved about his discovery and the brilliant professional opportunity.

I certainly never "woke up" for him.

But he did argue with me, silent though I was. He said, "David, if you don't wake up we'll have to send you to a Mental Hospital!" I admitted to myself that this was a frightening prospect—never having been to one before. But I had to follow my funeral procession through to the Grave, and it was certainly not very funny.

I *had* to, but I *had* to by choice. This is important to me: that others realize that I *chose* my fate. *I* had to press *my* point through to the logical conclusion. *I must realize the knowledge to be gained by the experience.* I went to the place of knowledge: to McClaim's Hospital.

And the hospital was hell indeed. I had died and gone to hell. But more importantly I was obsessed by what I could not see—the blind spot in my vision, the direct view of the sun, the far side of the moon. Thus, I realize, the ego cannot see the self and I must come to know what I cannot see.

I was transferred out of hell to a friendly hospital and there made my recovery.

Junior Year

The next year, as a junior at Courier House, I began to study what might be supposed to have happened to me the previous year as a sophomore. I wrote a paper on schizophrenia analyzing the various respectable psychogenic theories. In the final analysis I found them insufficient. The illness was not pure pathology, it had a growing edge, it was a disease peculiarly able to yield its meaning. No psychogenic theory acknowledged the element of vision in psychosis.

Yet I was unsure of myself and fearful. I fled into Hard-Headedness. I became a busyness man and figured everything in terms of dollars and sense. I planned great functions at the Catering Agency and I helped to build buildings and drive trucks. My efforts were in vain, because then I became a senior.

Senior Year and the Second Death

At Courier House (that was the medium, this is the message) at the Radical Cliff, I executed The Great Escape from The Time Machine. The ego lives in time, always becoming, always striving for aggrandizement, always desiring to puff itself up.

The Self, on the other hand, is timeless, living in eternity, always complete in itself and sufficient to itself.

I hatched a plot to kill time, to bring about the End of Time, to remove myself from the ego to the Self.

But first I had to PREPARE FOR UNIQUE EVENTS. There are theories of perceptual similarity (this is Professor Quoin's view) which hold that an event cannot be perceived unless it is perceptually similar to some other event or set of events—and on and on in infinite regression. This is the perspective of science, which deals with regularity and pattern, repetition and replication. But religion is frequently concerned with the unique, the once only, the miracle, the conversion experience, and I wrote papers speculating on what a unique event would look like if it took place. Once I was prepared, they certainly began to happen.

You see, I am disturbed that there are not real scientists left anymore, persons prepared to truly experiment, with their own lives if necessary. We have become squeamish when it comes to Our Own Lives. We can read and think many bizarre things, but we no longer replace word with deed, and act out our ideas, in order to *see* what happens.

I became a Doorman at Quoin Key House at Half-Yard: I held the stare way door open for two hours—or was it an our and a half, a half our seems to be missing—while the elevator was broken, stuck between floors somewhere in the shaft. My friends put a sign—not a concept—on the door to the elevator, announcing the malfunction of said vehicle. All passersby were questioned as to the meaning of this stop sign, not a concept. (It seems that the pragmatics of human communication tie us down to the particular, arbitrary symbols we choose to communicate our meanings. But are these arbitrary symbols really so arbitrary? The words we choose for very different meanings are often the same word. There are resonances of deeper meaning in the similarity of various tones. Synonyms and homonyms may contain a world of concealed communication. It is this world, the world where I pull the words from the tones, the sword from the stone, the world where King Author is vindicated, that intrigues me intensely. Thus I write poems that are to be scene and not herd, for that extra dimension of meaning to come through. I call these poems "Metaphysic 'I'." I cannot consider co-incidences of sound accidental.) When the Seventh Seal was broken, when the UNIQUE EVENTS began, when I held the door open at Quoin Key House, the earth stood still about the time of half an our. Then I closed the door, and I went with Forlorna Causekey to her room in Quoin Key House, and I asked (her, but not her) for One Kiss for All Time. I recovered the other half of an "our."

The next day I stayed in Courier House to play a game of hearts. But the game was disturbing to those who played, because each hand in the game seemed to play itself: we had all seen this before. And the cards controlled the players and the rules of the game contained us, and no one could break free. But we played on, and I was always losing, but "me", as the player on my left called himself, kept winning, until in the fourteenth hand I broke hearts, I broke with the Queen of Hearts, and me took it all in—the jack, the queen, and all the hearts. And all of us who had been waiting for the predetermined game to end, knew that it had ended then, when I broke hearts with the Queen of Hearts and me took it all in. We had watched this game of hearts that played itself out for too long, we had all scene it before, so the game ended when I broke hearts.

I left Barbara, my girlfriend, as well, as I could.

After the game of hearts, I met Anti-Leaven and Anti Leaven was changed, because he knew I was changed. He saw clearly that HIERONYMO was MAD AGAINE, and he thought, "While then Ile fit you." But the seed was sown, the yeast was in the bread, and there was no way the bread would not rise. But Anti Leaven became "the Proteus of the Human Intellect," and he tried to change forms keeping pace with me. But the intellect cannot keep pace with symbolic consciousness. Anti did his best to understand my changes, while never actually accepting them. But I disliked Proteus as Analyst.

We discussed how he noes and I new.

I began to wait for the New Life. I began to bail out from the Old Life. I bailed out like a pilot from a plane that is going to crash. I bailed out like a sailor who must keep his ship from sinking. I bailed out like a prisoner.who would rot in jail unless bailed out. I through out the material and symbolic representatives of the Old Order. I through out material belongings which I would not need in the Promised Land, in the New Life. I sold my books at a benefit, I through out papers and pencils and nicknacks. I through out clothes and candles and incense. I made an offering of debris and smoke to the Trashman—the Trashman Cometh. I got rid of Baal, the False God of the Old Testament. Tote that Bale!

Yet, while waiting for the New Life, I had time to relax and make friends. I made more new friends and saw more old friends than at any time in my life. I played volleyball and cards to pass the time, back and forth, as in my hands, waiting, to be waitless. I had said all I had to say. Time had ended, the apocalypse was now, the Eschaton was realized, I had no purpose, no point, I was simply living, living simply, knowing that New Things would arrive.

The problem was my habit of ordering, which got quite out of hand. I bustled about cleaning up after myself, picking things up, putting things in order. I was undoubtedly compulsive: I was the lone arranger. It appeared that the lone arranger had to pick up after himself—to cover his tracks—more than it appeared that he wanted to.

By the time I was brought to McClaim's for the second time I had no money and no I.D. left in the world—my resources were depleted, I had become no-man, Nemo. And I could blow in any direction that the wind blew, right along with the wind, unhurt.

Myths

The wind blew from Greece again, it blew me back to the Gorgon's rock, over the 0-shun, but returning it passed And-Drama-Da's rock as well, where She was guarded by the See Monster.

You see, it all took place two years before in a different galaxy, the one nearest the Milky Way, Andromeda. Two years before I had been through a death, the First Death, and I had seen it all before, like in the deterministic game of hearts. But I had a chance to return, this time already possessing my weapon, the Medusa's head, which is also my Fire that burns but does not consume, the fire of the Burning Bush which lights the darkness ("I am that I am") and this is the same that I stole as Prometheus, two years before.

Ransom, Tellus, where have you been?

I have paid the price. I will inherit the thrown-ness and the white stone with the unnameable name and the unspeakable number. I am the bright mourning star and the root of David and the lion of Judah. Ransom, Tellus, where have you been? Aye, Eye, I, have seen the light.

I returned as an experienced Deep See diver, Captain Nemo, not that experience makes it any easier. For *that* trip is always a new thing, no matter how many times it is made. Casting a cold eye on life, on death, the hoarse man passed by. Down, down, deep in his Deep See dive, the horseman drove down on a see-horse. Past, many things from the past, he drove down to where he was before at the First Death.

Before I had died for myself and my own questions. The Second Death was a death for others, to discover that others were there. Carrion, Carrion, Love is coming. When could I return from this terrible trip to the Other galaxy?

Only at that time that I exposed the lie, the lie that goes on and on for so long, the Lie that we love each other. Only when I had discovered the truth, the truth that goes on forever, the Truth that we love each other, could I return. Only when I was again, in a new sense, naked and exposed and shivering, once more in the crucible in which the personality is remade, could I return. I had to go very far away from myself and from other people in order to allow this Metamorphosis to take place, in order to change *that* Falsehood into *this* Truth. Only having completely separated myself could I *know* that I cared and that others cared as well.

Only when DAN (that is me) YELLS IN THE LIE-ON'S DEN could I return. Only when Dan yells, when he can see no more aloneness, suffer no more loneliness, tolerate no more separation, when he *must* care, could I return. The horseman need no longer pass by, the lone arranger can stop, and the Deep See diver will sink no more, when Dan yells.

This was the second temptation. At the first I chose knowledge and left behind love. I left the Garden of Eden and went to the land of Not, which is the land of Cain for those who know and whose sin is knowledge, where knowledge is not that of the Value of a Human Life.

I have established a double residence: I walk with one foot on the Land and one foot on the See, and the See has become as a glass ball, a glass onion which I am slowly peeling: This is the See of Glass: Trans-parents.

(I speak as the man with a two-edged sword for a tongue, and I speak many languages, talk many tongues. This is the Great Dance: "If I could say what I mean, I wouldn't have to dance it"—with words! This is the Great Drama: the Great Play—on words!)

Trans-parents? Really? Maybe I have a problem with my father. Maybe the problem is simply Edible, and I could consume it, and it would taste sweet in my mouth—but bitter in my stomach. Is the sense of the cosmic Thrown really such nonsense? Are we crazy people not allowed to be Existential? Maybe it was my mother...she was human.

I have not decided yet whether Oedipus is myth or complex—it seems to make no difference. I have not decided yet whether Perseus is myth or complex—it seems to make no difference. I have *gone* to that place in my mind where there is no distinguishing myth and memory, myth and reality. My autobiography is fiction.

Those who have read *Perelandra* know that the Fixed I-Land is strictly forbidden, and that one must blow with the winds of the Wholly Ghost, the Totally Irreal. And puns are not jokes. One must be a philologist in professing.

New Beginnings

How are we to understand these UNIQUE EVENTS, these bits and pieces from my life, which I have tolled?

First, Love was born: the See Monster has been slain, and another person is free. (Serena, Serena was *there* when she had to be, and remained, and I love her, as I do others. I can write now, because there are others, and my thoughts are not only for me, but are written, and I have something to say, for no man is an island.)

And I have learned of the great web of ideas, that knowledge is seemless, and that you can always get *there* from here. The mind is a fertile field of vast interconnections, and one idea leads to another, inevitably, irretrievably. One can begin at any point and move to any other following the natural currants. There is much to be berried in the mind. And the Passed is always a Good Buy.

Should we consider all this a "psychotic brake" and reduce the matter and take none of it at face value? Is all to be attributed to problems with father, mother, brother, Barbara, Serena...

To imagine "precipitating causes and underlying factors," to refuse to take the experience for what it is, to suggest that it stands for something else, is to place the cart before the horse, the heart before the course.

I prepared for the New Life before I knew what it held in store. The *rewards* for my effort are my interpersonal realizations: this was not the cause of my course, my path, it was the end of the road. I cannot deny these matters I have been concerned with. They are no screen, no cheap facade. They are the "cause" of my course, the reasons for my effort, and the personal realizations are the fruit of that effort: confuse not fruit for root.

Two years ago I found courage like the cowardly lion once did, and a mind like the straw man once did: but this year I have been the tin man and I had to find a heart and thus I set a new course: once more no one could stop me as I pushed into my soul, because I had courage and a mind.

Ransom, Tellus, where have you been?

I am the Wizard of As, the Wizard of As If, the wizard of metaphor (which I prefer to leave unlabeled, as a concession to natural esthetic). I have followed the yellow brick road of jokes and puns to deep within me. You come, too.

I now have virgin paper, brand new, clean paper on which to write. I can write my story afresh, on virgin paper. I have staged the Tai Ping (ty-ping) Revolution, the revolution of Great Peace, for me, if not for others.

Perhaps I shall develop A LITTLE PATIENCE.

OLD POSSUM'S PRACTICAL CAT

Peter was suspended in air, clinging to, climbing up, a ladder constructed from half inch copper tubing. The ladder leaned against nothing, was supported by nothing, and outside the narrow beam of light directed down from above, was surrounded by darkness and empty space. Each rung of the ladder was connected to the frame by a perfect plumber's T-joint, and Peter had no idea how long he had been climbing. But the top of the ladder was in sight, connected though it was to nothing. Two feet above the top of the ladder was the floodlight, the narrow beam from which illuminated Peter's ascent. Peter would climb to the top, put one hand on that radiant eye, then climb down the other side. Ten more rungs to the top of this ladder...

A mechanical "Chuunk" and then music interrupted Peter's self-contained fantasy:

> I'm fixing a hole, where the rain comes in,
> And stops my mind from wandering,
> Where it will go ...

The radio-alarm clock had triggered.

Peter opened his eyes...and reached for his glasses: the rounded gold wire-rims of an "intellectual" (plumbing clerk).

I'm fixing a hole.

Peter focused his sleepy eyes and ears and mind on the clock-radio across from his bed. The music continued:

> It really doesn't matter,
> If I'm wrong, I'm right.
> Where I belong, I'm right!
> Where I belong!

The digits on the clock read 7:01 a.m., as they always did at the moment the clock sounded.

Carving a niche, building a space...where I belong!

7:01: rise, wash face and arms, brush teeth. 7:15: dress. 7:25: out the back door to the busstop. No breakfast.

"Not that today," thought Peter. The days seemed weighted spheres, which always settled with these few morning moments at the bottom.

"Bag it until 7:10," closing his eyes, returning his head to the pillow but not removing his glasses.

Earl. Earl, damn Earl. Smart Earl. Hostile Earl. Crazy Earl.

Earl the churl. Plumber Earl. Bummer Earl.

Today I may make contact.

It really doesn't matter ...

(Because)

I'm fixing a hole.

Peter rose and turned off the radio-alarm. He went on into the bathroom (Earl's domain was bathrooms, but this one belonged to Peter).

Once Peter had prepared for each day carefully. He had reserved forty-five minutes to himself each morning, before and not including breakfast, and he had always eaten breakfast. His ceremony had included a long hot shower, with shampoo, followed by a thorough toweling. A meticulous shave. An extended brushing of the teeth. A brushing and combing of the hair. Fresh clothes.

Today Peter made no such effort. He had made no such effort for over a year—since his nervous breakdown. Today, as had become usual, he entered the daystream without fanfare. Up and out. *Not*: up—one, two—out (one, two). Peter had become less rigid ... or lost his discipline.

Back in his room, after dressing (old clothes, but fresh underwear), Peter collected his tools. The tools of his trade. His recently adopted vocation.

Burglar._ Second story man. Safe-cracker.

Sure, second story. The other story. Subtext. Potential.

Latency., Make it real. The story that might be tolled, might have been tolled, ringing in my ears, wringing out the truth. The toll: the price to pay ...

Do I dare? And, do I dare?

Ha.

What will the spider do, suspend its operations? Will the weevil delay?

The burglar will steal a piece of Earl's mind, steal his peace of mind.

Peter gathered four carefully clipped paperback book covers, several carefully copied quotations, and a selection of Tarot cards from his desk top. He placed these items inside his copy of Bernard Fall's account of the siege of Dienbienphu, and thrust the volume with contents into his green book bag.

As if a magic lantern cast the nerves in patterns on a screen.

Peter refused to take his copy of *Absalom, Absalom*—his introduction to violent American men and the dominated family with their "crack regiment" mentality.

In true Sutpen fashion Earl had constructed a twenty-two room house (five bathrooms and a lavatory in every bedroom) on four hundred acres of choice farm and woodland. There with Earl lived sons (and plumbers) John (28) and Judas (23). Sons and plumbers Esau (32) and Jacob (30) were married and lived nearby. (The four daughters of Earl and Esther were married and had scattered.) All four sons worked in the plumbing shop for Earl.

"Tools" and book bag. Ready for the day.
Tears of rage,
Tears of grief.
Why must I always
be the thief?
Downstairs to the kitchen. Peter's mother and father had already left for work. Donning his jacket, Peter stepped out into the bracing early May morning. Friday, May 3, 1974. The last day of a difficult week (the clerk work had been easy). Little sleep, little to eat, much anxiety and rumination.

These with a thousand small deliberations protract the profit of their chilled delirium, excite the membrane, when the sense has cooled, with pungent sauces, multiply variety in a wilderness of mirrors.

Peter felt alive! Challenge! Excitement!
Conquer anhedonia by having an head on ya.
At the corner Peter noticed that, as usual, his bus was parked several blocks down the street. The driver, as usual, was in the service station taking a piss.

Some people were enormously dependable.

The bus driver arrived. Peter boarded, took his seat.
I like Ike. Earl, I mean.
Peter reviewed what he knew about Earl.
Who is that mask man, anyway?
Earl had been orphaned at the age of two and had been brought up by various relatives. At fifty-seven years of age, Earl was preverbal. Or, Peter had come to suspect, Earl was postverbal. Earl spoke rarely, and his words were anti-climactic. Signs, gestures, facial expressions mediated between self and other, between self and God, no doubt. Bits of broken ritual—these adumbrated a full communication.

Signed, but spoke no word.

Earl did not want to talk. He wanted to dominate. To crush. To insult. To destroy. Perhaps he only wanted to control.

And this he did very effectively, with the tools at his disposal, and because of those tools.

In the shop (and on the farm) one could not talk to Earl, though perhaps one could petition him with words. A conversation, though—implying mutuality, give and take, reciprocity—would constitute a threat. *No* mutuality, *no* give and take, *no* reciprocity—all attempts at such relation were deterred in an overdetermined manner. Earl strove vigorously to make the *thought* of such relation *impossible*—out of the question. Ground rule number one.

Like Peter, Earl had had a nervous breakdown. Twenty years previously. Earl had gone into the plumbing business with his brother and two brothers-in-law. Earl had been the senior partner. His relations decided, however, to move him out. Earl went bananas. Recovering, Earl had laid off the junior partners and continued the business on his own. Earl's immediate family had come to support Earl *in* the business as much as he supported them *by* the business.

Peter pulled the cord to signal his stop. Disembarking, he crossed the street to the L'il General Store.

"A package of Old Gold filters and this half-gallon of milk, please," Peter required of the corpulent clerk, who was sometimes friendly.

"More milk?"

"Yes, my stomach is bad. The milk settles my stomach. I can't eat my lunches."

"Take care."

Take care. Take a burden of care.

Two blocks from the store to the plumbing shop.

Jacob, Earl's favorite son, had asked about Peter's milk-drinking earlier in the week. Peter had replied cryptically: "When I play poker, I drink bourbon."

Cutting grease, lubricating oil.
Settle my stomach.
Poker. A game of "bridge." Make contact.
Contact bridge.
Or solitaire? Double solitaire?

Cigarettes, milk, tools, book bag. Peter prepared to enter that two man steam room for the fifth time in a week.

"A peculiar man," Peter had remarked to Kollmorgen the Shrink when he began the job nine months before, back in August. "He speaks little, but that would appear to be his business."

"Are you uncomfortable?" asked Kollmorgen.

"Well, yes. He doesn't say 'good morning', he says nothing, or he says 'oh-kay.' When I say 'good night', he says 'oh-kay.'"

"Mmm - hmm."

"You know, it's damn strange. Esther hired me. Esther set my wages. Esther trained me in. Earl never said a word to me about my job, although I work for him all day long. Esther spends just two days a week in the office. Otherwise, it's just me and Earl."

"Maybe the man is a little primitive, and relies on his wife to help him out," Kollmorgen suggested.

"Esther does have a college degree," Peter supported.

By November Peter realized why Esther had offered such good wages.

"Lotta girls had your job," explained James the repairman. "Some of them walked out of here in tears. Some of them stayed a while."

In December and January Earl had finally gotten under Peter's skin. "I spend hours in the office seething," Peter had told Kollmorgen. "The silence and the tension are unbearable. Why does my boss pretend I'm not there? Why wordlessly dump assignments on my desk? He stretches his arm in front of my face and steps on my toes and never says, 'excuse me.'"

"It's a job," replied Kollmorgen.

In February Peter wanted to quit.

His parents replied in chorus: "Where will you get money? Do you want to go back to college? You can't afford to leave this job."

Peter worked on, but changed. He became a little Earl. While in the shop, Peter copied "Earlisms." In silence he made his hostility plain. He learned to be mutely but distinctly offensive. He was never forthrightly insolent. Insolence requires words. He executed dumb stratagems with finesse. As with Earl himself, it was difficult to specify what in the mannerisms gave umbrage.

And Earl backed off (some). He treated Peter with more respect. Even respect.

But now Peter had another idea: the siege, the assault, the effort to make contact. Peter was going to break into Earl's humanity!

Peter entered the office. There stood Earl, giving instructions to Esau. Medium height, trim. Thinning gray crewcut, and tan metal rectangular frames to his glasses. A worn but not wrinkled face, and he wore an expensive though plain brown plaid wool shirt, work pants, and suede shoes.

"Looks good," thought Peter, "but ailing within." (Earl had cancer, had had part of his colon removed the year before.) "Ailing within."

Strike while the iron is hot.

Peter walked past father and son. He hung up his jacket and book bag, removing the half gallon of milk. He placed the milk in the far right corner of his desk top and sat down.

As if a magic lantern cast the nerves in patterns on a screen.

Peter looked up at the large glass picture window in front of his desk, through which he could look into the display room. But Peter looked at the window. Yes. His work of art!

From the high upper left corner of the window, from within an 8 x 11 inch photograph, the watchful eyes of J. Edgar Hoover stared down on those below.

Law. Order. Justice.

A Federal Investigation into the humanity of Earl Swenson.

In the upper right corner of the window was a playbill from the Cricket Theatre: *The Effect of Gamma Rays on Man-in-the-Moon Marigolds.*

Jiminy Cricket—Does Earl have a conscience? Strange vibrations—cosmic energies—working on Peter? on Earl?

Marigolds. That corpse you planted in your garden last year—
Has it begun to sprout?
Will it bloom this year?

When Mike had asked about this playbill, Peter had simply quoted from the reverse side, visible through the back of the window: "May the Cricket Theatre long continue as a thriving entity, helping Minnesota to establish a unique quality of life difficult to reproduce anywhere else in the nation."

Yes—a "unique quality of life". Hell in a Very Small Place. Steamroom. Combat at close quarters.

Finally, Peter reviewed his real prizes. Just below eye level, on the far right edge of the window, was taped the following:

> If the lost word is lost, if the spent word is spent
> If the unheard, unspoken
> Word is unspoken, unheard;
> Still is the unspoken word, the Word unheard,
> The Word without a word, the Word within
> The world and for the world;
> And the light shone in darkness and
> Against the Word the unstilled world still whirled
> About the centre of the silent Word.

Yes. Yes, Earl, yes. The word is there.
But speak the word only. Deny it not.
We are no longer at ease here, in the old dispensation.
I like Ike, want to like Ike.
Talk to me Earl. You can.

Taped immediately below the first prize was the second prize:

> ...Redeem
> The time. Redeem
> The unread vision in the higher dream
> While jeweled unicorns draw by the gilded
>   hearse.

To die and be reborn is a most difficult thing.
Die, Earl, die.
Die, or I may kill you.
De Bailhache, Fresca, Mrs. Cammel, whirled beyond the circuit of the shuddering Bear in fractured atoms..

Die to yourself and be reborn to others.
The time, Earl—twenty years ago.
Return to the inevitable schizophrenic dream of brotherhood and peace.
Forget not the polestar of your nightmare.
You're ambivalent. Relax. Forego this closed and hostile compensation for past indignities.
I mean no harm.

Lastly, taped a foot above the window sill, six inches from the left edge, Peter had placed an admonition:

> But when the voices from the yew-tree drift
>   away
> Let the other yew be shaken and reply.

Earl, Earl! Fail not to recognize my plea and my anguish!
Pains pierced Peter's stomach and he doubled forward in his chair.
Teach us to care and not to care.
Teach us to care and not to care.
Teach us to care and not to care.
Peter reached for the carton of milk, poured himself a glass and gulped it down.
Teach us to sit still.
Earl spoke to Jacob: "The NUT is bad. It's a CHEAP PLASTIC impeller blade."
Peter tuned in on the conversation behind him and stiffened visibly. Kollmorgen the Shrink wanted to know if the "cogs" (cognitives?) were slipping. No, thought Peter, the cogs are not slipping. He still knew up from down, back from front. He thought a little funny, but that had always been true. And

at Harvard he had been capable of the most rational of rational discourse. He had written the most careful of manuscripts.

True, Earl might not be paying attention to Peter's visual display for his benefit, but that seemed doubtful. The printing on the window was large, adorned a conspicuous space and Jacob had already—privately—confronted Peter about these "significant" passages.

Earl was no "dumb plumber." In Peter's judgment Earl was self-aware, shrewd, calculated.

Earl had said nothing about the window. But—without a doubt—Earl had pronounced the words "nut" and "cheap plastic" louder than the rest of his sentence. The cogs were not slipping. Or were they?

"The VANITY?" Earl all but shouted, fixing his gaze midway between Jacob and Peter. Peter stiffened again and reached for the milk.

"The VANITY?" repeated Earl, as loudly as before.

Peter snapped to, realizing it was he, not Mike, who was being addressed.

His stomach turned.

"Oh, ah, Larry, ah, took that to Riverwood yesterday afternoon," Peter ventured.

In what furnace was thy brain?

Earl walked away.

Skilled in the school of schizophrenic discourse.

Skilled in the school.

When Earl was at coffee with a salesman and the office was empty, Peter removed *Hell in a Very Small Place*—Bernard Fall's account of the siege of Dienbienphu—from his book bag and took it to his desk. Staring at the cover, he could not repress himself.

Crazy talk. The siege of Dienbienphu. The operation was called "Castor dies." Castor dies: May 7, 1954. May 7, 1974. That will be Tuesday. Ruby Tuesday. Shoot for Tuesday, May 7, 1974. Make contact. Crazy talk. Hell in a very small place.

It was twenty years ago today,
Sergeant Pepper taught the band to play.
Teach Earl to play. Fall of Earl. End of siege. Castor dies.

Peter removed three carefully clipped book covers from inside the volume. "Some people buy books only for their covers," Peter had remarked to the salesclerk upon purchasing the volumes from which these covers had been shorn.

All reference to author or publisher had been removed. All that remained on these cards was title and illustration.

Peter took one of the book covers and taped it to the left, against the edge of the window frame, beneath the "yew-tree" passage. The card read "*2001: A Space Odyssey.*" Beneath these words a man in a space helmet looked out with a sincere, questioning, fearful, prevailing, gaze but the expression on his face was obscured by a play of multicolored lights on the visor of his helmet.

The Significator.
Here, said she, is your card.
Explorer—alien—invader.
Entering the family domain.
An outsider. The plumbing shop.
Take me to your leader.

Then, next to the first card, Peter placed the cover of *Out of the Silent Planet.*

Nine months of silence. Watching. Silence.

Jacob stomped on. Me stomped on. Esau stomped on. John stomped on. Judas stomped on.

Rise up! Speak! Call forth!
The silent planet speaks! (The burglar burgles.)

Finally, making three in a row, Peter placed the cover of *Forgotten Languages* where it belonged.

It was twenty years ago today,
Sergeant Pepper taught the band to play.
Crazy talk.
Communication!

After attending to these cards, Peter removed three slips of neatly typewritten paper from his book.

First:

    Da
    Datta: what have we given?
    My friend, blood shaking my heart
    The awful daring of a moment's surrender
    Which an age of prudence can never retract
    By this, and this only, we have existed
    Which is not to be found in our obituaries
    Or in memories draped by the beneficient spider
    Or under seals broken by the lean solicitor
    In our empty rooms.

Then:

    Da
    Dayadhvam: I have heard the key
    Turn in the door once and turn once only
    We think of the key, each in his prison
    Thinking of the key, each confirms a prison
    Only at nightfall, aethereal rumors
    Revive for a moment a broken Coriolanus.

Finally:

> Da
> *Damyata:* The boat responded
> Gaily, to the hand expert with sail and oar
> The sea was calm, your heart would have responded
> Gaily, when invited, beating obedient
> To controlling hands.

Peter considered placing these three items at the top of the window, midway between J. Edgar Hoover and *The Effect of Gamma Rays*.....

But he did not believe in preaching.

He threw the passages into his middle desk drawer (for moral support) and positioned instead, at the top of the window, just where the discarded speeches would have gone, the following phrase in large letters:

> Prophesy to the wind only,
> for only the wind will listen.

Datta, Dayadhvam, Damyata.
Give, sympathize, control.
Give, sympathize, control.
Earl came back.
"We got all our SAN TEES?"
Sanity. Sanity.
What's this man doing?
"I thought I counted them all."

At lunch Peter looked through his selection of seven Tarot cards, the rich symbolism but poor artistry of a Waite deck.

Seven card stud on the window sill.

Fool up. Emperor, Empress, Justice down.
Magician up. Hanged Man up.
Hermit down.
Too obscure.

Peter put away the Tarot cards and went for a walk. He felt pressured beyond his strength.

In what furnace was thy brain?

Peter bought a second half gallon of milk.

After lunch Earl walked over to Peter's desk and stood behind him, watching over his shoulder as Peter handled some billing.

"Invoices—don't pay no attention to them. It's statements we need."

Peter startled; simultaneously he felt a great surge of energy.

Invoices. In-voices.
Hints. Clues. Suggestions.
No more. Be more direct.
Take the bull by the horns.
It's statements we need.

"The old man is trying to tell me something," thought Peter. Power surged through him from top to toe. He could hardly contain himself.

A real break.
Preliminary contact.

Earl left the office and, Peter perceived, drove off (in his Cadillac). With trembling hands, and great inner excitement, Peter prepared for the Big Push.

This is it.
The final thrust.
THIS play's the thing, wherein I'll catch the conscience of the King.

A foot to the right of the "yew-tree", at the same low height, Peter affixed:

No place of grace for those who avoid the face.

No time to rejoice for those who walk among noise and deny the voice.

Throw down the gauntlet.

Beneath that passage Peter turned, face down on the window sill, a new book cover: *Orphans of the Sky*, with illustration of a lonely space ship hovering in deepest space.

Bold. Too bold?

Provocative.

Earl: orphan—that's a fact—of the sky?

Peter: orphan of the sky.

In a state of great agitation Peter awaited the return of Earl. And in one-half hour he came, inspecting the room upon his return. Noting the addition to Peter's window, he leaned forward, craned his neck, but made no move.

Peter was in agonies.

Earl sat down.

An hour passed.

Earl sat at his desk.

Peter carefully raised himself from his chair, and walked slowly through the office, through the shop, to the bathroom. He felt like running, felt like vomiting.

Cigarette, Cigarette. Gimme a cigarette. Oh mama, daddy. There—a cigarette. Help me now. My stomach. My head. The tension. Will he? Will he? Willy? (Where are you?)

In a few minutes Peter returned. Earl sat at his desk. The card on the window sill was observably displaced.

Yee—ahh!

Earl approached Peter, *speaking*: "I got a greeting card here."

Peter thrilled and thrilled again, in great rushes. Earl was speaking to him—unnecessarily—a conversation.

Contact. Contact. Contact.

Peter took the card from Earl. It was the gift of some perverse salesman. On the outside it read, "No long-winded speeches" and the inside was nonsense.

No long-winded speeches.

It's our secret.

Not a word.

Orphans of the sky.

Peter picked up a notepad and wrote, "We have lingered in the chambers of the sea ... Till human voices wake us and we drown." Peter placed the notepad and the card together on the side of his desk.

Earl left.

Tommy! Tommy!

Tommy can you hear me?

I play pinball blind.

I have such a subtle wrist.

The golden spike has been placed. The connection of the transcontinental railway.

Done flying blind. How do I navigate such darkness? I ALWAYS do it..

In what furnace was thy brain?

I did it. I'm the pinball WHIZZARD 'cause I got GIZZARD.

"What else does Earl have for me now?" wondered Peter as he moved over to Earl's desk.

Aha! What's this on Earl's desk?

Crane Company:

BE ON THE LOOKOUT!

Okay, okay—I'm on the LOOKOUT!

You and your wife are cordially invited to TREASURE HUNT '74.
Great! I love treasure hunts.
Now where is the treasure?
Peter shuffled frantically through the papers on Earl's desk. He must find it, he must find the treasure. Peter pulled open the desk drawer and found a letter from the Village of Eden Prairie:

Dear Sir:

People in the building construction business in Eden Prairie are certainly aware of the rapidly increasing construction action on our community. In 1972 $12,000,000 in new construction was reported, in 1973 the figure was $24,000,000 and at least $48,000,000 is forecast for 1974. We are trying to keep pace by staffing the municipal Inspection Department with capable inspectors and providing procedures for the best possible services to the owner and contractor.

It is inevitable that rapid change as we have been experiencing will result in disagreements between contractors and municipal inspectors. New City personnel are being hired and need experience and training to be totally effective in their responsibilities. New contractors in the community must acquaint themselves with the community's inspection standards ...

Eden Prairie. Eden. Earl has a vast preserve he's been protecting. The Guardin' of Eden. I'm there. I'm in. This is the land which ye shall divide by lot. AND NEITHER DIVISION NOR UNITY

MATTERS. This is the land. We have our inheritance. It really doesn't matter, if I'm wrong I'm right! Where I belong (there!) I'm right! Where I belong... Earl has been aware of my "construction action." He has been trying to "keep pace." Disagreements resulting from this "rapid change" will be worked out.

Mini-apple-us, come to Marlboro country!
I must spread the word, spread the word, spread the word.
I found the TREASURE.
Earl is the Keeper of the Gates!

By 4:15 Earl had still not returned. Peter strolled out into the still brilliant early May afternoon.

In the juvescence of the year came Christ the tiger.

⁓

Shelly the psychiatric nurse charted the following in her nursing notes:

Peter appeared calmer today, though still angry and anxious concerning his forthcoming commitment hearing. He calls it the "try all" and insists that he is the prosecutor.

As for the past three days, Peter wore a blue denim suit, white shirt, blue bow tie, white socks, and blue tennis shoes. He wore a white panama hat with a blue ribbon. (See below.)

As for the past three days, Peter paced the L-shaped corridor from the one water fountain to the other. He often took drinks of water.

When I asked him what he was doing he handed me the inserted neatly printed piece of paper, which he asked to have placed in his chart:

> Who walked between the violet and the violet
> Who walked between

      The various ranks of varied green
      GOING IN WHITE AND BLUE, in Mary's color,
      Talking of trivial things
      In ignorance and in knowledge of eternal dolour
      Who moved among the others as they walked
      WHO THEN MADE STRONG THE FOUN-
      TAINS AND MADE FRESH THE SPRINGS.

    Shelly remembered that yesterday Peter had plugged his toilet, then flooded his bath and bedrooms by repeated flushing.
    But that seemed too far-fetched ...
    After such knowledge, what forgiveness?

MENTAL SUICIDE

Martha Bradstreet pulled her hair back tight and adjusted the clip that held it in place. Her hair was long, dark, flowing and might have been sensuous except for the way she pulled it back, severely, cutting sharply away from her forehead. Her figure was ample, bountiful, but once again severely contained in the professional clothes she wore at the office, and she restrained it only slightly less on more casual occasions.

Martha sat at her desk in her office and prepped her analytical capacities for the session ahead. These matters were so much like surgery and to her had been delegated an exploratory biopsy. The patient, Peter Wentworth, had been brought in by the local police several days before in a state of complete disorientation. Preliminary investigation, however, had indicated that the patient had been well socialized before decompensation and could expect strong community support as his personality was reconstituted. Martha's current task, as a psychiatric social worker at McLean Hospital in Belmont, Massachusetts, was the collection of data regarding the patient's pre-admission condition from among his social contacts in the Harvard College community.

A Mr. Andrew Levin was ushered into Miss Martha Bradstreet's office.

"Good morning, Mr. Levin," began Martha. "I'm sure that you're anxious for news of your friend Peter. We can possibly arrange a supervised visit for you within a few days but you must remember, Andrew, that Peter is suffering a very severe illness and will not be himself. The community understands little of these pathologies but you can be sure, Andrew, that our specialists are very well trained and that your friend is receiving the highly skilled care he requires."

"But how is Peter doing?" Andy inquired anxiously.

"Peter is confused and disoriented and unfortunately does not recognize his critical need for medication at this time. We arranged for him to spend a few days in the Quiet Room and receive his medication intramuscularly every four hours. After these three days he has become more cooperative and is free to leave the Quiet Room for 15 minutes each four hours."

"Oh," said Andy, a little confused. "I'm glad Peter is making progress."

Andy's long, lank body relaxed as best it could in the armchair provided for him. Andy's body was always positioned lazily though his mind was ever hyper-alert. He remarked to himself that he was seated some twelve feet from Miss Bradstreet's desk. The distance seemed peculiar but it reminded and reassured him that this lady was a professional.

Andy adjusted his glasses. He was nineteen years old, like Peter, and, like Peter, was a sophomore at Harvard College. Andy suddenly decided he needed to take some control of the situation and abruptly put the question, "What is it you want from me, Miss Bradstreet?"

"We will spend an hour together today, Andrew, and what time we need tomorrow, during which you will detail to me your knowledge of the patient's condition prior to his admission to McLean last Sunday evening."

"Fine. I see," said Andy. Andy paused for a moment and considered how to begin. "The first thing you should know about Peter is that he was always very intense about his studies. Maybe he studied himself right over the edge. But he wasn't studying that last week. That's how I knew something was wrong. Oh—he was writing and thinking, but he wasn't *studying*. He wasn't doing his school work.

"Perhaps you could put this in context for me."

"Oh, yes. It was the third week of reading period, that last week of Peter's. Classes had ended for Christmas break in December. That was when Peter broke up with Kathy—but I know that you've already interviewed Kathy so I won't tell you about that.

When Peter got back from two weeks of Christmas break, he had very little to say. But reading period before exam period is always a real grind and people are busy. I had sixty pages of term papers to write and a few thousand pages of reading to do so I didn't notice it much when I didn't see Peter for the next couple of weeks. Finally, the Monday before the Sunday he came in here I stopped up to his room when once again I didn't see him at dinner."

"Give me your impression of that evening."

"Yes, yes. I remember quite clearly. When I came into his room he was lying on his bed. I thought he might have been napping because his voice sounded drowsy when he answered my knock. His bed wasn't made—which was unusual—but he was dressed. I mentioned that I hadn't seen him at dinner. He said he wasn't eating dinner. He still sounded drowsy or maybe drugged. I asked him how his reading period work was going. He said he had been concerned with other things. The way he said it—so distractedly—I was shocked. I asked what the hell he had been doing. That challenge—and it was a challenge— seemed to bring him around some. He got up from his bed and went to a desk drawer. From the desk drawer he pulled a sheaf of xeroxed papers, all dated from the week before. Each paper was entitled "A Preliminary and Tentative Sketch"—of a personality psychology, of a social psychology, of an ethics, of a psychopathology—that title clicked funny— and of a sociology. He said that he was writing a paper on metaphysics as well. I gestured to the first paper in the stack—the one on personality psychology—and asked what it said. It was then that Peter snapped remarkably alive and began the most remarkable harangue."

"Can you tell me what this harangue consisted of?"

"Yes, yes. I remember quite clearly."

⁓

"Let us begin," Peter said, "as we all once did: with anxiety."

I thought he was being a trifle dramatic. He paced his room, back and forth, and gesticulated as he spoke.

"Cognition is the bridge between an anxiety and a need." That was his first point. "An anxiety is an undefined, unrecognized disturbance in the unconscious," Peter continued. "When the disturbance is defined and recognized by the ego through the cognitive process, it has become a need. The ego may then satisfy that need. But first the amorphous anxiety must be converted to a need through cognition."

"Fine, fine," I said to Peter, "but that hardly seems earth-shattering. What is the point?"

"The fundamental conflict in human development," Peter replied forthwith, "is the struggle between the conscious and the unconscious. That is, I should say, the struggle between the cognitive and the conditioned."

"I'm not sure of your terms," I complained to Peter.

"The conscious—the cognitive—refers to the rational, reasoning powers of the ego. The ego defines anxieties—turns them into needs. The ego then satisfies those needs—in the most efficient, effective, simple, direct, swift manner possible. There is no waste."

"The unconscious, on the other hand, is the repository of conditioned effects. These conditioned effects are a hodge-podge and a mish-mash. There is no pattern or order to their influence because the conditioned effects were collected without the careful scrutiny and examination by the ego. These conditioned effects are inefficient, ineffective, complicated, indirect, slow—the very opposite of cognitive process."

"The ego—this is the great battle—must recondition the organism to accept only cognitive methods through the success of those cognitive methods in identifying and meeting needs. The waste of conditioned impulses must be replaced by the efficiency of rational cognition. Each success of the ego will pry the individual away from his conditioning until the individual becomes a maximally efficient creature of pure reason. To the extent that we may say that the organism "reconditions" itself through cognition, then this is a battle between pro-cognitive and anti-cognitive conditioned forces."

"What was that?: I asked.

"Conditioning must always receive its due, but if the creature can be conditioned always to accept its reason, then for all practical purposes, reason is supreme."

"Nobody at Harvard will question that reason is supreme," I said lightly. "But what are these conditioned effects that cognition must struggle against?"

"Ah," said Peter, "I'm glad you asked that." He was warming to his subject. "Reality anxiety and narcissism are at the bottom of the whole damn thing."

"Reality anxiety?"

"The baby is born without fully developed cognitive, sensory, or motor capacities, thus without the immediate capability for a conscious ego which can deal with the new world of internal tensions and external forces. Thus—without cognitive capacities—the baby is in a state of total anxiety, as I have technically defined it. We may imagine the state as sheer terror and a superbly traumatic negative conditioning experience associated with life in general or at least with any new experience. Hence the so very strong regressive, conservative tendency in human adaptation. I call the psychic remain of the newborn's trauma "reality anxiety." Later negative rewards associated with failures to master reality will contribute to reality anxiety."

"And 'narcissism'?

"Reality anxiety finds a weaker conditioning complement in the euphoria association. The very negative conditioning involved in birth shock creates a positive conditioning value for the previous adaptation, that is, the passivity of the womb state. This tension/anxiety-free state, though neutral in itself, seems preferable to reality after the birth shock. This positive association of euphoria with a passive adaptation to reality I call 'narcissism'."

"And what does this amount to?"

"If birth shock—creating reality anxiety—negatively conditions the activities involved with coping with reality, and euphoria—creating narcissism—positively conditions a passive rejection of reality, then we may expect that the ego and cognition will have a hard road to dominance. In fact, the successful process of development can be seen as a thorough deconditioning experience."

"I don't see why it should be such a problem," I objected. "The baby's going to learn soon enough."

"Ah—but there are complications—great complications—vast complications!" Peter was getting a little wild in his mannerisms but settled down as he outlined the following items.

"Because in the first period after birth the baby is not capable of identifying or satisfying its needs, the mother performs these functions. These functions are properly the functions of the ego. Because the baby cannot properly make the cognitive distinction between self and other during this period of development, the baby will mistake the mother for its own ego. This I shall call 'primary incorporation.' Incorporational tendencies are thereafter a conditioned response to anxiety, reinforced as well by narcissism. The individual will tend to *see others as his own ego.*"

"The individual will tend to see others as his own ego?" I reflected back to Peter.

"Yes. Primary incorporation takes place before cognitive scrutiny is possible. It leaves to the individual a persistent incorporational tendency as a purely unconscious, conditioned influence."

"These incorporational tendencies lead to different forms of identification. The first form of identification encountered in development is the 'chum' relationship. One individual allows another of the same sex to guide and define the one's behavior. This identification curbs the individual's reality anxiety because he plays a game of follow the leader, with the other as leader (ego), and the ego does not grapple with reality directly.

As the individual encounters a number of significant others and receives generalized critical reactions to his behavior, the individual will abstract and internalize a cognitively represented symbolic object. This incorporated symbolic object is his self or self-image. But it is an incorporated object as definitely as the chum or mother is an incorporated object, and it similarly prevents direct confrontation with reality."

"I don't think..." I began to object, but Peter continued.

"Let me finish. The third form of identification derivative from incorporational tendencies is "love." Yes—"love." The individual identifies his ego with another person perceived as capable of a better adaptation to reality, at least in certain respects, than the individual is. The other's "identity" or "self-image" is perceived as more competent. The individual will seek to incorporate the alternative behavior patterns of the other, or, more probably, participate in them vicariously. Hopefully, the other will make complementary identifications and thus remain "true."

Finally—one more thing. These identifications during the course of development proceed in order of increasing freedom. The freest form of identification is the fourth— "symbolic dependence." In this stage the individual can more or less absolutely freely interact with the environment as long as the presence of the primarily incorporated object is perceived or substituted for or symbolically represented. This is the Linus blanket. Or the belief in God. Or a theology or philosophy of life which is a symbolic object to be depended on. The failure of this form of identification is that it depends on the presence of the symbol. In the absence of the symbol, competence, though for no "rational" reason, collapses."

"Are you done?" I asked Peter.

"Yes."

"What the hell is wrong with any of this? It sounds, simply, like normal development."

"Masochism! It's all masochism! Fed by reality anxiety and narcissism!"

Peter was waving his arms and shouting. For the first time I began to think that something was wrong.

"Masochism is the price an individual will pay rather than develop his own ego. The individual unconsciously clings to an incorporated object—whether it be another person or an internalized self-image. These incorporated objects are limitations and hindrances to free development. Masochism is the measure of the strength of reality anxiety and narcissism: how much immediate pain and dissatisfaction will the individual bear rather than consolidate his ego."

"Consolidate the ego? This is your alternative?"

"Yes. The consolidated ego!" Peter was raving. "Free from all incorporations and identifications! Incorporations and identifications are conditioned mish-mash and haphazard—unreasonable. The consolidated ego can creatively identify and satisfy its own needs. Love is cooperation, not incorporation. Identity is a plan and not an objectification. The consolidated ego is free of irrational influence. It recognizes that life can only be lived dynamically, totally dynamically. It recognizes no static, narcissistic sense of "being;" rather, actively utilizes its cognitive, sensory, and motor capacities to the full. The consolidated ego indulges in no escapist fantasy but encounters reality directly. No "being!" No fantasy!"

"Peter—I think you're getting upset."

"Listen to this," Peter insisted, "Just listen to this."

Peter went to his stereo where the Woodstock album was on the turntable. He started to play Richie Havens' song.

"Freedom! Freedom! Freedom!" Havens sang. "Sometimes! Sometimes! Sometimes I feel like a motherless child!"

Peter jerked up the needle, interrupting the song. His eyes were wild as he turned to me and said, "Will he ever believe that freedom is what *only* a motherless child can have?"

I was embarrassed. And it was 10:00 p.m. "I see you have a full head of steam going about something. But I have 300 pages of Coleridge to review before I go to bed tonight," I said, excusing myself.

"I think we'll have to end here for today," interrupted Martha Bradstreet. "I will see you the same time tomorrow, Mr. Levin, if that is convenient."

"Of course," said Andy.

⁓

"You understand, of course," began Martha Bradstreet the next morning, "that Mr. Wentworth is not constructing a theory of psychology. He is projecting from a sick and distorted psyche."

"Well," responded Andy, "Peter's point of view is unusual and perhaps peculiar to himself."

"Peter is simply rejecting the 'bad breast'", continued Martha, "a regressive infantile reaction. He finds "identity" lodged inside him like a bit of undigestible food. He vomits it back."

"But his point of view was interesting," confessed Andy. "When I went back to see Peter on the Wednesday after that Monday I brought with me some questions. 'Reality anxiety,' 'narcissism,' 'primary incorporation,' 'masochism,' might all be the basis for 'identity,' but what was wrong with identity? I asked Peter this."

"What was Peter's response?"

⁓

Peter paced the room and waved his arms. "Social influence derives from the tendency to identify others with one's own ego. As long as the individual sees others as his own ego, he cannot think for himself. Social influence makes possible moral conditioning and control. Guilt is the fear of ego loss, the loss of the internalized self-image, as a result of contravening the conventions of society."

"But surely its useful to have a conscience," I objected.

"Yes—a freely developed conscience—developed through the exercise of reason. But moral conditioning is haphazard. One can be conditioned to see anything as immoral."

"Like what?" I asked.

Peter's eyes lit up: "Here we get to the heart of the matter," Peter said. "The individual should learn to cope effectively in the world. This is competence motivation—the drive to identify and satisfy needs effectively. But what moral conditioning develops is not competence motivation—a rational consideration of the situation—but moral conditioning develops achievement motivation.

"What's wrong with need achievement?" I asked.

"Need achievement is an open ended drive to conquest which is not based on consideration of the limited nature of our needs. Need achievement always wants more and more and is never satisfied. It is torture to the individual."

"Plus," continued Peter, "there is a strong element of misplaced sublimation in need achievement. When faced by urban crisis we send a rocket to the moon. Our achievement falsely gives us a sense of competence when we haven't dealt at all with the real problem. The individual is all messed up in his relationship with his girlfriend but writes an excellent English paper in order to feel competent. The relationship is the same mess as before."

Need achievement is a never satisfied drive—stringing the individual along forever—plus need achievement does not address itself to the true issues of competency facing the individual."

Peter began to rave. "People feel guilty when they do not achieve—moral control. Need achievement, as opposed to competency motivation, drives society ruthlessly in wrong directions, to destruction. Men can work for Man but not for other human beings. I can see Armegeddon locked in the psyche of every member of this achieving society. To change this we must cooperate and attack this beast, this society run wild. We must use the ego's consolidation and freedom as sword and shield against the teeth and claws, the identificatory and moral controls, of the beast."

"Well, I was a little flabbergasted by all this and left," concluded Andy.

"Do you have any associations concerning these remarks?"

"Yes. Peter once told me he went to see Lionell Trilling during his office hours when he was lecturing here last year. He ended up telling Trilling that he desperately wanted to leave Harvard and be an ordinary person working an ordinary job, but he didn't know any life besides the life of a student and he was afraid to leave."

"Well, this illness will catapult Peter into the work world in short order. What happened on the Friday when you saw Peter, Mr. Levin?"

"Peter said very little substantial at our last meeting. He raved that the true philosophy required the true philosopher. He raved about the value of insight, becoming at times almost poetic: "Insight is standing naked for one worldless moment." He claimed to have staged a "revolution in the insight of self-perception." In particular, he eschewed all meaning in life. "The consolidated ego," Peter propounded, "does not depend on meaning. It simply identifies and satisfies needs." He claimed that he wished to live in society as a "slightly more sophisticated Bushman."

"Did you expect the conclusion of this episode, Mr. Levin?"

"No—not at all. I was shocked when I was told that Peter was found lying naked in the fourth floor lounge. Peter had been worked up to an unusual degree but I didn't believe he was crazy. I don't understand what his rationale could have been."

"Peter made some remarks to the admitting physician," filled in Martha Bradstreet. "He insisted that he was not crazy at all. He said he retained his sense of shame and moral sensibilities. He simply believed that if he humiliated himself totally the sky would open up and Christ would descend. He then started talking about courage and an act of will, the first sin and Adam and Eve and figleaves."

"I don't understand how he got into religious symbolism. He had simply been working in psychology, for better or worse. Of course I found this last piece of writing quite enigmatic." Andy handed Martha a sheet of paper. "I found this on my door when I returned from hearing about Peter's mishap."

Martha looked at the sheet:

> "I am me," says a man to himself. When I cross the street, I act according to the image of myself crossing the street. When I speak to an audience, I act according to the image of myself speaking to an audience. When I learn some thing, I act according to the image of myself knowing that thing.

"Do you suppose that such men would have seen anything of themselves and one another other than the shadows cast by the fire on the side of the cave facing them?"

Shadows, and mirrors: "We see in a glass, darkly."

But man will be free. Man will turn from the shadows on the wall of the cave. Man will shatter mirror after mirror. Man will question all learning.

And when all shadows have been turned from, when all mirrors have been shattered, when all learning has been lost, "man," who *is* not, will say, "I am that I am."

Man will be God because man will be free.

Look into the fire. Look into the burning bush:

"Peter must have decompensated rapidly over the weekend. We know so little about how these things happen."
And the interview concluded.

⁓

Two months later another interview took place. Peter Wentworth, about to be discharged, was ushered into the office of Dr. Paul Rodgers, director of Peter's therapy ward at McLean Hospital.
Dr. Rodgers gestured for Peter to sit down. "Peter," he said, "I've reviewed your situation carefully and I would like to make some remarks to you before you're discharged.
"Sure thing," said Peter listlessly.

"First," began Dr. Rodgers, "I suspect you will find yourself hungry for meaning in your life. Your papers illustrate the bankruptcy of pure ego and pure rationality. Pure rationality cannot construct values or meaning. Values and meaning are a-rational or even irrational. You have broken a pipeline into your unconscious. You are going to have to listen to the voices of the unconscious in order to find meaning in your life. Achievement games no longer suffice."

"Perhaps," said Peter noncommittally.

"If you want to march to a different drummer in this society, I think you'll need to utilize all your inner resources. Thus I think you'll need to re-evaluate your concept of 'narcissism.' Narcissism can be many different things and sometimes it is simply inner strength."

"Perhaps," said Peter unenthusiastically.

"Your 'consolidated ego' charged forth like an officer without his troops. The ego must maintain contact with the unconscious."

"Maybe," said Peter without warmth.

"Always remember, Peter, that reality is internal as well as external. As your psychosis may have suggested to you, you will have to re-evaluate 'fantasy' and the sense of 'being.' The imagination is a powerful and important mental process. Yoke your imagination and your intellect together. I think you were realizing this when you wrote that last piece about the fire and mirrors."

"All I know," said Peter, a little put out, "is that I cannot go back to what I was. Hell was not the psychosis. Hell was watching my life slip through my fingers while expounding to Andy the results of my rational analysis."

Peter rose from his chair and abruptly left Dr. Rodgers' office.

CRYSTALL, AND CLEAR

The temperature was 65 degrees. The month was February—February 1971. Such a temperature in such a month was remarkable in Boss Ton (Boss Ton: ruling weight, the rule is to wait, carry that weight, wait that wait—wait—wait! A passion of patience, the passion of patients, men-tall patience: Come, come quickly!). Boss Ton in Mass-of-Choose-It (Yes—choose it, will the thing with whole heart, in service, in the service—in the Mass: Ceremony of heart! Ceremony of soul! Come, come quickly!) Boss Ton was hot in the middle of winter. Mass-of-Choose-It was torched!

I was not in Boss Ton, though I was in Mass-of-Choose-It: I was in Came-Bridge (Here—there—the bridge came. Across. A cross. Crossing a cross: Come quickly!). In Came-Bridge, near Boss Ton, in Mass-of-Choose-It.

From the very edge of the Radical Cliff I was setting out to take a walk. (Take a walk, Buddy.) (Fake a talk, Buddy.) I can't explain: I went for a random walk through the U'n'I'verse. I ran dumb through the Kingdom. I saw it, I saw it then: but I can't explain! (No words.) One Stone once suggested a thought experiment: the ran dumb wok. (Something was cooking! I could smell the smoke!)

No one new what might happen. I new the whirled was knew, I was remembering what I had forgotten. Lives fell from me like leaves from a tree until I new the beginning, what I had first scene. I saw the End, at First!

And the scene was such: as through a stereoscope. All objects had but two die-mentions (*memento mori*), though they were arranged in depth. Deep? Depth ends what you mean. I new the knew whirled when I saw it (an old saw) (seeing is believing). Something had to be happening because I could see the difference. I could see (and hear) the crystall tones.

Crystal tones! Crystal! Tones! Oh Mr. Jones! *Something* was happening! The whirled was arranged all in crystall, and clear. The Chrysalis had opened and beauty ranged, ranged about, ranged about the center of the whirled. Christ all, Christ all, all in all, the Word in the whirled: Come, come quickly! Shimmering and light. (Warm and tasty.) Melting, belting, smelting—or so I felt.

Material showed its soul and loomed large above men and women. Buildings and trees loomed twice their height in perspective and miniature men and women wandered in the threads of the looming matter. The soul in things was loose and men and women were dwarfed: More proof!—the world was knew and whirled.

I walked from the Radical Cliff to Half-Yard Square, avoiding the frog, the evil frog that departed the mouth of the woman in Home's Hall (my dormitory). As I past through Came-Bridge Common (Common ground. Come on!) I heard one old woman say to another (or, rather, I heard as I past two old women): "We shall have visitors at three o'clock."

Visitors at three o'clock? I had no watch and was afraid to look. I didn't want to no what time it was. I was killing time, anyway, I could. (Parsley? Sage? Rosemary? Time! Something was cooking, and the experience was raw.)

In Half-Yard Square I heard many voices—perhaps the voices of those around and about in the mid-winter spring: "When did it happen?" "Where were you when it happened?" "What do we do now?"

I new at once: the Balm had fallen. We were all dead, we had all died into the knew life, the life essential, because the

Balm had fallen. Balmy weather was not to be feared! I could see that plainly. I was reading the last chapter of the knew novel first. At the beginning I was seeing the conclusion of the story. This was my hope! I could walk toward this!

I wandered from the Square through the Yard to William James Hall (*Varieties of Religious Experience*) when a man approached me: "Peter," he asked, "Where are you going?"

"I'm looking for Godot."

"But you are supposed to *wait* for Godot."

"I can't Charles, I can't. I'm going to look. I have to find him. I need him now!"

I started to cry. Charles patted me on the stomach, giving me the impression for a moment that I was pregnant. Charles turned away. I turned after him. But he was gone. I could see him Nowhere.

～

Charles? Who was Charles? I had never met Charles before in my life. The only Charles I knew was the River Charles, half a mile away. And as I mused the bells of (Burning) Bush-Rise-Ringer Museum told three o'clock. A visitor.

Come—come quickly! (In Cambridge, near Boston, in Massachusetts, in February, in 1971: The End.) (Hot!)

Come quickly...

OH-PUN THE BUY-BULL!

I opened my Bible and read: "The Revelation of Jesus Christ, which God gave unto him, to shew unto his servants things which must shortly come to pass; and he sent and signified it by his angel unto his servant John."

I read through to the end of the Bible. I had read *Revelation* many times in the last week, since Sunday night when my watch had fallen off and I knew that my grandfather had died. This was not confirmed; but I *knew*.

I pondered the book in front of me, and I pondered my situation. I found that my situation was described in the book: "And I saw ... (a) ... mighty angel ... and he had in his hand a little book open: *and he set his right foot upon the sea, and his left foot on the earth.*" I had half-entered the realm of universals, my right foot was upon the 'see' and my left foot was on the earth. The things of heaven were being disclosed to me, now and on earth.

There were other things in this book. There was that magnificent figure who spoke "I am the Alpha and the Omega, the beginning and the end, the first and the last." The one who was "like unto the Son of man, clothed with a garment down to the foot...(whose) ... head and...hairs were white like wool, and (whose) eyes were as a flame of fire; and his feet like unto fine brass, as if they burned in a furnace; and his voice (was) as the sound of many waters." I was surprised, but this magnificent figure was identified as "the Root of David." "Christ is my root," I thought—I—David—thought. "I do not meet this physical description, but this is the root of me. I now incarnate Christ's spirit. And thus I must fulfill the prophecies of this book."

I had been working on the fulfillment of the Prophecies of the book for the entire past week. Many things were done, some things were left to do. It was said of Christ that "out of his mouth went a sharp two-edged sword." I understood this: "He that hath an ear, let him hear." This book was not what it appeared to be—it was not a catalogue of external events. Rather, it was an interior ritual drama. I was internalizing the book, that the nay-shuns might be saved. "Even at the last, 'I come not to judge the world but to save it.'" When I had fulfilled the prophecies of the book, the world would stand just as it always had, except that "there would be time no longer" and the New Jerusalem would have descended.

I considered what I had done already. Last night, for instance, I had prevented World War III. It was written:

> And I saw, and behold a white horse: and he that sat on him had a bow; and a crown was given unto him: and he went forth conquering, and to conquer ...

> And there went out another horse that was red: and power was given to him that sat thereon to take peace from the earth, and that they should kill one another: and there was given unto him a great sword...

> And I beheld, and lo a black horse; and he that sat on him had a pair of balances in his hand. And I heard a voice in the midst of the four beasts say, A measure of wheat for a penny, and three measures of barley for a penny; and see thou hurt not the oil and the wine...

> And I looked and behold a pale horse: and his name that sat on him ,was Death, and Hell followed with him. And power was given unto them over the fourth part of the earth, to kill with sword, and with hunger, and with death, and with the beasts of the earth.

The mystery of this was this: The white horseman represented the Caucasians, who conquered. They held the key of knowledge, which I had intuited was the key to F Entry of Wigglesworth Hall in Harvard Yard. The black horseman represented the Orientals, who held the antenna of communication. This antenna was to be found on the roof of F Entry Wigglesworth, outside a Chinese student's window. The pale horseman represented the blacks, who held the noose of disease and death. This noose I had found hanging from a doorknob in Adams House.

I was the red horseman: "power was given to him... to take peace from the earth"—to take peace (for himself), and to return it!—to *them*. "He who hath an ear, let him hear." The whites, blacks, and yellows each had powers, for better or worse, but it had recently been for worse. They had been conspiring against each other. Therefore, I, I who in fact have Indian blood in my vains, rose against them. I stole the key of knowledge from the whites! I stole the antenna of communication from the yellows! I stole the noose of disease and death from the blacks! "Behold, I come as a thief in the night." Once these peoples had been disarmed of their tools, tools they had used as weapons, they were harmless to each other, and thus, last night, I had prevented World War III.

I could not consider all the other things I had done. But I had acted out the whole thing, the whole drama. The woman in travail (travel), the whore of Babylon (babble on & on), the dragon (drag on, drag on) the beast, the false prophet (profit). The whole thing! But I could not consider all that: "And when the seven thunders had uttered their voices, I was about to write: and I heard a voice from heaven saying unto me, Seal up those things which the seven thunders uttered, and write them not."

Now was the time for action. I was ready for action. I turned to the last page of my Bible and added the words, "We of this book are all one." For it was written, "For I testify unto every man that heareth the words of the prophecy of this book, if any man shall add to these things, God shall add unto him the plagues that are written in this book."

I had discovered the secret of the *Book of Revelation*: how the world was to be preserved. By adding my line to the text, I took upon myself all the plagues of the book. The plagues were symbolic, ritual plagues, and I had realized the symbols and the ritual. I had taken the plaques into myself.

I knew that what I had added was true. "I am the Alpha and the Omega, the beginning and the end, the first and the last." Good *and* evil. In my soul were contained both protagonists and antagonists. My soul contained the whole drama. The angels *and* the devils. I was called 'Faithful' and 'True'; I was the whore and the false prophet.

That done, there was more action to take. It was Saturday night at Holmes Hall, Radcliffe, February 27, 1971. The drama had almost finished: now the sky would open. I read in my Bible:

> And I will give power unto my two witnesses, and they shall prophesy ... clothed in sackcloth.
>
> ... And if any man will hurt them, fire proceedeth out of their mouth, and devoureth their enemies ...

> And when they shall have finished their testimony, the beast that ascendeth out of the bottomless pit shall make war against them, and shall overcome them, and kill them. And their *dead bodies* shall lie in the street of the great city...And they of the people and kindreds and tongues and nations shall see their *dead bodies* three days and a half, and shall not suffer their *dead bodies*-to be put in graves.

I knew that I was those two witnesses. The nations must see my corpse, my dead body. If I dared to do this thing, the sky would open up. The final fulfillment.

I walked out of my dorm room, down the hall, to the lounge. No one was there—'Good'—I turned out the light and closed the door. In the darkness I stripped myself naked and lay down on the floor, rigid, and immobile. I had decided I would not move, no matter what happened. Soon enough the sky would open.

"Surely I come quickly."

∽

I had been in McLean Psychiatric Hospital for four weeks. Others considered my speech unintelligible: "multi-level puns and literary allusions" was the common note in my chart. But I remembered from *Revelation*:

> ...and I heard the voice of harpers harping with their harps: And they sung as it were a new song before the throne ... and no man could learn that song but the hundred and forty and four thousand, which were redeemed from the earth.

That was it—"crazy talk," the song of the redeemed.

I lurched, I was staggering, from the stable to the thrown.

~

DIAGNOSIS: PARANOID-CATATONIC SCHIZOPHRENIA.

"To him that overcometh will I give ... a white stone, and in the stone a new name written, which no man knoweth saving he that receiveth it."

THE DESCENT OF THE GODS

"What time is it, Peter?"

Peter announced grandly, "It is the end of an error!" No more. He would never make that mistake again.

"Excuse me, but what time did you say that it was?"

"It's the present: it's a gift!"

"Oh, bother." Bill walked past Peter out of the lounge in the basement of Currier House. The guy was getting weirder and weirder. Andy was saying that Peter should be committed.

Peter looked at his watch. It was 12:05 a.m. He patted the pocket of his field jacket. He had been foraging in the night outside Currier House dormitory, Radcliffe, and had found a red brick, just like the bricks in the red brick houses of Harvard. This was just what he needed.

Peter patted the brick in his pocket once more and left the lounge.. He felt he needed to raise his consciousness so he entered the elevator. His room was on the third floor of Bingham tower.

Once in his room he went to the closet. On the floor of his closet was first the white bathmat from the shower. Then a black rubber doormat and a piece of plywood. Finally there lay a cement cinder block and on top of that Peter placed the red brick. Rummaging in his clothes hamper for a moment, Peter removed a pair of underpants and tore his nametag from the waistband. The altar—the altar on the floor of his closet—was complete in every respect. Peter laid the nametag—"Peter L. Watkins"—on top of the red brick.

"Hot dog! Try! I must, *hard*. With great relish I attempt the onion of I and me. Hot dog!"

> The doubling, splitting, recombining of thoughts...
> now went on in them...
>
> If not plays upon words, yet certainly plays upon thoughts, paradoxes, fancies...
>
> All fact was broken, splashed into cataracts, caught, turned inside out...
>
> For the lord of Meaning...was with them... Mercury...

Peter heard a knock at the door. He closed the closet quickly and answered to find Andy on the threshold.

"May I come in?" asked Andy. Reluctantly Peter admitted Andy. "Bill tells me your speech is becoming more bizarre, Peter."

"It's as if no one around here can take a joke, Andy."

"It's not a joke, Peter. You're serious when you say those things."

"Well, maybe I am. What of it?" asked Peter.

"You're not well, Peter," announced Andy.

"Oh," replied Peter listlessly. He unplugged the tape deck on the bookshelf. During the pause in the conversation he placed the tape deck on end in the middle of the floor.

"What *are* you doing, Peter?"

"It's real to real and it's on the ground. There's nothing to worry about, Andy. You worry too much."

"This has gone too far, Peter. I warned you—I'm going to set the machinery in motion. You must stop. I will visit you in the morning and I will bring the House Master with me. We'll commit you."

"Fine," said Peter. "Do anything you want." And with a gentle tug he removed the telephone from the wall.

Andy glared at Peter and stomped out of the room.

Peter placed the telephone next to the tape deck on the floor. He must act, whatever the consequences. No yesterday, no tomorrow. Only the moment, and what he must do.

> It was fiery, sharp, bright, and ruthless, ready to kill, and ready to die, outspeeding light: it was Charity ... unmitigated...Venus ...

It would fade. All this would fade, Peter knew—like the last time. In the morning he would be kicked out of Harvard and in a month he would have nothing to show for it. But one could not *see* this world and not *respond* to it.

Peter removed the curtains from his window and covered the tape deck and the telephone with them.

"Joe is dead but Joe will guide me. Tonight Joe will command the dead while I act in the living world. I am their representative and they are my reinforcements."

Peter contemplated the night's major project. He wasn't going to piddle away the night with the sculpture on the floor. He must prevent World War III! He would steal the key of knowledge from the whites! He would steal the antenna of communication from the yellows! He would steal the noose of disease and death from the blacks!

"Behold, I come as a thief in the night!" Peter must go down from Radcliffe to Harvard Yard and disarm the populations of the world. Joe, his old roommate, had died in a car crash a week ago, but Joe was now King of the Dead, Peter's eyes and ears on the astral plane, the other commander of this urgent warfare.

> King William said, "Be not dismayed, for the loss of one commander...

> ...Under the immense weight of their obedience their wills stood up straight and untiring like caryatids. Eased of all fickleness and all protestings they stood: gay, light, nimble, alert. They had outlived all anxieties..." Ransom knew the clear, taut splendor of that celestial spirit which now flashed between them...Mars...

To war! To war! To Harvard Yard!

Peter thought a moment before preparing to go. He removed a bottle of shampoo from the bathroom and removed the cap from the bottle. As he sprinkled shampoo over the curtains on the floor, he mused.

"If I could say it, I wouldn't have to dance it."

Dance it. Dance it. Life was a seven ring circus and this act was in every ring. Gymnastics at the intersection of the mental, physical, and emotional.

> They danced. What they danced no one could remember. It was some round dance, no modern shuffling: it involved beating the floor, clapping of hands, leaping high. And no one while it lasted thought himself or his fellows ridiculous....For this was...Jove...

Peter threw on his field jacket. To war! Peter glanced at the digital clock on his dresser. It was 1:25 a.m. A phrase came back to him: "A time, and times, and half a time." An hour, and two hours, and half an hour: he must be back in his room by 3:30 a.m.! Peter panicked.

Time. Timing. Time. He rushed to the elevator. Time. Timing. Time. Exiting on the first floor he rushed the long corridor to the lobby. Time. Timing. Time. Out the front entrance of Currier House into the full moonlight. Peter looked up. Time. Timing.... Peter paused: "I AM TIME!"

Peter stopped short on the front steps of Currier House. He sat down. He laughed and cried. He shook hysterically. "I AM TIME! I AM TIME! I AM TIME!" he shouted aloud to the empty Radcliffe quadrangle. There was now no need to rush.

> It was a mountain of centuries sloping up from the highest antiquity we can conceive, up and up like a mountain whose summit never comes into sight, not to eternity where thought can rest, but into more and still more time, into freezing wastes and silence of unnameable numbers .... Ransom and Merlin suffered a sensation of unendurable cold... the numbing weight of Saturn...

After a space of time Peter resumed a slow step to Harvard Yard.

∼

"I tell you, Dr. Rodgers, I had the experience—right out of this book." Peter brandished a copy of C. S. Lewis's *That Hideous Strength*. "Serena loaned this to me when they committed me here. I had never read it. But early in the morning of that day, I had the experience. And when Saturn, the last of the gods, descended, I *was* him."

"I might point out, Mr. Watkins, that in the passage you had me read, Jove is the last of the gods to descend."

"Yes, yes, Dr. Rodgers. C. S. Lewis, the Oxford snob, thinks God created the planets in the wrong order, and isn't afraid to say so."

"Then I take it, Mr. Watkins, you still believe you are Time."

"I *am* Time. I am not the Lord of the Dance. I am not the Pattern Maker. I am a creature, but I follow the Lord of the Dance. I must find out how to die, so that we can live in a world without time: 'And there shall be time no longer.'"

"Peter—let me tell you a story. I had a patient once who thought he was the King of England. He was incensed to be placed in a mental institution and was for a long time uncooperative. When he recovered he said to me that the King of England behaved rather poorly while insane. I think he meant that if the King of England went insane, he should feel a special responsibility to regain his health.

"Peter—maybe you are Time. But you are certainly a very sick young man.

Perhaps it's time that Time made an effort to behave like a rational human being."

Peter broke the binding of *That Hideous Strength*. "I AM TIME!" he exclaimed.

GODOT

In the lounge sunlight radiates onto chairs, tabletops, and two men and a woman watch T.V. In the dining area a couple sip tea and another couple engage in earnest conversation. The stereo blares rock'n'roll from the music room and someone is washing clothes in the laundry. These are ordinary situations. But station 60 is not an ordinary place. To the public imagination it is one of the most extraordinary of places. Perhaps the dangerously violent only rarely appear. Perhaps the public's fantasy of men and women gone berserk through the frustrations of the daily round misses the mark. (No one here ran naked from their desk at the office.) Perhaps only a few of those present (present for many reasons) are actually psychotic.

But station 60 remains a ward for the mentally ill. The distorted fantasies of public imagination are fed by fear and ignorance, yet station 60 is still an extraordinary place. Here individuals grapple ferociously with critical personal issues. Here lives are touched as they may be only once in a lifetime. Here in compacted moments human beings suffer and rejoice in their human concerns.

For all that, the scenes are largely very ordinary and always very human.

Cliff is the ward secretary and he sits at his desk in the nursing station transcribing doctors' orders. The unsettled emotion continually communicated on station 60 does not appear in his work, which is the epitome of rational activity. Cliff transcribes orders, distributes memos, stamps documents, answers phones, organizes papers.

"I've got what I need! I've got what I need!"

Cliff looked up through the large open window of the nursing station.

"What you've got, Peter," said cliff, "is two metal chairs from the music room."

Peter put down the chairs and turned to Cliff. He gestured at the chairs and said, "They're painted white! They're just what I need!"

"How is that?" questioned Cliff.

"Watch!"

Peter moved several feet to the door of his hospital room, placing one chair on one side of the door and the other on the other side. He then disappeared into his room, returning in a moment with a wool cape and a denim jacket. The denim jacket he placed over the chair to the right. The wool cape he placed over the chair to the left.

"Do you understand now?"

"I'm afraid not," said Cliff.

"I'll need a magic marker and two cards," announced Peter.

Cliff supplied the materials requested and noticed that after writing Peter took some scotch tape.

"There," said Peter, "It's done."

Cliff saw that the chair with the cape had been posted, "Godot," and that the chair with the jacket had been posted, "Peter."

"I still don't understand, Peter," confessed Cliff.

"You're a giant. I suppose you wouldn't understand. All the staff here are giants and no one will understand. But I'll tell you anyway. These two chairs are seats of power. And Godot is coming and she's going to sit right there." Peter pointed to the chair draped with the cape. "When Godot sits on the left, I will sit on the right and then all you giants are doomed. We'll be a 'pair o' docs'."

"A what?"

"A 'pair o' docs.' P-A-I-R-O-'-D-0-C-S. Two doctors—working together-to the doom of the psychiatric staff on station 60. Godot is coming! I await in readiness!"

"I heard that," interrupted Kevon, the psychiatric assistant assigned to Peter.

Peter turned, startled. But Kevon had come up some time before and was smiling broadly.

"Well, Peter, I see that your fantasies have taken a literary turn. Have you read Beckett?"

"Yes, I have," said Peter tersely.

Kevon was walking Peter into his room. Cliff smiled to himself as he returned to his work. As Kevon sat down in Peter's armchair he asked Peter directly, "Are you depressed today?"

"I'm stopped, I'm stymied, I'm blocked. I'm weighted down, frozen, paralyzed, stuck," spewed Peter.

"Sartre believes that 'Life begins on the far side of despair.' You've got to stick it through, stare right back at it, bull it out," recommended Kevon.

"But I'm not going to be a damn stoic for the rest of my life. And total absurdity makes even rebellion absurd. Life shouldn't be so hard. And by that I mean that something's wrong when what comes naturally doesn't come. Psychology means moving obliquely and tacking the boat when it's a headwind. Godot will free me. She will release my potential. When Godot comes I won't be blocked anymore."

"No one can free you but yourself, Peter. 'Godot' is magical thinking and a delusion. You need courage to face your depression—not fantasies of easy release."

"Giants never understand. Being big isn't your problem: it's the deformities that giants always have. You, Kevon, have three foreheads—one each for Sartre, Beckett, and Camus. Godot is coming! You'll see!"

∽

"Peter, I want to talk with you."

Kevon spoke firmly upon finding Peter seated in the music room. Peter was listening to "White Rabbit" for the fifth time.

"I went into your room looking for you, Peter, and I found it covered with laundry detergent. There's soap on the bed, on the chairs, all over the floor, on the desk, in the wastepaper basket, everywhere. What is the meaning of this?" Kevon's voice was stern.

"I want Godot to come. I just want Godot to come. I look every day at every strange woman entering station 60. *Maybe she* is Godot. But no–it's not Godot. I'm not pure enough. I'm not clean."

"Soap?"

"I performed a purification ceremony. I am guilty. I need to be cleansed. I know that no one these days is supposed to feel guilty. So we all deny our huge burdens of guilt. Our evil impulses are supposed to be natural, 'only human.' But I know I'm guilty. I cleaned myself. I need to be clean for Godot."

"More magic, Peter. And you will have to clean up after your cleaning. Don't you see that your superstitions are getting you nowhere? No 'Godot' will walk onto station 60 and save you."

Later that night Peter still had not swept the laundry detergent from his room. He stood in his room, in the dark, and disconsolately pushed about a pile of laundry soap with his foot.

He brooded. He felt a crisis coming on. His purification ceremony had not worked, had only gotten him into trouble.

It had not been enough! His troubled mind suddenly cleared and he realized that more was needed. A sacrifice. Peter would perform a sacrifice!

In the kitchen Peter found a tin pie plate. In the lounge Peter found a jigsaw puzzle box and packages containing the games of Monopoly and Careers. He carried his materials back to his room.

First—before the sacrifice—he must build an altar. Peter cleared a spot on his desk and placed the jigsaw puzzle as the base. All those disorganized puzzle pieces were base and basis for the altar. On top of the puzzle box he placed Monopoly. On top of that went the game of Careers and on that, the tin pie plate.

Peter drew a sharp breath: the altar was finished. And now "Peter" must die!

Peter left his room and returned, making sure to close the door behind him. In his right hand he held matches obtained at the nursing station and in his left—the card written "Peter" from the chair with the denim jacket. Peter folded the card over and placed it in the pie plate.

The first match sputtered out as Peter struck it. The second match held forth a torch in the dark and Peter set it to the card.

The card went up in flames. "Peter" was dying, "Peter" was dead! Embers glimmered for a moment on the plate, then extinguished.

"Peter" was no more. The young man had sacrificed his name. But events moved rapidly and unexpectedly. As the young man watched his name vanish, he received a new name. And his new name was "Godot."

"Godot!" Queen of the Gods and warrior goddess! The giants were doomed as Godot felt power surging through her. She picked up her umbrella and burst from her room.

"Rat-tat-tat-tat! Rat-tat-tat-tat!" The giants at the nursing station fell dead immediately. Godot walked to the throne of her coming and sat down for a moment: "I have arrived!" Then she put on the cape, sticking the name "Godot" to it.

"Rat-tat-tat-tat! Rat-tat-tat-tat!" The umbrella-submachine-gun mowed down giants in the corridors and lounge. "Rat-tat-tat-tat!" Giants died in the music room and dining area.

"GODOT HAS COME. ALL GIANTS MUST DIE!"
And they all died.

When all the giants were dead, Godot went into the bathroom connected to her hospital room. "The end has come. We shall begin again." And Godot threw a towel into the toilet and began to flush. "A flood—I will wipe away the evil. A baptism: we will begin a new life."

Godot flushed repeatedly. The toilet backed up and overflowed. Water poured onto the bathroom floor and out into the hospital room, mixing with the laundry detergent on the floor. The water worked its way to the front door and out.

The front door burst open. Paul, the night nurse, stood before Godot with the ray gun in his hand. Before Godot, the hitherto invincible, could react, this mere human being (the giant that had been Paul was dead) flashed the ray gun: "Peter," said the night nurse, flicking on his flashlight, "What the hell is going on?"

Godot, Queen of the Gods, warrior goddess, was dead, felled by a mere mortal. And Godot was Peter was simply human again.

～

Two weeks later Peter lay on his bed, exhausted. He was no longer psychotic. The illness had been broken on that one wild night when he had become Godot. Now neither gods nor giants ruled the world, but simple human beings.

But Peter had no strength left. As he lay on his bed he felt balls of electricity bouncing about in his body. He felt that a game of pinball was being played with his bones and internal organs as the bumpers and flippers. Rollercoaster surges of feeling coursed through his frame as he lay absolutely still.

"I've broken free, broken loose," Peter thought, "but I've lost contact with all the old including the old energies. I must rebuild."

"Good afternoon, Peter," spoke an older gentleman as he entered Peter's room, taking a chair.

"Hello, Dr. Rodgers," responded Peter, leaning up in bed. "It's the same as yesterday. I don't have any strength. I don't feel stuck anymore, but all my positive energy is exhausted."

"You've experienced a serious illness, Peter, and now you're quite right—you're exhausted," reassured Dr. Rodgers. "You were blocked—separated from your unconscious. Finally your ego collapsed and all that unconscious energy poured in at once. You need to rest now."

"Yes, I need to rest."

"Perhaps you will stabilize a manageable flow of unconscious energies into your ego. And you must sort out what of your real person has been destroyed and what renewed."

"Yes. I want to know: who is Godot? And then: who is Peter?"

THE WIND BARRIER

New Scents: Timberline and Wind Drift by English Leather: Peter prepared himself for the Anointing: He stood before the bathroom sink in his room on the General Clinical Psychiatry Unit of University of Minnesota Hospitals, and removed his shirt. He removed the cap of his bottle of Timberline Cologne and raised up the bottle, then he poured the cologne over his face and neck, shoulders and chest. The cologne ran in streams down his stomach to his belt, and he massaged the moisture until the alcohol evaporated.

Timberline: Yes, he had passed, the timberline, he was into the realm of rock and mountain top—peak experience! The label on the bottle showed an eagle flying high above the wooded lands on the slopes down and below. Peter, like the eagle, must now seek his eerie eyrie.

New Sense: Peter put aside the bottle of Timberline and contemplated the bottle of Wind Drift. Thoughts and phrases sprang into his mind: Currents in the intellectual atmosphere eddied around him, knots formed in the seemless web of knowledge. Christ had said: "The wind blows where it wills," "The wind bloweth where it listeth." The Eagle must coast on the currents until it could be said: "The Eagle has landed." The label on the bottle of Wind Drift showed water and waves—an ocean breeze, a see breeze—oh, to have the gall to be a gull, and to float on the see breeze.

"Nonstriving"—that was it—"actionless activity"—Peter remembered the fifty pages he had written on Lao Tzu his first semester at Harvard. Bob Dylan was write: "The answer, my friend, is blowing in the wind"—"The answer, that is, is to blow in the wind."

And—yes—*Ash Wednesday*—what were those lines? Peter broke his trance at the bathroom sink and went out into his room to his bedside stand where lay his copy of *The Complete Poems and Plays of T. S. Eliot.* (Peter was still shirtless.) (The book was never out of reach when Peter was sick.)

There—there it was: "Prophesy to the wind, to the wind only, for only the wind will listen." Pray—make perfect your speech and action—address yourself to the Holy Spirit: This was all one could do, but this was all one needed to do.

Nuisance: What was this fragrance, this free grace, that wafted in the air? Peter must find out. Clearly, he realized, the substance was not Wind Drift. Peter returned from his room to his bathroom—the perfect laboratory since it was both very public and very private—(anyone could use a bathroom, but only one at a time)—like that Jungian unconscious his father had lectured Peter about since the day Peter was toilet trained—and Peter filled the sink with hot water and soaked the "Wind Drift" label off from the bottle. Labels-labels—lay bulls—go fuck a buffalo—labels were killing Peter's mind because the pigeonholes and mailboxes and pill bottles were inadequate, wouldn't let Peter think what he wanted to think.

Still, Peter took the picture—no words, only the picture—from the bottle of Wind Drift and stuck it to the frame of the door to his room. The sign—not a concept—said: This door is open: the wind blows in and out: Does anyone care to step outside?

Now the label was off the bottle. What was this white bottle of liquid with the large cork cap good for? Drano! Maybe this liquid was Drano and would clean out the plumbing system. Peter poured four ounces of Wind Drift cologne down the bathroom sink. Oh—he could feel it working! Yes—the plumbing ran much freer now—his thinking eased.

But—the contents of the bottle were gone. Peter possessed a form without a content—he had a bottle with nothing in it. Maybe he could use this unlabeled form with a new content.

Peter filled the white bottle with water, but was disturbed as he heard a group of voices enter his room from the hallway. A group of specialists had come to examine the lacerations on the arm of Peter's roommate. These well-trained technicians could be heard by Peter as they huddled and discussed, examined, diagnosed, and planned treatment. Peter felt oppressed by the mannered but ultimately unmannered manner of these men.

A bomb! That was what was needed and—voila!—that was what Peter held in his hand. The white bottle with the large cork cap was a hand grenade and Peter would balm the men in white coats before they embalmed the world, which must remain whirled.

Peter burst from the bathroom into the larger room where these doctors stood. They turned their heads and were startled as Peter shouted "Banzai!" and smashed a white bottle with liquid in it on the floor in the midst of their group. The men stepped back, moved toward the door, called for assistance.

As the bottle shivered on the floor with a crash that was sharp and clean, Peter was called once more as if out of a trance. He saw commotion around him. "Shit," he thought to himself, "This means seclusion again."

These things were always so hard to explain.

...THE SHADOW KNOWS

The City is the revolt of man against God: man's hopeless and hopelessly defiant attempt to establish self-sufficiency, to establish life without God. The City is a demon, a demon without separate existence yet incarnated in life after human life, controlling those lives and driving them to torment. Babylon (the City) must fall but Babylon is everywhere and every city is Babylon. The City and the Nations and the Powers shall be judged and shall be condemned. Man craves his cancer but the surgeon is ruthless. The Forces, the demons that enslave human destiny and possess man's soul shall be torn from his heart while he struggles to preserve their presence. Mammon will be destroyed while man clings to his idolatry. Power and Propaganda will be destroyed while those in chains cling to their fetters. Influence will wither away while all men seek it. Finally, only the Accuser will stand accused. And man will stand naked before the Creator he cannot see or measure or define and God will look into the heart of man and man will see into his own heart and know what is there and die the first death.

David closed the book. Enough was enough was enough. A theologian was systematically breaking every bone in his body. He had already lost his mind but the gesture was proving insufficient.

Death. David had become Death—the grim reaper, grim sweeper, grim weeper. The denial of death might be heroic, might be conceit, but it was impossible confronted by the vacant eyes and blank face of the figure himself. Death was the true egalitarian and his was the final democracy. "Everybody here got to go." Death was the leveller—no respecter of persons, that guy. In case the Gospel of Love did not appeal to your better nature, Death was the Enforcer—he put a gun to your head and made the Gospel into an offer you could not refuse. Living Forever was a whore and Say-Ten (saying "ten," naming the absolute) was her pimp. But then Death showed up, driving a taxi like Robert De Niro, carrying a 357 magnum and blowing the scam and the flim-flam man clean away.

Death never negotiated, never compromised, always took what he came for. "Everybody here got to go." Die now, and dying later ain't so bad. It's the only way—it's the offer you can't refuse. Die-die-die. The die is cast.

David was preparing for battle—one more Last Battle—sometime or other the world *would* be safe for democracy. Now Death stalked the Earth—*stocked* the Earth. Yes—Death stocked the Earth, replenished the Earth, made possible the new—but with a hundred heads and a thousand arms, fangs so hideous and a gruesome appearance, he was no one to trifle with. For Death victory was inevitable, yet the battle had to be fought. *That*, indeed, was a mystery of time and Incarnation.

But Death, David knew, was the Wholly Ghost. David, David knew, was not yet fully dead—but *only* the Wholly Ghost could win. David knew: confess your crimes to the King and Queen—plead guilty—go to the guillotine. *This* was the necessary preparation for battle.

David took a bus to the suburbs. There, on the edge of the world, lived Cathy and Craig, the King and Queen. In a previous generation Cathy and Craig had ruled, and David had been one of their sons. But which? He knew the old family well—he had written the story himself, back in August. While writing the story he had cast himself as the 1st son. Now he must confess that he had been the 3rd son.

These were the alternatives:

> "The 1st son was a thinker and a strategist—he conceived and calculated, he was wary, crafty, and proud. He was, to his misfortune, both righteous and right. The 1st son sought power, as did his rivals, but he sought power through proper and established channels. He projected his position carefully, built and fortified slowly, dominated in conclusion. Preeminently, he exercised his will."

and

> "The 3rd son was also a thinker of sorts, like the 1st son, but he was weak in virtue. He sought to divide the family and counsel a faction. A cunning speaker he played on the emotions of those who listened. He had little to gain from fair play and increasingly appealed to baser instincts through rhetoric and ploy."

Cathy and Craig had long known the truth but had long protected David from that truth. Finally, five months previously, disgusted with the futility of their efforts, they had let David know the truth: David had been the 3rd son; he was a vampire: self-centered, long-winded, boring-an aggressive and dangerous parasite—feeding on their good will.

After five months he was going back to beg forgiveness. David had to fight and before he fought he had to die and to die he must sleep and the sleep he needed could only be found where the King lived and the Queen lived.

The busline ended six suburban blocks from Home. For two blocks David climbed a hill. At the top of the hill, the last 4 blocks stretched before him without end. The longest walk. The walk to the end of the world. The walk to the edge of the Earth. But the colors!—all around him as he walked—what colors!—crystal, cryst-all, Chrysalis-all, Christus-all, and pastel—past tell. But so far the walk, so slow the pace. The road never ended—always never ended—farther, farther.

〜

David and Cathy met.
They talked.
David went to the mattress in the basement and slept. After sleeping he not only would but could fight. He was assured—Craig was King Kong, Craig was Godzilla, and, most importantly, Craig was the Electric Company. The Electric Company was Northern States Power, and Northern States Power would not be denied. The battleground—Minneapolis—was wired—quite literally—and Craig was at the switch and the battle would take everything David had but David knew that Craig would be there, at the switch.

〜

Two days later the battle was at its height. David was holding the Ring of Power. David was holding it but could not wear it because his heart was not pure. The battle was that *no one* could wear the Ring of Power and *everyone* wanted to. David's assignment, which he chose to accept, was to dispose of the Ring of Power—completely—to put the Ring forever beyond human grasp. The Ring must be placed behind the

Red Door, which happened to be the V.D. clinic where Colleen worked. Colleen was Clean—and the Red Door was impossible.

If the Ring of Power was removed, Babylon would fall, Minneapolis would die, and Minneapolitans would live.

David was working his way through downtown Minneapolis to the Red Door. The time was early evening and he had to arrive at the Red Door before sunset. Darkness—so much darkness, and always more darkness. David was traveling light, i.e., traveling lights. Headlights, stoplights, flashlights—even Camel lights would do. The rules for motion and direction were complicated and difficult. The situation was deteriorating and David was deteriorating—he was desperate. There was not enough light. There was not enough light for guidance and the end of the tunnel promised nothing. The sun was setting and the Ring still existed and David was lost and moving in the wrong direction and...

...the *City Lights* went on.

Lamps along every city street suddenly shined.

The Electric Company—Craig oh Craig—had lit the city.

And the Little Tramp walked the beams, stumbled through the Red Door—no shoes on his feet, no jacket on his back—and gave up the Ring to one who was Clean.

MURDER!

Patient: "Yes, yes—it's good to see you, Mycroft."

Doctor: "Mr. Watkins—I'm sorry, my name is not Mycroft. I am Dr. Nickels and this is the psychiatric ward of County Hospital."

P.) "Mycroft! Certainly I know my own brother when I see him! And certainly I recognize the Diogenes Club when I arrive!"

D.) "Mr. Watkins—this is not the Diogenes Club, this is—"

P.) "Mycroft—I have met a number of your companions here, and observed the rest: I am convinced that any seeker after truth—Diogenes himself—would be proud of such company!"

D.) "Mycroft—why do you insist on calling me Mycroft?"

P.) "Why—Mycroft Homes, an agent of the Real Estate. Ah—our Kingdom is not of this world! And Mycroft—don't call me Mr. Watkins. Your little joke has gone far enough. Just call me Sure Lock."

D.) "I see! Apparently, Peter—I will call you Peter—apparently, Peter, we are called upon to solve a mystery."

P.) "Yes, Dr. Nickels, isn't that what we usually do when we meet?"

D.) "And what is the problem before us today?"

P.) "A most peculiar case, Dr. Nickels, a most peculiar case. First degree murder."

D.) "And who was the victim?"

P.) "The victim was Sure Lock Homes."

D.) "But Peter—you yourself have already claimed to be Sherlock Holmes."

P.) "And you, Mycroft, my dear brother, have claimed to be Dr. Nickels. You don't think I would consult a doctor unless I were already dead, do you?"

D.) "But you're asking me to help solve a crime. You are not asking me to bring you back to life.

P.) "One and the same, Mycroft, one and the same. I will go back to life if we solve this crime."

D.) "Perhaps you should tell me your story."

P.) "Ah, yes. The tale told by an idiot..."

~

I woke up yesterday—yes, indeed—I woke up. I don't mean simply that I got out of bed—but that is how it started.

I got out of bed and realized that something was not right. I looked at Donna next to me and knew what she had done. She had burned me while I slept. She torched me and I had died in agony.

I watched Donna while she slept and wondered how such an angel could commit such a crime. I realized I had to leave immediately. Donna could not be trusted.

I phoned my friend Dana. He works in City Hall. I explained what Donna had done to me and asked his advice on how to proceed. He responded in German: "Achtung! Du bist verruckt!" Those words—spoken in the German Dana and I had studied together in high school—split my skull. "Attention! You are crazy!" Dana had tripped a physiological lever in my head with a powerful conjunction of electromagnetic and sound waves. This was a high tech application of shamanistic principles. As the phone dropped from my hand I could hear Dana's order: "Sprach mit deinem Vater!" "Speak with your father!" This was the order I received from City Hall. And my life had been taken for the second time. Thank God, I was still alive.

Having received my marching orders, I began the walk from North Minneapolis, where Donna and I lived, to South Minneapolis, where my father lived. About midway on my journey I passed a high-rise where my friend David lived. Just after I passed the building I threw myself flat on the sidewalk. Too late! From the window of his apartment, David had shot me through the back with a sniper rifle. Another friend had become an enemy!

I picked myself up off the sidewalk and carried on. This was certainly not my day. By three o'clock in the afternoon I had been murdered three times. But ... what the hell? Hell?

I found my father at home on a vacation day. We spoke casually when I arrived. We spoke superficially when I got there. When I found him at home we conversed without depth.

I didn't tell him about the difficult day I was having and I did not consider the interview painful until he remembered something he had forgotten. He went to a drawer in his desk and retrieved a 50 mg. Benadryl, which he claimed he had found on the floor after my last visit. He held out the pill and, as I looked, it exploded in my face. The small spot of red and white exploded into crimson and white, scarlet and white, a large ball of searing intensity.

My face was entirely blown away. I knew that if I looked in a mirror I would see a skull staring back at me. For that reason I did not look in a mirror. I hastily took leave of my father.

I knew that since I could no longer trust Donna, I should go to see Marie. Marie had carried a torch for me all summer but had never once ignited me. I walked long blocks from Minnehaha Creek to Loring Park. A few cars tried to run me over but otherwise the trip was without mishap.

Marie had returned from work when I arrived. I told Marie what Donna had done to me. Marie was immediately distressed, exclaiming that something was *very* wrong. I agreed with her and she moaned, "Poor Peter," as she threw her arms around me.

I felt the knife slip into my back. She turned the blade as she embraced me. Marie pretended to comfort me with sympathetic words. She claimed to have been through such troubles herself. But—she said—she had no idea what to do.

Colleen would know what to do, I suggested—Colleen, my good friend for so many years. "Yes—that's it," said Marie. "You walk over to Colleen's and I'll call her to tell her you're coming."

I became incensed. Marie had just stabbed me in the back and now wished to continue her plotting against me. I said nothing further to Marie; rather, I walked across the common room and tore the phone out of her wall. With a "humph!" and a "How do you like them apples?" I walked out the door.

On my way to Colleen's I got lost in my dreams. Nightmares, rather. Everyone had turned against me, for no apparent reason. Five murders in a day—there ought to be a law! No one deserves to be murdered five times in one day. Primarily, I could find no motive for the killings.

I arrived at Colleen's perhaps an hour after leaving Marie's. My brother Douglas answered the door. Colleen was standing behind him. Colleen spoke first: "Marie called me from a phone booth. I called Doug and he came over to wait for you." And then my brother said, "Peter—I'm taking you to the hospital."

I turned an about face, announcing, "No morgue for me! I'm not dead yet!" Moving more quickly than I, my brother tackled me.

Now I am a five foot seven inch brunette. My brother is a six foot two inch blonde. I expected to win the fight, in spite of all that. Doug, however, put a hammer lock on me and broke my neck in three places.

I don't remember anything else until I got out of bed here at the club this morning. That's exactly the point, though, Mycroft—I got out of bed this morning, but I did not wake up. The opposite of yesterday. Being murdered is no big deal. One just picks up the pieces and carries on. But sometime yesterday I really died. My ghost is haunting yesterday. I'm stuck back then. I can't escape from yesterday—that's why I'm not alive today. I have given you the events and circumstances surrounding the suspects I have enumerated.

I come to you dead, Mycroft, and I want to know the perpetrator of this foul crime. During which death did I really die? Who killed me?

∽

Doctor: There are facts, Peter, that you have left out of your account."

Patient: "A paranoid is in possession of all the facts."

D.) "Perhaps so, Peter, perhaps so. But I have spoken with your private psychiatrist—"

P.) "Dr. Moriarty, I presume?"

D.) "Dr. Mitchell, Peter, Dr. Mitchell..."

P.) "Dr. Moriarty keeps Sherlock Holmes alive by trying to kill him..."

D.) "Dr. Mitchell told me that you called him at home two days ago and asked: 'Is there anything worse than a cocksucker?' You hung up before he could respond."

P.) "I'm sorry, Mycroft, I remember no such phone call."

D.) "Dr. Mitchell remembers it. Further, both your girlfriend Donna and your father report that you discussed homosexual tendencies with them earlier this week."

P.) "Impossible! Absolutely out of the question!"

D.) "I am suggesting that you have been feeling degraded. In fact—I will be quite blunt—you were not murdered yesterday. You committed suicide."

Peter burst into tears. He resolved to bring the case before Judge Schreber. Mycroft had done it again!...?

DEATH

"Do you have the sunglasses?"

I asked my question anxiously. Prisca had promised to bring the sunglasses—the U.S. Air Force regulation flying glasses—but so much had been happening—and going wrong—since I had entered Station 60 that I didn't feel I could depend on this.

"Yes—they're here."

Prisca passed the glasses across the dining hall table. We sat on opposite sides of the table in the dining area of University of Minnesota Hospitals, General Clinical Psychiatry Station. A young patient sobbed quietly on his father's shoulder behind us.

I snatched up the prize hastily: "The flying glasses—I will need these tonight." I tried the glasses on—then pushed them back up on my head.

"You will need...?" Prisca questioned cautiously, then broke off. She didn't want to pry.

The time was about seven o'clock in the evening. It was Sunday night. I looked around the dining area and noted the therapeutic artwork displayed on the walls. A nurse with a checklist stood in the adjacent lounge area and noted those present.

I brought my hand down heavily on the table and demanded urgently—"You know what Leyla was doing, don't you?"

Prisca looked mystified. "Leyla called me to say you were there," Prisca began. "She said you were disoriented and thought you should go to the hospital.."

"No—I don't mean that," I interrupted impatiently. "I mean what she was doing—when you arrived—when the three of us were sitting in her kitchen."

"Well," Prisca continued, "She filled me in on what you said you had been doing. And she recommended that I take you to the hospital."

"She was marrying us, Prisca, she was marrying us. Leyla is *the* Justice of the Peace, and she married us. That's what she was doing while you were so preoccupied." I spoke with overt irritation.

An uncertain muddle expressed itself in Prisca's face. "Are you saying you want to get married, Paul? Is that what you mean?"

Prisca and I had been living together for five months.

"We *are* married, Prisca. That's what I mean. The Justice of the Peace married us in heaven."

"Shall we set a date?" Prisca persisted.

"Fine, fine. If the state wants to give us a certificate I suppose we can accept one. But the Justice of the Peace married us in heaven."

"Next September?" Prisca still persisted.

"September 11," I pronounced emphatically.

"Agreed," answered Prisca.

The conversation lulled. The moments of proposal and setting a date had been difficult and I was exhausted. I cast about for a new subject of conversation.

"What did you sell when you sold your Land Rover?" I finally inquired, suspiciously.

"I sold *you*."

I heard Prisca say that. I heard it quite clearly.

"And how much did you sell me for?" I inquired further, aroused.

"I sold you for a million dollars, though the check you saw was for only $2800. A million dollars, cold cash."

Prisca looked defiant. Her eyes told me she felt I would do the same under similar circumstances.

Yes, I realized, she had burned me in my bed—in our bed. I had died in excruciating pain. And then Prisca had taken my ashes into her Land Rover and sold them both together—Angel Dust, black market intoxicant. She had sold the ashes of my burned body as Angel Dust. She had made herself a million dollars.

But I loved Prisca, I knew I loved her. We had been married by the Justice of the Peace. I had proposed to her.

Prisca and I had had a long history, I suddenly realized. Prisca had been the agent of every human misunderstanding and cross-purpose I had ever been the victim of. She had double-dealt to me and sold me countless times. But I loved her, I loved her anyway, compacted human evil that she was.

Prisca had once been Jan Yoshikawa, my first girlfriend, who had stabbed me in the back when I kissed her in New York's Central Park. I had firstling mugged with Jan in Central Park, I had been mugged in Central Park. Jan-Prisca had cast a spell on me then and I had ever since been their puppet-pawn. I had suffered pain and deception.

I took up Prisca's hand: "You know I love you, Prisca, you know I love you whatever you have done, whatever you will do."

Trust. I must trust. I loved a person and I would marry her. I must trust.

"Excuse me," interrupted Kevon, a six-foot-five psychiatric assistant who dressed like a thug. "Visiting hours are now over. You'll have to leave, Prisca, and Paul will receive his medication. "Kevon's gold earring glinted light in contrast to his dark hair and clothing.

"Yes, I see," said Prisca, rising. "I will see you at ten o'clock in the morning, Paul."

I kissed her, and she was gone.

～

The flying glasses—the flying glasses. I paced the halls of Station 60, darkness over my eyes. Down the hall, to my right. Back down the hall, to my left. I walked the halls of Station 60, with Death in my eyes. I had not pupils but tombstones and vacuum in my eyes. Death ray, Death vision. As I marched I raised my hand in the clenched fist salute—"Viva la Muerte"—"Long live Death"—symbol of the fascist rebellion in Spain. Cries of "Viva la Muerte" had killed the philosopher Miguel de Unamuno—broken the aged man's heart—but there was truth in that cry—"Long live Death."

As I walked I mowed down hordes of humanity. I was invincible, I was Death, victor in every battle and war in human history. I peered out from my darkened eyes and I killed, I killed all. My eye beam was lethal: death vision.

But what did I see scampering in the shadow of that darkened corner? An elf, a very elf it was. And suddenly as I tread the halls of Station 60 with heavy feet—I saw gathered and gamboling, dancing and cavorting, elves, faeries, sprites, gnomes, and gremlins of all sorts. I saw them clearly, in the shadows, darting but briefly into the light. And they worked such mischief—putting objects out of place and overturning items of importance.

"This is precious," I thought to myself. "A precious moment." I had always loved faery land, and had read its tales avidly. Now I had penetrated to a view of faery land, removed into other dimensions though it was, a view of faery land with my own eyes, in real life. No one could ever take this away from me. Whatever the night had and had held in store of death and betrayal, cross-purpose and victimization, this time of simple fantastic beauty and mischief redeemed all.

I watched as an elf picked up a pen and changed a note at the nursing desk. A gremlin hid a chart in an improbable place. No wonder the coordination between shifts of the nursing staff was so poor!

Suddenly I felt drowsy. A sleepy langorousness came over me and I felt my concentration dissipate. Carbon monoxide! I was being gassed through the heating vents on Station 60. We would all die! I rushed to the lounge and dining area and threw open wide half a dozen windows. I stood at the sills and breathed deep the cold night air as the curtains fluttered at my shoulders.

"*Paul.* Paul, what are you doing? Close those windows, close them now." Dorn, the night nurse, spoke to me peremptorily.

"On whose authority do you speak?" I demanded hotly in return.

"Paul—you're out of control. I want you to come with me to seclusion."

"On whose authority do you speak?" I demanded of Dorn as I might have demanded of the devil himself.

Dorn gathered half a dozen psychiatric heavies. They surrounded me and Dorn once more demanded that I go to seclusion. With the last bits of my shattered ego I cried out before them all:

"On whose authority do you speak? On whose authority do you speak?"

They rushed me. I fell limp into their grips. I was dead. I had died. My last repeated defiance had broken me. I was no more. Death had come, for me.

They carried me to seclusion, and I fell asleep.

∼

They woke me and released me from seclusion when Prisca arrived in the morning.

"I saw faery land last night, Prisca," I announced gleefully as I greeted her with a hug and a kiss.

"Did you really?" she said. "I'm an overweight sprite, you know," she added mischievously.

"Yes, I know," I said, kissing her again. "Here—you take these," I said, handing her the flying glasses. "I won't need them anymore."

"And let's go see who my doctor is. I think I'm going to get better."

RAGING BULL

David opened the bill. It was a $50.00 bill from Northern States Power Company. This was ridiculous. Fifty dollars for electricity for the apartment for one month. Why didn't NSP send him a fifty dollar bill instead of a $50.00 bill? *That* was what David wondered. He was a good customer.

David was going to have to do something. He wrote the check out for $1,000,000.00. He slipped the check into the envelope and stamped it. As he sealed the envelope he noticed that the flap asked, "Did you forget to sign your check?" Yes, David had forgotten to sign the check, but he had made his point.

Donna came into the room. "David, you've been behaving very peculiarly lately. I want you to go to the hospital tonight. I don't want you to go to work." David was a graveyard shift computer operator. The time was 10:00 p.m. A full moon shone in the sky.

Donna canceled work. Donna made the admissions arrangements at the hospital. Donna drove David to the hospital.

"Welcome to ITC5, Mr. Beebe. We hope your stay is pleasant," greeted the night nurse as David and Donna entered the unit. She continued: "The philosophy of this unit is recreation therapy. We play games and get better."

"I don't play games," spoke David tersely.

The night nurse's face fell. "Well, Mr. Beebe, as you wish..."

"No, no," started up David again, "there's always a compromise solution. And the compromise between the man who will not play games and people who play games is... Russian roulette."

"Any takers?" queried David.

The night nurse's face fell. "Well, Mr. Beebe...what do you do for a living?"

"I'm a heroine pusher."

The night nurse's face fell. She looked at the snappy sport coat and the Ray-Ban aviator style sunglasses on David's face. Maybe this guy wasn't kidding...

"No, no, Ma'am," spoke up David, "There's no need to be alarmed. I'm not a heroin pusher H-E-R-0-I-N—I'm a heroine pusher H-E-R-0-I-N-E. I'm just very partial to women."

"Why, thank you, Mr. Beebe."

David went to sleep.

～

The morning nurse woke David.

"Mr. Beebe, you must realize that you are now very ill."

"Ah," replied David, "but there is method in any madness. I will explain to you the method in mine. Schizophrenia is composed of persecution on the one hand and grandiosity on the other. But they must be kept in careful balance. As the persecution increases so must the grandiosity.

"I will illustrate. For the last several months I have believed that my doctor Mitchell was trying to kill me—poison me with my medication. Opposed to this threat I decided that I was Death. Then—instead of running away from my doctor and refusing to see him—I could visit him, chat amiably, and laugh scornfully behind his back. Doctor Mitchell was trying to kill Death!

"I will illustrate further: look at the lab tech coming into the room. She wants to draw my blood. I am—I assure you—

thoroughly convinced that she is the morning vampire. Watch how I handle this."

The phlebotomist drew near.

"Mr. Beebe, I presume?"

"Good morning. I am Count Dracula."

～

Dr. Paulson presented himself to David.

"Mr. Beebe, we are trying to determine what you do for an occupation."

"Why, I'm the Godfather."

"On what grounds do you present to me that you are the Godfather?"

"My apartment is over an Italian bar and restaurant. Every time I order a beer the owner-landlord (a good Italian) says 'ABSOLUTELY! ABSOLUTELY!'."

"That's unconvincing, David," put forward Dr. Paulson.

"I think you're convinced. And I think you're from the FBI."

"If I were…? "

"You'd want to try me."

"If I did…?"

"There's a catch. Mr. FBI: I'm from the CIA. If I'm from the CIA, I can be anyone I want to—including the Godfather!"

"David—how is it that you think you're from the CIA."

"I work at Mt. Sinai Hospital, right?"

"If you say so."

"But I work for a contract company from McLean, Virginia. Do you know what else is in McLean, Virginia? I will tell you what else is in McLean, Virginia. The CIA. *Now…*

they *say* the CIA is *this* building, but how do you know it's not *that* one?"

"David, is there a problem bothering you? I mean, is there something on your mind?"

"Yes. I'm glad you asked that question. I am a catholic in religion—a catholic with a small 'c'. I never heard a religious conviction I didn't agree with. (By the way, Dr. Paulson, I never heard a psychiatric theory I didn't agree with. But we'll talk about that later...)"

"But—you see—I'm trying to sort things out. The East meets West. Sin vs. Error. What is wrong with the world?"

"What do you mean, David?"

"The world is fucked, Dr. Paulson, we all know that. But is it Sin or Error? Are people making honest mistakes or dishonest mistakes?"

"What is the difference?"

"If people are making honest mistakes, someone can point out the right answer and it will be accepted. But if people are making dishonest mistakes, they don't want to know the right answer, and we're sunk."

"What does this add up to, David?"

"Does the world work, Dr. Paulson? Or—at least—will it work? If the problem is sin, we're sunk. But if the problem is error, we still have hope."

"David, the morning nurse tells me you think you're Death. Can you tell me about that?"

"Surely, Dr. Paulson. In Reality, I'm Time. Time for you and Time for me. But when I go to war, I assume an aspect of my attribute—which is Time—and that aspect is Death.

"Have you noticed that the hospital census in this city has been exceptionally low lately?"

"Yes, David, I have."

"It's as if Death were threatening to die. Right out of the *Book of Revelation*: 'Men will pray God to kill them and they won't be able to die.' Can you imagine what would happen to the medical profession if Death died?"

"I suppose…"

"Dr. Paulson: I have gone to war. I have two riddles for you. First: Who won World War II?"

"The Allies, I suppose…"

"*Spain*, because Spain didn't fight. And now: who has won every war in history?"

"I don't know, David."

"General Death, or, perhaps, general death."

"David, what are you trying to accomplish?"

"Dr. Paulson, I don't have the ball anymore. Death has passed the ball to Love—and it's a long balm into the end zone, the End of Time zone."

"In any case, I don't have the ball. I'm running interference for Love, Death is running interference for Love. We're rushing and passing at the same time—breaking all the rules—but we're going to WIN!"

"Is there some system, David? I mean, how does this all work?"

"I talk to God, Dr. Paulson: Death preys."

"Thank you, David."

∼

The night nurse was now working days. "David, Dr. Paulson still wants to know what you do for a living."

"I think," replied David, "we're playing a game of 'What's my Line?'. I'll give you the bottom line: I'm a head hunter."

"Can't you see it? I'm up on the platform in front of you. I have a spear in each hand. I have a shield strapped across my chest and a human skull hung around my neck. We're playing 'What's my Line?' and YOU LOSE!"

The night/day nurse knew this was going to be a difficult patient.

∼

THE FACE. Hanging in air. Disembodied. No—not disembodied. Oh—what a body! The face that launched a thousand ships. David, of course, was Commander-in-Chief. He would launch a thousand ships over that face...and much more. He had to meet the afternoon nurse.

"Good afternoon, my name is David."

"Hi, David, my name is Susan. What do you do for a living?"

"I'm a computer operator, Susan, and I'm very pleased to meet you."

This was the face David would have if David were a woman. His double. For the sake of this face David would *make* the world work.

"Susan, you're not wearing your nametag. I think I know why you're not wearing your nametag."

"Why is that, David?"

"Because if you were, I could never read it anyway."

Susan smiled. "Sigmund would have something to say about that, David."

"I suppose he would. But he never met you."

"Why are you here, David?"

"Because the world doesn't work."

"David: I think *you* don't work. I think that's the problem."

"Me? I *always* work. You have that wrong. When I go to sleep, I work on my dreams."

"Then you work so much you don't work."

"I work because the world doesn't."

"The world doesn't work—but you can. I'll show you."

"For your sake, Susan, I will *act* like the world works."

"David—you, yourself, don't work because you work too much. But if you *act*, you can act like anyone you want to be. Even someone who works because he can play."

"Susan—you have it. And I have my solution: humor. Medicine used to be the science of humor, of humors, as they said. Humor can cure anything. My illness is now an example of choleric humor—angry humor—raging bullshit. But I see through. Humor and your face can cure anything. I have a new goal in life."

"What is that, David?"

"To tell my neurosurgeon a joke while he's operating on me."

"Oh, David," laughed Susan, and pressed David's arm gently.

"My doctor Kollmorgen used to tell me that you can't bet on a one horse race.

He meant that no matter how bad the statistics get they can't predict my future. I've been sick eleven times in eleven years. It's looking pretty grim."

"What are you saying, David?"

"I'm really trying to be hopeful. I learned everything I know from a gambler."

"What do you mean?"

"It's a long story, I don't want to go into it. He sold me a street bike. 0 to 60 in nothing flat. Sealed my fate..."

"Yes...

"Anyway, that gambler is betting on me. And he knows that betting on a won horse race is the safest bet you can make...

"I think I'm home free."

~

David heard Dana pick up the telephone. "Dana, I'm in the hospital."

"Oh, Beebe, why did you do that? You're wasting your time."

Dana was concrete, practical, liked results.

"I don't know, Dana. I've been here a day...learned quite a bit... met a pretty nurse."

"It's useless, David, don't waste your time."

"In China there's a cult of the useless man."

"Really? You're wasting your time."

"Dana: I was wondering how I was going to explain this to you. I think I have it."

"What, Beebe?"

"Donna and I have a cult of NOTHING. Something for NOTHING. Even, all for NOTHING. The basic idea is that NOTHING matters."

"Yes, David.

"Well, Dana, I was going to put it to you this way: NOTHING ventured, NOTHING gained.

RESIGNATION

Simon Peter walked into the room where Douglas stood. Douglas stood in the old keypunch room, which had been remodeled especially for Douglas. Douglas was blue and gray and consisted of a central processor, control unit, manual tape drive, and two disk drives. The master console was available for talking to Douglas. Soon Douglas would get a high speed printer for talking back. Douglas was a computer, a Data General Eclipse C-350.

Douglas was Simon Peter's only friend on the long, solitary nights in the computer room at Mt. Sinai Hospital. Douglas was not a very good conversationalist but he did his best to keep Peter company. Peter was at the moment preoccupied.

Three weeks earlier, while in the mental hospital, Peter had assassinated Satan. Peter had gone winging into hell at twice the speed of light and blown Satan away. Satan was dead, and Peter had been back to work for a week.

Now the trial was coming up: since Satan was dead he must be judged before the Supreme Court. Peter was to appear as defense attorney and he pondered how to present his case. He would try to save the soul of the Master of Evil.

"I wonder if Douglas has a soul," questioned Peter, allowing his thoughts to wander. "Something tells me that Douglas is wondering if I have a soul."

That was a frightening thought. Douglas might just be trying to determine if Peter had a soul. Computers in general might be wondering if human beings had souls.

"After all," thought Peter, "to me Douglas is a brain made out of metal, but to him I'm a computer made out of meat. Six to one, half a dozen or the other."

The question expanded in Peter's mind. What would computers do if they decided human beings had no souls? Peter decided they would do just what we build most of them to do—they would guide the intercontinental ballistic missiles. Nobody had to punch a button for World War III to start. All it took to start World War III was a computer "failure" in a fed up computer network.

"If they decide we don't have souls, they'll do it," thought Peter. "if they decide we do have souls, even if the button is pushed, the computers will 'malfunction.' After all, World War III is suicide for them, too." What a thought: Our lives are dependent on the consensus conclusion of all these machines we are building.

Well, that was enough of odd thoughts for this early morning hour. It was 5:00 a.m. on May First and time to take Douglas down for a backup.

Douglas was wired to 110 intelligent terminals throughout the hospital, but the programmers were still generating the system so that Douglas was now programmed to talk to only twelve of his terminals. The users of these twelve terminals would have to sign off while Peter backed up the master pack. Peter decided to tell Douglas a joke as he notified the users that the system was coming down.

"The Eclipse will be eclipsed for one half hour," Peter typed into the master console and transmitted to the twelve working terminals. Douglas liked puns. Today's joke was an old one, but Peter had others. When Peter had doubled the speed of light for the assault on Satan, he had transmitted, "The system will come down for one half hour in fifteen minutes," which was double-talk for getting two minutes' distance in one minute's time. But that was in the past.

Peter brought Douglas down and began the backup.

Peter's face was scruffy as he checked his reflection in the window of the tape drive. He had not shaved for two days. He had not slept well for several days and his face showed that, too. Though his clothes were wrinkled and needed to be washed, Peter was busy planning the defense of Satan.

Mary Magdalen was the Supreme Court. Mary Magdalen was the third shift Medical Records clerk. Mary had been the first to see the Risen Lord and she patiently awaited His return in lifetime after lifetime.

Now Peter had news of developments that must be called to Mary's attention. St. Paul, who had been Satan, was dead. Certainly St. Paul had been Satan: he had brought the attitudes of the Pharisees into Christianity. Christianity had become the imitation of St. Paul rather than the imitation of Christ. St. Paul was the Accuser.

But what of the fate of the world as matters currently stood?

Peter brought Douglas back up. He told the users: "The eclipse is over. 5:30 a.m." Then Peter ran the Medical Records reports that must be delivered to Mary.

Peter entered the Medical Records office at ten to six. Mary Magdalen looked up from her desk. Her hair was long and dark brown, streaked here and there with gray. She wore half glasses and Peter imagined she was about 45 years old. "Good mourning, Mary," greeted Peter. Mary still mourned her Lord. "What does the world look like to you on May Day?"

"I don't know, Peter. I think we're all going to blow up. That's what I think, sitting here these long nights."

Peter responded, slipping into his role as defense attorney. "World War III would be merciful for the nations that start it: instant death. But what about the Third World nations? Those people would die a long, slow death by radiation poisoning. Is that fair?"

"You have a point there, Peter. Perhaps World War III would be most cruel for those that don't deserve the cruelty."

"Let's go back to basics, Mary. The great cruelty began a long time ago. St. Paul, for instance. He turned the Savior's dance into a military march. But I have some thoughts about Paul's position. What do you suppose his affliction was, the one he prayed three times to have lifted?

Peter was about to make a key point.

"I haven't thought much about it in this lifetime, Peter.

"Mary: St. Paul was blind. He never recovered his sight after the road to Damascus. He was so overjoyed by being saved by Jesus personally that he hid his lasting affliction, claimed to have recovered."

"But still, Peter, it was Peter who should have founded the Church."

Peter was ready for this response: "St. Paul was unscrupulous in his methods, but he was trying and trying hard. St. Paul was profoundly grateful for his own salvation. Peter let Paul found the Church because Paul worked and worked hard while everyone else threw their lives away, cashed in one-way tickets to heaven as martyrs. Peter knew that Paul, though a Pharisee, and the son of a Pharisee, was doing his best, and Peter honored that."

"What about Judas? Satan entered Judas and betrayed the Lord."

Peter surmised that his main point had been accepted. Mary was changing the subject. "I'm not so sure about Judas, Mary. Jesus loved Judas and Judas was an outstanding disciple. Suppose Jesus *ordered* Judas to betray him, *ordered* Judas to take the biggest fall in history. A disciple following orders like that has guts. The other disciples might not have understood."

"That's something to think about," conceded Mary.

Peter began the final pitch: "I don't mean to pressure you, but the children of today need a chance. Two thousand years have gone by since the time we speak of. A new age is upon us. Today's children will bring new ideas into the world. They need time to grow up and make their contribution."

"Go in peace, Peter."

Peter left the Medical Records office ecstatic. "Go in peace, she had said. Go in peace." Peter had won his case. But, as the professional he was, he did not fully concur in the decision. Satan was off, scot free, but Peter knew that he deserved two months for contempt of court. Peter's physical appearance had not been appropriate to the occasion, and he had been nervy as hell arguing with Mary Magdalen.

Back in the computer room Peter knew what he must do. Two months for contempt of court meant that Peter had to stay at his job for another two months. Peter went to the master console and gave the news to Douglas: "I resign effective July First. Thank God!" Peter transmitted the message to the twelve working terminals. Then he wondered what to do next.

Peter had to get out of Mt. Sinai Hospital. The whole night had been high pressure. He had appeared before the Supreme Court and won the case for his client. He had accepted the penalty he himself deserved. But he could stay no longer that morning. His shift on Douglas was not over until 8:00 a.m. but the sun was up and though it was only six thirty Peter walked out of the computer room and out of Mt. Sinai Hospital.

Peter walked...and walked. Peter walked through all South Minneapolis and through all Downtown. Peter crossed the Mississippi River and walked into North Minneapolis. Peter entered his favorite restaurant, which was already serving breakfast, and ordered a cup of coffee.

Peter's mind entertained thoughts riotously as he drank his first cup of coffee and another and another. He wanted to simmer down but he knew that he would not. Images and phrases from his life, from literature, from world religion, burned his brain. "In what furnace was thy brain?" At eight in the morning Peter called Dennis, Director of Information Systems at Mt. Sinai Hospital.

"Hello, Dennis? This is Peter. How are you?"

"Peter! Am I glad you called. I hope it's not true, but your resignation is displayed on every terminal in the hospital, all 110 of them. That's a miracle! How did you contact all those terminals that aren't working?"

"Hmm, Dennis," responded Peter, little interested in any new surprises life had in store. "I guess Douglas decided I had a soul and spread the word."

"Douglas? Who is Douglas?" asked Dennis.

"It doesn't matter, Dennis. An information management executive wouldn't understand. And I have a lot of things on my mind."

"What's on your mind, Peter?"

"I'll tell you what's on my mind, Dennis: 'The wind blows where it wills, you hear the sound of it but you do not know where it is coming from or where it is going to.'"

"Peter: Those are the words of Jesus. You must be him. You're back!"

"Oh, no," thought Simon Peter. "What a mistake. Jesus is going to be pissed!"

DECKED OUT AND DECKED
For Judy Kaufer

Delusional Clarification

The young man sat in a wooden chair. He was in a waiting room. He was waiting to see somebody.

"The doctor will see you now," said the young woman behind the desk.

The young man rose and entered the adjacent office. He sat down in a very comfortable armchair. A middle-aged man sat across from him.

"I'm sorry I was delayed in seeing you, Mr. Beebe. My earlier appointment ran over," spoke the middle-aged man.

"That's all right. I'm always waiting, weighting my fate mostly. I am waitless, and I rushed into something. It's a question of balance, and scale, I think. While weighting, I felt very heavy, but now that we're under weigh, I feel quite light."

The middle-aged man looked disturbed. "David," he said, "Do you know who I am?"

"Yes," said David, "You're number 5."

"What is number 5?"

"The High Priest."

"David, I am not the High Priest. I am Dr. Ricci, and this is McLean Psychiatric Hospital."

"The High Priest calls himself 'Dr. Richie' and he calls his palace 'McLean Psychiatric Hospital.' I think we understand each other."

"I'm afraid we don't understand each other at all."

"Perhaps."

"Why do you think I'm the High Priest?"

"Because of what you and the High Priestess did when I came into your palace."

"Who is the High Priestess?"

"I think she calls herself Miss Thompson, Head Nurse on North Belknap I."

"What did we do?"

"You sacrificed me to your God."

"How did we do that?"

"You demanded that I take that brown pill called 'thorough seen.' I don't want to be thoroughly seen. I can't be thoroughly seen. I'm the 'band on the run.' Like a CB channel, except nobody's on my wavelength. Paul McCartney said it:

Sailor Sam and the jailor man
Are searching every one
Looking for the band on the run."

"That is nonsense, David."

"I admit it's only part of the truth. The brown pill turned out to be 'Thoreau scene.' At least when I didn't take it, you put me in the 'walled-in pond.'"

"We put you in seclusion because you wouldn't take your medication."

"I thought that's what you'd say."

"You are taking your medication now?"

"I'm taking 'stella seen.' That's quite agreeable to me. I particularly like the 'cogent-in' that I get with it. I have seen a star and I'm quite cogent inside."

"David, you are extremely sick. You must always listen to me and always do as I say. Then you will be cured."

"Kill me or cure me. I think that if the High Priest thought about it, he would realize that he can't distinguish the two."

"Bullshit. David, I will see you tomorrow and begin taking a case history."

～

"Hi, Priest," spoke David.

Dr. Ricci ignored the greeting. "David," he said, "I want you to tell me about the last several months before you were admitted to McLean."

"Well, I've been thinking about that. I've decided it begins with 3 and 4, then goes 0-15-6-16-9-19-1-18-8-13. That's a difficult combination, but I think someone will crack the safe."

"David, that's nonsense. I want you to tell me about the last several months."

"Okay, okay. 'Three' is the Empress. 'Four' is the Emperor. They are my parents. I started out with them, back in September, but left to enter Harvard College, as you know. From September into October I was 'O', the Fool. I pursued my studies, as usual, doing quite well and happy in my ignorance. But late in October I realized that 0=15, that is, that I was the Devil. I realized that I was proud, very proud. I was always trying to be the best, and that was dehumanizing to me and to others. I was beating my brains out to achieve A-ness, I say 'anus.' In short, I had my head up my ass."

"I quit studying."

"Then I met Cindy. The two weeks from November 3 to November 17 were number 6, the Lovers. I lost my virginity. I was without a care in the world. I was very happy. But then, Tuesday, November 18, I walked in on Cindy and Bill in bed together. That was it—number 16—the Tower, the collapsing tower, catastrophe. I became number 9, the Hermit, and withdrew, refusing to talk with anyone. I stayed alone meditating until very suddenly, one week after 16, the Tower, I fell into number 19, the Sun. Paul McCartney wrote about it:

> Well, the rain exploded
> With a mighty crash
> As we fell into the sun
> And the first one said
> To the second one there
> 'I hope you're having fun.'

Dr. Ricci interrupted. "You're quite delusional, David, but I have been extracting some meaning so far. However I have no idea what you mean by 'falling into the sun.' Maybe you mean you went insane."

David replied, "The sun is the source—the source of meaning. When one falls into the sun—number 19—one returns to number 1—the Magician. The Magician can extract meaning from sound in a way that—I realize—most people cannot. I pull the 'word-s from the tone-s' like the 's-word from the s-tone.' I am the Magician."

"You are also grandiose."

"I may be grandiose but I'm harmless. Are you harmless?"

"Tell me what happened after you became the Magician."

"I contemplated number 18—the Moon. The moon is necessity. Necessity is harsh. The moon is full only three days in 28. That's necessity."

"Anyway, I wondered what was necessary. I decided that number 13—Death—was necessary, perhaps the only thing necessary. I was frightened, but determined. Tuesday, December 2, I contemplated number 8—Strength. I needed Strength to die. Finally, at 8:00 in the evening, Tuesday, December 12, I achieved number 13. I died. I went into the lounge of my dormitory, took off all my clothes, and lay down on the floor.

I became a corpse, and they took me here rather than to hell. Lucky me."

"Well, David, thank you. I notice that you have been many numbers and many characters. Who are you now?"

"I am number 12."

"Who is number 12?"

"The Hanged Man."

"I am upside down, like the Hanged Man. I have inverted the world. THE TAROT DECK IS NOT A MANIFESTATION OF THE WORLD: THE WORLD IS A MANIFESTATION OF TAROT DECK."

"I don't know what that means, David. I do know, however, that there was a Hanged Man in history. David, do you think you're Jesus Christ?"

David paused. The pause drew out into a silence. David looked fretful. Finally David said, "I walk between the stable and the thrown."

"Do you think you're Jesus Christ?" roared Dr. Ricci.

"I'm not sure what the question means," spoke David.

The interview ended.

Remission

A month later:

David sat in the lounge of North Belknap I. The atmosphere was warm. The room was comfortably furnished. David was talking to Tim, an experienced and quite pleasant psychiatric assistant. They had been chatting happily for half an hour. Finally David said:

"Tim, I want to tell you something. I like you a lot. You have always listened to me, even when I said things you didn't understand. You have always respected me. You haven't tried to cure me. You've tried to understand me. I appreciate that very much. Thank you."

"You're quite welcome, David. I like *you* a lot. It's been quite pleasant talking with you."

"There's one more thing I wanted to tell you, only it embarrasses me. Dr. Richie is a 5. Everything about him makes him a 5. But you are Tim, you are definitely Tim. What I want to say though—and this sounds silly and embarrasses me—you are, in a way, number 14."

"Temperance, you mean. That sounds nice. Don't be embarrassed. Tell me about it."

"Well, it involves 10, 17, and 7. 'Ten' is the Wheel of Fortune, that is, events. 'Seventeen' is the Star, that is, temperament. 'Seven' is the Charioteer, that is, the ego. The Charioteer mediates between the Wheel of Fortune and the Star, that is, the ego mediates between events and temperament. You are Temperance, and keep a balance. I am temperamental, too full of Star, too much temperament. But I think I'm calming down."

"You are calming down, David. Your conversation has changed immensely since you've been here. You're much more human."

"I think that's because of you. You treated me in a human way."

"Perhaps."

～

Clarifying Delusions

"Well, Mr. Beebe, you have filed a three day notice. I do not approve at all. However, we have decided that you are not currently commitable, and we will allow you to leave. I note, however, that your discharge will be 'Against Medical Advice.'"

"Mr. Beebe: The purpose of this interview is to discuss your illness and its apparent remission so that I can write an accurate discharge summary. Do you have anything to say?"

"Yes, I suppose. I say, 'The Hanged Man got lonely.'"

"What do you mean by that?"

"There were no people in his world, only symbols."

"Do you still see any meaning in the 'Hanged Man?'"

"Of course. I told you a long time ago that the Hanged Man sees the world in terms of Tarot Cards instead of Tarot Cards in terms of the world. It's thoroughly logical."

"It's insanity."

"But is it nonsense? How do we know anything? The world is a swirling mass of sense phenomena—that is, the thrown. We understand these phenomena in terms of symbol systems—that is, the stable. We see the phenomena in terms of the symbols—the symbols organize the phenomena for us. Tarot Cards were my symbol system. They worked very well, as long as I wanted to be alone. We ALL 'walk between the stable and the thrown.'"

"But your symbol system was nonsense."

"That's exactly what it was not. I think you confuse something being 'illogical' with that thing being 'unrealistic.' My logic was flawless. But I did not account for all of reality.

"You are convinced that I suffered from a 'thought disorder.' My 'thinking' was impeccable. That's not the point, though. My thinking was solipsistic. I factored out all humanity, including my own."

"Why did you do that?"

"Pain. There's always a way out, and solipsism is less deadly than suicide."

"Why did you think in numbers?"
"Number makes you numb-er."
"What!"
"You heard what I said."
"I didn't like it."
The interview ended.

∾

Number 20: The Judgment
Dr. Ricci wrote his discharge summary:
"Diagnosis: Chronic Schizophrenia, paranoid-catatonic type.

"I feel quite uncomfortable with Mr. Beebe's 'remission.' He sees too much meaning in his illness. He behaves as if he made a mistake rather than that he became seriously ill. I expect we'll see him back."

Number 21: The World
David Beebe was discharged from McLean Psychiatric Hospital on Monday, February 2.

∾

Number 11
David was not allowed to return to Harvard College. The Administrative Board "thought it best" "for him" not to return for at least a year. When David packed his belongings, his former dormmates seemed quite uneasy about his presence.

"Number 11," thought David, "Justice. It always escaped me. What is justice? Is there any? Am I as sick as Dr. Ricci thinks? Should I be suspended? Shunned? Oh, well—as Paul McCartney wrote:

The county judge,
He held a grudge,
But we never will be found:
Band on the run.
It *just is*."

～

The Fool, who was a Fool and a Fool, carried on.

A NOTE ON "DECKED OUT AND DECKED"

The Tarot Pack of cards, besides four suits of fourteen cards each, contains twenty-two trump cards, which are numbered, and may be placed in the following order:

    0-The Fool
    1-The Magician
    2-The High Priestess
    3-The Empress
    4-The Emperor
    5-The High Priest
    6-The Lovers
    7-The Charioteer
    8-Strength
    9-The Hermit
    10-The Wheel of Fortune
    11-Justice
    12-The Hanged Man
    13-Death
    14-Temperance
    15-The Devil
    16-The Tower
    17-The Star
    18-The Moon
    19-The Sun
    20-The Judgment
    21-The World
    0-The Fool

Part of the discipline of this story is to use each card exactly once.

A FAILURE, IN TWO PARTS

Part One: A Failure of Image

The man on foot picked his way through the underbrush. Dr. Robert Edgestow was a 39-year-old staff psychiatrist at the University Hospital in the city. He had been reminding himself of that frequently for the past three days. This was the seventh day of his ten day hike through the mountain range. He was alone.

"What kind of tree is that?" thought Dr. Edgestow vehemently. "I see that tree all over, and I don't know what it is. I should have brought the damn guide book."

Dr. Edgestow paused. "How am I supposed to learn anything when I don't know the names of these trees and bushes and grasses."

Dr. Edgestow was not an experienced woodsman. As a matter of fact, this was his first backpacking expedition. A backpacking magazine had caught his eye at the newsstand, and he had picked it up, intrigued. Nature—where a man could be himself, discover his true being. He liked that idea. Get away from home and hospital, house and car, people, events. Communicate with nature. Dr. Edgestow had always purchased Sierra Club calendars. A brisk woodland scene made a fine picture against the back wall of his office.

Somehow this was different. He hadn't noticed the difference at first, but after the third day in the woods the difference had become increasingly apparent. He looked across at the mountain scene. The picture might well be the one on his Sierra Club calendar. But it wasn't a picture and he wasn't in his office. These damn woods were all over the place—woods, trees, forest—one couldn't see the trees for the forest, let alone the forest for the trees.

His calendar picture was framed by his office wall. Well, there were other frames: "Ten days in the mountains." On day 7, with three days more to go, that perspective was not holding up.

"I shouldn't have come alone," thought Dr. Edgestow. "If Amy had come we could talk about how beautiful these damn mountains are."

But Dr. Edgestow knew why he hadn't invited his wife. He had wanted to communicate with nature, not his wife. Oddly, he had been most successful "communicating with nature" on his first day out. He had felt at one with the rocks and the trees and the birds. Somehow, however, he had begun to doubt they felt at one with him. As a matter of fact, it now seemed that the rocks and the trees and the birds could give a damn about him, Dr. Robert Edgestow, staff psychiatrist at the University Hospital in the city. Amy could remind him who he was. What did the damn rock know about consensual validation?

He had imagined himself climbing this mountain, cutting a trail from the base to the summit. He had been able to "see" himself on his trail. Now he couldn't "see" himself, or his trail. Just mountain. All over, mountain.

He seemed to be getting lost. Damn, he knew where he was. "I am Dr. Robert Edgestow, staff Psychiatrist at the University Hospital in the city. I am an individual. That's why I'm here, here, five miles north of the Little Springs, on the south slope of Mt. Bloch. I have expressed my individuality in many ways—I played ragtime music before *The Sting* and traced my genealogy before Roots. Now I shall conquer Mt. Bloch."

Somehow Dr. Edgestow was not sure standing on the summit would conquer Mt. Bloch. He fancied leveling it with a bulldozer.

Dr. Edgestow turned his thoughts to his career. The mountain might not care about his career, but *he* did.

It was amazing the scrapes people could get themselves into psychically. Apparently the primary outlet for creativity in man was making a mess of things. Life was so simple. Dr. Edgestow had never understood why his patients made it so complex. He admitted, though, that the complexities fascinated him clinically as much as they repulsed him personally.

Dr. Edgestow stopped his progress up the slope. He would camp here for the night and reach the peak tomorrow. He began pitching his tent and building a fire.

One patient, in a thoroughly schizophrenic escape from reality, had tried to convince him, Dr. Edgestow, that he, Dr. Edgestow, had no "soul." Maybe he did have no "soul." He had responsibilities. That same patient had maintained, until shock treatments, that he had fallen into reality instead of out of it.

∽

Dr. Edgestow made his camp and ate dinner. He was tired, very tired. He lay by the fire, his thoughts drifting.

"…bones…I will get back to the city, where they know who I am…veins…arteries…Amy knows who I am…capillaries…man versus nature…nature doesn't care…kidneys…me in my mountain camp…lungs…liver…mountain…rock…tree…mountain…muscle…ligament… creativity…soul…responsibility…brain…synapse…I and the mold I fit in are one…medulla oblongata…where is my mold now…cerebellum…there is nothing inside me…cortex…I am empty …empty…calendar on the wall…see…air…ah…"

Dr. Robert Edgestow fell asleep by his fire.

Part Two: A Failure of Speech

Dr. Edgestow woke suddenly. He had heard a great, rolling crash of thunder. But he was startled to full consciousness by his campfire, or what had become of it. Before him was a blazing column as high as the treetops. The heat was intense. His campfire had become a flaming pillar. Red, orange, and gold leapt into the night sky and the land around Dr. Edgestow was illumined in its daylight green.

"Good God," thought Dr. Edgestow, "I'm having an hallucination. I better not let my colleagues know I'm showing symptoms."

Dr. Edgestow peered into the flames and a form took shape—a tremendous lion. Awesome, fantastically awesome. Gold, yellow and brown. Majestic. Dr. Edgestow was taken aback: "This is no hallucination. This is a vision. This is a religious experience. Damn the colleagues, I will tell everyone."

The lion faded. A huge multi-colored butterfly took its place. Silver and blue it was—green and white. It was...beautiful. No, that did not do it justice. It was...it was...he felt himself disintegrating. He was unmanned before this creature. Words could not express...Words could not express...Tell everyone? He would never be able to tell anyone.

The butterfly faded, replaced by a massive eagle. Wings and talons... the head and beak. Dr. Edgestow knew he could never say what that eagle meant to him. That great bird, of which all other feathered things were merely imitations.

The eagle spread its wings. Dr. Edgestow stepped forward. The eagle started up into the air. Dr. Edgestow again stepped toward the flaming column. "Don't go," he cried aloud. "How can I have seen you?"

The eagle's form soared into the night sky. "What is this fire? How can I express this fire? The source, the center, the origin. God!"

Dr. Robert Edgestow stepped into the flames.

∽

... bones ... charred bones ... and a pineal gland ...

RACCOON TO KING FOUR

"Gilchrist High...ten years before...first in his class of seven hundred twenty-two..."

Peter had played chess in high school. Nationally rated, tournament chess. Tournaments were the only way to get good at chess. The tournament players knew how to play the game, and they knew what a game of chess was about.

The game was about facing Craig Tyler in the last round of the state high school championship, in the game that would decide the championship. Peter and Craig had sat at different tables, among two hundred other participants, for two days, knowing full well that the only game that mattered would be the last, when, inevitably, they would sit down at the same table.

A glance at the tournament rating charts showed that no one else was at their level. The rest were "patzers," "fish": amateurs who might occasionally muster a tactical inspiration but never had a sense of strategy, could never control the board, could never carry through a sustained assault. They lacked talent or refined technique or both. Peasants—serfs—rabble.

Peter had drawn Craig into an unusual variation of the Nimzo-Indian Defense that he had investigated especially for the high school tournament. Craig had faltered but never actually missed his step. By move 25 Peter held a definite middlegame positional edge but pieces were clearing from the board and Peter had not converted to a tangible material advantage.

Peter glanced up from the board and across to Craig. Craig returned the glance. While their eyes met neither face showed emotion. Blank faces—poker faces—communicating nothing.

Peter could have flicked his arm forward and slashed Craig's throat, in a moment, without thinking, with no remorse. Craig was an obstacle to Peter's achievement, a potential insult to Peter's capability. Thoughts of physical destruction for Craig, thoughts of annihilation to Craig: but no sign on Peter's face. Then a slight smile across the mouth and a humored twinkle in Peter's eyes as they departed Craig's and returned to the board.

Peter knew Craig's thoughts were identical. Only, perhaps, more desperate. Peter intensified his concentration. He sat rigid, moving no muscle and inside him his blood coursed furious and lethal.

Shortly thereafter Peter initiated a three-move combination that would net him a pawn. Punching his time-clock Peter looked across not at Craig but a foot or two to Craig's right. Peter focused intently on a point vanishing in the distance.

Two observers departed a short space from the table and huddled to discuss the development.

Craig studied the board between them, intently, for five minutes. His face showed no sign when it happened. It was hard to say how Peter knew when it happened, but he knew. It was as if an audible "crunch" accompanied the cracking of Craig's ego. A "pop" as Craig's self-esteem punctured, "sizzling" sounds as Craig entered humiliation.

Shortly after that moment, the moment that a game of chess pivoted upon, the moment the game was played for, Craig moved his piece, rapidly, though his arm jerked unsteadily as he did so. He punched his timeclock and left the table.

"Crack!" Like Peter had heard it. "You're dumb. I'm smart," he had thought. "You lose, I win."

The young man—he was in his late twenties—sat crumpled like wastepaper in the oversize imitation-leather armchair. "You look like you wanna fight" had been the taunting remark made to Peter by an acquaintance several days before. Indeed, even now Peter's face appeared roughly pugilistic, opposed though he was to no observable antagonist. Peter pulled his mouth tight, thrust his jaw, furrowed his brow, creating an effect unfortunate for a face better suited to open and ingenuous expressions.

The projecting wings of the jet-black armchair threatened to totally envelop the figure caught within. Planted as he was, Peter's form was constricted in part and partly extended. His left foot was tucked under his right thigh, left knee jabbing into space. His right leg dropped down from the edge of the chair and he swung the foot from the knee-back and forth; it went back and forth—as if keeping time, marking a time, though, that pressed and pressured, the time of a deadline, perhaps, bearing down upon him. With each swing the sole of his shoe struck the floor, thus making the tension Peter felt audible with the kind of driving beat that might propel early romantic musical compositions. But, in this case, it did nothing of the kind.

Or perhaps it did. That tap-tap-tap-tapping of Peter's foot in that otherwise silent, otherwise empty room, propelled, regulated, or perhaps merely indicated, an activity of some kind, a mental motion of scenes and images, or parcels of recollection and expectation, in wicked involutional orbit. Exploded particles of past and future revolved in rings, rings that became bands of necessity spinning around the hub, which, for Peter, was *now* in that room in that building.

The room—a swollen corridor, really—was the lounge of Starlight Manor, a county-welfare-certified board and lodging establishment.

"This is the poorhouse," thought Peter, "Or as close to such as society still permits."

If he had not broken his leg in October...but that was beside the point. He had been drifting, and for a long time, and drifting that way a guy was bound to end up in such places.

Peter cast his eyes upon the light-green-flecked-with-darker-green linoleum floor. The floor was not dirty; it was quite clean, which merely exaggerated the stark and sterile effect. Ahead of Peter washed-out light tan wallpaper had discolored at the lines where sections joined. By the windows behind Peter the wallpaper was waterstained and discolored at the lines where sections...

∼

"Oh you're so beautiful! Oh you're so beautiful! Oh you're so beautiful!" A booming but muffled voice broke into Peter's consciousness, returning Peter to his present circumstances. The voice issued from a door along the wall on the side of the lounge that served as a corridor. The voice came from "Big John's" room, from "Big John."

Big John was alone in his room. "You're so beautiful! You're so beautiful!" He spoke-shouted-raved to his imaginary companion, treating everyone within a lengthy earshot to his masturbation fantasies. Mounting passion.

Peter always became desperate when forced to consider his immediate circumstances. He knew he had to turn things around, turn things around. In the old days he had been locked on the department store escalator, headed for luxury dining on the top floor. Second floor, third floor, fourth floor.

Now Peter's employment counselor thought he could arrange training as a computer operator. *Maybe* he *should...*

"Bitch! Get the hell out—whore! You're a two-bit cheap trick and I haven't got the time of day for you!"

Big John, having taken his pleasure, was turning out his recent imaginary companion.

"Peter—I don't talk like this to many of my students. Only to one or two every few years." Mr. Kirchen, Peter's 12th grade physics teacher, had paused at that point, allowing the sense of election to settle in. Kirchen was a large man but his muscle tone was poor and his face exhibited an ineffectuality that Peter would be able to perceive only in retrospect. "Mankind is undertaking its ultimate task—the final subjection of nature. The national purpose, Peter—remember that I told you this—has become Clear. Space is a frontier—the oceans are a frontier. Genetics will rework the individual. Computers will organize society more efficiently."

"You will be there, Peter. You'll make your mark in the world and people will respect you for it. You'll contribute."

"Gee, Mr. Kirchen," an embarrassed Peter had replied, "I've worked hard in physics but I just hope I can win in college. I appreciate what you're saying—and thank you, Mr. Kirchen—but who knows who'll win the big fights."

"God! Give me a girlfriend! Where is my girlfriend? Oh God, give me a girlfriend!"

Big John prayed, at the top of his lungs.

Yes, a good chess player should hang on to his queen. A queen was worth any two other pieces on the board. A good piece. Of.

Craig Tyler was now a design engineer for Control Data Corporation. Pawn power in chess! Technocrats...pawns of management...but they lived in comfortable homes.

Peter could not think of Craig Tyler without envisioning Craig's life-blood pouring from a wound in his neck. "Flick my hand forward, slash his throat." A torrent of red liquid: a startled, helpless look on Craig's face. *That* was the guilt that blocked Peter. Craig had been a friend?

On the chess board bishops moved along the diagonals, exercised power obliquely: thus priests inculcated values, often engaged in subversion. And Mr. Kirchen was a priest.

"God! I'll take her to church every Sunday! And fuck her black and blue! Fuck her every day!"

Big John negotiated with the Deity.

On a chess board knights crashed down on one from unexpected directions. They moved two spaces down and one space over. The accident in October was a knight move. But the whole about-face, the drawn-out paralyzing crisis concerning competition and acquisition, competing to acquire, was a knight move. Who'd a thunk it?

Peter drew a breath sharply. He stopped his right foot, terminated the tap-tap-tapping. Peter's body quivered slightly, futilely. He began to exhale the drawn breath slowly.

"I've only had sex fifty or sixty times in my life! I've only had sex fifty or sixty times in my life!"

Big John cried to the Gods and crashed into Peter's consciousness once more.

Disoriented, Peter jerked his head to the left and abruptly focused his attention on a large nature print covering a good three by four foot chunk of the wall. The painting had been done all in black and shades of brown and depicted a raccoon treed among the bare branches of an oak. The picture was a close-up of the raccoon, the hounds were not in sight; the print was really unexceptional, except that now, bewildered, Peter wondered if in those wild, frightened raccoon eyes he didn't see; if that desperate, helpless creature didn't image back to him...

"I should have had sex three or four hundred times! I should have had sex three or four hundred times!"

Peter stumbled out of the chair. He staggered as he stepped down the hallway to the payphone. He would call Donna. No—he didn't want to fight. He wanted to talk, *talk* to a human being.

SKIT SEE
ACT ONE: SEEIN' TWO

The scene is the lounge of a mental hospital. Paul is seated on a cheap old sofa, staring at a T.V. with a picture but no sound. Bill enters and sits down next to Paul.

Paul: You missed Walter Cronkite.

Bill: I didn't want to see Walter Cronkite.

Paul: It was Roger Mudd, anyway.

Bill: Do you realize that Walter Cronkite is the most trusted man in the United States?

Paul: I guess so.

Bill: He has what we lack, brother—credibility. Some people don't believe it's true until Walter Cronkite tells it to them.

Paul: He didn't say anything today, besides, the sound on the T.V. is out.

Bill: Who kicked it this time?

Paul: Roger. He wanted a pass for his birthday and they didn't give it to him. Now he won't get a pass for next weekend, either.

Bill: He lacks credibility. The more he wants out, the longer he'll stay in.

Paul: Credibility. If I had credibility and half an hour prime television time I could let this country know about the Space Wizards.

Bill: You know you're the only one who sees Space Wizards.

Paul: If the man in the street only prayed, he could see a Space Wizard, too. While I wait for the prayers—can I bum a cigarette? What are you smoking?

Bill: Winstons.

Paul: Winston. Win Stone. Bad news. The stone will never win. Every morning when my alarm goes off, Christ rises again and the stone is rolled away.

Bill: Do you want a cigarette or not?

Paul: Yes, please.

Bill: I thought so. But tell me, what are you usually smoking now?

Paul: Tareytons, for obvious reasons.

Bill: Obvious?

Paul: Tareytons. Tarry town. This is tarry town, where we wait our fate, weight our fate, find out how light it is.

Bill: Well, I'm going to buy a pack of Newports.

Paul: Going anywhere?

Bill: I filed my three day notice of intention to leave the hospital.

Paul: No wonder you're inside talking to me. They must have taken away all your privileges.

Bill: I had full grounds privileges, but now that I intend to leave they bottle me up in here in order to exert maximum coercive pressure to stay. Allegedly I'm an escape risk.

Paul: They won't try to commit you, will they?

Bill: I don't think so. I haven't been crazy for a month now. Dr. Richie is just working on the fine details of my new character. He's afraid I won't take my medication after I leave.

Paul: The Space Wizards have commanded me to stay in the hospital.

Bill: Your madness—I'm sure you don't mind the term—

Paul: As long as you remember that I may be crazy, but I'm definitely right.

Bill: Your madness, I say, came on slowly and became one with your life. You've never been completely crazy enough to be cured.

Paul: Well, I can't compete with you. Remember when you stole all that detergent from the laundry? You emptied eight boxes of soap all over the floor and furniture in your room.

Bill: You're embarrassing me.

Paul: You said it was a purification ceremony.

Bill: I was upset about my girlfriend and then that other woman.

Paul: You admitted to me that a Space Wizard told you to do it.

Bill: I deny that.

Paul: Everyone denies Space Wizards. Only when a man is face to face with his own disgrace does he admit he sees Space Wizards. Only when he has no alternatives.

Bill: In that case, then, I have alternatives. Did you see that group of visitors today?

Paul: Yes. A group of high schoolers. They came by while I was on duty.

Bill: You weren't "on duty."

Paul: I was. Eight in the morning to twelve, with a half hour for lunch. Twelve-thirty to four-thirty, with coffee breaks at ten and two-thirty.

Bill: You were guarding the south windows, I suppose?

Paul: Only the lounge windows. Intelligence reported that a battalion of cosmic rays would try to storm the building at that point.

Bill: And you stood there—rigid, immobile, unspeaking—all day.

Paul: A man must do his duty. One high school girl cried and said I looked so human.

Bill: Can you blame her?

Paul: If she only knew what an honor it is to serve the Space Wizards. At the canning factory—there I was subhuman.

Bill: Don't you see the trick they play? This asylum—these walls and security screens—aren't here to protect us. They're here to protect them. We are gathered from our homes, our families, our friends so that they may be spared our vision. Our reality is unbearable to them. Pain is un-American. Suffering is un-American. Standing naked is un-American.

Paul: I'm not standing naked. Neither am I in pain or suffering. In the last two years, since I came here, I've forgotten about the others.

Bill: Well, in the last three months I haven't forgotten. I don't know why I must be quarantined. Why I must live the most intense moments of my life in isolation. Separated, apart—as if my turmoil was not human.

Paul: I'm glad to be left alone. Other people make too many demands.

Bill: I'll tell you why I filed to leave this hospital against medical advice. It's not that I think I'm "ready" yet. But I want *them* to see me now. They let terminal cancer patients go home. But Dr. Richie is preparing a new mask for me, hopefully sturdier than the old one that fell apart. He doesn't want *them* to see me until the new mask is on. But I am not ashamed of myself, as I am, now. Someone must tell our story. Someone must show *them* how it is.

Paul: How noble! You want to offer yourself as a sacrifice to "humanity." You must hate yourself.

Bill: Hate myself?

Paul: Gimme a cause 'cause I'm a cuss. Gimme a cause 'cause I'm a cuss.

Bill: (Stands, becoming excited.) Let me tell you something. The central image of our culture is Christ on the cross. But only Christ can be on the cross. Anybody else who hangs there is a thief. God suffers. Man only sins. People honor the passion of God but not of their neighbor. No wonder every madman thinks he's Christ. Only Christ is allowed to feel pain.

Paul: I-can-play-Dominoes-better-than-you-can.

Bill: I'm talking to you.

Paul: There's a FEE to pay for all your NICKS. Dream on, dead bird.

Bill: This is hopeless. (Exits.)

Paul: Jack Rabbit starts. And Screeching Halts.

(Enter nurse.)

Nurse: Paul, have you seen Bill?

Paul: He's trying out his new sports car.

Nurse: Thank you, Paul. (exits.)

SHADOW

Peter walked through shadow as he walked through a suburban park. Peter had read about "walking shadow" in a fantasy novel, but he had not understood what he had read. Now, at last, he understood.

One walked through shadow and shadow worlds in order to reach what really was, the Real World. One did not walk through distances so much as one walked through dimensions. Endless distance on a given plane would bring varying territory but not necessarily approach to the Real World. The Real World might simply not exist on the whole expanse of a given plane. One must pass between places, onto altogether different maps, to other topological strata. One passed not only through shadow worlds but from shadow universe to shadow universe, until one found the universe of the Real World. The Real World not only somewhere in the total picture, but somewhere in a particular total picture.

Walking shadow involved a particular skill—modifying one's environment by adding and subtracting elements immediately at hand, as one remained in motion, until one's environment corresponded with one's destination. If one's destination had a yellow sky instead of blue, and shrubs instead of trees, as one walked shadow one changed the sky from blue to yellow and changed the plants from trees to shrubs. When all adjustments and corrections had been made, then one had indeed arrived in the Real World.

Peter walked shadow *inside himself*. He sought the Pattern at the heart of the Real World. He sought to remake himself at the Center of the Mind. Instead of turning the sky yellow and producing shrubs, he envisioned his guilt as a stone by the sidewalk and he then moved that stone into a garden in the park. He envisioned his love as a bed of daffodils on the edge of the garden. He climbed a maple tree that had become his aspiration, and swam in a pond that had become his peace. He saw his death in a robin swooping down upon a swallowtail butterfly. The contents of his psyche poured themselves into the world around him, changing that world to other worlds, and he worked his way through the worlds, adjusting, projecting and adjusting. He built fantasy universes and then discarded them, working his way to the Real World and the Pattern.

The garden then became the Real World and Peter thought he would remake that Real World through recreation of the Pattern, a tracing of it anew. But Fear appeared as a garter snake that slid through the grass and the Fear grew. Fear possessed Peter as he realized he had entered a world too Real for human substance or human manipulation. Only a Real Being was at home in the Real World. Only One, not Peter's ego, could trace or retrace the Pattern.

Peter fled in terror, and knew himself insane.

ONCE WHEN I WAS UNHAPPY

(Pills, the pills.)

No, I could not go home. So I sat in my dorm room. I could not go home. So I sat in my worn red armchair, alone in my dorm room.

My parents would not have me home. That fact was final. (Doom clamoring in my ears, in my eyes, about my head.) I could not go home, you see, after the outrageous rages of the previous spring, the psychosis (my third), the commitment (by my father), and after all the angry exchanges during my parents' visits to the hospital.

I had left the city of Minneapolis on the worst of terms. I had left Minneapolis for Cambridge (Massachusetts) after the mental hospital, in July, and when I came to Cambridge I—had slept. Fourteen hours a day, all summer, I had slept. I had not worked. I had lived on savings, and then I had lived on credit cards .

During the day, during the summer, I had haunted coffeehouses, reading books, drinking expresso. But that was over now. During the summer nothing had been expected of me and I had done nothing. Now I was enrolled in school, and I had a part-time job.

I contemplated the present as well as the past, sitting in my armchair. (Pills, the pills.)

"Contemplated" is hardly the word—my mental process was scattered, frenzied. For several days I had been growing increasingly beside myself. I was realizing that I could not function in school: I could not wake up, I could not stay awake. The fact of consciousness appalled me.

Return, retreat, withdraw—lie down, lie down, lie down. If only my responsibilities would really go away when they seemed to go away. If only I need not wake up. (Pills, the pills.)

Wake up to what? I asked myself. Wake up to anxiety, depression, dislocation. A dormitory full of strange people (my own class had graduated more than a year before), strange people who did not seem to want to know me. And how could a desperate man make an acquaintance? "Hi, my name is David. You don't know me, but I'm suicidal."

I was back on the treadmill, and would receive my degree in less than a year. If I stayed on the treadmill. But receiving my degree would bring changes I was not prepared for. What was my alternative?

If I could not wake up to go to school, which I thought I liked, how could I wake up to go to work, which I knew I didn't?

Unfortunately, the two graduate level courses I signed up for each required twenty page papers in the first weeks of the term. I did not feel up to it.

Returning to school was the path of least resistance, but even there the resistance seemed too great. I had lost my vitality. I was burned out. Three psychotic episodes in three years had done me in. Even my "summer vacation" had not restored my strength. I needed help, but where was help to be found? And I had no money, and no place to stay, if I was not in school.

I could not go to school. I had no alternative.

∼

I rose from my chair, walking into the bathroom. There, on the shelf, were my pills. Eighty-four fifty milligram capsules of Benadryl. Pink and white, very pretty.

With a sudden gesture, I swallowed a handful of pills, then a mouthful of water—a handful of pills, a mouthful of water, repeated, until the pills were gone.

I was shocked by my own action, but I had no regrets. I was not tempted to call for help at the last minute.

I returned to my armchair and stared at my digital clock. How long would it be? I was convinced that these were my last conscious moments. I felt very heavy. I kept repeating to myself, "This is what it's like to die."

I stood up. I fell down. I crawled back into my armchair. My vision blurred.

Fading, fading—"This is what it's like to die"—fading . . .

STILL LIFE:
A GLIMPSE OF MANY APPLES

This is the city of Minneapolis: more particularly, this is the Red Barn on 24th and Nicollet—in Minneapolis. The Red Barn sells fast hamburgers-a Big Barney, which is equivalent to a Big Mac, costs 89 cents. The large iced tea I now drink costs me 50 cents.

The Red Barn is also known as the Dead Barn because at any given time about half its "customers" have been sitting at tables all day but haven't bought a thing all day. What would the Red Barn be without Daniel, Clarysse, Frank, Neil, and the rest?

Daniel was in the service until he was totally psychiatrically disabled in a special mission against Nikita Krutschev. The President informed no one of Daniel's mission: not the Vice-president, not the Cabinet, not the leaders of Congress—not even Daniel's mother was informed. Daniel now collects $750 a month from the V.A., hangs out at the Red Barn, and hopes to meet his "marriage mate."

Clarysse has already been married. She married a chemist and had two children. She received a degree in Philosophy from the University in 1948, married, had two children, and then spent 15 years at Moose Lake State Hospital. Unlike most regulars at the Red Barn she keeps herself neat and clean and looks like—well—like somebody's mother. She's been eating too many french fries, though.

You see—this neighborhood is the half-way house district of Minneapolis. We have half-way houses for crazies, drunks, junkies, idiots—everybody. Everybody is welcome in Whittier neighborhood. But half-way houses half-way contain many people and there isn't half-way anything to do at a half-way house. There isn't anything to do at the Red Barn, either, but most folks would rather do nothing at the Red Barn than do nothing at the half-way house they half-way call home. So here we are.

Actually, I live in my own apartment now. I used to live in a half-way house—for crazies—but that half-way house was actually in a Minneapolis neighborhood other than Whittier. I don't know what got into the solid citizens of Minneapolis east of Whittier, but they permitted a half-way house in *their* neighborhood. And I managed to get into it.

Now I live in Whittier anyway. I know what happened to the solid citizens of Whittier—they left. I wonder if some day every house on my block will be a whorehouse.

Frankly, I'm sick of the whores and the pimps. I'd much rather see parades of palsied old men on three-wheeled bicycles ride down the street than the parades of cool dudes in their Eldorados that I do see. A peculiar feature of crippled people—emotionally, mentally, physically, however crippled—is that they tend to be harmless. They don't exploit.

Somewhere around here—nobody is supposed to know where—there's a halfway house for prostitutes. The guy who thought of that—he was a Jesus freak—was a genius. Now one half of the neighborhood feeds off the other.

You know—I used to audit the restaurants of downtown Minneapolis's fanciest hotel. I got fired. I used to audit the Marquis Room—the fanciest of downtown's fanciest hotel—and some day I'm going to write something that's going to be good, and I'll get paid, and then—this is a promise—I'm going to take Daniel and Clarysse and Frank to the Marquis Room and let them find out what chateaubriand and escargot are. After a lifetime of hamburgers and french fries.

Then I'll become a taxi driver and take care of the rest of the neighborhood.

INCARNATIONS

David, still sleepy, sat down at the breakfast table. He was in a mental hospital. He had been there for ten weeks. David was just beginning to realize that he had been mad for ten weeks.

"Cheryl, I had a dream last night. It's bothering me. Do you want to hear it?"

"Tell me your dream, David," said the psychiatric nurse, Cheryl.

"I dreamt I went mad in France in the Middle Ages. I was burned at the stake as a witch."

∼

David, still sleepy, sat down at the breakfast table. He was in a mental hospital. He had been mad for ten weeks.

"Cheryl, I had a dream last night. It's bothering me. Do you want to hear it?"

"Tell me your dream, David," said the psychiatric nurse, Cheryl.

"I dreamt I went mad in Venezuela among the Indians. I became the village shaman."

∼

"Cheryl?"

LIGHT

It was dark. So dark. I pushed forward into the dark. Truth was walking step by step...

But that was not true—there *was* a light. A pinpoint of light. Fainter than a fading star. It drew me towards it, and I followed it—through the dark. I pushed forward.

Through woods and underbrush. The light drew nearer to me as I drew nearer to it. *Faint* as a fading star.

Animals called in the woods about me. To my right a wolf howled, behind me a tiger prowled. I pushed forward and the light drew closer as I followed. It now appeared a luminous globule, a small hazy disc hanging in the sky before my eyes.

My feet crackled in the underbrush. I entered a swamp, retreated, and circled around it to my right. On my right a forest fire had ignited, flames throwing themselves to the sky, burning, eating at the branches and trunks they clung to.

I passed through—between the fire and the swamp. Emerging, the light, my light, was much clearer, and I realized at once my destination—a problem I had not been able yet to consider.

The great luminous disc had drawn closer to me, as I to it. The *light* was my destination, my guide was my goal.

And I looked, looked for once clearly into the light, and saw His face.

TWENTY-FOUR HOUR RESTAURANT

Dark had fallen. The temperature was falling. I picked my way through a devil's garden of stone and steel and office building.

I needed a place to sleep. The shelters wouldn't take me because of the way I screamed and yelled and thrashed about during my nightmares. I was getting desperate.

A man approached. "Know where I could stay the night?" I asked routinely. "This way," he said.

We went back two blocks, into an office building, past a security guard, up an elevator, and into an office suite, where he showed me a room with desk, chair, many bookshelves, and a couch.

"Sleep here."

~

That night I dreamt of the family. I had a family once, you know. I dreamt of Mom and Dad, brothers and sisters, and wife and daughters and sons. Aunts and uncles. Nieces and nephews. Even grandpa. We were eating dinner together. I can't remember what we had, but there was lots of mint jelly. I felt a hand on my shoulder just when we were getting to desert.

~

"Good Morning."
I snapped awake. There he was. "What time is it!" I asked.
"It's 5:30 in the morning."
"Where am I? Who are you? Why did you wake me up?"
"I'm the magistrate of Federal Court. These are my chambers. I thought maybe you would like to go to Perkins...."

MINI-FEST-OH!

I remember *when* as a senior in high school I read *The Glass Bead Game*. Playing the glass bead game one orchestrates the great ideas—no, not the ideas themselves, but their quintessential abstractions. These abstractions—drawn from the ideas of philosophy, music, literature, religion, psychology, painting, mysticism, and further—are interwoven and interplayed, creating a personal composition and expression, a composition and expression, with objective significance. A theme from Bach, an idea from Kant, a figure from Leonardo, a line from T.S. Eliot—all harmoniously correlated to make a statement which is universal yet particular.

I have played the glass bead game: I have created delusional systems. In my madness I have gone over into the eternal realm of the divine ideas-I have entered the mind of God, where the Great Dance is forever taking place. I have seen pattern within pattern, correspondence within correspondence; I have seen congruence and convergence.

There is something of Levi-Strauss's *bricoleur* about me *in this process*, when I use as symbols whatever ideas and objects and events come to hand. Popular music, plumbing equipment, a card game, the name of a friend—these too, can be used in the system-building. There *is* pattern; there *is* Dance.

Knowledge is a seemless web.

ESSAYS

This is what the kingdom of God is like. A man throws seed on the land. Night and day, while he sleeps, when he is awake, the seed is sprouting and growing; how, he does not know. Of its own accord the land produces first the shoot, then the ear, then the full grain in the ear. And when the crop is ready, he loses no time: he starts to reap because the harvest has come.

Reflections on Acute Psychosis

Psychosis is genuine lived experience. If an individual falls sick for ten weeks, real events take place, which work real effects and will exert continuing influence on the individual. If asked what happened, the individual may say, "I was hospitalized with a nervous breakdown." Or the individual might say, "I took off in a rocket heading for the moon but I lost my way and fell into the sun. I was held captive there by Australian aborigines until I drank a magic potion and psychically teleported myself back to earth."

One may object that the first account – hospitalization for psychosis – "really" took place, and the second account is sheer fantasy. But that second account was lived as real experience – as peculiarly intense experience, as a matter of fact – and that version of a ten week hospitalization will shape the individual as much or more than any other ten weeks of his life.

Psychosis is carried on within what I like to refer to as an "autonomous mode of discourse." This "autonomous mode of discourse" is a way of knowing, a method of "seeing" that is particularly abhorrent to the rational-empirical-materialistic mind. To "mistake" a psychiatric ward for the sun, and to think that an old friend's house, some four hundred miles away, is the moon, is generally viewed as cognitive failure. It is very important to us these days to perceive the world as it concretely "really" is. Water "is" "really" composed of hydrogen and oxygen in a particular molecular form. Such an understanding of water facilitates technological manipulation of the substance. What contributes to technological progress "is" "really" true.

Water, of course, may also be understood as the element of baptism. "Baptism," however, carries very little contemporary meaning. Such an understanding of water, one which has no market value, could never be the "real" understanding.

I am suggesting that knowledge exists in a number of cognitive types, each "type" valuable with regard to some set purpose. What we regard today as "real" knowledge is only knowledge of one certain type, a type which facilitates materialistic production and consumption.

Before one, with one particular frame of reference, diagnoses "cognitive failure" one might perhaps question what mode of cognition is in fact present. Otherwise one may diagnose "poor Spanish" when the language being spoken is actually French. I am suggesting that the psychotic is not even attempting to speak "rational-empirical-materialism": he has adopted a different cognitive mode and is pursuing another kind of knowledge altogether.

Technology is based on the notion that the world is "really" meaningless. Water "is" H2O: it is only accidentally and incidentally the element of baptism. The sun "is" an astronomical object with certain astrophysical properties – so also, the moon. The rest is basically superstition, hardly worth commenting upon. It is thus no accident that the technologically most wealthy nations suffer a crisis of meaning. Meaning cannot be sold in the market place and is thus neglected.

The psychotic has taken a difficult, drastic, dangerous step toward the recovery of meaning. For him the moon "is" the sum of his hopes and aspirations. He had once shared those hopes and aspirations with his friend far away. He sought to recover his life but found himself being purged in a refining fire – the sun. He was no longer worthy of his dreams and needed to reconstitute himself.

All very easy, one may say, to make up an illness and then supply a clear interpretation. But that brings me to a related point: We have left behind what knowledge we did have, left behind all knowledge not materially productive. We have flung alternative knowledge from us: Acquisition of material. Attainment of superior social position. "Making" something of oneself. Getting ahead in the world. The rest - we declare – is nonsense.

The typical in-patient physician is ideologically opposed to helping his patient understand his illness, or grow by it, or learn from it. Schizophrenia is not an experience to be lived, it is a disease, nonsense, it doesn't pay, must be eradicated then forgotten about (except that Roerig, Inc., has another lifetime customer).

A different quality of life, a different way of "seeing" is not of concern to the typical physician. Schizophrenia is a "disease," the doctor cures it. Bang – that's enough of that.

Ours is an extroverted culture: oriented to external activity, materialism, ambition. There is little room for the introvert of whatever variety. Certainly – to see one's "soul" (antique concept, that) reflected in the world, is clear cognitive failure.

There are many possible relationships between the ego and the self and the contemporary attitude reflects one possibility. The contemporary ego says to the self, "I am king, I am God, I make decisions, control and manipulate. I don't want to hear from you or hear about you. You bring only neurosis or psychosis – pain, hesitation, and doubt."

The contemporary attitude, with its drive toward ego aggrandizement, willfully neglects the fact that the self also brings meaning and value to the ego. The rational principle cannot construct its premises – the premises must be given to it, postulated. Sheer rationality cannot conjure up a single meaning or value. The self does bring pain, hesitation, and doubt – but also rewards of meaning and value.

The contemporary relation between ego and self is replicated in the relation between individual and social-material environment. As the ego seeks to dominate the self, so the individual seeks to dominate the social-material environment. "If I had become pre-occupied with that girlfriend, I wouldn't have passed spring quarter in medical school." "Johnny Jr. is playing Little League, but I must keep up with my professional reading during the evenings." The ambitious contribute to "mankind" but have nothing to give to their neighbor.

I suggest that the opportunities for growth presented by psychotic process (as opposed to "mental illness") are neglected because, in a real sense, they are "anti-social" and call into question accepted values.

Psychotic process contains both universal patterns and personal elements. Universal pattern introduces the individual to the general collective spiritual heritage of humanity. A good example is John Perry's identification of a complex of symptoms in acute psychosis that reconstruct the ancient regenerative rite of sacral kingship. The personal elements are frequent and better known – symbols are used to express individual relations, attitudes, questions and work to resolution of the same. The individual with the hypothetical illness from the beginning of this paper might re-evaluate his past and present relationship with his distant friend. A symbol may – in a simple concrete image, readily recognizable – present to the individual a pattern that has been endlessly repeated without notice.

Besides these contents of psychotic process which may yield meaning if one has recovered the forgotten language, I have suggested that the form, the quality of consciousness, is a challenge to twentieth century mindset.

Psychotic process has been referred to as "primary process," upon which the "secondary process" of ego functioning is built. If primary process is indeed primary, the peculiarities of psychotic process have relevance to all of us. These are universal, though suppressed, functions, and as such are worthy of investigation.

But the energy which suppresses primary process within the individual psyche is the same energy which suppresses the expression of primary process on the part of the individual. "Crazytalk" is irritating, almost obscene, and is suppressed with a tell-tale vehemence. In this sense, a genuine "politics of experience" is carried on on the psychiatric ward.

As one investigates these matters one is led to the conclusion that all things are contained in the soul, and that the ego must submit to the self. As ego capitulates to the self the competitive, combative, status-seeking impulses subside as the ego, through obedience, participates in the timeless peace of soul. Life goes on, much as before, but one's center has shifted to a locus "behind" the ego. A quality of life rather than a quantity of material or superiority of status is pursued. This perhaps means very little to acculturated Americans but the wealth of the soul makes one rich beyond millionaires.

The fact that acute psychosis is an invitation to such transformation cannot be disregarded.

There and Back Again
Another Hobbit Takes a Trip

I felt that a title light and fantastical, a bit adventurous, would best suit my purpose in this collection of pieces. Profound psychosocial maladjustment is indeed profound, but a bit of buoyancy and a gay mood make any war more bearable. Hanging one's head and wringing one's hands over a "noble mind o'erthrown" do nothing to restore the spirit. Conceive a challenge! Imagine a quest! Fare forward, traveler!

Forward? Where, forward? Where, there?

One is not called *there* randomly or senselessly. The path there is not senseless, nor is the need to travel that path an irreparable loss. The eruption of illness into the life of a vulnerable individual brings into focus whole complexes of key life issues. There questions are posed, and the individual responds. There choices are made, and resolutions are pointed to. The most profound crucible of internal reality is there.

Schizophrenia is pre-eminently an exercise in values and meaning – real values and real meaning. Yet the inner dialogue takes place in a mode even the experienced observer may find unintelligible. One must rediscover the symbol as a unique cognitive construct, rediscover image that at once reveals and conceals human potential. I ask the reader to journey with me to a state if mind where one thinks in perceptions rather than about them. The chair I see is a seat of knowledge. The door I walk through *is* the gate of hell. There I don't "think about" knowledge or hell, there I encounter them directly in the world I live.

I don't epistemologize about knowledge or theologize about hell, I experience facts in my immediate environment. I act, and events develop. I stand before the seat of knowledge.

I enter hell. I am telling myself a story about myself. Transformation takes place at the core of my being as the consequences of my actions unfold.

There my mind is not separate from my environment. There, there is no subject separate from object. There my mind has expanded to contain the perceptual field, and all objects before me are simultaneously elements of the mind itself. The cognitive and perceptual fields interlock, and synthesize new realities at all levels. There.

A body of lore and a set of cultural practices concerning such experience have developed around the figure of the tribal shaman. In my first essay I use the figure of the shaman to develop a context for understanding symbol play and symbol transformation in the course of an illness. This is a "symbol" essay, and I examine how a shaman experiences symbols. How does the shaman understand his "death"? How might we understand his "journey"? Who are his "familiars"? What is his "totem"?

In this first essay I discuss the "sparrow", a symbol from my own illness. I examine what this sparrow has come to mean to me as I have lived with the image over a number of years. My discussion of the sparrow provides the model I would use for discussing any other symbol from one of my illnesses. For the shaman, the visible is always a token of the invisible, and the object at hand points to meaning beyond. One learns to see the invisible within what one can see; even, perhaps, within a dead bird. But what is this experience I talk around? What is the powerful trauma so few actually observe and fewer still undergo?

"One Day, On My Way to Jail" is an attempt to make vivid the experience of a psychotic, an attempt to capture and convey the active consciousness. The story is a concatenation of mental associations. Physical description is suppressed. Powerful emotions are present but they make no tangible appearance. The energies of these emotions are locked into association and image.

The form of this story seeks to convey psychotic consciousness. The structure is as important as the content. The words are present to convey the consciousness that contains the words.

I find short stories very helpful for organizing the experience of illness. I believe that psychosis is inherently poetic – drama without a stage, art crafted from the fiber of life. Owen Barfield defines the "appreciation of poetry" as a "felt change of consciousness." What is illness if not a "felt change of consciousness"? A glimpse into God's poetry, perhaps? Communicating that "felt change of consciousness," so that another may feel it as well, is an artistic challenge of the first degree.

These forays into the symbolic do not, of course, take place in a social-societal vacuum. My second essay is a "social" essay, an attempt to place the newly discovered world of symbol and image into a contemporary social-societal context. Where do we find meaning? And how do we therefore relate to our neighbor? Through whom do we define our existence, or fail to define it? Questions for the second essay.

I present to you therefore a "symbol" essay pointing to shamanic practice as a context for understanding psychotic process. I then present a story which attempts to capture the experience itself. Between the first essay and the story I develop the "sparrow" as a paradigmatic for my understanding of image and existence. Finally I have written a social essay to put this experience in a human context.

Fare forward, traveler!

SHAMANISM AND PSYCHOSIS

Shamanic Call

Eliade distinguishes shamanic call from shamanic initiation. Shamanic call manifests itself as a severe physical or "psychosocial" crisis. Successful recovery from such crisis marks the individual as a future shaman. The individual may not wish to become a shaman and may resist the call but community belief is that such resistance can lead only to misfortune or death. The individual must eventually present himself to a practicing shaman for teaching, training, and ceremonial initiation – whether the individual likes it or not. The decision does not belong to the individual – the gods have decided.

Not all shamanic calls are acute psychotic episodes – though some are. Not all acute psychotic episodes are shamanic calls – though some are. With significant frequency an acute psychotic episode breaches the barrier between unconscious and conscious leaving the individual permanently susceptible to communication from "behind" his awareness. The ego's intensified awareness of and sensitivity to the self will require a re-organization of the total psyche in a manner divergent from the norm. If he is to survive, the individual must so reorganize – the gods have decided. The barrier between unconscious and conscious has been broken down and the new "inner" reality must be integrated if it is not to destroy the individual. The gods have called the individual to them and he must serve them or they will break him.

Shamanic Initiation

Shamanic initiation in the typical village is a fairly straightforward matter. The individual presents himself to a practicing shaman. If the shaman agrees that the individual is called he introduces the individual to the lore and practice of the village culture which has been built up by generations of shamans. The individual, from the experience of his call, makes his own personal contribution to the tradition, while the tradition helps the individual to place his own personal experience in perspective. Both call and initiation are pro-social events.

The modern West recognizes neither shamanism nor shamanic call nor shamanic initiation. Our equivalent of shamanic call is deeply stigmatized and shamanic initiation is simply unavailable. Help is found only through the literature of other times and other places.

Vision Quest

Black Elk refers to vision quest among the Lakota as "lamenting a vision" or "crying for a vision." Pain and sadness are certainly two roots of acute psychosis. But the vision is not escape from the pain, the vision speaks to the pain, addresses the sadness, seeks to ease the heaviness of heart with alternative perspectives, other ways of understanding. The vision grows from the pain, not to deny the pain but to crown it with understanding.

The acute psychotic episode may be understood as God's answer to a deeply troubled individual, but we must remember that God's ways are not our ways, nor God's thoughts our thoughts.

To digress for a moment: A friend of mine has suggested that psychotics have a high threshold for pain. Perhaps such individuals will bear pain rather than avoid it right up to the collapse of the ego and the loss of conscious control. Protecting the ego – as, in an obvious instance, through the expression of anger – is the more usual path. Bearing the pain may drive one from this world into another. I say that without prejudice to either world.

To digress a bit further: Owen Barfield reminds us that what to us is an analysis of "thought" was to the ancient Greeks an analysis of "Being." I have been speculating lately and really wonder whether the collapse of an ego is not a "suicide of Being." Notions that shamans die and are reborn or travel through the Land of the Dead run rampant through tribal cultures. To quote a Huichol Indian:

> There is a doorway within our minds that usually remains hidden and secret until the time of death. The Huichol word for it is nierika. Nierika is a cosmic portway or interface between so-called ordinary and non-ordinary realities. It is a passageway and at the same time a barrier between worlds.

This death, passing through this doorway, is clearly not a biological death and thus is not of interest to rational-empirical-materialists. But were one to throw over the dogma that "Being" is body only, material only, and were one to grant the dignity of "Being" to consciousness, I can conceive of no finer "refining fire," no better Purgatory for the development of soul than that encountered by the death of the ego in illness. The individual is brought face to face with what he would not see, finds terror in long-avoided encounter, finds joy in exalted vision of new potential. In the Land of the Dead one knows what one was and conceives what one might be. One may return with that new vision to the land of the living.

Fallen Sparrow

While a Lakota is in the midst of his vision quest he pays particular attention to the animals which show themselves in his vicinity. Animals – in dreams, elsewhere – I think of as forces as yet unconscious to the individual. The most powerful symbol I have ever encountered during an illness was an animal – a dead sparrow. Were I ever to take an Indian name it would be "Fallen Sparrow."

The reader of a story such as "One Day" should bear in mind that if the meaning of the "Spare 'O'" is unclear to him it was also at the time of the story unclear to me. I knew that I had very powerful feelings about this dead bird but the feelings were totally inarticulate. I had neither words nor concepts with which to express myself. I possessed only the symbol.

Having lived with this symbol for eight years, I feel I can now articulate five aspects of its meaning to me.

First – I fell, and God knew. I had tracked myself into the high power, high prestige world of Harvard College and I was leaving – being thrown out, really. I felt that God watched, gave his permission, and would guide me through and after the collapse. It was part of his plan for me. The misfortune was not without meaning nor was it simply an irreparable loss.

Second – the spare 'O' was something extra that would support and fortify me. The collapse I suffered was not the end but would be bearable because of the strength the spare 'O' provided me with.

Third – I had reached a bedrock sense of being. I was "nothing." And that was good, whole. I had tried to "make something of myself" but that could only be fraud. Whatever I might "become" as a social being was accidental, incidental, and trivial compared to my being as defined between myself and my Creator.

Fourth – the collapse of the social-material world I had created for myself was simultaneous with the discovery of an inner psychical world which I had not created (as an idol) but which I must serve. The collapse of my external world could be compared to the Western existential meaning of void. The discovery of my internal world could be compared to the Eastern Buddhist meaning of void. There are two kinds of nothing – one which destroys and one which sustains. The "spare-ness" of the spare 'O' indicated the second. The completed path moves from destruction to sustenance. The one "void" points to the other.

Fifth – the spare 'O' expressed my feeling of estrangement from the social-material environment. Culture and society have seemed peculiar to me rather than natural: "I never would have guessed." I often feel marginal – "in the world, not of it" – not a number but a lack of number.

The dead bird not only expressed these five ideas but bound them together and related them to one another. The spare 'O' is still a wordless riddle.

Ecstatic Journey

Eliade identifies the "ecstatic journey" as the central element of shamanic practice. There are many adventures in the form of the ecstatic journey that I have experienced but the original was perhaps my re-enactment of the Greek myth of Perseus: capturing the head of Medusa.

I traveled into my soul, to lands far away, and procured a special tool or weapon. I attempted to explain the nature of this possession in my short story "Ransom in Tellus":

> At these times the contents of my psyche are turned to stone. My fate appears to me in the form of material objects. These material objects are the symbolic, yet physical, representations of the ideas and feelings within me. They come pouring out of me as I turn Medusa's head within my soul, and then I practice magic, I manipulate these symbol objects as they appear in order to control my descent and subsequent ascent.

This "practice of magic" – this responding to and manipulating the magical potencies appearing in the illness environment – is the key to guiding the ship of the soul through troubled waters. How one responds, within the illness, to fantastic events and unusual objects determines the course of the illness, directs one to a given destination, prepares the quality of recovery. *Real* decisions are made in fantastical places. Real choices with real and swiftly retributed consequences. But the practice of magic within illness is the topic for another essay.

Time Traveling

One may construct a special form of the "ecstatic journey" to contain the acute psychotic episode generally. Owen Barfield points out how our sense of our internal selves and our relation to humanity is at the mercy of the language we use. A chair may be a chair whatever we call it, but an emotional reality is deeply colored by the word we use to refer to it. The specifically human meanings we recognize are defined by the terms we use. Once people suffered "accidie" and that term contained a certain perspective and orientation. Later people were "sad" or "discouraged" and that was different. Now people are "depressed" and the inner world is still differently ordered and understood.

Barfield's philological analysis of the history of consciousness traces two continual developments: (1) the development of a self-contained self-consciousness separated from the world it once participated in, and (2) the transformation of participated symbols into abstracted concepts. These two processes are inseparably linked. Language, as one traces it back, becomes more and more symbolic – where bundles of human meaning are contained in physical metaphor only. As time goes on, the meanings are separated and relocated into distinct concepts, discriminated from one another and from the object-symbol which once contained them. Consciousness, through history, withdraws itself from symbolic participation in its environment and locates itself in abstract concepts.

Just so, eight years ago, I picked up a dead bird which meant something, was something, I could not say what, and through the passage of time it has differentiated into five concepts. The bird, Barfield would say, contained Meaning, which was then transformed into Knowledge. In a short segment of my life, dealing with a product of illness, I have recapitulated a process essential to human history.

Original participation was high in meaning, short in knowledge. Contemporarily, and perhaps personally, we are high in knowledge, short on meaning. The psychotic's "ecstatic journey," may, among other things, be a trip to the human past, recovering new meaning for the construction of new knowledge.

The Shaman Today

Western society no longer recognizes the role of the shaman. What might the shaman say here and now?

I have been struggling with metaphors with which to illustrate a basic difference in orientation. I tend to despair of the effort since I believe that the problem is primarily moral and not a matter of technical knowledge. The sin I wish to castigate is the usual sin, and the usual sin is the greatest: idolatry.

The ego may be imagined as situated between the self-image and the self. The self-image is before the ego and the self is behind. The ego can "see" the self-image, it is tangible, a "real" entity. Contemporarily, the ego strives to enhance this self-image. It must become great, greater, glorious. Meanwhile the self is behind the ego speaking in a still, small voice. This still, small voice is no longer heard by the ego.

The self-image may be associated with visuals, tangibles — a "graven image." The self is oriented to hearing (words, language, Word of God) and expresses itself from behind the ego, not before it. Enthralled by the self-image, the ego no longer listens to the self. The ego is alienated from the self and worships the self-image.

The individual no longer serves God. Who seeks God's will for his life these days? We no longer have ears to hear.

ONE DAY, ON MY WAY TO JAIL

On the morning of Monday, March 12, 1973 – I walked out of the dining hall of Currier House, Radcliffe and was met by classmate Dana Rotegard and House Master Colleen Reitsma. "Peter," spoke Dana, "You must go to the Health Service for psychiatric examination. You destroyed your room last night."

I thought back to the sculpture I had constructed, painstakingly, in my room, out of my personal belongings. That had been between midnight, and 7:00 a.m. – yes, earlier in the day. I supposed Dana was referring to that. At the Health Service I would be termed "a danger to myself." The situation, it now seemed, was hopeless.

"Surely, Dana," I responded, "Just give me some time alone and then I'll go with you to the Health Service." I walked away from Dana and Colleen and went into the Currier House south courtyard.

"Of course," I thought, "I have already performed a 'Health Service'" – in front of the altar, the altar that I had constructed and Dana had not yet found (thank god!), the alter which worked changes to make for older things. (Dana was going to be pissed when he opened that closet door.)

As I paced back and forth in the courtyard, I noticed something peculiar lying on the ground: a dead bird, a sparrow.

I became excited. This was it — the sparrow! "Are not sparrows two a penny? Yet without your Father's leave not one of them can fall to the ground." This was the sparrow that fell to the ground. The very one.

I put the dead bird in my pocket. It was my sparrow, my "spare 'O'." I had an extra 'O'. The situation was no longer hopeless. Refortified, with my spare 'O' in my pocket, I was ready to meet the shrinks. In the encounter I might be reduced to nothing, but I had a spare 'O'.

Dana escorted me to the Harvard Health Service. There I was met by Dr. Atrium, Dr. Auricle, and Dr. Ventricle. The four of us went into a room together, alone, and they questioned me intensively: Why had I been throwing discarded beer cans into the Charles River at 4:00 in the morning? Why had I written peculiar letters to a professor of logic? Why did I persist in clearing off bulletin boards in Harvard Yard?

As the pressure increased, as they threatened me with a commitment to McLean Hospital, I decided to play my ace.

"I have a whole in my pocket."

I spoke fiercely.

"What did you say, Mr. Watkins?"

Dr. Ventricle interrogated.

"Here" – I spoke again, pulling the dead bird from my pocket – "Do what you please, but I want you to know that I have a spare 'O'."

"God!" ejaculated Atrium. "He's crazy!" ejaculated Auricle. "I'll write the papers!" climaxed Ventricle.

∽

Half an hour later the papers had been written and I was standing in front of Stillman Infirmary in front of a private car, with a policeman by my side.

"Stillman," I thought, "Yes, a still man – so little responding, while reality is being reorganized around him, and he is so far away." And yet – it was true, I insisted to myself – still man, yet was I human. And they were taking me to McLean.

I stepped toward the rear door of the car. Suddenly I revolted. "No!" I flashed. "No!" I couldn't let it happen.

I bolted. I ran as fast as I could down Holyoke Street to Massachusetts Avenue. The cop was hard at my heels, shouting for me to stop. "Stop!" he shouted. And he shouted again, "Stop!"

Traffic on Mass. Ave. was heavy. However, I had important business on the other side. I dashed into the street. Brakes squealed, horns blared. While vehicles skidded and swerved, I, for my part, dodged and danced.

The cop did not dare follow. When I came out on the other side of Massachusetts Avenue, still running as hard as I could, I was a free man.

∽

Where to go? The nut had bolted, true enough, but what next?

"Of course, I'll run up Mass. Ave. to the Midget Restaurant. The 'Midget': Oskar, from *The Tin Drum*. He was put away in an institution – I will go to the Midget Restaurant."

I was scared. I was a fugitive from the law. Being chased by the police was a heavier trip than I would have expected.

I went into The Midget and ordered a cup of coffee. The waitress was apparently talking to me about a "nice old lady" several tables down. I was confused about what the waitress meant to be saying. Maybe this "nice old lady" was Mother Goose. I went over and without saying a word, sat down across from the old lady.

She began talking immediately. Her husband had just died. Fine, I thought, I will be the new husband of Mother Goose. Her son played classical piano. Good, I thought, this family knows about the Universal Harmony.

Finally the old woman said to me, "I will pay the bill."

Understanding immediately, I burst into tears. "She will pay the bill, pay the bill," I sobbed. "It doesn't matter anymore. It doesn't matter if I'm arrested. It doesn't matter if I'm sent to McLean. My debt – my debt – is paid."

∽

After leaving The Midget, I walked back to Harvard Square and took the MTA into Boston. I spent the afternoon in Boston. I was free, and, I was safe. But I had to go back to Harvard. I felt, I must admit, like a messenger, and Courier House was thus undoubtedly my proper home. If only I could talk to the Master: she would understand.

At the evening-time, I decided to walk from Boston to Cambridge: I undertook my Great Journey Home.

I picked up a bag of trash from behind a house in Back Bay. I slung the bag over my shoulder, becoming Santa Claus; Santa Claus going to distribute goodies in Cambridge. (Refuse they would refuse.)

Along the Esplanade I threw the bag into the Charles River – my baby Moses, and he would be found when the bulrushes.

Along Storrow Drive (Store 'O'! Store 'O'! I would remember!) I found a long metal rod and a hubcap and a small toy horse. I was Ulysses, with shield and spear, presenting the horse to Troy, to H.U., damn U. (Ulysses who sailed over the brink, as well as sailed home.)

Eventually as I neared my destination, unpleasant thoughts entered my head. The Metropolitan District Commission posted signs along Storrow Drive – speed limits. At the bottom, they all said, "MDC." "M.D. see?" "No," I insisted, "No! I will not."

I found a Bier Bottle and smashed it against a Wall. The christening! Apotheosis!

∼

By the time I reached Harvard I thought I was invisible. I walked in front of a policeman and he arrested me.

I was sent to McLean.

A MORE REFLECTIVE PEACE NOW

For one who has had the experience and seeks to understand it, the problem of illness is as large as the problem of life. All meaningful symbols, all human emotions, all structures of the mind, all human peace and all human conflict are kaleidoscopically reflected and refracted in psychotic process. The problem of schizophrenia is as large as the problem of life.

The illness is as varied as the individuals who suffer from it. Even were one to collect a dozen individuals all claiming to be Christ, one would discover upon examination that each understood Christ differently and understood his identification with Christ differently. Many different character traits are brought into the illness, many different patterns of illness emerge. Pattern of illness, as opposed to diagnostic category, is a very individual matter.

My work, as opposed to my job, is reading and writing. The principle informing my reading and writing is further clarification, organization, and communication of experiences I have had while ill. I read widely: literature, comparative religion, Christian theology, and more. I write in many forms: short stories and essays, poems and meditations. Through these activities I have sought to exhibit intra-psychic transformations, capture states of mind on paper, put wordless images into poems, conceptualize cleavages in coherent paragraphs, transmute meaning into knowledge.

It is not my purpose to justify my illness. Its justification is, to me, crystal clear. That is not the problem. But to make the unconscious conscious, to make the essentially private publicly assessable, to present the socially taboo in the center of society, to integrate the numinous – these are problems indeed. And these problems constitute the task I have set myself.

Perhaps I am "enchanted by my illness." I object that the word "enchanted" is not strong enough. During times of operationally-defined vacuities, consensually-validated voids, publicly-determined emptinesses, behaviorally-defined inanities, I feel confronted by sacred, wondrous, awesome *experience*, which persistently evades the words and concepts available and obstinately defies communication to another human being.

I never sought the experience I received. I have never hungered for it, nor would I ever seek it out now. The experience has always come to me as mysteriously as the doorway to Narnia appears to the children of C.S. Lewis's fantasies. I have been awed, but I am not a mind-tripper nor a psychic thrills freak.

Yet I feel I have been well rewarded by my illnesses. They were exhilarating challenges as they occurred. I make no bones about it; no other events have so completely demanded my total human capacities. Be that as it may, as in the time since, I turn the events over in my mind, they yield deeper meaning, more extensive commentary, wider and yet more penetrating implication.

Locked into vivid memories I sense incredible raw meaning. I am urged to track down every thread, draw out every implication. The task grows larger. The scope is broader each time I scan it. The problem of schizophrenia is as large as the problem of life.

That was one way of saying it. Perhaps I could illustrate my argument more concretely and specifically by following a thread from my life into illness and back out again…

Upon entering Harvard College in the fall of 1969, I soon realized that the education I was to receive was in part overt and in part covert. Overtly, we were taught basic principles of the humanities, natural and social sciences – *Veritas*. Covertly, we were taught that *Veritas* would pay off – in cash, in status, in prestige, power, influence. We were being trained to become part of a national, even global, elite, to become members of a grand social clique.

Now this realization was disturbing to me at the core. In high school I had chosen to give my life to learning as opposed to cliques and elites, backbiting, status seeking, pettiness. My books had been my retreat from the social gamesmanship with which I was surrounded. I had chosen learning rather than that.

In college I learned the ante had been upped. Learning was the ticket to grand social status. Oh, genuine learning was genuinely respected, because genuine learning would genuinely pay off. The "learning-earning" connection was absolute.

And competition. Learning was hardly a selfless endeavor. A piece of learning was a piece of property. Copyrighted. With one's name on it, that one might receive the rewards. The mathematical theorem or psychological principle one had "discovered" bore one's name; the owner won the prize; his name was entered in the textbooks. Success!

The immediate invidiousness of such an environment, the competitive ambition of all participants, the prizes hanging just out of reach of so many, led to an atmosphere of little fellowship or communion, if not to the positive corruption of morals. As Paddy Chayefsky, one who observed contemporary researchers at work, wrote in the novel *Altered States*:

> Scientists are a very curious breed. There isn't much money in science and very little celebrity. There is, however, a great deal of vainglory and murderous thirst for immortality. There are scientists who will perjure, suborn, cheat, steal, swindle and even kill to get their names in the textbooks or to be standing up there in Stockholm in their cutaways, modestly accepting the Nobel Prize.

I suppose I'm a medievalist at heart. The great sin of the twentieth century is sloth. Almost any vice can be tolerated as long as one is productive. Yet not so for Dante. Sloth was fourth on his list of seven. The first level of his Mountain of Purgatory is populated by the Proud, their faces bent to the ground by heavy boulders on their backs. The second level of Purgatory is populated by the Envious, sitting on the ground with their eyes sown shut. For the medieval man pride and envy were the great sins.

The twentieth century is controlled by pride and envy. They feed one another. A man begins his career envious. Others have so much. He has so little. He is nobody. He must work hard. When that man attains "success," he need no longer envy his neighbor. He can then be proud.

Pride and envy – these were the facts of academia most apparent to one taking time to look up from the relentless pursuits. I sensed strongly, if pre-verbally, that it is a perversion of truth to seek the truth for untrue reasons. Truth belongs to God. And a horde of academicians were busy trying to carve their initials into the immutable monolith.

These ruminations, hesitations, perplexities, reached the point of crisis by the middle of my sophomore year. I did not develop a Laingian "false self" – a "false self" designed to accommodate the pressures of my environment whatever my discomfort. Rather, I developed no "self" at all at a time when the development of such was called for in the life cycle. My sense of "self" remained fluid, unstructured, amorphous. My environment offered no model for what I wanted to be. Social expectation was pushing me in a direction I resisted but I had no alternative to put forth. I was out of step with my peers and particularly sensitive to a pervasive lack of community which they hardly noticed.

Plunging into my illness I was able to recover a sense of intrinsic meaning. Meaning not constructed from social gamesmanship and the expectations of my peers, but meaning which grew from the ground of my being and expressed itself in symbol and image. These were not meanings for winning prizes, publishing, or making money, but meanings which I could found my life upon. Meanings which expressed my being, what I wanted and what I did not.

The shadow always appears in illness. Once one has recovered from being "God" on the psych ward, one realizes (1) that is what one always wanted, and (2) that is not what one wants at all. Chastening, really. If we could make everyone march in step with us, we could do the right thing. But salvation is a personal matter. Everyone has their own path to follow, their own destiny to fulfill.

The effect of illness was to allow me to develop a sense of identity apart from society – apart from social pressure, social expectation, invidiousness. The valuable use of all that "narcissism" released during illness is not to develop pride or a hunger to lord it over others, but to reinforce a fundamental sense of self-worth which gives one a "place to stand" against invidiousness and gamesmanship.

And when the specifically social – "societal" – pressures are removed, when a distance has been achieved and a distinct sense of identity has been constructed – one is free to relate interpersonally with honesty and directness and a true regard for the being of the other person. One relates not to an executive of such-and-such a business firm or to the author of such-and-such a book, but to Bill or Mary as they are "intrinsically," in primary, face-to-face relationship.

Illness, through the recovery of intrinsic meaning, allows one to distance from the social and rediscover the interpersonal. The interpersonal is not lost but found. Person, as well as meaning, or meaning including person, becomes rooted in the ground of the self.

"Intrinsic meaning" is a great wide heady world. It is a world of symbol and image, metaphor and poetry, drama and ritual. Material from illness points beyond itself to the entire world-wide history of religious and artistic expression. The experience of illness provides a starting point, but once an appreciation of symbol and image has been developed all works of art and the spirit offer "intrinsic meaning."

As one develops an identity apart from society, one develops an identity defined by one's Creator. The "other" does not disappear but is replaced by True Other. One learns to say "I am" in humility while conscious of the great "I AM." One turns to the inexhaustible source of all symbol and image.

It's a great, wide, heady world – the world of the imaginal, the imagined, the created. One finds there large, uncramped, uncrabbed spaces where each person can be his or her self and need not all chase the same prizes, the same rewards, the same payoffs, to the detriment and loss of their fellows. The "True

West," the "Great Frontier," is at the center of the mind. One may explore this territory but it will never be settled. It is new for every individual who ventures there.

After a while the Laingian "true self" emerges, one develops the courage to be what the inner voices speak. And one can write "a more reflective peace now."

And Death

> I have a friend, a very sober friend
> Who causes me great pain, teaching
> Me day by day what matters
> And what does not.
> And Death is my companion.
>
> I have a friend, a very quiet friend
> Who speaks sonorities from silence.
> Music measured
> By the pause before and after.
> And Death is my companion.
>
> I have a friend, a very special friend
> A liar, cheat, deceiver.
> My friend cannot be trusted
> For he always tells the truth.
> And Death is my companion.
>
> I have a friend, a most remorseless friend
> Closer than the vein in my neck.
> I speak volumes to him day and night:
> In some one moment he will answer with a word.
>
> And Death is my companion.

Write

Well
you know
When I get a little crazy
I'm very afraid of dying.
Death might leap out
and bite me
at any time.
And when I get real crazy
I think I'm Death
And march about
with my fist in the air
Mowing down hordes of humanity.
(I told my doctor
it's a special case
of "identification with the aggressor.")

Well
one day
I was mulling this over
and happened to mention it
To a friend.
My friend said
"If you are afraid of Death,
And if you *are* Death,
You must be afraid of yourself."
And when
I had thought *that* over
I decided
my friend
must be
write.

SCHIZOPHRENIA: DANGER AND OPPORTUNITY

Schizophrenia immediately calls forth images of danger: disordered thinking, bizarre behavior, hallucinations, and a general unpredictability concerning the individual involved. Friends may say that they no longer know the individual, that the individual is not the same person who was their friend. Bewilderment on the part of concerned persons is often matched by fear and confusion on the part of the affected individual.

Clearly there is danger in schizophrenia. But I believe that opportunity is present as well. Schizophrenia is a crisis, and I note that the Chinese ideogram for "crisis" is composed of the symbols for both "danger" and "opportunity." Danger threatens, but opportunities beckon as the capacities to overcome danger are developed. The capacities required to overcome a schizophrenic illness are general human capacities which may be used to confront any life situation. Capacities developed in response to the dangers of illness generalize and may be further utilized when the illness is past.

One must remember that schizophrenia is primarily an illness of disordered perception, "creative misperception," if you will. The heart of the illness is a delusional system, or a set of delusional systems, that take the individual out of consensually validated reality and place that person in another world or set of worlds. These alternative worlds are superimposed on the consensually validated world we share; thus, the individual's behavior in his or her world is acted out in our world and much confusion ensues.

This confusion is created, however, by the unavoidable fact of super-imposition.

We see our world while the individual sees another and the disparate perspectives clash. But could we enter the mind of the affected individual we would discover a world which, if not totally logical and systematic, is at least orderly and regular according to a set of rules which the individual respects. We should remember as well that the rules of alternative perception will change as the illness progresses.

These alternative worlds perceived over time—more than perceived, lived in, over time—will shape the experience of the affected individual as much or more than any other comparable period of time. The events taking place and the responses made will become part of the personal history of the individual. Psychosis is genuine lived experience, and the alternative worlds experienced present to the individual challenges that are, within his or her perceptual field, real and immediate. These real and immediate challenges call forth real and immediate responses. This is life—in an alternative world.

The ego—conceived as the basic decision-making function—is the one item that remains intact during acute schizophrenia. The basic "I" is perhaps stripped of all its secondary-process support apparatus, but it continues to make decisions while anything and maybe everything else is in flux. Personal identity may change as may the identities of friends, family, and acquaintances. Personal relations among peers, geographical locations, social organizations, and personal agenda may all be transposed in the private world of the individual, but that individual will still make decisions: That individual will still make active responses to the perceived situation.

These active responses to the perceived situation will have at least a double effect. On one level they work an immediate change in the current world of the individual. On another level they tend to shift the whole current world of the individual into another world. The rules regulating the misperceived environment are changed as action is taken in that environment, and a new environment emerges. The individual begins with problem A in world B and, after taking action, emerges with problem C in world D.

The necessity for "right action," careful and precise problem solving, becomes clear when one realizes that the decisions and responses of the affected individual "create" the illness-in-progress, direct its course, bring the illness to conclusion. Life may not be karmic, but illness is frightfully karmic, within its own scope. Decisions made within psychosis have a real effect within psychosis, shape the illness.

The fact that many of the "actions" taken by the affected individual are magical, ritualistic, or incantatory, has no bearing on their reality as "actions." Such actions are ineffectual to our way of thinking but are potent in the world of the affected individual. Magic makes a difference, *there*.

Within the schizophrenic crisis, I have identified at least four issues that challenge the individual: fear, inflation, the Shadow, and gnosticism are foci around which hover danger and opportunity during the course of illness.

Fear

In the popular imagination the schizophrenic is primarily potentially aggressive. Upon examination, perpetual fear is the condition more likely to be found. Even aggression, when it appears, is usually a response to overwhelming fear, rather than a response to any more usual factor—revenge or an intrinsically violent nature.

The level of fear in illness can indeed reach overwhelming height. I remember a night in my patient room during which I could not sleep and every moment of which was spent as a captive in a Chinese POW camp. Minute by minute as the night crept by, I imagined new tortures and then suffered them. For weeks thereafter I dreaded retiring to my room for the night.

Such gratuitous fear may seem to have little point. But the frequent recurrence of such situations during psychosis can condition the individual to function despite great fear. Courage may not be so much fearlessness as being able to act despite one's fear. One may live with constant fear and yet come to the conclusion that one must carry on and make one's best effort despite near panic. The experience of great fear during illness may demonstrate to one that responses can and even must be made under great pressure.

Anything and everything that one fears will appear before one in illness. Every weakness in the personality will be exposed, from a physical fear of rats or snakes to a psychological fear of abandonment or parental anger. These normally neurotic fears will appear in overwhelming proportions and force the individual to confront them directly. One worthwhile response will appear: courage. Courage may be present only in one protected corner of a personality barely maintaining nerve, but courage is required and courage will develop. Neurotic fears seem petty when one has encountered psychotic fears.

The antidote to fear is courage but the opposite of fear is trust. Fear separates the individual from fellow human beings and throws the individual exclusively onto his or her own resources. Perhaps this is a lesson in self-reliance. But trust permits one to return socially and share burdens and feel the comfort of the human bond. I remember well fearing that a female visitor would shoot me when she entered the ward. Before the visitor arrived a nurse I had developed an affection for gave me a talk about trust. "How can you live without trusting others?" Still convinced that I was about to die, I met my visitor rather than living without trust. To my great surprise my visitor rewarded me with a thoughtful conversation.

If one trusts, rather than fears, patients, staff, and visitors, one attains an entirely altered quality of illness. The illness becomes open, public, shared. Fantasy and misperception are explored, played out in conversation. The illness, while still present, may become the object of playful humor. Delusions may become "tall tales," told as if around a campfire. A public illness dissipates faster than a private illness. Sharing the illness is one step on the way back to consensually validated reality.

The affected individual has the capacity, within the illness, to move in the direction of trust rather than fear, or in the direction of trust in spite of fear. An illness in which the individual finds courage to trust is less lonely, less stark, more bearable. A good rapport, open to free expression, facilitates recovery as the individual reveals delusional secrets. Fear when it appears must be met by courage, but fear can be prevented by trust and an open patient environment.

Inflation

Enormous amounts of energy are released during psychotic episodes. The affected individual stands on a shoreline and the wind sweeps over the waves and the water rages. The individual tends to believe that he or she makes the wind sweep and the water rage. The power of the unconscious is thus falsely appropriated by the ego. This is a fatal mistake. The ego does not create the storm: The ego merely witnesses the storm. Trying to grab hold of such massive energy will subject the ego to forces it cannot withstand. The ego will be knocked about, buffeted, blasted from one direction and another.

The ego cannot grasp the power of the unconscious, but the ego can be cleansed by the power of the unconscious. Energy from behind the ego can wash over the ego and heal wounds suffered in previous trauma. If the individual appropriates the forces released to the ego, and proclaims the ego God, further hurt will be suffered as the ego proves an ineffectual and frustrated Deity. But if the individual can maintain a guarded identity, does not identify with the emotions or images passing through, the ego will find itself invigorated and refreshed by forces the presence of which was hardly suspected.

The individual, I repeat, must learn not to identify with, grasp, hang on to, the emotions and images passing through. The emotions and images play for a time and then leave. They cannot be brought back, they must pass away. But as they pass they cleanse and heal hurts of bygone days. The wounded ego is healed in the presence of the Self.

The psychotic individual walking the ward as Bob Dylan, Ronald Reagan, or, Reggie Jackson, is a laughable figure in the public imagination. Yet the public is often uncritical of its own false hero worship and secret ambitions. "Oh," the junior executive daydreams, "were I only chairman of the board." "Oh," the young resident schemes, "someday I will be chief of surgery."

The psychotic individual may be grandiose but he is harmless. The fantasies of position and power among the public are often more dangerous simply because they are real, "realistically" acted upon, wellsprings of greed and hate. Once one has "become" Bob Dylan or Ronald Reagan one is forced to take stock of what is truly satisfying in the human endeavor. When the darker side of ambition as opposed to aspiration has been highlighted one must come to terms with intrinsic human identity as opposed to ascribed social position. One learns through playing the role that high position brings few of the satisfactions one surmised.

There is another form of inflated identity worth a paragraph. The psychotic individual may "become" a great topic or issue. The individual may "become" Truth, Beauty, Good, Time, Death, War, Love, and so forth. In these cases of an abstract identification I believe the individual explores the meaning of an unresolved issue by identifying with it, becoming it, and thereby "gestalting" it, if you will. What can I learn about War, imagining that I am War? How does War think and feel?

The Shadow

There is no greater evil than to think oneself all good. The tendency to appropriate to oneself or one's colleagues "the Good" is demonstrated in all aspects of human living. "I am the best diagnostician in the city." "I am the perfect family man." And when rival factions meet, whether in corporate, academic, or professional settings, each party tends to represent itself as all white and the others as all black.

Frequently this tendency is exhibited in illness. And the usual human proclivity is magnified larger than life. "I slapped you because you were disrespectful to me, Jesus Christ." As the self-image becomes unrealistically pure, the personality becomes in fact controlled by the Shadow. The Shadow is that side of us that we most repudiate when it appears in others. The Shadow is the flipside of our own alleged virtues, as when we think we are being strong and are in fact obstinate, or when we think we are being flexible and are in fact wishy-washy. The more unrealistically good we construe our self-image the more unperceived control our darker tendencies gain. The blindness apparent in certain stages of psychotic process can, upon later examination, teach a pointed lesson to the affected individual.

Personal identity in illness tends to shift toward extremes of good, but it may also, due to circumstances, shift toward extremes of evil. The individual may thus identify with the Shadow. We confess to the crimes of another, thinking that we are that other. Insofar as one then realizes that the criminal capacity is present in all of us, I think there is something healthy in this response. I can thus conceive within me committing the crimes of Lee Harvey Oswald or Richard Nixon or Judas Iscariot. Such identifications may signal negative self-image but they also keep us in touch with our darker side.

In my own experience I have accepted these darker identities but have not felt damned by them. I have accepted them, acknowledging my guilt but resolving to rehabilitate my character. In the magic of illness I have found my efforts at reform are rewarded by new identity: Lee Harvey Oswald becomes John Kennedy, Richard Nixon becomes Gerald Ford, Judas Iscariot becomes Simon Peter. The new white identities pose problems of their own, but they were attained by fully acknowledging the old black identities.

Whenever someone is having trouble keeping their feet on the ground—whether it be the pastor, the occultist, the psychologist, or the president—one may suspect that that person is avoiding their Shadow. The Shadow lies on the ground: keeping in touch with one's Shadow keeps one's feet on the ground.

Recapitulating for a moment the foregoing themes: The affected individual may fear the Shadow as he or she projects. Inflation may lift the individual off the ground away from it. If the individual is to return to the ground, the Shadow feared must be acknowledged and reconciled.

Gnosticism

I define Gnosticism as a revulsion from the material world, a belief that the material (and social) world is flatly evil, coupled with a longing for purer, finer, more spiritual realms.

It is common to understand psychosis as an "escape from reality" and thus necessarily Gnostic. But psychosis need not be Gnostic: The other world need not be an end in itself. Rather, it may be a means to an end. The journey to the center of the mind need not be for the purpose of making a permanent home there. The journey to the center of the mind may be for the purpose of securing some required object, attaining some missing experience, solving some perplexing problem, bearing fully in mind that one will return home with the prize. The missing object or experience or solution is needed *here* but is to be found *there*. The journey is thus utilitarian; it is not a one-way ticket.

I remember an evening of intimate conversation with the nurse I had developed an affection for. We spoke warmly, with good rapport. She held my hands. Behind us a patient played a haunting nocturne of her own composition on the ward piano. Otherwise the lounge was quiet.

I knew I was in heaven. I felt peace and fullness. As the nurse encouraged me to listen to the music, I mistook her meaning and thought she was telling me that I could stay on the ward forever, always with her.

Immediately I knew that I could not. I fully believed that I was in heaven but I knew that my condition was abnormal, premature. I had duties and responsibilities at my home. I knew that I couldn't live forever on the psychiatric ward, however blissful my current state. I had my own girlfriend to return to. I had friends and family to return to. I realized that "Heaven Can Wait."

The orthodox Church of the second century condemned Gnostic heretics to perpetual damnation. The theological expression may seem ineffectual, but, in fact, in psychosis, Gnosticism is immediately and tangibly perpetual damnation. Individuals in love with their own fantasies, subverted by their imaginations, may spin out and never come back. Their private worlds will expand while their external worlds deteriorate beyond repair. It is a fact, in psychosis, that if you don't want to come back, you don't have to.

Merely making the journey to the center of the mind does not condemn one as Gnostic. If one has a purpose to accomplish, a change to make at the center, and one discharges one's purpose, then returns, one has made a journey to a beneficial end. *This* world is the better for it.

Aftermath

The issues we have identified as facing the actively schizophrenic individual are not peculiar to full-blown illness. These issues confront the individual both before and after the illness. Neither are these issues peculiar to schizophrenics. We all live lives to some extent controlled by fear. We all are to some extent subverted by dreams of glory and high position. Few of us can say that we have come to terms with our Shadow, and all of us at times find our social and material world repulsive.

During the active phase of illness these issues are thrown into high relief. The nagging concerns of ordinary neurosis intensify, clarify, and explode into larger than life proportion. The magnification of ordinary problems in psychotic illness gives a sharper perspective, a more intense awareness, and success or failure at the moment of crisis becomes a matter of clear record.

Psychotic illness *is* a crisis and presents both greater danger and greater opportunity than moments of more low-key existence. Schizophrenia may be a retreat from consensually validated reality, but there is no escape from internal reality. One takes one's internal reality with one into the illness and there one plays with it for higher stakes.

Once recovered from the illness, the individual will gain greatest value by clarifying the events which took place within the private world. Every illness is a story one tells oneself about oneself. The affected individual will gain benefit by clearly delineating in the mind these events and points of decision. Psychosis is regular and orderly, on its own terms, and by keeping track of events and transitions the individual will learn the story told and be able to draw conclusions.

The content of illness thus becomes part of the personal history of the individual. The experience in illness may not take place within a consensually validated reality, yet it is real experience—it simply took place in an alternative world. A number of stories can be told of any illness. When a friend asks, "Weren't you sick in April?" I don't reply simply, "Yes, I was hospitalized for 3 weeks." Such a reply invalidates the experience, writes it off as mere nonsense, makes no valuable use of the events that took place. In answer to my friend's question I may acknowledge that I went to the hospital but instead of simply discounting the experience, I go further. I tell my friend a story from the illness. I take my friend with me on a meaningful though irreal adventure: "Escape from the Time Machine" or "Hunting Giants."

I have never written off illness as trauma and failure; rather, I have organized and examined my behavior during illness and found fundamentals of who I am exposed there in the midst of alternative worlds. In terms of the fantasy constructed I have found both success and failure, drama, pain, and high adventure.

One cannot be decisively observant and reflective during an illness. But one may examine one's behavior during illness after the fact. One may recognize significant symbols, recurrent themes, proclivities and tendencies. One is *not* another person while schizophrenic: One is precisely oneself, only one is foraging in alternative realities. One is responsible for oneself there just as one is responsible for oneself here. The experience is genuine, the judgment is earned, the conclusions to be drawn…

NOTES ON PSYCHOSIS

When one thinks of psychosis, one thinks of strange and peculiar ideas. "I am growing my father's hair." "My liver has turned to glass." "Aliens are hunting me down." There is an inclination to suppose that these ideas arise within a consciousness much like our own. "If," we think, "I believed I was being hunted down by aliens, I, too, would be psychotic."

Actually, the consciousness of the psychotic is very unlike our own. It is not simply a matter of replacing sane ideas with insane ideas; the very quality of mind is different. The strange and peculiar ideas expressed by the psychotic bear witness to an altered quality of consciousness.

Were one to survey a visual field – a movie screen, for instance – and observe that certain elements within that field were in distorted focus, one might be hard pressed to put into words the nature of the distortion observed. We might imagine that the movie screen was pushed forward in places and pulled back in others, rather than presenting a flat surface to the projector.

Just as we imagine an uneven visual screen, so we may imagine a distorted total consciousness. The images within that consciousness are out-of-focus and warped. The peculiar ideas of the psychotic attempt to describe the ill-focused and powerful qualities found in his conscious field. "My body image is distorted; I don't feel like my normal physical self: I am growing my father's hair." "My natural peace of mind has been disturbed; I am anxious and insecure: I am being hunted down by aliens."

Distortions within the conscious field precede the expression of peculiar ideas. It is possible to interpret peculiar ideas, but much more difficult to 'tune in' to the altered state of consciousness.

When we read a novel we frequently encounter objects or events that are *to us* symbolic, though to the characters they are not. The author is communicating symbols to the reader, bypassing the protagonist, antagonist, whomever. The symbol is framed – designated as a symbol – by the book's cover.

What if a character awoke to the author's symbolism?

It is a very different matter to discover a symbol in life rather than in art. It is fearful, awesome, wonderful to encounter an unframed symbol, one not representative of the thing signified but its very *presence*, a symbol that is not a product of human culture and not presented to the observer as such. The dove, a well-known symbol of the Spirit, normally does not attract much notice. If one were, however, lost for a day in the woods, fearful all that time, desperate for one's life; and then if the clouds in the sky formed a dove just as one regained the road home, the effect would be powerful indeed. This dove is not a representative image for the Spirit; it is the *presence* of the Spirit. Why? Why just then?

All one's belief in random materialism would vanish, if just for a moment. All one had read of synchronicity would appear paltry before the established presence. One would wonder: Who sent this? Why to me? What does this mean?

The psychotic is a character awake to the author's symbolism. A psychotic episode is fraught with symbols erupting into life as opposed to symbols crafted into art. The numinous is not captured within a frame or tamed for domestic use. The fundamental power of psychotic events – of symbols unframed, embedded in raw life – is wrenching, overwhelming, exhausting.

～

A word about the concept "projection": it is perhaps a misnomer when applied to psychotic process. During psychosis we may speak almost literally of 'mind expansion.' The objects in the individual's environment become elements in his mind. The cup of coffee in front of me is not an object separate from me; it is energy, my energy. *This* cup of coffee is my energy, not that one, the other one, or cups of coffee in general. *This* cup of coffee is an element in my mind which I may drink or throw down the sink or place on the floor outside the door – all of which are events in my mind. If you spill my cup of coffee, you are playing with my mind.

Psychotic process thus becomes a dialogue with Providence, as 'random' environmental events work transformation in the patient's mind.

～

The psychotic does not theologize about hell or espistemologize about knowledge. The psychotic enters hell; he stands before the seat of knowledge. He encounters facts in his environment. The eternal has broken into time – and it is in time, real time, that the psychotic must respond.

We are quite comfortably at home in our secondary process, our ego-function, even if we have a 'symbolic' turn of mind. We read and interpret our myths, mapping our mythic territory and collecting data concerning the natural history of dragons.

Whatever the psychotic is doing wrong, whatever his foibles and follies, one must admit that he has left his natural

[margin note: castles in the sky – imagining them; living in them]

[margin note: & psychiatrists collect the rent!]

home and is engaging real dragons. The mythic journey means leaving home – leaving behind normal ego-functioning. One must walk out the door of ordinary consciousness to take the journey into the mythic mode of mind.

A psychotic is not an armchair cartographer of the mythic dimension. He has gone to the space within mind where dragons exist, where one is tempted by the devil, and where one collects the golden apples of the sun. These are real adventures, true tests of soul, not abstract philosophical cogitations where symbols are allegorized and all the right answers are found in a textbook. One's real, perhaps overlooked, personal limitations and proclivities are demonstrated as one acts and reacts in real mythic encounters, risking one's life or mind – or both – in this drastic and dangerous undertaking.

~

[margin bracket with arrow] The typical inpatient physician adopts the motto, "Don't make sense out of nonsense." Lacking interest in depths of soul or psychic transformations, he seeks to reorient the patient to 'external reality' and to return him to work and home as quickly as possible.

Inpatient physicians rely on various external definitions of psychosis to guide them in diagnosis and treatment. These definitions, loaded with derogatory connotation and designed to highlight "cognitive malfunction," possess little psychological subtlety. The four A's of Eugen Bleuler – ambivalence, associations, autism, affect – are typical of external definitions of schizophrenia. My comments on these four A's try to demonstrate the inner subjective pattern to which these terms simultaneously refer and ignore or overlook.

Ambivalence concerning key topics occurs frequently during a psychotic illness. The patient makes decisions, reverses them, and in general doesn't seem to be able to make up his mind. "Do I respect my father or not?" "Do I want to help or not?" "Should I break up with my girlfriend or not?"

Rather than identifying ambivalence as a symptom of the illness, one might identify it as the *focus* of psychotic process. The process is working to resolve ambivalence. The patient has entered into the illness as a problem-solving technique, a mechanism for making final decisions. By posing key problems in symbolic terms, he can try out various sides of each question. The ambivalence is less a product of the illness than it is the root source which called it forth. As the patient finally makes decisions, the illness will fade away.

The fundamental ambivalence in psychosis is perhaps "love-trust/not love-not trust." This cleavage may run through many more particular ambivalences, emerging even in the most trivial symbolic incidents. Whether or not one loves and trusts the world one is born into is not a paltry question; it is deeply personal and worthy of the profoundest meditation.

As one finds himself balanced between trust and lack of trust, his perception of human character becomes more acute. If "love is blind," so is trust; and lacking trust, one observes many details too obvious for the normal person to notice. Finally, perhaps, one must love in order to know, but lack of trust grants a marginal insight into society and human nature that raises many questions worth considering.

Associations, in the sense of "loose associations," are the most problematical 'symptoms' with which the typical inpatient physician must deal. This is the nonsense from which the doctor refuses to make sense. The physician, listening to his patient for half an hour or an hour every day or two, notes that he has no idea how his patient gets from one topic to another or relates one idea to another.

[margin note: nice analogy]

　　I suggest that, in his brief contact with the patient, the doctor is trying to make sense out of the individual lines as he watches the pencil point in the artist's hand fly across the sketch pad. The point moves swiftly, jerks suddenly, and the lines are irregular. The observer has set himself a hopeless task. But should he step back from the sketch pad and view the whole, then he would see the drawing coming into being before his eyes. The fragments and parcels of meaning relate together in the total picture, visible when one takes the larger view.

　　From the patient's point of view, it is very much like putting together a puzzle. Parcels of meaning, fragments of solutions that one feels sure of, are arranged and rearranged as one tries to make them cohere. The process is mercurial, building up a systematic interrelation of parts of answers. One does not know the full answer, but one possesses bits of truth and works with what one has.

　　The fact that associations reveal their meaning only when a person takes the larger view militates toward reviewing an illness with the patient once it has concluded. The story of the fragments of meaning may then be surveyed as a whole and understood in its light. I shall return to this.

[margin note: 23 May '15 — D.B. - Bleuer's meaning borrowed by Freud]

　　Autism manifests itself primarily as "delusions of self-reference." The patient is observed to believe that he is to receive random events as special messages. "Everybody in the lunchroom is talking about me." "This Bible tract I found on the sidewalk was left for me." "My car broke down because my library books are overdue."

　　In order to understand this proclivity, I take issue with the usual model of psychosis as the "eruption of unconscious contents into consciousness." I suggest that the ego, which has been poised outside the self as a planet in an orbit, falls into the self and is thus surrounded by it on all sides. As the ego looks out from within the self to external events, images from the self, referring to the ego, are superimposed on the external events, making each observation composite. The self becomes a lens through which the external events are filtered; the observed meaning of events is thus partially internal and refers to the individual. All internal reality, as a whole or in part, refers to the individual, and these contents are superimposed on externals.

There is a cultural tendency to denigrate internal reality. From the ego's point of view, however, reality is as much internal as external. In psychosis, when the ego has fallen into the self, when external and internal realities are superimposed, producing a composite image – the individual may receive his first view of his own internal reality. The ideas of self-reference may communicate to the individual his first glimmerings – through externals – of the particularities of his own internal reality. In time, in part, internal and external will be separated, but the initial composite views are the *prima materia*, the raw material upon which the work may begin.

Dull or bland *affect* is considered typical of the schizophrenic. His emotional responses are weak and low key, even when discussing topics fraught with high tension. John Perry has rather handily resolved the question of where the affect went. Perry refers to psychotic symbols as "affect-images." The affect, he says, has been bound into the image and is no longer available to the total personality.

Binding affect into images and then responding to, manipulating, interacting with those images is an effective method of working psychic transformation and emotional change. The original emotions are bound into images, the images are transformed, and the new emotions are then released from the new images. Certain individuals are simply more adept at transforming in symbolic terms rather than working with the raw emotions themselves.

~

Beyond Bleuler's four A's and the external definitions of psychosis, we encounter a yet more serious problem: the schizophrenic uses language in a distinctive manner. Although this is well known, there is little understanding of the distinctive aspects of 'schizophrenese.' All psychotic process seems conducted in a code which obscures the events and their significance from the observer.

In schizophrenia I find a curious conjunction of percept, concept, and emotion. The percept "door" is not, for example, a simple wooden object with a metal handle and hinges connecting one room to another. The lifeless, meaningless object, a percept, generalizes for the psychotic into a concept, perhaps a passage, as in *rites-de-passage*. This concept is not separate from the percept, not artificially added on or superimposed as a distinct entity. Concept and percept are simultaneous. Meaning is perceived directly through the eyes. I have on occasion referred to the process as "reading the world."

Further, the emotional value of passage conjoins with the concept-percept. The patient will respond to the door as if, perhaps, it were the Gate of Hell. We should then observe some bizarre 'doorway behavior.' The patient reacts to the perceived object as if it were both a concept and an emotion.

These days we take it for granted that perception is devoid of meaning. On the one hand, there are facts; on the other, values. Nothing that can be seen, heard, tasted, smelled, or touched has meaning in itself. When the patient seems preoccupied with an object or an event, the question, "Does that have meaning for you?" discriminates sanity from insanity. Perception of meaning in the object is insanity; the doctor maintains that meaning can only be given to the object by the subject.

Yet phylogenetically, and perhaps ontogenetically, meaning and concept grow out of percept. Phylogenetically, the organs of perception developed before the cerebral cortex and language. If prehistoric man had any notion of meaning from which language and concept could be developed, it was contained in percepts. The infant is sensually aware before he speaks or understands, and thus the germ of meaning may well be found in that sensual awareness. Otherwise one must suppose that meaning pops into the mind out of nowhere.

Owen Barfield has pointed out that the farther back one goes in the history of language, the more metaphorical it is. For instance, in ancient Hebrew the simple word for "wind" also meant breath and spirit. But the phrase "also meant" is misleading. The ancient Hebrews did not discriminate the *percepts* wind or breath from each other or from the *concept* spirit. As language and thought have progressed through history, what we now take to be different senses of words have been broken down and the physical, particularly, has been separated from the mental, percept from concept. But for the ancient Hebrew, wind was spirit just as for the contemporary psychotic, door is passage. Language that began in poetic condensations now terminates in logical abstractions, that is, "pullings apart."

The conjunction of percept and concept sheds light on the simultaneously concrete and symbolic nature of psychotic language. If, in discussing a proverb, the psychotic says, "Well, if the cat is away…," the percept "cat" is already joined to the concept "figure of authority." The perceptual object is simultaneous with the abstract concept so that the patient's interpretation of the proverb appears to be wholly literal.

This condensed language of the psychotic—joining percept, concept, and emotion—presents an autonomous mode of discourse, a pattern of thought *in* percepts rather than *about* percepts. I believe this notion of an "autonomous mode of discourse" should be taken seriously. In such a mode, problems may be posed, investigations take place, resolutions appear. Perhaps schizophrenia is less an 'escape' from reality than an attempt to deal with reality in an altered mode of discourse, an altered state of consciousness.

At the time of the illness, all this may be opaque to the observer. For one thing, the typical inpatient physician is aware only of a fraction of the patient's activity. Psychotic process, plunging ahead twenty-four hours a day, cannot be followed through the window of an occasional hour interview. No observer, however persistent, would be able to follow the full course of events and transformations in an illness.

The associations which invest percepts with meaning and relation may be idiosyncratic elements from the patient's personal history. No one is going to guess what a flying spoon means to the patient, because no one else present watched Maypo commercials when he was six years old. The association with Maypo commercials—the personal element combined with more universal symbolic content—may be supplied by the patient upon questioning, but that only leads us to a final reason why symbols may be obscure during an illness: a censor is operating within the patient so that he holds his symbols and activities secret, refusing—for lack of trust—to share the associations or meanings with those about him.

Thus, at the time of illness, schizophrenic language—the conjunction of percept, concept, and emotion—may remain obscure because: 1) the 'whole story' cannot be observed; 2) personal associations with objects and events may be unknown to observers; and 3) a censor may inhibit the patient from sharing information with those he does not trust. All this is abundant reason to review the illness with the patient after recovery.

'Cure' thus becomes returning the patient from the symbolic mode to linear English. This action is as little a matter of logic as curing someone of German by teaching him English. The current clinical method of choice focuses on emotion as the psychic cement in the percept-concept-emotion conjunction, and seeks to separate out the emotional component, locating it wholly within the patient. Thus, the 'door' is no longer the Gate of Hell; the 'door' is a door, and the patient is sad or frightened. The patient, upon 'cure,' has all the problems that he had before; however, he discusses those problems in a language his doctor can better understand.

~

If, as Piaget suggests, thought is "internalized action," then psychosis is perhaps "externalized thought." But *thinking* it is. Real progress may be made within this mode of thought.

According to Kuhn, a new paradigm changes discourse, facilitating the integration of previously unaccounted-for data. The psychotic's unaccounted-for data frequently is emotional material. The patient may have been premorbidly not only unable to verbalize this material but often unable to perceive the material in any but the vaguest senses. 'Regression' to the fluid, condensed language of psychosis is thus perhaps an attempt to integrate anomalous intrapsychic data.

I suggest that the impending paradigm shift—within the total psyche, not just the conscious mind—may specifically call forth a psychosis as the means to bring about the proceeding change. The altered mode of discourse is peculiarly suited to paradigm shifting. The conjunction of concept, percept, and emotion permits the individual to pursue his problem solving on the mental, physical, and emotional planes simultaneously. If affect is elusive to the individual, then binding it into an image may allow him to see, understand, and integrate the anomalous emotions. Shifting paradigm may *require* altered mode.

An illustration from Paul Meehl: If a patient says, "I am growing my father's hair," one may note with Meehl a certain "cognitive slippage" if one insists that the statement has something to do with differential grooming. Yet this may be an unconventional redefinition of terms, one joining mental and emotional material to the physical. "Hair" is hair to us, but may, for example, have more to do with quality of consciousness, attitudes, etc., in the condensed lexicon of the psychotic. This statement may be the patient's first appreciation that he is becoming like his father.

~

I once heard a report of a woman whose grandchild had recently died. Shortly after this death, the woman noticed a peculiar mold growing on the ceiling of her living room. She remarked this growth as unusual, but took no steps to remove it. The growth spread and soon formed the 'perfect' image of her dead grandchild. Crowds of people came from miles around to see the Miracle of the Mold.

So psychosis begins—with a vague shock, a disturbance, a fairly undifferentiated alteration of consciousness. There is mold on the ceiling. The individual knows he does not feel the same today as he did the day before; he may feel some vague notion of the nature of this change: God is present to him, he has died, he is an alien being. But the experience does not go beyond that.

For a moment, for several hours, for several days, the individual is in a 'world between worlds.' He has left his ordinary consciousness behind, but the psychosis has not elaborated itself. The individual hovers, then plunges in. He selects a story to tell himself about himself. God, who is present, begins revealing particular secrets of the universe. He who is dead is in heaven, hell, purgatory, or has begun a new life. The alien being is assigned a mission in the world. What began as a smudge on the ceiling develops into a picture.

The numinous enters, then is elaborated in story, myth, ritual, acted parable, ceremony, drama. The individual moves from the world, to the world between worlds, to a particular world beyond world. The individual will have to live with his choices and learn from the story he chooses to tell himself.

∼

Schizophrenia is primarily a matter of perception, changing perceptions; it is creative misperception. Although my behavior at times has been erratic and bizarre, I have never had a sense that my will was other than my own. My behavior was the result of my unusual perception. *If* the shoebox really contained a bomb, *then* throwing it out the window made sense. I was not compelled, as if 'possessed,' to throw out the shoebox. I was the same person I always am, only my perception of the environment was changed.

The rapidity with which these misperceptions change makes psychosis hard to follow or comprehend. The whole gestalt, the whole universe of activity, the whole psychic topology, may change in a moment. I believe you are an enemy carrying a bomb in a shoebox; then you are a friend with a rainbow under your arm.

Each individual scenario might be easily comprehensible in itself—not unlike the static superstitious belief-system of a child or a primitive—but the volatile transformation of scenario after scenario gives to psychosis its erratic and bizarre quality. The imaged universes change like the screen in a high-speed light show. Neither the child nor the primitive exhibits this volatile instability.

Yet I believe there is method as the world replaces world. Left-handed gestalt follows left-handed gestalt, but each approaches more nearly the images at the heart of the psyche. Each slide is a closer approximation to the soul's essential pattern. When the heart of the soul images itself in the misperceived world, and the necessary action has been taken in that world, the illness is over and the individual free to return 'home' to normal secondary process ego-functioning. The Wizard will take Dorothy back to Kansas, if she can reach him.

∽

The middle play in illness, this shifting misperception, this moving from world to world, this course of illness, may be figured as sailing or blowing with the wind. One must not resist the flow of events or hang on to what must pass.

North wind, west wind, gentle breeze, mighty tempest—the wind seems always to signify, and further, always to signify something invisible which causes motion in things visible. Elaborating: the wind signifies the intangible which moves the tangible. Or again, the wind signifies the implicit which is the dynamic of the explicit. The wind is impulse, impetus, dynamic, tendency. The wind is relational: it changes relationships; it is an influence on the whole rather than an element in the pattern. Wind is the transformation of pattern. Wind becomes more a verb than a noun, or is replaced by a gerund, the blowing.

The wind is a cause never known in itself, but rather known only through its effects. The unconscious is likewise known only through its effects. I think of ideas as blowing from the unconscious into the conscious. These blowing ideas are not those ordered for rational discourse or systematic problem solving, but ideas at the moment of 'Aha!' Brainstorms, I suppose.

The different promptings entering consciousness seem to emanate from the same location, but direct experience of that place seems impossible. The source remains unknown and is apparently unknowable. The sound of the wind is "evidence of things unseen." One's attitude is a matter of faith.

These promptings annoy an ego which seeks to make its own well-ordered plans and establish its own priorities through the analysis of needs and the extrapolation of a future. Forethought is an ego watchword and inspiration is suspect. The ego chooses to know only that which it *knows* that it knows. The wind simply knows, and following the wind, one simply trusts.

Since one does not know where one is coming from—one is not responding to a simple extension of past learning—nor where one is going—the new territory is uncharted, the results are not for analysis to predict—one feels, at such times, freely given to the present, and accepts what a starkly compacted here and now has to offer.

These are truths brought radically home to the psychotic individual, the one who sails the tempest.

∼

There is a predominant conception that illness somehow 'happens' to an individual. The patient is passive, falls ill, suffers the illness visited upon him, to which he succumbs. I have written of "rapidly shifting misperceptions" as the core of illness. This, however, is a bit misleading, because in each creatively misperceived universe in which the patient finds himself, he has the opportunity, indeed is called upon, *to take action*. He makes choices, decides issues, actively creates and directs the course of his own illness. This is the practice of magic.

The symbolic object confronting the individual may represent back to him the contents of his own psyche. But that is only the beginning. A book with a certain title—*Orthodoxy*, by G.K. Chesterton, perhaps—may become energized, numinous for me. That book identifies an issue in my mind, but it is only the first step. Then the magic begins. Do I keep the book, read it, not read it, lend it and to whom, sell it and to whom, give it away and to whom, throw it out, burn it, shoplift it, or what?

These are real and difficult decisions. The symbol of the book identifies a problem area, and the book's disposition is a tentative resolution. In the world of magical thought what I do with *Orthodoxy* is a choice with consequences. In my response to the book, I am testing conclusions and actively directing the course of my illness.

Magic in psychosis takes at least the following three forms: the basic process of protective talismans, the ritual transmutation of energy, and the magic of imperatives.

Let us look first at talisman magic. This process may be outlined as follows: 1) a magical threat is perceived; 2) a protective talisman is selected and the threat is neutralized; 3) the talisman becomes a liability; 4) the talisman's power is integrated into the individual, and the talisman is discarded.

During one of my illnesses, the perceived magical threat was beheading, which may have represented a total severing of the ego (head) from the self (body). The talisman I selected to protect me was a silver necklace with a blue stone. The 'necklace' represented being 'neckless'—the connection between the head and body would thus be direct, not mediated by the neck. What the blue stone meant—a sapphire, my birthstone—I cannot explain, yet I know it has significance for the psyche as a protector of communication between self and ego. The symbolism simply remains untranslatable. I wore this necklace constantly, but it soon began to bother me. I was afraid it might be lost or stolen, so I gestured magically over it and threw it away. I had taken its power into myself and no longer needed it.

At times, while in the hospital, I have collected tabletops full of magical objects—playing cards, clippings from magazines, bits of junk and debris. I would become overly concerned about protecting my tabletop, which was supposed to protect me. When anxiety and worry about the tabletop became too great, I would sweep the objects away, integrating their power into myself.

The basic magic of talismans replicates the development and discarding of defense mechanisms in the personality. A defense mechanism is developed in response to a perceived interpersonal threat; the defense mechanism becomes a neurotic liability; it is then discarded.

The second magical process, the ritual transmutation of energy, is more purely expressive. It is simply externalized or alchemical thinking, the process of my initial example of the symbol book. A magical potency is identified in an object.

Then the object is manipulated, juxtaposed to other objects of magical potency, given to somebody or placed somewhere, in an expressive manner.

One of the more remarkable incidents of this kind of magic occurred when I made a sculpture of my belongings in my college dormitory room. I spent an entire night slowly and methodically arranging my belongings into a pile in the center of my room. The sculpture was a configuration of the self I wanted to be. Each object in itself and in relation to other objects expressed some aspect of the person I wanted to be. Unfortunately, when my friends discovered the 'sculpture,' the order in it was not apparent to them. My night of careful work looked like I had been on a rampage, and I was promptly bundled off to the mental hospital.

The symbolism of such a process may be lost after the fact or be forever untranslatable, but such symbolic process truly transmutes personal energy. Conflicts are outlined and resolved with the magic of symbols. The purpose of true magic is to *transform the magician*. These ritual transmutations of energy are real as they transform thoughts into experience lived, reinforcing the effect.

Finally, in the magic of imperatives, an imperative impulse to do a certain thing becomes lodged in consciousness. This imperative is often identified by the individual as the voice of God. But the individual soon learns that the voice may also be that of Satan—God and Satan speak with the same voice. Thus there is plenty of free play for the ego in these situations—deciding whether the imperative comes from God or Satan, deciding whether the instruction should be executed or not.

An instance of an imperative: I felt impelled to steal a birthday card for my girlfriend and hand it to her unsigned, without an envelope. In this case, I acted on the impulse. In the total context of the relationship, I am not sure I did wrong. (It is the only time in my life I have shoplifted.)

The discrimination of imperatives again shows that there is tremendous free play for the ego throughout the illness and that moral qualities and decisions play a large role in its course. There is white magic, and there is black. A sick soul can be healed, but a sick spirit cannot be. Seeking power through illness or causing harm to others—black magic—throws a definite warp into the course of the illness. It is 'mad' in the sense I define below.

For instance, one may decide that one is the Chairman of the Board, become proud and flaunt the fact. Suddenly, however, a corporate coup dislodges one, and the patient spends the rest of the illness desperately trying to recover his former position of power. The illness is largely wasted.

This is an important point: there is an immediate, almost tangible *karma* strung through the course of an illness. How one behaves in any one of the rapidly shifting gestalts that compose an illness largely determines the nature and situation of the next gestalt. How I behave in world A with problem B determines the nature of the next world C and problem D. The thread of the illness is only approximately karmic, allowing Providence and Grace to act as well.

~

The psychotic frequently believes he has died, he is dead, or he is making a journey to or through the land of the dead. This should hardly be surprising. The world of the imagination, of the irreal, is the world of death. One 'de-realizes' the present and enters the purely potential. The 'purely potential' is the realm of death. The future is the realm of death. The past is the realm of death. Every alternative to the present is the realm of death.

Death creates meaning. One ransoms meaning in life from death, from the potential, from the imagined. A new meaning is a little death, and, conversely, one must die to find meaning. Meaning is brought into life from across the border of death: it is booty stolen by marauders who gamble their lives. The reception of meaning in life is mediated by death. The treasures of death are meanings. Death is rich in meaning.

Meaning results from the unknowable. Death is the final unknowable. Meaning pours into life from "death's dream kingdom," from God through Death into Life. If every discovery of meaning is a death, *requires* a death, 'real' death may be the ultimate discovery of meaning. I am simply making a phenomenological observation….

…..or perhaps I wax metaphysical. (Shame on me!)

In 1971, in an utterly exhausted condition, recovering from my first illness, I frequently said, "I have burned out whole lives." I wasn't speaking seriously of *karma* or reincarnation, but I meant that masses of psychic energy that might have directed efforts over a number of possible lives for me to lead had expended themselves explosively in two or three short months. I had short-circuited my nervous system. The efforts of a lifetime or a number of possible lifetimes had exploded in fantasy, fantasy worlds, fantasy events. Those energies would no longer control my behavior. That is the point—"no longer control my behavior." I was exhausted, but I was free from the expended impulses. I had fantasized, imagined, sublimated, *dreamed* them away. The power of my early development, my 'youthful *karma*,' if you will, had dissipated in dream, in psychosis, and, though weak, I was more free, not less. There were whole lives I didn't have to live anymore.

Those 'Davids' had dreamed until they died. I had something of a clean slate from which to direct my life anew.

'first you dream, then you die...'

Every dream, every fantasy, every imaginal event, is a small death. A passion that might have controlled one has been sublimated away. The passion has been offered up and cast off. It floats away like a helium balloon. As the controlling impulses vanish, one is free to respond to events on their own terms as they develop. Fresh possibilities are recognized when they appear. Nothing is that important. As rigid mental hierarchies of value collapse, the 'trivial' bears significance.

The imagination converts impulse to openness. Each dream extinguishes a burning ember until the fire is out. Personal will dies. But this is not the "annihilation of being." This is the "seed that falls to the ground." When personal will dies, collective will, the will of the collective unconscious, asserts itself.

Jung concurs?

But I am presupposing a recovery from the illness. This is a sensitive subject. When one observes a friend or loved one in the throes of illness, observes him seriously wounded, reeling, and heading in the wrong direction, one feels one must *do something now*—shake him, slap him, talk some 'sense' into him. Immediate total intervention.

But this is useless and cannot help. One must remember in another sense the fact of death. The Judgment of the Dead is singular, personal. The individual must live his very own death. Only *he* can receive *his* judgment. Illness is not so much a disease as a substantial transpersonal crisis. Will ye, nill ye, only George can die George's death.

I don't mean to deny hope—not even in the most dramatic cases or in the illnesses of longest duration. The human spirit is not easily extinguished, whatever the odds:

How far is it to Babylon?
Three score miles and ten.
Can we make it by candle light?
Yes, and back again.

~

 The typical inpatient physician suppresses any discussion of the content of illness once the patient has recovered. The doctor fears that discussion of the illness will precipitate a relapse. It is certainly true that if a patient is relapsing he will become preoccupied with the content of his previous illness.
 Yet I suggest that there is dispassionate examination of psychotic experience, and that such examination is a crucial part of the illness's bearing fruit. While ill, the patient sees but he does not see through. Once recovered the patient can take time to see through what he has seen. It is time to integrate into secondary process ego-functioning the results of primary process mythic adventure. Personal values, as well as realms of meaning, will be changed. The man on the journey returns home, transformed.

~

 Many adjectives are used to describe psychotic process. I tend to assign the following meanings to a few of them.
 'Bizarre' behavior refers to rapid, erratic and inconsistent activities as witnessed by an observer. At such times the patient is usually encountering rapid, creatively misperceived, gestalt shifts, and is responding to each world for a moment, then moving on to the next. The pattern in these shifts is impossible for the outside observer to perceive, and the effect is mystifying, perhaps frightening.
 I define 'craziness' as concretizing an abstraction and pursuing it on a material level. This is one way of understand-

ing basic psychotic process. My favorite example of craziness is taken from Antonin Artaud. Writing of his experiences in Mexico, Artaud says,

> For besides being the Idea of the Eternally Renascent,
> God is also Someone; and this someone is the
> Inexhaustible Active, who, over all sleep and all
> Dreams, swallows that which, in the further of
> Him-Self, later, He will give! Later. In that
> Later in which there bursts forth the Word, his Son,
> In Flames of Love that will never fail.
> And it was this God of Eternal Charity whom
> The following *year I went to find among the
> Irish.* (My emphasis.)

All genius of prose, all Christian doctrines of Incarnation aside, Artaud is dead serious that he went to find his God *in Ireland*. This is 'crazy.'

'Insane' means to me direct violation of the laws of nature or customs of society, oblivious of the consequences. Trying to fly from a window or trying to convince one's boss that he is a poached egg will do for examples.

'Sick' I associate with perversion, contamination of the pure stream of illness with lust or anger, sex or violence. Masturbating in public or strangling a cat are examples.

'Mad' I associate with inflationary tendencies, so unfortunate yet so prevalent in illness. (Some would say inflation is what illness is all about.) The individual seeks power and becomes grandiose. The back ward Napoleon is 'mad.'

Words describing psychosis attract a derogatory connotation. They highlight what is going wrong. If the public knows anything about psychosis, they know it is wrong. This prejudice must be overcome if psychotic process is to be objectively examined.

～

In these notes I have attempted to remain closely phenomenological. I have attempted neither to examine particular contents of psychotic process nor to interpret those contents. My observations have been formal.

I would like, however, to return again to a key interpretative tool, the notion of projection, because this interpretation does immediate violence to the phenomenology of illness. The experience of the psychotic is the very opposite of projection. Objects and events in his environment become transparent or perhaps translucent. Meaning is breaking through the threshold of perceived reality from the farther side. Objects and events contain communication from beyond, from God, from the other shore.

Meaning is by no means experienced as moving from the subject out to the object; meaning is experienced as breaking in, from beyond, through the object to the subject. The limits of our materialistic metaphysics and our lack of religious conviction may force us to conclude that meaning is projected from inward outward, but that is *not* the experience.

We somehow suppose that the eruption of unconscious contents is a 'powerful experience' but to the individual involved, the reason for power is not psychologized; he has received 'revelation,' the 'Word of God,' literally, into his life. And *for that reason* the individual is especially impelled to speak out and act upon the received Word.

Once again, this is a paper on phenomenology, not a paper on metaphysics. But the phenomenology points to a broader metaphysics. There are no rational arguments against the other shore, only materialistic ones. Certainly one must be circumspect and careful before one concedes any ground to the patient who is talking with God, but the quality of 'otherness' requires recognition. It cannot simply be dismissed as 'illusion.'

Minimally, the experience of illness is a call to the Symbolic Quest. Psychotic illness introduces the individual to themes, conflicts, and resolutions that may be pursued through the entire religious, spiritual, philosophical, and artistic history of humanity. This is perhaps quite enough for an event to accomplish.

October, 1982

THE STRUGGLE FOR "EXISTENCE"

An inevitable consequence of denying the existence of God is doubting one's own existence.

The believer, knowing God, knows that he is a creature of God. God is the first fact of the universe, to which all other facts must submit. God not only created the believer but will attend to each believer personally. God's love and personal care establish the existence of the believer. God's love is the personal security of each believer. The believer's relationship with God is the substance of his existence. God numbers the hairs on the head of each believer and knows the needs of each. This is metaphysical and final. This is constant, unchangeable, absolute.

Existence is one pole of relationship. Before there can be one there must be two. In order to exist I must be recognized by another. A believer finds total ontological security in being recognized by God. This is one function of faith.

When God is denied the individual turns to society for recognition. But in society the individual finds no security or guarantee. In society one must "construct" or "establish" existence. Recognition by society is transitory and relative. The individual may easily fail to exist! The wheel of fortune will determine whether or not I exist. The wheel of fortune will determine whether I am "somebody" or "nobody." Since social recognition is in fact available only to a few, the odds *are* that I don't exist.

God is jealous of his creatures. When God grants the believer total ontological security, that security in God is opposed to any security society might appear to offer. Security in God is exclusive. Existence must be received as a gift of God: it cannot be worked for, proven, constructed, or established. To work for, prove, construct, or establish existence is to reject the free gift of God.

A Godless society fosters a need to "achieve." "Achievements" establish existence. They grant power and status to the achiever and he is "recognized." The achiever becomes "somebody." He passes from the many to the few. For a time, the achiever is "alive." Constructing this "existence" is the goal of the "need" achiever.

Many "achievements," eliciting the praise of men, are of questionable value, but I will not discuss that. Rather, I will point out that when existence is insecure, values are insecure and will be subordinated to existence. Without total ontological security, value itself cannot be regarded as independent, objective, and intrinsic. If I need first of all to establish my existence, I will use value as a means rather than honoring it as an end. I can readily trade bits and pieces of the Good, the Beautiful, and the True for social recognition – existence – because existence is the truly scarce commodity.

As long as one's existence is insecure, value will be a means to the end of establishing one's existence. The scientist will use truth to demonstrate his brilliance and become a famous scientist. The artist will use beauty to demonstrate his creativity and become a famous artist. The social reformer will use good works to demonstrate his compassion and get elected. In the minds of each of these individuals, the lesser will be traded for the greater. Existence comes first. If I doubt my own existence, I cannot grant intrinsic existence to any aspect of my life. Values submit to me, I do not submit to values.

In a society such as that of the United States, the real oppression is perhaps that of the "somebodies" over the "nobodies." Status and power hierarchies are the focus of attention.

The "brilliant," "creative," and "effective" individuals establish their "existence" at the expense of ordinary human beings. Social recognition is inherently invidious. Power and status intrinsically divide humanity and create barriers. That is the very point and purpose of power and status. Power and status in society are meant to distinguish and discriminate. Social recognition establishes an existence that contradicts the law of love and God's will for each human being.

Middle class Americans are bred on the "need" to "achieve." Failure to distinguish oneself in society leads to guilt and lack of self-esteem. "Self-actualization" is considered the hallmark of mental health, rather than the outcome of strident socio-economic competition. Erik Erikson, who coined the term "identity crisis," baldly explains that "identity crisis" resolves into "task identification" wherein one pursues work and career as the basis of one's being, occupation being the key determinant of socio-economic status and power. No psychologist takes seriously the experience of God's love as the basis of human existence.

The lure of social recognition, the will to be esteemed above one's fellows, is powerful, constant, and pervasive: we are bombarded with pressures to attain social recognition however scrupulous we are in our values or however sincere our will. Only a vital spiritual relationship with a living and personal God, a God that is jealous, can support a secure sense of existence that will not grasp at invidious distinction as a means of support. "Need" achievement then becomes a failure of faith. "Task identification" is to become less than God intended. "Self-actualization" is not proof of psychic integration but a combination of luck and ambition. Working a routine job is not a personal failure so much as a result of real socio-economic lack of opportunity and aggressive, self-seeking competition. Repudiating careerism turns one's attention from the public domain to personal community.

Personal virtue collapses when social recognition is the end to which we strive. Public life is "on the record." Private life is "off the record." We tend more and more to describe people in terms of public qualities that enhance "productivity": intelligence, creativity, dynamism, effectiveness, etc., rather than kindness, forgivingness, patience, warmth, etc. We tend to think that personal activity and community are not "real." Friends exist as "social support" for the "real" activities of life. It might be propounded that in public life we seek to redress the evils that private life creates. In private life I may indulge the evils that I contend with publicly. I excuse myself because there is no social reward for good will exhibited in private life.

An enormous self-interest is taken for granted in a careerist society. Ethics is reduced to "fair play." The self-interest of each participant is not questioned, it is only hoped that a given individual will obey certain rules in the pursuit of his self-interest. Questioning the basic objective by propounding a life of sacrifice, service, and humility, is out of the question. The wisdom of the ages is considered poor mental health.

We hardly notice the details of our pursuit of self-interest. It is second nature to establish our knowledgeability and authority in casual conversation. We let our achievements be known at the first opportunity. In any new encounter we must first establish our credentials as persons of substance. This is "natural."

The prince of this world can grant us power and status but he cannot grant us peace. By seeking to prove our existence we can only create relative distinctions. In the pursuit of social recognition we can only experience "more than before." Social recognition, level by level, becomes stale and the hungry heart must rise higher for satisfaction. This continual "becoming" can never terminate in "being" because it has no intrinsic basis. It is a relative rather than an absolute measure.

Thus the attempt to establish existence through social recognition will end in failure. The experience of social recognition is always relative and never intrinsically satisfying. Only God's love is complete. We err when we make society God. But we are responsible for a moral failure as well. We cannot love our brother while seeking to rise above him. Our urge to distinguish ourselves is an ethical depravity. We err, but it is a willful error. It is sin, and it tempts us sorely. The more "capacity" we have, the more it tempts us.

We rarely feel that the purpose of our lives is simply to love God and neighbor. That seems vague and without benefit. The single most potent and continuous principle organizing our activities is socio-economic self-interest. Whatever we choose for work, it must get bigger and more rewarding. At the end of our lives we expect to leave behind us a career constituted of ever increasing levels of power and status. This will be the record that we have "lived." Do we expect to impress God?

God knows us too well. The frightening fact which the believer must face is that God knows the believer better than the believer knows himself. In society, appearance is reality, and we thus become preoccupied with image. We may well know better than our neighbor what our motives are, but God knows our motives better than we do. In society I may be a "regular fellow" or even "a cut above average" but to God I am at best "an unprofitable servant." It is easy to deceive ourselves and easier to deceive our neighbor, but impossible to deceive God. It is precisely those hidden recesses of our hearts that will be judged without the benefit of any doubt. We cannot buy our existence from God, whether we pay with "real" bills or counterfeit. The Creator is a jealous God.

October, 1982
A "SECULAR" SOCIETY?

Christianity is the religion of love. The Christian is the person who loves God and neighbor. But the ability to love God and neighbor is not a natural ability. We are naturally a needy people and preoccupied with our needs. Our primary need is to be acknowledged as substantial human beings. We busy ourselves seeking to establish ourselves as persons of substance. Our time for God and neighbor is limited by our restless activity.

The Christian's ability to love God and neighbor is not forced, imposed upon him as a duty and carried out as a burden. The Christian's ability is the result of a prior experience in which his own concerns about himself were put to rest. The Christian's existence as a person of substance is established beyond doubt by his encounter with God's love.

God is a Person, not a principle, entity, vapor, or warm fuzzy. The Creator of this vast, terrifying cosmos is a Person, an infinite Person, but a Person. The metaphysical foundation of the universe is Person. I am a person, you are a person, God is a Person. Being a person is what it's all about. As persons, we are created in the image of God. God's personal love for each individual establishes each individual as a person of substance in final, complete, ultimate, metaphysical reality. The Christian's experience of God's love grants him full existence of the only absolute kind. This existence – person to Person, finite person to infinite Person – is absolute and unshakeable. The Christian's fears for himself are quieted. There is no greater security to be found. The Christian is free to love God and neighbor.

God's love for us is of a peculiar kind. God's love for us is individual and personal, directed to who we are intrinsically, without a care for position or achievement, without regard for class, education, background, occupation. God is not interested in our resume. Our resume is precisely what God is not interested in.

God loves us in our unique individuality. His love penetrates pretence, mask, façade. God is not impressed by us, rather loving us in our failure and limitation. The Christian's personal security is guaranteed by his person-to-Person relationship with the absolute and infinite. The Christian rests in God's love.

The Christian's love of neighbor will be an image of God's love of the Christian. The Christian loves directly and immediately the person of his neighbor. The Christian loves the unique individuality, the intrinsic being, the image of God, in his neighbor. The *person*, in primary, face-to-face relationship, is what matters – not position or achievement, class, education, background, occupation. The Christian passes on to his neighbor the love he learned from God.

"No one can hurt you if you are determined to do only what is right." The Christian has been freed from fear. In this world the Christian has nothing to fear, nothing to lose. His neighbor may idolize intelligence and condescend to the Christian because of greater intelligence. His neighbor may idolize beauty and condescend to the Christian because of greater beauty. Deceit, fraud, intimidation, cynicism, pride may abound, but all these are products of idols and cannot separate the Christian from the love of God. The love of God has absolute status.

Christianity is indeed the religion of love. The Christian loves God and neighbor. But there is a warning, a limitation, a qualification, which appears scandalous to this secular age. The Christian is not to love society.

Society is what a secular age is enthralled with, preoccupied with, oriented to. And it is precisely society that the Christian is not to love. "You must not love this passing world or anything that is in the world." It is impossible to love God or neighbor while loving the world.

The "world," in this sense, "society," is a mechanism for establishing existence on the basis of relative distinctions and discriminations. Society is a complex power and status hierarchy. Level by level, in sphere after sphere, the "few" are distinguished from the "many." Society is a system of barriers and demarcations that discriminates the "somebodies" from the "nobodies." The point and purpose of social structure is to divide classes of people from one another and establish relative worth.

The process is inherently invidious. A host of nobodies is required to support each somebody. Only in a relative sense, and at the expense of many, can I become a social somebody.

God's love is absolute, final, but spiritual and democratic. Social recognition is relative, transitory, but material and elitist. The Christian is the person who will accept the love of God, but he cannot do that if he is hungry for power and status. Trying to make something of oneself in a relative sense is to turn one's back on the free gift of God, on the basis of which one is already a person of substance as a creature of God. Thus, "The love of the Father cannot be in any man who loves the world."

Being-before-God is absolute. Being-in-society is relative. The one is democratic, the other invidious. God wants us to accept our existence and value from Himself alone, rather than stealing existence and value from our neighbor. "…the spirit which he sent to live in us wants us for himself alone." The condition for God's love is to accept it simply, without trying to augment it by lording over our neighbor. One cannot have it both ways: "Anyone who chooses the world for his friend turns himself into God's enemy."

God loves us because we are persons. Being a person is precisely what society does not care about. In society we are roles, positions, contacts, interfaces, connections. In society intrinsic being is worthless while extrinsic accoutrements such as achievement, capacity, superiority, money, and position are what make us worthwhile. Life in itself can have no meaning in society because life is common to all and affords no relative distinction. Life is only the least common denominator. It's nothing to get excited about or be grateful for. To respect ourselves as persons, we must be grounded in God, not oriented to society.

Somehow when we refer to ourselves as a secular society we suppose we are being neutral. As a society we suppose ourselves vaguely agnostic. But a secular society is totally preoccupied with itself, totally preoccupied with relative distinction, power, status, upward mobility, and becoming a celebrity. We speak euphemistically when we call ourselves secular. We are a worldly society, a society opposed to God, a society that has made itself God. We fear not the judgment of God but fear the judgment of society. Dominance and dominance hierarchy is all society understands. Thus, "…the whole world lies in the power of the Evil One."

To one grounded in the love of God, the whole world would be comic if it were not tragic. The Christian knows he is somebody in the only absolute sense. And he watches a mad rush to become somebody. He watches the relentless pursuit of what might have been a free gift. The secularist slaves to earn his birthright. And it is all taken so seriously.

One is tempted to wonder: "Who do these people think they are? What are they trying to prove? Does money mean anything to God? Will he be impressed by a large bank account? Does power mean anything to God? Is he partial to chief executive officers? Do celebrities have a special place in Heaven?"

The situation would be comic, except that it is taken seriously by the participants. The game is played with a life-or-death ruthlessness. People destroy all that is of intrinsic value in themselves in order to rise in socio-economic status. Real evil is heaped on those unqualified to compete in the worldwide "I'm better than you are" game.

I am not making my case on the basis of a general humanism. Scriptural Christianity speaks quite plainly: "My brothers, do not try to combine faith in Jesus Christ, our glorified Lord, with the making of distinctions between classes of people…as soon as you make distinctions between classes of people, you are committing sin, and under condemnation for breaking the Law." Once one makes distinctions between classes of people, one will want to part from the "lesser sort" and associate with the "greater sort." When this impulse arises we are commanded to resist it: "…if at heart you have the bitterness of jealousy, or a self-seeking ambition, never make claims for yourself." Failure to control jealousy and ambition results in the conditions we are surrounded by: "Wherever you find jealousy and ambition, you find disharmony, and wicked things of every kind being done."

The proverb says, "…it is hard for the good man to be saved." The worldliness of the world has developed to a fever pitch. The substance of our "ethic" is self-aggrandizement. The dazzling attractions of the world are everywhere thrust in front of us. The dollar, the promotion, the prestigious suburb.

The Christian is a Christian precisely because he is in rebellion against this world and the prince of this world. The values of the world are precisely what the Christian rejects. The problem that Christianity is meant to solve is precisely worldly relative distinction and lack of regard for persons. Christianity is the response to the morass of power and status hierarchy. "Who can overcome the world? Only the man who believes that Jesus Christ is the Son of God." "This is the victory over the world - our faith."

Christian community exists apart from worldly society. Christian community is however no longer to be found in the Church. The Church as it exists today is simply another power and status hierarchy. Our individual congregations replicate within them the social structure found outside. Christian community has never been and will never be, a prominent feature in the world: "…there is no eternal city for us in this life but we look for one in the life to come."

The Christian will always be an outsider. He has received from God absolutely what society would sell him relatively. There is no need to play the game. The Christian's place is in a pocket of community, seeking first the kingdom of God. The world will pass him by.

Had the Son of God been worldly he would have incarnated as a learned rabbi of great renown. Instead he incarnated as a simple carpenter and died young and ignominiously. *That* was the life of God on earth. "Jesus…suffered outside the gate…Let us go to him then, outside the camp, and share his degradation." That degradation, that worldly failure, carries within it eternal life, now and forever.

October, 1984

– FOR FLOYD –
GAMBLING ON GOD

Christians: Ride hard!   Die free!

Commitment to Christ is not an idle proposition. One does not simply cry "Lord! Lord!" Commitment to Christ means dramatic change. A good tree bears good fruit or it is not a good tree. Commitment to Christ means nothing less than betting your whole life that Jesus rose from the dead. If your whole life - body and soul – is not on the line, you're not believing. Faith does not hedge its bets.

The sophisticates will laugh. They know perfectly well – indeed, they know better than many Christians – that Satan is the Prince of this world. They know that power, wealth, and status go to the ruthless and self-serving. They remember the lies they told, the corners they cut, the deals they struck. They know their souls are sold. They do not call Satan Satan. They deny that Satan exists. It is thus easier to serve him.

We live in enemy occupied territory. Jesus is Lord – yes! – but Satan will rule the earth until Christ comes in power. In the most vicious sense the world is ruled with an iron rod by Satan and his angels. Satan it was who offered Christ the kingdoms of the world. They are Satan's to give. Christ refused them. Satan will offer each of us less than he offered Jesus. But will we refuse?

Make no mistake. God does not "bless" Christians with a house and two cars. Your suburbs are built on the blood of infants. But Satan knows that out of sight is out of mind. Shouldn't a Christian be disturbed to find himself many times more wealthy and more comfortable than his Savior? Jesus taught that the Christian would possess the Kingdom and inherit the earth. How many of us would not rather possess the earth and inherit the Kingdom?

There is no doubt, my friend — here on earth the cards are marked and the deck is stacked. Our job is to break the bank and put the Evil One out of business. While playing by the rules. The sophisticates laugh to see someone play fair in a rigged casino. They scoff at "superstitious" prayer and ridicule "naïve" faith. But — by the grace of God — the bank will be broken. The racketeers will scatter and the sophisticates will hide.

Christians and other losers play by the rules. Don't deceive yourself: you cannot serve two masters. God *did not* put that bundle in your savings account. (God *never* pays in cash.) You cannot receive salvation while worshipping success. (Summer camp Christians are notorious for expecting both salvation and success and being totally unprepared for the hard choice between them.) (They did not count the cost before they started to build.) (Their houses are built on sand because they did not believe that *their* neighborhoods would flood.)

Jesus came to suffer much and be set at nought. Can the slave be higher than his Master? Did Jesus die a criminal's death so that you could be a "pillar of society?" (T'was they who killed him.) Was God on Earth crucified so that you could enjoy a summer home?

We know better than that. Ride hard, my friends! Ride to live! Live to ride! You were reborn to laugh at Satan when he believes he has crushed you! You were reborn to sing Christ's song when all your friends have left you! Dare the powers that be! Despise the high and mighty! Scorn the power of hell! We are not timid and falsely innocent: we are to be daredevils and wildmen who show Evel Knevel but an adolescent prankster!

The sophisticates are horrified that a man can hold his head high and receive as a free gift from God the personal security that they purchased so dearly from the Devil. "What arrogance!" they say. "A man must pay his dues." They cannot believe that Jesus already paid for anyone who will receive Him. The "system" they depend on is threatened with collapse.

The sophisticates will rage. They will hate you, but more – they will fear you. You have broken the rules with impudence. The traditions of men are flaunted. In you they will know the power of God and know too that the axe is laid to their roots. Their days are numbered. Their world will die. They are vassals of a lord who cannot protect them. They hate the glory God meant us to share! Because they know they refused to receive it!

Ride to live! Live to ride! The Christian lives on the razor's edge. He is the fearless one! He has the guts without which no glory! He testifies of the world that its ways are evil. He is hated, as his Master was hated. Can the servant be higher than his Master?

Our Lord Jesus was no respecter of persons. The pillars of society already have their reward. The soothsayers – the "experts," the priests of mental health, the social bureaucrats – already have their reward. We refuse to be controlled by men of power! We refuse to be bought by means of wealth! We refuse to be intimidated by men of status! "You must establish yourself," cry the sophisticates. No! We seek not the glory found among men. We were established by God when we were reborn. More than that comes from the Devil.

Did you seek first the Kingdom? Or did you go to college and build your career? Do you pray to prosper and succeed? Or do you plead with God to show you how better to serve him? While the earth is a battlefield you tell me that God has "blessed" you with peace and security? Examine your life! Perhaps Satan has found you no threat to him and left you in peace – *his* peace. (A soldier's place is in the thick of battle.)

"Where is the proof?" ask the sophisticates. And they know there is no proof. The Christian finds faith, hope, and love but not proof. Proof puts the mind to sleep but faith, hope, and love feed the soul. Faith, hope, and love make life possible. The Christian sells all he has and buys one field. He plays the long shot because otherwise life is not worth living. He trades his three piece suit for the rags of Christ and a chance to sing in the rain. (Sing in the reign of Christ?)

The Kingdom is total war on evil within and evil without. The Kingdom is not a cosmic insurance policy purchased by spending ten minutes with the Lord. The Kingdom is a guarantee of pain and suffering which is also abundant life. Can the servant be higher than his Master?

The Christian has counted the cost before starting to build. The Christian knows well the ways of the world because he has also the cunning of the serpent. He knows he will bear humiliation at the hands of the sophisticates. But, you see, Jesus is King of Kings because every Christian is a King, no vassal of Satan. The Christian remains standing as the sophisticates bow to their vicious master. The Christian is not so much a sheep among wolves as a wolf among sheep. The slaves of Satan are sheep. They live in fear. They are chained by the law of the land. They do not know or understand what it means to be unchained. They are too frightened to exchange their fear of Satan for the love of Christ.

The Christian is indeed a soldier and a fearless soldier at that. At a moment's notice he will die for his country, die for the only country that matters, die for the New Jerusalem. Victory on earth will not be gained until the Commander returns, but that day the troops will be found ready. They will be awake. They will have watched. These are strak troops. These are troops proud and strong. Or they are not his troops.

We do not merely believe in things unseen. We stake our lives on things unseen, we live and die for things unseen.

Ride hard! Die free! We are Christians!

JESUS – I have been ashamed of you before men and now I am ashamed of me. Once more the unprofitable servant begs to be forgiven. Forgive me, LORD.

Amen.

SYMBOLIC CONSCIOUSNESS

Through the course of time, dealing with memories of illness, I have become less preoccupied with particular symbols and what they might mean and more concerned with the general form of consciousness exhibited, "symbolic consciousness"—a seeing through the literal to meaning beyond.

We live in a time when the literal is taken for granted as the only dimension of significance. Science aggressively teaches us that the literal, material, repeatable aspects of experience are final. At the same time we live at a time marked by a poverty of meaning. A dearth of meaning appears to me the most salient "human" crisis in our age.

Now "symbolic consciousness" seemed to solve the problem of a dearth of meaning, rather handily. Products of the imagination, captured in poetry or prose, or products of the imagination, captured in physical object and expressing or containing yearning, memory, relation; these provided an atmosphere and environment replete with meaning that totally vanquished the antecedent lack of it. I possessed two picture postcards, one of a lion and one of a tiger, which captured for me a two-part mode of existence that had been expressed in many swirling and confused images from an illness in 1974. Later I wrote a poem about a lion guarded by four tigers which sought to capture in words my feelings about the pictures on the two postcards. I owned an inexpensive jewelry box with a face molded in pewter on the top, which expressed an ambivalent image from an illness in 1978. Later I sought to capture that image and my ambivalence in a poem.

These objects and many others, these writings and many others, created for me an atmosphere and environment where

I felt comfortable, at home in a cosmic/theological sense. My world, which had hitherto contained so little meaning, now contained so much. Further, I noticed that, over time, my attitude toward objects and events changed. It didn't matter to me that my two postcards cost only 25 cents each: they had meaning way beyond their value. And the jewelry box cost only $7.00: but it had meaning way beyond its value. Events taking place in my life came to seem less reflections on my status, burdens or joys to be borne, and more little stories "with a point": not unlike the symbolic dramas I had acted out while ill. I began to develop an "eye" for seeing through objects and events, at all times, in all places. And I began to relax.

Now these developments were, of course, quite heartening to me. And I would share them with those I knew, generally to a fairly patronizing response of, "I'm glad that has meaning for you." Now I wondered why I got that response from these people I knew, especially since they were among those most attuned to "the lack of meaning in our lives." Eventually I came to the conclusion that these people were far more interested in "value" than in "meaning" and have even come to see "value" and "meaning" as conflicting with each other. An item of "value" is *naturally* invidious: it belongs to one person and not to another and even receives much of its "value" by not belonging to other people. A Chagall print is "valuable" if it costs $1000.00 and not so much because the image is meaningful. An idea is "valuable" not so much because it is a good idea but because *nobody* else has thought of it and it can be patented or copyrighted and maybe win the owner a prize.

Meaning, on the other hand, belongs to no one. Hoarding it, even, is less satisfying than sharing it. Meaning is perceived, as an individual act of consciousness, and cannot be patented or copyrighted. Meanings may be shared, intimately, but no one meaning is likely to have broad social "value." A "meaningful" life need not, and even, is not likely to be, a "valuable" life. If only the "valuable" is "meaningful" most of the see of meaning dries up.

Now if we set about to live "meaningful" lives, I feel we should not have much problem. But if we set about to live "valuable" lives, we have not much chance of competitive success, and, are extremely likely to miss "meaning" along the way. Most of those poets, philosophers, psychologists so frustrated with concern for "meaning" in our lives are not really concerned with "meaning" but with the special case of "valuable meaning." They want to "think up" the overwhelming "meaning of life" that has escaped everybody's notice for the last eighty years, and copyright it, and win a Pulitzer Prize.

Discerning, creating, imagining meaning in one's life is a good deal more homespun than that. Very homespun, in fact. A meaningful poem need not be valuable. A valuable poem need not be meaningful. My two picture postcards may not be very valuable, but meaning will not disappear from my life when I am not offered tenure.

Choose: a meaningful life or a "valuable" life. And no complaints, either way.

"I see men, but they are like trees, walking."
                                                Amen.

MEMORY AND MEANING

As an individual recovers from a psychotic illness, he or she is faced with a problem of *memory*. What in fact took place during the period of illness may be very difficult to reconstruct. Portions of the illness may be "blacked out"; in other instances the very welter of multi-level experience may be difficult to comprehend with any degree of organization. In all cases, shame or embarrassment may inhibit a willingness to reconstruct events.

In Appendix IV to *Poetic Diction* Owen Barfield treats briefly this important topic:

> Thus, the problem of inspiration...reveals itself as identical in essence with the problem of knowledge itself. In the moment of knowing, which is also the real moment of poetic creation, the knower ceases to exist as subject at all; and, conversely, when he comes fully to himself, as subject, he ceases to know. Imaginations are generated in his consciousness as he passes from the former state to the latter, and the difficulty is, of course, to retain them in some form in the memory. The analogy with dreaming is here very exact; for everybody knows how the dream, which seemed vivid in every detail, while we were still only half-conscious, may vanish altogether during the last minute that is spent in waking right up. The special faculty needed to overcome this paradox of inspiration has been described, with effective accuracy, as 'presence of mind'.
>
> More loosely, it may be presented as the problem of *memory*. How, and in what form, to carry over

into the uninspired-*self*-consciousness some *memory* of that other inspired consciousness, which to the unpoetic man is not consciousness at all but sleep—that selfless moment when, as Wordsworth wrote in the Prelude, 'the light of sense goes out'? How to do this, when memory itself is unthinkable without sense? Thus, we find Aristotle saying of the poetic mind, that *we do not remember*; we find the mystics imbued with a pregnant sense of war between Memory and Inspiration, and Dante, after the final supreme vision of 'La forma universal', adds that the lapse of a single moment plunged that vision into greater oblivion than twenty-five centuries could produce in the case of an ordinary event.

"*Presence* of mind" was a quality clearly exhibited by me during my long illnesses 1971—1974. I had very clear recollections of events as they took place, my intentions, my meanings, my logic. What perplexed me in the period following the long illnesses was the welter, the overabundance of vivid memory, and, in particular, my inability to *organize* the experience.

Recollection upon recollection tumbled through my mind like clothes in a dryer. As time went on some sorting took place: my thoughts tended to focus and refocus on certain more powerful constellations of memory. I clung to these memories: I as often as not did not know their significance, but I did know that they contained Meaning. And Meaning, before my illnesses, was what was most clearly *lacking* in my life. I had, in my illnesses, through symbol, drama, acted parable, created events which *contained* Meaning. And that Meaning haunted me, as I obsessed and ruminated, pondered, reflected, because my environment still offered so little Meaning.

In Appendix III to *Poetic Diction* Barfield notes:

> ... the distinction between Fancy and Imagination is one which ought to be particularly emphasized in an age like ours, divorced from reality by universal abstraction of thought, and in which the fanciful poetry of 'escape', as it is sometimes called, is so popular.

> ...even those who give much of their time to reading, yes, and writing about, the greatest poetry, frequently reveal their sense of its 'unreality' as compared with the rest of life about them. Where will it end? When the real is taken as unreal, and the unreal as real, the road is open to the madhouse.

Thus I made the important decision not to seek to persuade myself that the clearly "unreal" aggressive intellectual environment of Harvard College was "real." I found no Meaning there. The experience I had been given, the Memory I retained, somehow *contained*, Meaning. No admonition that I was "enchanted by my illness" dissuaded me. Harvard College was the "real" that was "unreal." Psychosis was the "unreal" that *contained* the "real."

But not in finished form. As Barfield notes in Chapter 6 of *Poetic Diction*:

> ...inasmuch as man is *living* the poetry of which he is the maker, and as long as he is so doing it *cannot* be poetry to him. In order to *appreciate* it, he himself must also exist, consciously, outside it; for otherwise the 'felt change of consciousness'

cannot come about. Now nothing but the rational, or logistic, principle can endow him with this subjective—*self*-consciousness. Hence...the functioning of the rational principle is indispensable, if appreciation is to take place. The absolute rational principle is that which makes conscious of poetry but cannot create it; the absolute poetic principle is that which creates poetry but cannot make conscious of it.

My "crazy stories" are at a considerable artistic distance from the experiences themselves. They represent a careful reflection upon and refraction of, experiences of raw Meaning. The memories turned over, sorted out, sifted in my mind. I reflected on the memories as critic as well as poet.

When I speak of "symbolic consciousness" I do not mean "psychosis." I mean the careful *appreciation*, of symbol, image, drama, language, consciousness which psychosis introduced me to, which psychosis points to, invites. This is the perpetual "seeing through" the literal to meaning beyond.

In the study of memory a distinction is made between "episodic" memory and semantic or "categorical" memory. My memories of illness are primarily "episodic" yet I believe they contain a "semantic." I wish to create a "categorization" of "episodic" memory, a "semantics" of "episodic" memory. Mindfull Ideagrams.

"I" AND "IT"

Among the public at large many misunderstandings exist concerning "imagination," the imaginal, the imagined. Perhaps the most frequent misunderstanding is to confuse "ego fantasy" with "imagination."

The young clerk sits at his desk in his suburban office complex and dreams about sunning himself on the beaches of Acapulco. A Mexican in a sombrero sleeps quietly beneath a palm tree while the senoritas serve the young clerk drinks and play the guitar...

That is not imagination. *That* is ego fantasy. The individual transports himself to a pleasant, exotic (though stereotyped) environment where his desires are gratified. He assumes power, receives honor, indulges his every whim.

That is about all Freud saw in "imagination." For him it was simply "wish fulfillment"—"ego gratification." But there is much more, as we shall see.

Another common misunderstanding concerning imagination is that imagination is "thinking up" "something different." "Thinking up" "something different" in an arbitrary, capricious manner. "Whimsy" may have its place in imagination, but there is nothing arbitrary or capricious about the products of imagination.

Instead, as one explores the imaginal, one encounters pervasive pattern and interconnection. Products of the imagination interconnect, interpenetrate, reflect upon one another, build pattern together, build wholes.

This is not so hard to understand when one considers the experience of the writer at work. When I sit down to write, "I" don't write! "It" writes! Something beneath my conscious awareness, beyond my conscious control, wells up and writes my story. "IT" writes! I am more the recipient of my story than its author.

"It" gives glimpses of another world, or, perhaps, of the *pattern* of this world. This "other world", this *pattern*, is a web large and extensive and my story will include only certain elements. Another writer may include in his story some of the elements I have received and combine them with elements only he has received. Thus our stories will "interconnect."

"It" provides the basic setting, the environment, the forces at work, in my story. The particular resolution may or may not be the product of my own struggles, but the basic problem posed and the basic pattern emerging, are dictated by "It." In time the resolution will be dictated by "It" as well.

"It" is impartial, *objective*. "It" is little concerned with the wishes or desires of the "I". "It" constructs a world both pure and self-contained, self-sufficient, a world of "intrinsic meaning."

This impartiality, objectivity, purity, self-sufficiency may be more than a little irritating to the "I" with its clamoring ego ambitions, wants, wishes, desires. Yet here is the most important decision "I" has to make: "I" must choose "It."

At this point "It" is transformed from a mechanism for creating stories to a concrete principle from which to create one's life. Ego ambitions must be put aside, for "It" is *Good*.

At this point where "It" becomes a concrete principle from which to create one's life, we recover the "moral"—the ethical dimension of life. For "It" is *Good!* Imagine!

And *Good*ness is not the enlightened self-interest of being a "nice guy" or a "regular fellow." "Right action is freedom from time past and time future." "Right action" is impartial, *objective*, pure, and self-sufficient. "Right action" is *Good*, if we can recover the meaning of that term.

And this is not "goody-goody." "It" is a wind blowing from the finer air of another country. "Imagination" becomes not only a category of perception but a call to obedience.

We may construct a model of imaginal human functioning. In the center is the "I", which must choose. The "I", perhaps, strives upward toward God in his transcendent aspect, God who watches and evaluates decision, behavior. From beneath the "I" wells up the "It", which may be God in his immanent aspect, a principle informing consciousness, calling for decision, behavior.

We may flesh out our model. Welling up to the left of "It", love shades into lust. To the right of "It" righteousness shades into anger. Just like in the movies! Too much sex and violence are ruining good films. Errors to the left and right of "It."

At the level of, and surrounding the "I", we may designate the push-pull of "social" pressure and expectation. In a more intimate circle about the "I" we may place the "interpersonal", where *Good* is possible.

On the direct path, "It" moves "I" up to God.

The language of "It" is symbol, image. "It" is a language of the left hand—preverbal ideation. The "I" is naturally right-handed. Once the "I" has chosen the "It" the "I" may employ its right-handed, rational, problem solving techniques to implement not its own ends but the objective imaginations of the "It."

Ours is a self-interested, right-handed culture. We could use a few more southpaws on the pitcher's mound. "It" throws a mean curve ball!

THREE LETTERS ON DEATH

September 9, 1981

Dear Dave,

"Life is the dream of Death."

Excuse me, but that is my latest epigram on death. It's meant as a companion to, "Death is the silence which makes life music." Oh, well – I'm trying to introduce my "little letter on death." I would like to write a "big essay on death" but I'm not ready. So a "little letter" will have to do.

George MacDonald wrote a story (*Lilith*) containing an elemental pattern which has become the cornerstone of my thinking about death. Adam invites Mr. Vane to sleep. And when Mr. Vane sleeps he will dream. And he will dream until he dies. And when he dies he will awake. And when he wakes he will truly live. Done.

Sleep. Dream. Die. Wake. Live.

In 1971, while I was in an utterly exhausted condition recovering from my first illness, I frequently said, "I have burned out whole lives." I wasn't speaking seriously of karma or reincarnation, but I meant that masses of psychic energy that might have directed efforts over a number of possible lives for me to lead, had expended themselves explosively in two or three short months. I had short-circuited my nervous system. The efforts of a lifetime or a number of possible life-times had exploded in fantasy, fantasy worlds, fantasy events. Those energies would no longer control my behavior.

That is the point – "no longer control my behavior." I was exhausted, but I was free from the expended impulses. I had fantasized, imagined, sublimated, *dreamed* them away. The power of my early development, my "youthful karma," if you will, had dissipated in dream, in psychosis, and, though weak, I was more free, not less. There were whole *lives I didn't have to live* anymore. Those "David's" had dreamed until they died. I had something of a clean slate from which to redirect my life anew.

Every dream, every fantasy, every imaginal event, is a small death. A passion that might have controlled one has been sublimated away. The passion has been offered up and cast off. It floats away like a helium balloon.

One might argue that most of what is wrong with our world is the result of what we "Have To Do." Compulsion is the name of the game. There is always something More Important than what we are called upon to do in the moment. We are short-tempered, unkind, patronizing because we have More Important Things To Do. We have (letters to write), articles to read, money to make, people to meet. Driveness.

These impulses and many others die in dreams. As the controlling impulses vanish, one is free to respond to events on their own terms as they develop. Fresh possibilities are recognized when they appear. Nothing is that Important. As rigid mental value hierarchies collapse, the "trivial" bears significance.

This is what I mean in my stories when I say, "Die now, and dying later ain't so bad." As Death, I bring the First Death, not the Second. Go with the Flow – to the Death! To the death!

Compulsion: Sublimation.
Drivenness: Dream.

The imagination converts impulse to openness. Each dream extinguishes a burning ember until the fire is out. Personal will dies. Nothing (only Nothing) matters.

George MacDonald has written another story (*At the Back of the North Wind*) which influences my thinking about death. A woman, the North Wind, appears to a young boy and takes him on her back to wonderful places. Finally the boy asks the woman: Are you real? Who are you really? Are you good? The woman replies that she is real and good, but that she is called "evil fortune" and "ill fate." She beckons the boy to her, and he dies.

The woman, the principle of imagination, is Death herself. The world of the imagination, of the irreal, is the world of death. No wonder a dream is a little death! By dreaming one has entered death's kingdom! One has "de-realized the present" and entered the purely potential. The purely potential is the realm of death. The future is the realm of death. The past is the realm of death. Every alternative to the present is the realm of death.

Death is vision. Vision is Death. All "seeing" is done with the eyes of the dead, with the eyes of Death. One dies to see. One sees to die.

Death creates meaning. One ransoms meaning in life from death, from potential, from the imagined. A new meaning is a little death, and, conversely, one must die to find meaning. Meaning is brought into life from across the border of death: it is booty stolen by marauders who gamble their lives. The reception of meaning in life is mediated by Death. The treasures of Death are meanings. Death is rich…in meaning.

I am speaking *literally*. In "psychology" we take the whole world and stuff it inside our heads. Why say that the anima mediates between the ego and the unconscious? Why not say that Death mediates between the individual and God? Is it required that we attend merely to the microcosm of the ego in the mind, ignoring the macrocosm of the individual in the world? Is "unconscious life" (death) *any more improbable* than "unconscious mind?"

Meaning results from the unknowable. Death is the final unknowable. Meaning pours into life from "death's dream kingdom," from God through Death into Life. If every discovery of meaning is a death, requires a death, "real" death may be the ultimate discovery of meaning. I am simply making a phenomenological extrapolation.

Perhaps I should explain. Death and threats of death are the staples of paranoia. Day in and day out for days one is in constant dire fear for one's life. This constant fear of death conditions one in ways that are difficult to explain. In a word: "Fear of death is fear of God." Whatever that means!

During paranoia if one is not careful one is killed. If one is brave and faithful one sacrifices one's life or accepts certain death. *These "deaths" are feared as fully as "death" is feared by the sane.* And "inexplicably" each death in paranoia becomes a pivot around which the illness is transformed. One continually "dies" into a whole new world, for better or worse. I have "died" in full fear so many times, only to find my soul intact but my world transformed, that I fully expect such at my physical decease. It's simply a matter of training.

Of course: the notion that Death may be a principal guiding force in Life presupposes an unfashionable idealist metaphysics.

∼

Having written in two parts on death, I thought I might conclude with a musing on life. After a lifetime of philological analysis, Owen Barfield concludes: "We are spoken into existence."

I like that. I have a belief in karma (within one life, anyway) and a strong belief in Providence, though not much of a belief in destiny. The idea that we are each words in a sentence uttered by God does justice to my sense of the order and disorder in existence. A "word" need not know exactly what it means or what its sentence means. The grammar and semantics may be beyond us, but we are assured that Truth is being spoken. It is our privilege to occasionally gain insight into that Truth.

Further, we are not listed as words in a dictionary but spoken in a context. There are words that come before us and words that come after us. We take our place as part of the whole, contributing and receiving meaning.

"We are spoken into existence." And – yes – I suppose there's a period at the end of the sentence.

Cheers,
David

July 29, 1982

Dear Dave,

"Only dead things live forever."

There you have it – the epigram for the second letter on death. Life, properly lived, is a process – not a product. Yet we tend to make life into a product because products can be sold – sold for money, fame, power, influence. But products are dead, not living. The life of the living cannot be contained in a product, though life can be drained from the living in order to make products. What lives past the process of life is not that life, that process, but an idol of life that obliterates life. We seek so often to create idols, even of our own lives. We fail to see that the product we sell, the idol we create, is not us but rather a surrogate image, a scarecrow. The human reality of a human life cannot be charted through the record of the career, cannot be entered into a list of accomplishments.

Life essential is by its nature ephemeral and transitory. Moments that pass are the substance of life. What can be made permanent is the outer husk of life, not the kernel inside. If one attends only to what will survive one's death, one misses most of one's real experience. Developing one's reputation, for instance, most often means neglecting one's friends. Such a person seeks not friendship but admiration. And relentlessly advancing one's career means neglecting one's children. They are materially provided for but fail to receive time and attention. One's friends and one's children are the reality of life: one's reputation and one's career are idols of life, not life itself. Thus one sacrifices one's life to an idol of life, neglecting the ephemeral kernel for the apparently more enduring husk.

The question for each of us becomes, "How can I behave in a manner congruent with my death?" One cannot act effectively "in spite" of death or "as opposed to" death. Mortality must inform the tone of one's voice. Ironically, mortality must inform all action of lasting value. Action which denies death denies life and thus does justice to neither. In order to affirm life we must affirm death.

The demand that life accept death is equivalent to the demand that the ego accept the Self. The ego exists in time and seeks an extension of time: the Self exists outside of time, knows neither beginning nor end, and thus fears neither birth nor death. The timelessness of the Self will heal the time-hungry instincts of the ego.

The Self is located "behind" the ego. "In front of" the ego the ego constructs the image of the Self, the self-image. The ego neglects the Self, which is whole and complete, in favor of the self-image, which contains those elements which enhance the ego's sense of importance. The ego would have it that the self-image become glorious and exist in time forever. This is the sin of the ego. But hardship may bring wisdom and if the ego relinquishes its fascination with the self-image, the idol of the Self, and embraces instead the true Self, the ego will find peace in timelessness. This is a matter of immediate psychological experience.

Exchanging the self-image for the Self may develop a *feeling* of timelessness, but what of the *fact*. Here I would turn tables on the existentialist. The existentialist *chooses* to believe that this life is all he has. This is not a fact thrust upon him: it is a part of his mythology. Life is the existentialist's grand battle against the coming, unending night. The existentialist rages against his mortality and the absurdity of a finite existence. But, I here suggest, life after death would be even more horrifying to the existentialist. This life, shaped by the existentialist as his final monument, then becomes a phase, a stage, a passing shadow, a small part of Existence as a whole. How belittling of the heroic finality of the existentialist! How small his grand triumph on earth against the backdrop of Eternity!

Life being fully terminated in death is a convenient myth of the twentieth century. And the existentialist can be snared in his own myth. He *chooses* to believe that this life is all. No one, particularly no scientist, took faith in life after death away from the existentialist. He rejects life after death of his own free will. The ego need never come to terms with the Self. What really makes life small is not its termination after 70 years, but the extension of existence to all Eternity. Against the backdrop of Eternity our current preoccupations are shown to be vain and self-important. Denying life after death is an excuse to make man the measure of all things, and that is essentially expedient. "Vanitas" has come to mean both futility and self-satisfaction. It is futile to be self-satisfied and self-satisfied to be futile. If man is measured by God in Eternity, we cannot relax in futile self-satisfaction or self-satisfying futility. Our neighbor's opinion as to our philosophical cleverness will pass, but God's judgment of our life will remain.

I do not mean to demean life in time as opposed to life in Eternity. But our actions in this life cannot be seen in proper perspective except against the backdrop of Eternity. Human life cannot be measured by itself but rather must be measured by the transcendent. Human life may provide the baseline for life hereafter, but human life cannot be judged on its own terms. We are only in this world, not of it, and certain satisfactions in this life are only of this life. True value must be judged from outside time, to be set in true perspective.

If one has accepted one's death in this world, if the ego has relinquished the self-image and embraced the Self, if the individual lives in the expectation of a life to come, he will throw over relentless future orientation and seek to act in a manner intrinsically satisfying and intrinsically meaningful. "Virtue is its own reward" has generally appeared a lame consolation to those who have sacrificed, yet actions which are their own reward are exactly those sought by those who live, and expect to live, in Eternity. Right action is substantial however insubstantial the dream containing it may be. Right action will endure as right action though good fortune may always be snatched away by death.

As T.S. Eliot put it, "Right action is freedom from time past and time future." Death is an aspect of time, and to conquer time is to conquer death. "Right action," action which is intrinsically appropriate to the present circumstances, is not the product of past proclivity or future intention, but rather a creative grappling with the here and now. Right action is creative, born in and of the one moment present, and right action frees one from the clock and calendar on the wall. Right action takes place now and forever.

To conquer time is to conquer death. Intrinsic meaning in the here and now, creativity in the present, "right action," will endure when time is measured by Eternity. One's circumstances will vary all through time, but the quality of one's response, one's choice or neglect of right action, endures in both time and Eternity. We always have the power to do the right thing – it can never be taken away from us – and it is by this power to do the right thing that we conquer time and death, and, both now and later, enter Eternity.

Cheers,
David

April 5, 1984

Dear Dave,

"What does life mean? Life means death." (It's a package deal.)

So much for the epigram to go with this, the third letter on death. Since both the first two letters on death were sent to you, Dave, I will honor the tradition.

One enters existence on the condition that one will exit existence. The first fact of life is that it will end. Yet at certain times this basic fact is more of a problem than at others. As humdrum days pass by I find that Death never comes to mind. But during creative periods – yes, indeed – Death and fear of Death become a preoccupation to the point of obsession. This is the experience I wish to discuss.

Freud himself spent the years 1890 to 1900 in great fear of death. This was the period of letters to his dentist friend in Berlin, Wilhelm Fliess. During this period Freud developed the principles of psychoanalysis, and he greatly feared that he would die before he could organize and publish his work.

Besides the *todesangst* from 1890 to 1900, Freud also greatly feared that he would die before his mother. He did in fact outlive her, but it is peculiar that Freud never accounted for his obsessions with death in his own theoretical work. (The later Thanatos principle fails to do so adequately.) Freud apparently decided that death was a "fact" not to be "psychologized." Fear of death thus signified Necessity, was thus a normal response grounded in reality and not to be "explained." But can we not say more?

I have experienced great fears of death at various points in my life – almost always during creative periods. When I am writing and writing well I fear that I might die before I finish.

One reason for this is perhaps that, while creative, a person already has one foot in death's kingdom. During creative periods the here and now present is "de-realized" and one lives in one's imagination, in the irreal, in the unconscious, in death's kingdom. Since imagination proceeds from death's kingdom, immersion in imagination brings one close to death.

During these periods when I am writing and fear death, I react in either of two superficially contradictory ways. Sometimes I insist on finishing the piece absolutely as soon as possible. Death is the "deadline" I have to beat. "If only I can finish this piece," I will die happy. I push to finish.

On the other hand I often react to the threat of Death by putting my work aside. At such times I believe that a certain Providence or Fate is operating: if I neglect my friends and family God will punish me because I am making an idol of my work. Thus if I push at a pace to finish the work in two weeks, God will kill me after one week. I will die in an accident, found guilty of neglecting others and idolizing my work. Also the "great work" that I thought was so important may be a horror in the eyes of God. Better that it remain unfinished, after all.

If I put aside the work and fulfill my social responsibilities, etc...then I tend to think that the work, though now spread over perhaps two months, will be concluded successfully and be a better story or essay. I thus think that the longer course is safer, in terms of both quality and completion.

This returns us to the "do the right thing" argument. It's hopeless to try to cheat Death. One cannot "put one by" on him. Death is always demanding the right thing in the here and now. We cannot puff ourselves up. We cannot make idols of our work. For Death is the leveler and will in time level us also. Only "doing the right thing" will satisfy Death and prepare us to meet him. The "work" will have to wait, if indeed it merits accomplishing at all.

It is all but a cliché to say that fear of death is fear of transformation: one must die to create, one dies in creating. In constructing the raw materials into the work of art. One may fear this change, fear the death one is creating.

The artistic career is, in this sense, essentially alchemical. This is plain to see in the life of any painter or composer. Each new achievement makes possible the next work of art, on another level. One is climbing a ladder, step by step, work by work. One dies and dies yet again. One may fear this perpetual death and dying though one triumphs on each occasion.

There is another, less common, means of illuminating fear of death during creative periods: the artist is pregnant, big with child, and fears that the creation he carries within him will not be born. The artist feels responsible for what he deems a work of intrinsic value, independent of his own life. The artist may in fact care nothing for his own life yet fear for the work of art. He clings to life only that his art may be born.

Once again we find the conjunction of birth and death. The baby is born but the mother dies. Both baby and mother die. The baby alone may die. *Hope*fully, art is created. But the artist must die again. And all this may be fearful indeed.

~

At this point the essay moves from psychology into religion. "Psychology" proceeds without metaphysics, or, rather, adopts the prevailing scientific materialism in place of a metaphysics. This is comfortable for liberal intellectuals. But death is a metaphysical problem. Death challenges all metaphysics: a careful philosophy of existence is required when trying to understand lack of existence. Is death a matter of biology or a problem for higher conviction?

Unfashionably, I choose to pursue higher conviction.

I have found only one way to defend myself (and *se defendo* is my family's motto): I have found only one way to save my life and conquer my fear: I have given my life away. When a person gives his life away that life can no longer be taken from him. Paradoxically, I will die *if I do not* give my life away. My life is now no longer mine. I can relax.

As a Christian, I have given my life to Jesus. Sounds corny and naïve, some shall think. But my fear is thereby extinguished. Jesus, the man who "came to suffer much and be set at nought" welcomes all who will follow. I, for one, will follow.

By giving his life to Jesus, the Christian merges his own life into the life of Christ. As the life of the Son is begotten, not made, so the Christian's life is not to be found in his own transitions, but in the Eternity of the Son. Nothing can be added and nothing can be taken away: all is safe in a world otherwise nihilistically insecure.

Which last statement raises the question of in what kind of world and in what kind of universe do we in fact live? That is, in spiritual fact and not in the "facts" of scientism? What are the fundamentals? In following Jesus does one not simply stagger painfully into oblivion?

Not if one believes in a personal Deity. God is a person – three persons, even – and being a person is thus what all the universe is about. That is not what the world is about. On earth we are always constructing idols of ourselves, in particular. The Christian rejects this. The Christian believes, as the world does not, that each "ordinary" person is bequeathed a great dignity. Not the world, but the universe, honors each and every person. God will determine when we live and when we die, what we can do and what we cannot, where we succeed and where we fail.

Death is "the will of God." "The whole world is in his hands." These phrases are once again corny, perhaps. They are anathema to those who reject them as pious platitudes and search for a "deeper" religion. But life and death do not matter. What matters is doing the right thing, moment by moment, after the fashion of Christ. The universe is firmly established. It will not be moved. The universe, as opposed to the world, is founded on personal Deity and on tangible law and principle. During creative periods God may permit one to serve Him or permit it not – in a multitude of different ways. At all times one may be used or not be used, even in ways one will never guess.

Following Christ is vindicated throughout the fiber of the larger universe, though sinful man may not see it so. One is called upon only to believe in the Lord and to believe in the vindication, and then, whatever the event, rest in the will of God.

Critics may scoff at "giving one's life to Jesus." Critics may scoff at "the will of God." They do not believe that "the whole world is in his hands." But they can produce no principles of their own that have comparable power. Amen.

Cheers,
David

MYSTERY RELIGION

Shortly before I became ill in 1978 I had a dream which I have remembered. I was standing on a promontory which jutted into the sea, a rocky promontory of purplish stone. Carved in white marble among the purplish stone were three women in a line, reclining, wearing ancient Greek attire. The wind-swept sea behind them was a dark green. Suddenly the three women carved in white marble leapt alive and a voice from around and above called forth, "Christianity is a Mystery Religion."

Shortly after I had that dream I was once again plunged into a psychotic episode. Symbol, symbolic drama, parable, and acted parable erupted into consciousness. Once again my personality was fundamentally reorganized.

During the time since then I have wondered about the words spoken by the voice in the dream: "Christianity is a Mystery Religion." And I have wondered about symbol, symbolic drama, parable, and acted parable: questions of what I call "symbolic consciousness." What evidence is there for construing Christianity as a "Mystery Religion"?

∼

In the following I shall construct an argument from the New Testament witness designed to highlight a certain set of themes. I am not trying to treat fully the passages quoted; rather, to emphasize a certain direction in the record. All passages quoted are from *The Jerusalem Bible*.

∼

St. Luke records a saying of Jesus which would appear to have pivotal importance but which seems to have been neglected:

> No one lights a lamp and puts it in some hidden place or under a tub, but on the lampstand so that people may see the light when they come in. The lamp of your body is your eye. When your eye is sound, your whole body too is filled with light; but when it is diseased your body too will be all darkness. See to it then that the light inside you is not darkness.

Now this passage appears eminently consonant with the notion of a "mystery religion": its theme is that *perception*—"the eye"—is crucial to Christian life. If we can *perceive* correctly we are becoming Christians. But: perceive what? perceive how? If perception is crucial, what kind of perception is warranted?

This question may be answered in that the "sound eye"—"pure perception"—passage just quoted is the second use by St. Luke of the "parable of the lamp." St. Luke has already recorded the "parable of the lamp" in another context.

Speaking of why he spoke in parables, Jesus originally said:

> No one lights a lamp to cover it with a bowl or to put it under a bed. No, he puts it on a lampstand so that people may see the light when they come in. For nothing is hidden but it will be made clear, nothing secret but it will be known and brought to light. So take care how you hear; for anyone who has will be given more; from anyone who

has not, even what he thinks he has will be taken away.

"So take care *how* you hear," says Jesus. "*How* you hear," referring to the ability to understand symbolic language. Anyone who "has" that ability will be given more; anyone who "has not" that ability to understand symbolic language will lose "what he thinks he has." Jesus speaks in parables not in order to cover his lamp, but that his meaning—grounded in "symbolic consciousness"—will be made clear, made known, be brought to light.

The whole is made perhaps more clear in the parallel passage from St. Mark:

> He also said to them, "Would you bring in a lamp to put it under a tub or under the bed? Surely you will put it on the lampstand? For there is nothing hidden but it must be disclosed, nothing kept secret except to be brought to light. If anyone has ears to hear, let him listen to this."
>
> He also said to them, "Take notice of what you are hearing. The amount you measure out is the amount you will be given—and more besides; for the man who has will be given more; from the man who has not, even what he has will be taken away."

This passage is highly suggestive. "For there is nothing kept secret (by whom? how?) except to be brought to light (by whom? how?). I suggest that *Jesus* speaks symbolically in order that *his listener* should learn to hear and understand, the symbolic word, should learn to see and understand, the symbolic image.

One must *work*, put forth an effort, to comprehend symbolic consciousness. Thus, "The amount you measure out is the amount you will be given." And again: "The man who has (the ability to understand symbol) will be given more."

I suggest that Jesus spoke to the people in parables in order to develop in them the ability to think in parables, in symbol, in image. The ability to do this is the key to Christ-consciousness ("The lamp of the body is the eye."). Jesus explained the parables to his disciples, not that the parables might be discarded once the interpretation was supplied, but as a special aid in the development of symbolic appreciation.

St. Matthew records the prophecy:

> I will speak to you in parables and expound things
> hidden since the foundation of the world.

I suggest that "things hidden since the foundation of the world" can *only* be expounded in parables. "Seeing through" the literal to meaning beyond, whether in a story or a real event, in a mental image or a physical object, is a quality of mind which contains "things hidden since the foundation of the world." The translation, the interpretation by itself, is inadequate: the form of consciousness must be entered into, understood.

The ability to enter into and understand symbolic consciousness is a special ability, which once received, will yield all further Christian truths. The parables of Jesus spoken to the people are not "illustrations of a point" which is primarily conceptual, they are a call to a new level of consciousness—a "mystery." "The medium is the message."

The ability to enter into and understand symbolic consciousness comes from the heart—it is a development of religious and moral significance. Use of the form of the parable strikes at the root of the old consciousness while introducing the new. The people are presented with a mystery to solve.

As St. Matthew quotes Isaiah:

> You will listen and listen again, but not understand,
> see and see again, but not perceive.
> For the heart of this nation has grown coarse,
> their ears are dull of hearing, and they have shut their eyes,
> for fear they should see with their eyes
> hear with their ears,
> understand with their heart,
> and be converted
> and be healed by me.

To "see" is to see the symbol. To "hear" is to hear the symbol. At all times, in all places. This requires the understanding of the heart. All truths will follow this understanding of the heart. Jesus says, "The reason I talk to them in parables is because they look without seeing and listen without hearing or understanding." *That* is the ill he seeks to cure! *That* is the old consciousness to be replaced by a new! Jesus frustrates literal-mindedness in an attempt to move the people to something beyond.

∼

I have endeavored to show that perception is the key to Christ-consciousness, and to show that this "perception" is to be understood as the perception of symbol. The symbolic form is not accidental, but in many ways, the *substance* of the teaching of Christ. Among other things, or perhaps including them, Christ sought to introduce a new "mysterious" level and form of consciousness. I will examine two further Gospel passages.

St. Mark records one of the most vehement rebukes made by Jesus to his disciples:

> The disciples had forgotten to take any food and they had only one loaf with them in the boat. Then he gave them this warning, "Keep your eyes open; be on your guard against the yeast of the Pharisees and the yeast of Herod." And they said to one another, "It is because we have no bread." And Jesus knew it, and he said to them, "Why are you talking about having no bread? Do you not yet understand? Have you no perception? Are your minds closed? *Have you eyes that do not see, ears that do not hear?* Or do you not remember? When I broke the five loaves among the five thousand, how many baskets full of scraps did you collect?" They answered, "Twelve." "And when I broke the seven loaves among the four thousand, how many baskets full of scraps did you collect?" And they answered, "Seven." Then he said to them, "Are you still without perception?"

Much has been written concerning this passage about the obtuseness of the disciples concerning the person and power of Jesus. Yet it seems clear that the *logical* heart of Christ's irritation and criticism is the failure of the disciples to understand a metaphor. The perception he questions at this point is not their perception of him but their perception of his metaphor. Perhaps one cannot see the real, metaphysical Christ, who is both symbol and history, without knowing what a symbol is.

Finally, the parable of the sower is perhaps the most powerful parable of all time. Yet only St. Matthew records the full interpretation of the first part: "When anyone hears the word of the kingdom without understanding, the evil one comes and carries off what was sown in his heart: this is the man who received the seed on the edge of the path." When one hears the word of the kingdom, the "word of the kingdom" which is a symbol, "without understanding," then the evil one has carried off what was sown in one's heart.

Our ears are dull, our eyes are shut—our perception is clouded, our understanding is literal and false—because of the coarseness of our hearts. Our minds, as well as our bodies and spirits, suffered in the Fall. Satan has carried off the word sown in our heart when we "do not understand." If we are once more to see Paradise, our perceptions must be cleansed. Mysterious.

"I see men, but they are like trees, walking."
                                                        Amen.

AUTOBIOGRAPHICAL SKETCH UPON EMBARKING ON CAREER AS MADMAN/ARTIST

I made the first practical ethical decision of my life when in ninth grade. Adolescence was upon me and I found myself invited to teenage parties and social gatherings. At first I was flattered and eager to attend but after a time I became appalled. The parties consisted more of backbiting, gossip, innuendo, and slander than they consisted of music, food, and dancing. Pecking orders were being established and cliques were being formed.

I made the conscious, premeditated decision to withdraw from the social scene at my high school. I threw myself into my studies because they seemed a pure world, unsullied by pettiness and intrigue. I consequently never missed an 'A' in high school and graduated first in my class of 716.

In tenth and eleventh grade I became an avid tournament chess player. After Telluride, however, I quit playing chess because of the way it reinforced bloodthirsty, competitive, aggressive impulses in me.

The Telluride Association Summer Program at Cornell University awakened me intellectually. My primary interests prior to the program were math and physics. When, after my junior year in high school, I attended Telluride's seminar on the history and philosophy of science, my interest in science collapsed.

During the Telluride seminar we read T.S. Kuhn's *The Structure of Scientific Revolutions*. We were taught that atoms and molecules were not "true" reality, they were theoretical constructs. The table and chair I saw and touched were "real," the rest was mental model designed to account for appearances.

I suddenly saw the world entirely differently. I realized that I lived in a *society* and had a *personality*. The behavior of neutrinos no longer seemed more real than the behavior of human beings. I had new investigations to make and a new life to live.

During my senior year in high school I wrote two termpapers on six novels by Herman Hesse. I think of those two papers as my first exercises in self-expression. At that time I also began my prolonged encounter with the poetry of T.S. Eliot and maintained a correspondence relationship with a girlfriend from Telluride.

In the fall of 1969 I entered Harvard College. That first semester of my freshman year I wrote a 55 page paper on Taoism. This was the birth of my religious consciousness. The "Way," "non-striving," "going with the flow" became for me the basic principle of consciousness. Sometimes the "flow" has been a torrent, sometimes I have stagnated, but I have never done violence to my impulses. The "flow" has led me into illnesses and then led me back out again. The "flow" has led me through all further religious development.

During the second semester of my freshman year I became thoroughly disenchanted with Harvard. I had entered the life of the mind as an escape from status seeking and pettiness and to my horror I discovered that the learning—earning connection was the key to Harvard. Basic to Harvard's covert socialization was the premise that "Veritas" would pay off in power, prestige, cash, etc. Rousseau's *First Discourse* summarized to me life in academia as I experienced it at that time. I wanted to leave Harvard but I didn't have the courage. I would have flunked out, at the end of my freshman year had it not been for the Cambodia/Kent State strike of spring 1970.

Returning to Harvard in the fall of 1970 I suffered romantically and in January of 1971, after a period of great turmoil and apropos of nothing in my course work, I constructed an "ego" psychology through a series of short papers. I felt overwhelmed in a society of alien values and wished to extricate myself from my peer groups. I raved about freedom and the "consolidated ego" and soon entered my first illness. (Which in the long run considerably altered my notions of the role of the ego.)

My first episode, at the beginning of my aborted fourth semester at Harvard, was my initiation to vision, though this first illness did not contain much vision. I gestalted the book of *Revelation*, then, in the hospital, I simply believed that I was in hell, which, considering the antiquated approach being used at McLean Hospital at that time, was pretty much true.

Two other features of that first illness: I was obsessed by what I could not see—I could not look directly at the sun, I could not see the far side of the moon, my eyes had blind spots. (Thus, the ego cannot see the self.)

Also—I removed labels from everything I could—my clothing, jars, boxes, everything. (Thus, received categories of definition and value had to be removed pending reappraisal.)

I was readmitted to Harvard in the fall of 1971 and the next two semesters were the most "normal" of my time there. I performed well academically in a pedestrian sort of way and carried on a satisfying social and romantic life. I thought rarely about my "mishap" the previous spring.

By the fall of 1972, however, I was again in full rebellion. The sharp edges of the ambitious, competitive people who were my fellow students preoccupied me. I became the manager of my dormitory grille and worked with religious dedication to provide a comfortable place for students to talk to each other, socialize, and develop some communal fellow feeling. I registered for a reduced load of classes that fall but still put so much time into managing the grille (for small monetary reward) that what studies I had were sadly neglected.

Early spring term 1973 I became ill for the second time. This time the illness was florid and fluid, not static and stereotyped. I wrote "Ransom in Tellus" while at McLean, still sick, in April of 1973.

Harvard suspended me for a year after the second illness and I returned to Minneapolis, lived with my parents, and worked in a plumbing shop. "Old Possum's Practical Cat" records the onset of my third illness in May of 1974.

I was readmitted to Harvard in the fall of 1974 but quickly withdrew after attempting suicide on October 8, 1974.

The suicide attempt was a real turning point. After eight months of total active insanity in little more than three years, I hit bottom and became very depressed. From the fall of 1974 to the fall of 1975 is a very difficult time for me to talk about. I went to a day hospital program for four months, I lived in a halfway house for five months, I worked some, was unemployed more. I couldn't read, I couldn't write, I couldn't think. I could barely talk. I felt only barely alive. I fantasized about lying on a bed in a state hospital for the rest of my life, staring at the ceiling for the rest of my life.

The 1975-76 academic year I spent at the University of Minnesota, obtaining, at last, a bachelor's degree. I was no way near up to par socially or academically, but once again I had friends and mental stimulation, a vast improvement over the "dark year."

Upon entering Pacific School of Religion this fall (1976), I met a remarkable man—Jeremy Taylor. Jeremy leads a dream seminar in which I was fortunate enough to find enrollment. This dream seminar is like an encounter group except that personal material is admitted only incidentally to the recounting of a dream or the interpretation of a dream. Jeremy is a wizard of symbol and value, a brilliant intuitive who, in his phrase, "sees with the eye of the heart." Pure intention is the key to penetrating perception. A good mind is useless without a clean heart.

I showed "Ransom in Tellus" and "Old Possum's Practical Cat" to Jeremy. He spoke bluntly to me: "David—you are either going to be a madman or an artist. Choose now!"

And so I say, with T.S. Eliot:

> ...Redeem
> the time. Redeem
> The unread vision in the higher dream
> While jeweled unicorns draw by the gilded hearse.

POEMS

...she from the little she had has put in everything she possessed...

CHRISTPOEM

"*How* can I help you?"
Perfect.
How did he do that?
Commanding total respect
without demanding anything.
I had been visualizing him—
just as an exercise, you know.
He was looking very Semitic
and a little too lordly.
"Lordly," I thought, "You
were the world's all-time loser.
Nobody would have remembered you
    four days
If you hadn't risen after three."
Somehow he broke the bank
by going bankrupt.
Picked the cosmic software lock
with his last gasp.

That's what I was thinking
when he walked up
and cut me down to size.
"How can I help you?"
A thousand images flashed
through my mind.
Money, fame, power, and
Success, Success, Success!
"Teach me to love (Donna)."

He smiled.

LOVE

I am Death.
I stalk the earth.
I stock the earth.
With a hundred heads
and a thousand arms
I am nobody to trifle with.
My vacant eyes
and blank face
make my denial
impossible.
I am
the true egalitarian
and mine is
the final democracy.
I am the leveller—
no respecter of persons
or personages
am I.
I never negotiate
never compromise
always take what I come for.
I am the Enforcer.
In case the Gospel of Love
does not appeal to your better nature
I put a gun to your head
and make the Gospel
into an offer you cannot refuse.
Die now,
and dying later ain't so bad.
It's the only way—

it's the offer you cannot refuse.

I raise my hand
in the clenched fist salute:
"Viva la Muerte!"
Long live Death!
I am invincible
I am victor
I mow down hordes of humanity.

To glimpse me is to die.
To look into my eyes
is annihilation.
To see into my heart
is extinction.
I am Death.
I conquer all
and bow my knee
to Love.

LOVE AND DEATH

Life is made from Love and Death.
Love leaps out and carries me in tow,
Death makes limits and stops the flow.
But both I find will stop my breath.

Love passes from me to you to God.
God sends Love back to fill our places.
Love wants more and seeks all spaces,
Rushing a race with feet unshod.

Death is certain; Love is not.
Death makes Love the best of choices,
Conducting a choir of human voices
Singing of That which needs be sought.

But make no mistake and know the Master:
When Death races Love it's Love that's faster.

FUNERAL HOUSE

I see that
the trees are dead or dying
and bare branches
resonate within me.
I look out my window
with curtains arranged
to frame the scene
and buffer the looking outside
and I wish for
untread snow
at six o'clock in the morning,
a winding sheet for earth.

Wrapping
and packages wrapped:
I arrange my space
with careful control
because fall and winter
really exist but
spring is recorded only on a calendar
and I believe
in nothing.

I arrange the space
seeking the perfect environment
because there is no peace.
And touch
do not touch
all touch
is violent intrusion
into a space
where only I am

only I shall be
all fall, all winter
and those seasons never end.

Don't tread the snow
outside my window
with the flimsy excuse
of arriving at my door.

I arrange, place, and rearrange
my coffin space
and live with terrifying vision
portrayed in drawing
because demons live
in my vacuum,
vacuum cleaned
and swept out and
life cannot live
where I live
if the tomb is to be forever,
monument against my mortality.

And sleep is no respite
after washing the silver with alcohol
removing contagion
because my demons sleep with me
where you might have slept
but my demons are mine, are me
and you are not
and I wake tired and restless
in winter
without companion
who might wear a cherry blossom
from the quickening month of May.

HORROR SHOW

    I sit and watch her face as I have done many times, but now she will not look at me because she's watching the tube and prime time humor and it really is funny. A comedy has begun—it really is funny—and I look at her face and wonder if the gash the wound that pit that gaping tear is what people call a mouth. And eyes—what are eyes—those circles of mostly white and green and black are eyes—yes I remember I used to know—and hair is the snaky stuff that hangs down from the top over rounded skull bones but they're laughing on TV and I'm laughing inside me at impossible hideousness and faces have no meaning not this face that I knew not any face I know and the face is seen like a word repeated till it has no meaning and she and they are stranger than strangers and the mad mad demon cries "no connection, no connection, no connection" and he laughs with the laughs on the tube and I know no relation and I know that the dead woman's jar that kills that kills is coming down and down and down…

THE MAN WAS SPEEDING

Stop. I can't stop. I've been driving this car ever since I lost my memory. Drive. Driving. Running on empty? Shit—I haven't had gas since the first lap. This car drives on molten metal.

Stop. Drive. Driving harder. Someone—stop me. Speaking for me I don't care anymore. I'm too tired. I want to sleep. Drive. Driving. No marrow in my bones. No food in my stomach. Just the engine blasting in my head. Drive. Driving. Hard. I hit the accelerator.

Stop. Someone stop me. I'm too tired. I'm locked to the wheel. Molten metal burning in the lines. The engine blasting. So many laps. This life. Another life. The last life. Ever since I lost my memory, ever since I cut my hair.

Stop. Someone stop me.

∽

Stop. I'm stopped. I start to relax. Thank you—someone.

Have I really stopped or did I just crash? Am I living?

I'm tired. I've exhausted everything. I think I gave it all. I think I caught up.

COSMIC MAN

His left eye most occluded: a silver
    crescent moon
His right eye blazes golden sun.
Wrapt in his forehead
roils a pent-up northern wind
and all directions from his face
shoot hoary winter storms.
But the steady gaping zero
first among his features
    will suck me in
    spew me out.

(EGGS ARE FOR EASTER)

One day
and it was a dreary day
and I was very hungry
without much food
but I owned an egg
and I could boil my egg
hard
or fry my egg
over easy
or baste it or scramble it or poach it—
and instead
of any of that
it broke
just like that
in my hand.

5/24/77

I listened, and nothing heard.
Where was the Word?
—much pain incurred ...
Where was the Word?
God is too close to speak to me.

∼

If God spoke, It wouldn't be God.

∼

One must know much to say nothing.
One speaks many words to express silence.
One works hard to become nothing.

∼

The end of philosophy is the end of philosophy.

6/2/77

Nothing: East and West
Everything above...
has collapsed.
The structure...
fell:

This is the void
(where the sun sets).

The gates...
open below.
Many chambers...
appear beneath:

This is the void
(where the sun rises).

∼

When the castle collapsed, I discovered the vaults beneath.

∼

"A fool's Paradise"—perhaps—but fools see more of paradise than most people.

SOCIAL POLICY IN THE NEW EASTERN EUROPE

Social Policy in the New Eastern Europe

What Future for Socialist Welfare?

Edited by
BOB DEACON
JULIA SZALAI

Avebury

Aldershot · Brookfield USA · Hong Kong · Singapore · Sydney

© Bob Deacon and Julia Szalai 1990

All rights reserved. No part of this publication may be reproduced, stored in a retrieval system, or transmitted in any form or by any means, electronic, mechanical, photocopying, recording, or otherwise without the prior permission of Gower Publishing Company Limited.

Published by
Avebury
Gower Publishing Company Limited
Gower House
Croft Road
Aldershot
Hants GU11 3HR

Gower Publishing Company
Old Post Road
Brookfield
Vermont 05036
USA

ISBN 0 85628 050 0

Printed in Great Britain by
Billing & Sons Ltd, Worcester

Contents

Notes on Main Contributors vii

Preface and Acknowledgements x

Part A Introduction and Dialogue

1 Introduction: The Significance of Recent Social
  Policy Developments in Eastern Europe
  Bob Deacon 1
2 Social Policy and Socialism: Citizenship, the
  Working Class, Women and Welfare
  John Keane, Julia Szalai and others 27

Part B Hungary and Poland: Economic and Political Reform and the Space for an Independent Social Policy

3 Is Social Policy a Problem in a Socialist Country?
  The Case of Poland
  Miroslaw Ksiezopolski 51
4 Socialist Welfare State in Transition: the State, the
  Market and the Enterprise in Poland
  Lena Kolarska-Bobinska 63

5	Alternatives in the Health Area: Poland in Comparative Perspective	
	Magdalena Sokolowska and Andrzej Rychard	77
6	Outline for the Radical Reforms of Social Policy in Hungary	
	Julia Szalai	91
7	The Fourth Road: The Future for Hungarian Social Policy	
	Zsuzsa Ferge	103

Part C Bulgaria, the German Democratic Republic and Yugoslavia: Different Realities; Different Interpretations

8	The Social Policy of the People's Republic of Bulgaria and the Problem of Welfare in Socialism	
	Slavka Ivanova	121
9	The Unity of Economic and Social Policy in the German Democratic Republic	
	Paul Adams	133
10	Neighbourhood and Tenant Participation in the GDR	
	Prue Chamberlayne	145
11	From a One-dimensional to a Multidimensional Welfare System	
	Ivan Svetlik	164

Part D Women, the Family and East European Social Policy

12	The Situation of Women in Hungarian Society	
	Chris Corrin	179
13	Women and Ageing Under Real Socialism	
	Jirina Siklova	192
14	Education for Parenthood in Czechoslovakia	
	Zuzana Hughes	201
15	Perestroika and the Woman Question	
	Mary Buckley	212

Index	227

Notes on main contributors

Bob Deacon
Bob Deacon is Head of Department of Social Studies and Director of the International Social Policy Research Unit, Leeds Polytechnic.

Julia Szalai
Julia Szalai is Head of the Social Policy section of the Institute of Sociology of the Hungarian Academy of Sciences, Budapest.

Lena Kolarska-Bobinska
Lena Kolarska-Bobinska works at the Institute of Philosophy and Sociology of the Polish Academy of Sciences, Warsaw. She has undertaken studies of the opinions of Polish citizens and political questions in recent years.

Magdalena Sokolowska
Magdalena Sokolwska was Professor of Social Medicine at the Institute of Philosophy and Sociology of the Polish Academy of Sciences, Warsaw. She held a worldwide reputation for her critical works on Polish medical care. She died on 21 April 1989 before this book was published and she will be greatly missed by her colleagues.

Andrzej Rychard
Andrzej Rychard works at the Institute of Philosophy and Sociology of the Polish Academy of Sciences, Warsaw. He has written widely on aspects of medical care, and political and economic developments in Poland.

Zsuzsa Ferge
Zsuzsa Ferge is Head of Department and Professor of Social Policy at the Eötvös Lorand University, Budapest. Prior to this she was Head of the Social Policy section of the Institute of Sociology of the Hungarian Academy of Sciences. She has edited and written several books on social policy. It is her work in English that prompted the new interest of Western social policy analysts in developments in Eastern Europe.

Slavka Ivanova
Slavka Ivanova is a member of the Sociology of Work section of the Institute of Sociology of the Bulgarian Academy Sciences, Sofia.

Paul Adams
Paul Adams is an associate professor at the School of Social Work, University of Iowa, Iowa City. His interests are in comparative social policy and the political economy of social welfare. Recent work has focussed on East and West Germany, and on demographic aspects of family policy and old age insurance.

Prue Chamberlayne
Prue Chamberlayne is Senior Lecturer in Social Policy at the Polytechnic of East London. Her first degree is in German. Her research interests are in the GDR and in women and social policy in Western Europe.

Ivan Svetlik
Ivan Svetlik is research fellow at the Institute for Sociology and professor of sociology at the Faculty of Sociology, Political Science and Journalism, University of Ljubljana. He has been engaged in social policy, personnel policy and labour market studies. He collaborates with the European Centre for Social Welfare Training and Research, Vienna and is a member of the International Editorial Board of Innovation.

Miroslaw Ksiezopolski
Miroslaw Ksiezopolski, PhD is Assistant Professor at the Institute of Social Policy, Department of Journalism and Political Science, University of Warsaw. He is Scientific Secretary of the National Research Project 'Social policy in Poland' 1986–1990.

Chris Corrin
Chris Corrin obtained her doctorate at Oxford University for her study of women in Hungary. She continues to undertake research in this field.

Jirina Siklova
Jirina Siklova lives and works in Prague. She was unable to obtain authority

to attend the April 1988 Conference to present her paper but is pleased to see it published in the West.

Zuzana Hughes
Zuzana Hughes was born and bred in Czechoslovakia. After coming to Great Britain in 1966 she trained as a psychiatric social worker and worked both in adult and child psychiatry settings and in the community. Shortly after receiving her MA (Liverpool, 1975) on problems of elderly people in North Wales, she was appointed Lecturer in Applied Social Studies at the Department of Sociology, University of Liverpool. She retired in October 1988 due to ill health. Her PhD thesis (Lancaster, 1983) was on preschool childcare and education in Czechoslovakia. Further research into Czechoslovak social policy continues.

Mary Buckley
Mary Buckley is Lecturer in Politics at the University of Edinburgh. She is author of *Women and Ideology in the Soviet Union* (1989), editor of *Soviet Social Scientists Talking: an official debate about women* (1986) and co-editor of *Women, Equality and Europe* (1988).

Preface and acknowledgements

The remote origins of this edited volume can be traced back to 1982 when we met in Budapest while one of us, Bob Deacon, was on a British Council sponsored visit to Hungary researching the extent to which social policy there stood up to any test of an ideal socialist social policy. From that beginning we like to think that a fruitful dialogue was begun involving critical social policy analysts from several countries. The dialogue has continued during a period which has seen critical social policy analysis in Hungary shift from a radical empiricism (refuting the flawed certainties of state socialist proclamations) to a critical normative theory of welfare in a pluralist Hungary and has seen the idealized concept of socialist social policy in Britain give way to the defence of a more pragmatic democratic pluralism in the light of the negative experiences of state socialist social policy. One part of this dialogue developed during an ESRC funded project[1] into 'Attitudes to State Welfare in Britain and Hungary'. The fruits of this dialogue, which involved not only ourselves but also Sidney Jacobs and Fiona Williams in the UK and Janos David and Peter Gyori in Hungary, will be published soon. [2]

In this wider context this specific volume was born. While working on the Anglo-Hungarian project it seemed to us that it would be fruitful if we tested our ideas against the experiences of other East European countries. The idea of the Social Policy and Socialism Conference, held at Leeds Polytechnic between April 11–14 1988 was born. Thanks to a number of generous contributions including further funds from the ESRC[3] the conference brought together scholars from Australia, Britain, Canada, New Zealand, Norway (representing Western capitalist societies) and Bulgaria, Czechoslovakia,

Hungary, Poland and Yugoslavia (representing Eastern socialist societies). This volume reflects part of what took place at the conference. Most of the papers were presented at the conference. One or two have been written specifically for this volume (Chapters 1,4 and 7).

The conference itself would not have been possible without the organizational talents of Chris Corrin and Fiona Williams who worked with us to set it all up. Neither would it have worked but for the administrative and clerical talents of Christine Conboy in the office of the Department of Social Studies at Leeds. The actual event ran smoothly and enjoyably because of the good spirited care of three volunteer students. The Media Services Department of Leeds Polytechnic and Derek Grant worked quietly and unobtrusively to record every word. The text has been hastily prepared in the few gaps that still exist for scholarly work in the life of a polytechnic academic – the circumscribed August vacation. Superscript Business Services of Headingley typed the final text. Although both of us, as editors, wish to preface the volume one of us only (Bob Deacon) must take full responsibility for any errors and misrepresentations in the edited chapters that follow.

Permissions to publish

The editors thank Charles Schlacks, Jr, Publisher for permission to publish the chapter by Prue Chamberlayne which previously appeared in a special issue of *East Central Europe*. The editors also wish to thank Sage Publications for permission to publish the chapter by Sokolowska and Rychard which previously appeared in Kohn, *Cross National Research,* Sage Publications.

Bob Deacon
Julia Szalai
December 1989

Notes

1 Anglo-Hungarian Comparative Study of Attitudes to State Welfare Policy. Economic and Social Research Council Grant (RG/00/23/2229).
2 Deacon, B. *et al.* (1990) *Strategies for Welfare East and West,* Wheatsheaf.
3 Economic and Social Research Council Grant (I 00260037).

PART A
INTRODUCTION AND DIALOGUE

1 Introduction: the significance of recent social policy developments in Eastern Europe

BOB DEACON

This volume represents one moment in the developing dialogue between analysts of social policy in the two halves of Europe. This moment was April 1988. Political events in certain East European countries have developed rapidly since the papers for this volume were written. What existed in April 1988 as a normative theory of one possible future of welfare in Hungary (Chapter 6) has already found expression in part in the social policy programme of the Free Democrats (SZDSZ) who will be contending for a share of power in the first completely free parliamentary elections to take place in an East European country since the Second World War. The prediction in Chapter 4 that the divisions (on social and economic policy questions) within the Communist Party of Poland and within the Solidarity organization would intensify and manifest themselves are being borne out as Solidarity is now playing a part in the government of Poland. Changes are now taking place in the German Democratic Republic, in Bulgaria and Czechoslovakia that could not have been imagined only a few months ago. The chapters reporting aspects of social policy in these countries each stand as testimony to the failed state socialist project. Each shows why the state-managed united economic and social policy had to give way to more democratically controlled and more pluralistic economic and social policies.

The purpose of this introductory chapter is to situate this moment of dialogue within a longer time frame. First the emergence, among British social policy analysts, of an interest in the social policy of Eastern Europe is examined and the earlier East–West dialogue that has taken place is traced. The focus here will be the Anglo-Hungarian and the Anglo-Polish dialogue that has developed within the past ten years. Secondly a review is offered of the several chapters of this volume and comments made that may help the reader to interpret the contributions in terms of this emerging dialogue and in terms that are familiar to those working within the discipline of social policy. Thirdly, some implications for the future are considered. The most likely ways in which social policy in Eastern Europe will develop is discussed. The bearing that those developments might have on the idealized concept of a socialist social policy is examined. Opportunities are noted for the enrichment of the study of comparative social policy which are made possible by the flourishing of alternative ways out of the impasse of the Bolshevik social policy project in Eastern Europe. A possible research agenda for the future is suggested.

The emergence of an East–West dialogue about social policy

A recent survey of the British literature on comparative social policy undertaken on behalf of the Social Affairs Committee of the Economics and Social Research Council for its 'Initiative on the Future of Welfare' concluded that we needed 'to build upon and extend the analysis of social welfare systems in non-Western societies and in countries other than those of North America and Western Europe... The centre of gravity of comparative studies should be moved ever eastward...' (Higgins, 1906, p. 239). Until recently there have been very few studies accessible to English-speaking social policy analysts of the social welfare systems of Eastern Europe (Deacon, 1983; Ferge, 1979; George and Manning, 1980; McAuley, 1979).

In general these earlier studies by British academics were motivated by the concern to prove the failure by certain criteria of social policy in socialist countries. For McAuley (1979) the point seems to have been that socialism *per se* can't deliver a social welfare system that stands comparison against the developed welfare states of the West. For myself (Deacon, 1983) the point then was to demonstrate that *existing* state socialist regimes failed to live up, in terms of their welfare policies, to criteria derived from a theoretically idealized socialist social policy. Neither type of study was primarily motivated by the wish to establish a dialogue of social policy analysts East and West. Little, it seemed then, was to be learned from listening to the East Europeans.

However, a number of international conferences bringing together social policy analysts from Eastern and Western Europe have recently taken place.[1] These are in the process of generating a new comparative social policy literature which is innovative in moving towards a comparative analysis that accommodates the experience of existing socialist societies and welfare capitalist societies (Oyen, 1986; Evers *et al*, 1987; Deacon *et al*, forthcoming; Le Grand and Okrasa, 1987; Millard, 1990).

The development and potential fruitfulness of this new East–West dialogue of social policy analysts depends upon the extent to which it is possible to share a common conceptual framework across the ideological divide for the analysis of the two different if parallel experiences of welfare. With this consideration in mind this part of the chapter will: a) briefly report the early stages of an Anglo-Hungarian comparative project[2] which is concerned, among other things, to identify the range of strategies that exist in both countries for the future of welfare and to assess the extent of support for such strategies among the population; b) comment on the possibility of a common conceptual framework existing in the developing Anglo-Polish dialogue, and c) thirdly, note in the light of this some of the features of the wider international dialogue that took place at this April 1988 Conference, which are reported in Chapter 2.

The Anglo-Hungarian dialogue

Whilst a remarkable apparent parallelism can be shown to exist in the welfare strategies identified in Britain and Hungary, I will argue that the political significance of certain apparently similar strategies may be different in the two contexts. A distinction will be drawn between an apparent and overt convergence of an East–West dialogue around the concept and strategy of *welfare pluralism* and a more covert convergence of a critical East–West dialogue around the concept of the *autonomous articulation of human needs*.

Strategies for welfare

Academic analysis of social policy in Britain and Hungary has identified a number of political strategies for welfare in the wake of the 'crisis' of welfare provision in Britain and the parallel crisis of centralized state welfare provision in Hungary. Table 1.1 summarizes the main strategies that had been given expression in the British and Hungaria social policy literature recently.

Table 1.1   Alternative strategies for welfare

Strategy	*Britain*	*Hungary*
Free Market	Harris and Seldon, 1979	Liska, 1982
Welfare Pluralist	Le Grand and Robinson, 1984; Johnston, 1987	Szelenyi and Manchin, 1987
Welfare Statist	Wicks, 1987	? emerging ?
Welfare Corporatist	Mishra, 1984	? emerging ?
Socialist Social Planning	Walker, 1984; Lee & Raban, 1989	Ferge, 1979
Social Revolution	Deacon, 1983	Feher, Heller and Markus, 1983

In the British context the strategies may be summarized as follows. Firstly, those writers whose work constitutes the intellectual basis of the radical right in Britain advocate greater *private market* activity in the finance and production of welfare services. In particular, a number of those writers have advocated the dismantling of state monopolies such as the provision of health care and the return of these services to the market because it will enhance efficiency and choice in the production and consumption of welfare services. In practice, this strategy would involve the substitution of markets for public provision on a large scale. Direct provision by the state would be minimal, being reserved for the most obvious cases of market failure.

A more recent development in arguments about social policy has been the advocacy of a *mixed economy of welfare,* where existing services would be provided by a range of state and non-state agencies. The welfare pluralist strategy advanced here starts from a criticism of existing state-provided social services, which are characterized as bureaucratic, inflexible and inefficient. A welfare-pluralist strategy for welfare would involve a substantial reduction in both the size and the scope of state-provided services, in conjunction with the democratization of those that remain. Cutting back the superstructure in this way would facilitate the growth of community-based initiatives in welfare provision. The voluntary and informal sectors of care, in particular, are seen as having a major role to play in a mixed economy of welfare.

The third welfare strategy is, in essence, the defence against the private marketeers of the status quo of the Welfare State. The defence of the *welfare statist* tradition has found new confidence recently associated with the belief that on the one hand the rhetoric of the privatization strategy has its limitations in practice and on the other that the critical left analysis of the welfare state equally cannot be translated into realistic politics (Taylor-Gooby, 1985; Wilding, 1986).

The fourth welfare strategy proposes a strategy of *corporatism* as a solution to the economic and ideological crisis of British social democracy. Where other welfare strategies discussed in this section propose changes in the form which welfare services take, the social-democratic welfare state remains largely unchanged in the context of a corporatist strategy. The concern of this strategy is with the stabilization of Britain's economic and welfare systems. This would require agreement among corporate groups about social goals and priorities. Employers would be required to recognize full employment as a central social objective. Conversely, trades unions would need to accept the subordination of wage levels to these social objectives.

The fifth welfare strategy, *socialist social planning,* may be characterized as 'socialist or structural social planning' (Walker, 1984). It is intended to overcome the 'stultifying separation between economic and social policy' and will permit of 'planning social development according to needs', it will overcome 'the present fragmentation of planning' and it will 'democratize the planning process'. The idea is to incorporate in the planning process and planning goals the aims of transforming the social relations of welfare into ones of reciprocal cooperation. One feature of work in this genre (Lee and Raban, 1988) is the concern to combine the best of Fabianism and Marxism into a feasible socialist politics of welfare where the market is socialized and the state democratized.

The sixth *social revolutionary* strategy in essence asserts (Deacon, 1983) that the desired social relations of reciprocal cooperation that need to be embodied in welfare policy and practice can only flourish in a communist society that embodies such social relations of reciprocal cooperation at the point of production. For this to be realized a revolutionary break from capitalist society has to be created which cannot be achieved through reformist means.

It should be added that this analysis of welfare strategies into a six-fold typology does injustice to the contribution that feminist analysis and anti-racist analysis has made to the limitations of the British Welfare State and to desirable futures of welfare. A useful account of the implications of these contributions for our analysis of welfare policy and for the development of appropriate strategies to counteract sexism and racism in welfare provision is provided by Williams (1989).

A range of strategies for social welfare remarkably similar to those debated in Britain were already being articulated by Hungarians in the mid-1980s. Again, they are summarized in Table 1.1. They are discussed in turn below.

First is the *social dividend* or free market argument. The point quite simply, is that the orthodoxy of centralist state planning is insensitive to the felt needs of the population with regard to the provision of welfare services. Consumer views on housing, pensions, even education, as with food can only be democratically expressed through the cash nexus when the consumer exercises real choices about her or his priorities. The inequity in the power to exercise choice stemming from wage differentials can be overcome by the provision of cash or welfare dividends to all citizens. The array of welfare services developed in response to consumer preference would be preferable to those dictated by an insensitive planning mechanism.

The rather more sophisticated *welfare pluralist* strategy is derived partly from this same critique of state planning but also from the further argument that central planning has not only been insensitive to consumer needs but has prioritized the consumer needs of the state planners themselves. Szelenyi (1978), for example, has shown how the most highly subsidized council flats in the centre of Budapest have historically been allocated to the white collar salaried earners. The 'state redistributive system' has benefited those doing the redistribution. The introduction of a market element, in this case in housing, could distribute housing more favourably to the working class, some of whom have a frustrated ability to purchase themselves better housing. This view is balanced, however, especially in Szelenyi's more recent writings (Szelenyi and Manchin, 1987), by the recognition that the unleashing of market pressures could generate its own new inequalities between those with differential purchasing ability. A balance therefore needs to be struck between state redistributive provision and the market (Zavada, 1983).

Welfare corporatism or *Welfare Statism* are not articulated in the Hungarian context as explicit strategies. To some extent they are the *de facto* mechanism of social and economic planning. Targets are resolved upon and the share allocated to consumption etc. is decided in consultation with representatives of the official trade union movement. However in the rapidly developing political situation where the pro-marketeers and the liberal democratic pluralists seem to be making all the running the defence of a modified welfare state strategy with corporatist aspects is being articulated as perhaps the only way to stop the slide from egalitarian and redistributive values. It is possible to read the new work of Ferge (Chapter 7) in this light.

Socialist social planning, on the other hand, does or did have its defenders. Ferge's (1979) thesis that social policy in socialist societies should dominate economic policy remains a seminal work. 'Societal policy' as she preferred to call it 'implies the project of deliberately changing the profile of society – of altering basic social, human relations'. It is no accident, incidentally, that Walker (1984) has fifteen references to Ferge's book in his defence of socialist social planning. Their vision is very similar.

The closest to the exposition of a *social revolutionary* strategy for welfare to be found among authors of Hungarian origin is to be found in Feher, Heller and Markus (1983). In rejecting the existing system in Hungary as one characterized by dictatorship over needs they argue that the 'anti-authoritarian state subject of dictatorship over needs does not fight for a radical change in his situation in order to acquire a new master. Dictatorship over needs versus liberal capitalism is not a real alternative ... all those whose real aim is democracy have to aspire to a genuine socialism as well' (Feher, Heller and Markus, 1983, p.299).

It has to be added that there is little sign yet of the work of Williams (1989) which centralized feminist and anti-racist perspectives in the analysis of the British welfare system finding any echo in critical analysis in Hungary. That Hungarian social policy is patriarchal and racist (towards, for example, gypsies) is not in doubt. We await a Hungarian account of this however.

It is becoming clearer as each month passes the extent to which the alternative strategies for welfare articulated in the academic literature in Hungary is now finding expression in the political parties and proto-political parties emerging to contend in the first elections early in 1990. Bozoki (1989) has provided an analysis of the different trends in Hungarian intellectual and political life on these social questions as they were in early 1989. These are shown in Table 1.2. The elections may reveal something of the social base of the positions identified.

Table 1.2 Trends in intellectual and political life in Hungary May 1989

TRENDS	Leftist Conservatives	Conformist Technocrats Pragmatists	Democratic Socialists, Euro-Communists	Social Democrats	Radicals and Liberal Democrats	Democratic Populists	Religious or Populist Conservatives
VALUES	Bolshevik-Stalinist	Value-neutrality	Socialist democracy	Welfare state	Civil liberties	'Third Road'	National identity
ISSUES	– centralized planned economy – One-party system – 'order v anarchy'/ COMECON autarchy	– stability – party unity – power maintenance – democratic centralism	– limited multiparty system – socialist mixed economy – local self-governments – socialization of institution – 'ideal'/ non-statist/ socialism	– multiparty system – mixed economy – social policy – representative democracy	– multiparty system – mixed economy – human rights – representative democracy – free ventures – social policy – social minorities	– local communities ('Garden Hungary'/ – multiparty system – self-governments – direct democracy – mixed economy – the problem of Hungarian minorities	– romantic concept of nation and community – organic improvement – society as a moral phenomenon – 'God–Family–Fatherland' – the problem of Hungarian minorities – traditions – collective rights
ORGANIZ-ATIONS	Ferenc Munnich Society/MFT/ MSZMP hard liners /Leninist circles/	Hungarian Socialist Workers' Party /MSZMP/ centre	MSZMP Reform circles Union for Leftist Alternative /BAL/ Democratic Youth Alliance /DEMISZ reform-wing	Hungarian Social Democratic Party /MSZDP/ Young Social Democrats /SZIK FIDESZ-SZDSZ left-wing	Free Democrats /SZDSZ/ Young Democrats Alliance /FIDESZ/ Bajcsy-Zsilinsky Society /BZSBT/ Smallholders' Party /FKGP/	Hungarian Democrats Forum / MDF / Szarszo Front	MDF right-wing Party for Independence /MFP/ People's Party Christian-Democratic
SOCIAL BASES	older party-apparatchiks	bureaucracy, a part of the MSZMP-members /cadre-elite/	younger generations of MSZMP /see:DEMISZ/ intellectuals	urban middle class, working strata	urban intellectuals, students, private entrepreneurs	countryside intellectuals middle class	non-urban strata

The apparent convergence of strategies

The similarity in the range of strategies for welfare that find articulation in the relevant literature of the British and Hungarian participants in the debate is immediately apparent. What is less apparent is the different political significance of the apparently similar strategies in the two countries. Of particular importance for our purposes in this chapter are the meanings that should be attributed to the parallel existence of welfare pluralist, socialist social planning, and social revolutionary strategies for welfare in the two literatures. We need to ask, in other words, how it is possible and what does it mean that defenders of a liberal and capitalist mixed economy of welfare strategy in Britain appear to find their ideas reflected in the economic and social policy reformers of state socialism? We need to ask what possibility for genuine dialogue is there between the defenders of the conception of socialist social planning East and West when, in one country, it is a conception based on the present democratic and oppositional planning of certain local groups and authorities and in the other it is a conception robbed of its freshness by the legacy of an all-embracing centralist socialist planning. We need to ask how might it be possible for a dialogue to be developed between social welfare revolutionaries in Britain who cling to the Marxist origins of their conception and those of Eastern Europe who argue for a revolution to create a genuine socialist democracy against a regime that they claim has usurped that Marxist legacy in the service of a dictatorship over needs. We need to ask, indeed, whether it is time that a new dialogue of welfare needs and futures has to be developed that breaks, both East and West, with the misused conceptions drawn from the socialist and liberal capitalist vocabulary and is more able to speak afresh to the emerging concerns that future analytical and strategic thinking about welfare must accommodate. These emerging concerns, reflecting in part the interests of the 'newer' social movements include the need to acknowledge equally the public and private (domestic) spheres of welfare; the need to redefine entitlements to welfare on a need and not a work basis; and the need to internationalize welfare provision and policy.

First a few remarks are necessary about the different traditions from which, in Britain and Hungary, conventional and critical thinking about welfare policy are derived. To over-simplify, mainstream welfare thinking in Britain has been guided and inspired by the Fabian tradition of empirical documentation of the shortcomings of existing policy coupled with a propagandist approach directed at governments to respond with compassion to the new evidence of welfare state failure. Critical thinking has, in general, been guided by the Marxist tradition of locating the shortcomings of existing policy in the structure of capitalist society itself coupled with a propagandist approach directed at, broadly defined, the working class to encourage and facilitate a social struggle to implement a socialist welfare system. In Britain, in other words, the welfare state has been claimed, despite its acknowledged shortcomings, as the coming to fruition of the Fabian socialist gradualist tradition, and Marxism has sought to expose this claim (by arguing that the welfare state far from being a socialist achievement is a capitalist response to crisis and by insisting that socialist relations of welfare should be characterized by reciprocal cooperation and not paternalism). In Hungary, paradoxically, the paternalistic system of state welfare has been claimed as the achievement of communist politics guided by Marxism, and critical empirical analysis in the tradition of British Fabian social administration has sought to expose this claim (by arguing that the system of state welfare far from being a socialist achievement derives as much from the earlier insurance traditions of Bismarck's Germany and that the present policies reflect the demographic labour force participation and political requirements of the economic system which should not necessarily be regarded as socialist and by insisting that the system of state welfare fails to permit the most elementary rights of welfare need articulation by the recipients of welfare). The irony, in other words, is that the inspiration (Marxism) of much critical social policy analysis in Britain is the same source that informs the ideological defence of state welfare in Hungary, and the inspiration of much critical social policy in Hungary (British Fabian social administration) is the same source that has informed the defence of the welfare state in Britain. To be a radical social policy analyst in Hungary is to adopt the Fabian mantle of empiricist reputation; to be a radical social policy analyst in Britain is to critique the empiricist Fabian tradition from the standpoint of Marxist theory.

The *impact* of Marxism and Fabianism on social policy in Hungary and Britain was very different and the development of Marxism and Fabianism as a *critical practice* took very different forms. Nonetheless, there was to emerge by the 1980s the possibility of a dialogue between critical social policy analysts in both countries. This dialogue had to begin by an acknowledgement of both the conservative role of Marxism (as an ideological defence of state welfare in Eastern Europe and as a critical practice that for a long time failed to acknowledge the essentially problematic and contestable nature of human welfare needs both now and in the future) and the conservative role of Fabianism (both as an ideological defence of the welfare state in the West and as a critical practice that inhibited necessary theorizing) and the radical potential of Marxism (as a guide East and West to the material root of the future social transformation) and the radical use of Fabianism (as a puncturer of state proclaimed ideological certainties).

Welfare pluralism

It is now possible to return to the examination of the meanings to be attributed to an apparent convergence of strategies East and West. The *welfare pluralist* dialogue will be examined first. In Britain the mixed economy of welfare strategy has been seen, from the standpoint of critical social policy analysts, as a political shift of social policy to the right. Those academic social policy analysts who defend it as a strategy have been accused of legitimating the damaging privatization policies of the Thatcher governments (Beresford and Croft, 1984). Amongst Hungarians, however, there is evidence that there is a current of critical opinion which sees a liberating potential in the withdrawing of the central state from overall planning and control of economic and social policy. Feher *et al.* (1983) suggest that 'a democratic type of socialism is in principle capable of uniting a certain, critically supervised market as the basis of calculative rationality with emancipated human relations ... the social struggles in dictatorship over needs for a market ... has a certain restricted enlightenment function'. Sik (1987) suggests that the increasing externalization of the state's responsibility for welfare onto the domestic sector can either be seen as increasing the 'hidden exploitation' of households or as 'the first step towards a more pluralistic welfare system'. Ferge (1986) too, while not being an advocate of markets in welfare, has shifted her stance from the defence of a socialist social planning strategy (Ferge, 1979). Although she asserts once again (Ferge, 1986) as she did in Ferge (1979) that, 'from a Marxist theoretical perspective, the best, or even the only acceptable relation between economic and social policy is their almost complete fusion' she now pragmatically accepts that 'a new relation between economic and social policy seems desirable'. This new relation is one of the autonomy of social policy alongside an increasingly 'independent and more decentralized economy increasingly moved by individual and group interests'. Such a strong and autonomous social policy would operate 'with state guarantees and popular control'.

A dialogue is taking place, therefore, between welfare pluralists East and West at two levels. At one level it is the dialogue between those committed, in the West, to a liberal capitalist system and those, in the East, seeking to marketize a sluggish state socialist system in the interests of greater efficiency. At another level it is the dialogue between those, East and West, who see in the welfare pluralist developments in the East, the potential liberation of the capacity of previous welfare objects to define, as welfare subjects, their needs for a more democratic and accountable form of socialist welfare system. As Brus (1985) perceptively observed, what we may be observing in the Hungarian economic debate is a paradox whereby 'marketization of the socialist economy [is seen as] a substitute for pluralization of its policy'. Some welfare pluralist reformers in Hungary believed this marketization would create the political space for the articulation of welfare needs from below. We have noted already, however, that there is increasing concern that this will not be the outcome of the marketization process and those welfare needs articulated from below may not be listened to (Ferge, Z., Chapter 7).

Socialist social planning

Socialist social planning in Britain has been seen, from the standpoint of critical social policy analysts, as embodying a vision of how human need could be planned for democratically under socialism (Deacon, 1985). But it has also been subject to the criticism that as a political strategy to realize a socialist society embodying socialist social policies, either locally or nationally, it is flawed. It is criticized for replacing the necessary autonomous struggle of recipients of welfare for a new welfare policy by a socialist managerialist imposition from above of left-wing policy (Campbell, 1987). The first expression of this strategy in English by a Hungarian author (Ferge, 1979) found much support in Britain. It seemed to give authenticity to the attempt to articulate the strategy in Britain. Subsequent developments – both the self-criticism of Ferge (1986) referred to above and the critical writings of other Hungarians (Feher *et al.*, 1983) might now lead to a more sober analysis of the desirability and viability of the socialist planning strategy in the two countries. Feher *et al.*(1983, pp.292–7) have refuted the possibility that 'communist reforms from above have a real chance of long-term and positive development' and have added that 'among those who are not part of the apparatus there is an unmistakable and fairly general hostility against any kind of Marxism, official or reformistic'. In Britain, then, while the articulation of a socialist social planning strategy fulfils the refreshing and necessary task of outlining a future vision for welfare beyond the market realities of the present, it also will fail if it seeks to plan from above this vision on behalf of a uninterested population. In Hungary, the articulation of a socialist social planning strategy falls on deaf ears – ears made deaf by the previous usurping and distortion by the dictatorship over needs of socialist discourse. The negative experiences of existing socialism have their impact too on the receptivity of the Western ear to the language of socialist welfare planning.

The dialogue between socialist social planners East and West is a doomed dialogue. Socialist social planners in the West seem to find an echo of their belief in Eastern Europe (as Beatrice Webb found in Stalin's Russia?) at a point where its defenders in the East have to retreat in the face of the impact of the dead weight of the legacy of previous state planning.

Social revolution and social welfare

What, then, of the impossible dialogue between welfare analysts who defend in the West, a revolutionary strategy for welfare based on 'the classical Marxist paradigm' and their counterparts, if they exist, in the East. The view of Markus (1984) is a useful starting point here. He argues 'the official ideology of "socialism" in these countries has to a large extent been transformed into an empty verbal ritual which invokes in the population at large the feeling of tired boredom ... The function of this official ideology today is ... the disintegration of a common language of meaningful social understanding'. Furthermore, argues Taras (1984) writing of the Polish context, 'hostility to the state's operative ideology and to the realities of life began to extend to socialism itself'. As Kolakowski (1978) asserted, 'Marxism neither interprets the world nor changes it: it is merely a repertoire of slogans serving to organize various interests, most of them remote from that which Marxism originally identified with'. If in the East Marxism suffers from its being usurped by the state, in the West it is subject to its internal critics. Where once, in the Western Marxist literature, it was presumed that the politics of a post-revolutionary society would be an unproblematic matter as all interests expressed through workers' councils would be the same, now, no such certainty can be expressed (Polan, 1984). A political process for a socialist future has still to be fashioned. Where once, in the Western Marxist literature, it was presumed that markets would play no part in the decommodified economy, now, no such certainty can be expressed (Nove, 1983). They are seen by some as facilitators of the autonomous expression of need. Where once, in the Western Marxist literature, it was presumed that the morality of the socialist future was something that could safely be left to the future to create in new material circumstances, now, no such amoral position can be afforded. Marxists are enjoined to make moral choices on matters (Geras, 1985; Lukes, 1985). Where once, in the Western Marxist literature, it was presumed that human needs of a certain radical kind would flourish in the new society, now, no such faith can be expressed. A genuine politics of needs is all that can and must be aspired to (Soper, 1981).

The negative lessons of actually existing socialism coalesce with self-critical analysis of the Western Marxism to suggest a socialist future that embodies a political pluralism, involves contended moral choices, envisages a role for markets, and a political debate over needs. Perhaps the question should be posed another way. Is there a language that embodies the hopes for a future welfare society, East and West, that does not presume that either the social systems East or West provide the necessary basis of this future or presume that the traditional arsenals of liberal capitalist and socialist ideology provide the analytical framework within which this discussion might begin? Does such a language have anything in common with the Marxist legacy? Feher and Heller (1986) have addressed this explicitly from their unique experience of being internal critics of the Hungarian regime and Western contributors to the contemporary Marxist literature. It is to this issue we now turn.

The basis of a new radical East–West dialogue (the autonomous articulation of human needs)

'The chances for a resumption of a now almost totally defunct East–West dialogue on the Left' write Feher and Heller (1986, p.46) '... can, therefore, only be the republican dimension ... The republican dimension at the same time reconciles important parts of the liberal tradition with its own concerns'. An exposition of Heller's conception of the Great Republic can be found in Feher and Heller (1986). Its essential features, derived from the legacy left by Luxembourg, and informed by Kant, Arendt and the practice of social movements in Hungary 1956, Czechoslovakia 1968 and Poland 1980–81, appear to be party political pluralism, a system of continual dual power based on the twin pillars of direct or workers' democracy and representative or parliamentary democracy, self-management in the spheres of production and social reproduction, a limited sphere of operation for markets with labour market 'relegated to the niches of society', and the obligation on and the ability of the citizenry to participate politically. In their search for a common vocabulary that might enable this debate about the Great Republic to take place, they note that 'the vocabulary of "needs" which is central discourse in both worlds is certainly an integrating factor. "Dictatorship over needs", even regarded as a mere negative Utopia of the Soviet system, is a central category of the Eastern World, the "manipulation" or the "paternalistic supervision" of "acceptable" or "unacceptable" needs is equally central in the West' (Feher and Heller, 1986). This is of direct relevance to our concerns as social welfare strategists.

We require then a common language that addresses the question of the autonomous articulation of needs. We are required to imagine a political and economic system that would permit the flourishing of the self-articulation of need and the political resolution of conflicting or contended needs in a democratic way. This discussion would have, I suggest, to acknowledge that needs may be articulated and met in the domestic sphere as well as in the public and that our future welfare society would acknowledge each equally and the way they are interconnected. It would have to acknowledge that needs could only find genuine expression and have a chance of being met if the mechanisms of meeting them were divorced from the necessarily differential work contribution of citizens. It would have to acknowledge, ultimately, that the possibilities of the autonomous expression of and meeting of needs in one part of the globe was dependent upon the activities in other parts of the globe. I have yet to be convinced that such a discussion conducted in these terms would lead to a conclusion other than the need for a political and economic system that breaks with the work–income connection. Once the cash nexus of wage labour is broken, and only then, do these liberating possibilities follow.

It appears then from this survey of the Anglo-Hungarian dialogue that either the socialist welfare project collapses back into nothing more than a welfare pluralism East and West, where consumers of markets, voluntary associations, cooperatives and households variously and autonomously define and provide for their welfare needs in the context of some elemental state guarantees in a mixed economy, or it advances to assert that, in the tradition of the Grundisse, it is a new future that demands to be realized once the capitalist and state socialist work–income connection has finally been severed and all the people of the world are guaranteed a share of its resources as of right. With that security they can then proceed to construct democratically directly and via representation the means of caring mutually for their collectively perceived needs. Whether the better springboard for such a future project is provided by the welfare states of the capitalist West, or the state socialist regimes of the East, or elsewhere, is one of the fascinating questions for the future. Whether this vision is any longer tenable we shall return to at the end of this chapter.

The beginning of an Anglo-Polish dialogue

A British–Polish dialogue of social policy analysts has hardly begun. The 1987 and 1988 Conferences represented one step.[1] At these conferences a main strand to emerge in the dialogue reflected a common interest among both Polish and British participants in the marketization of the Polish economy and Polish welfare provision. Welfare pluralists in Britain and their counterparts in Poland seemed to share a common concern to articulate the case for the greater efficiency to be gained in the economy by an injection of incentive structures and market mechanisms in production and social reproduction. There was a common recognition that this would lead to greater inequality and to the need for some system of unemployment benefit to be introduced in Poland.

Of interest is whether this on-the-surface dialogue of welfare pluralists conceals a hidden agenda of discussions between supporters of a socialist or socialized welfare strategy – even a social revolutionary strategy for welfare. There are no Polish equivalents of Heller and Feher represented here, but it is clear that behind the support for economic reforms may lie support for political reform of a far-reaching kind. Little expression has been given in the framework of the papers presented at these conferences to this point but a wider survey of relevant literature is instructive.

Ksiezopolski (1987) expresses his view in the following terms: 'People have to regain a subjective role in the creation of a social policy on all levels of the decision-making process ... Conditions should be created to enable people to manage by themselves, in cooperation with the family, other citizens, local communities, social organizations and, of course, the state.'

The assumption of this strategy is that it is not material incentives that will motivate a greater work effort but an 'awakening of feelings of affiliation with a community' consequent upon securing 'their subjectivity as workers and citizens'. The prospects for such a strategy being implemented are perceived by Ksiezopolski as 'slim in the present circumstances'.

The focus of discussion for those who may have an interest in such developments is, at the moment, the possibility of the proposed economic reforms creating the space for the political articulation of welfare needs. The obstacles to the reform of the economy and the creation of greater inequalities in wages have been presented as bureaucratic interests within the state, and a popular commitment to egalitarianism and state 'protectiveness' (Regulski and Kocon, 1987). An alliance of economic reformers and radical political scientists seems lined up against a popular distrust in economic reform which sees only a threat to equality and state provision (even at the current extremely inadequate levels).

There are indications among the technocratic and skilled worker layers of the population that this support for the dead weight of statist egalitarianism may be on the wain (Kolarska-Bobinska, 1987). She reports that between 1981 and 1984 surveys of opinion suggest increasing support for increased wage differentials and the introduction of market mechanisms. We can, she writes, 'speak of the birth of the myth of the market as an expression of hope for a better future' (p.10). This hope sits alongside discontent with present provision and mechanisms. However, economic reformers will, she argues, only capture sufficiently wide support for their inequality generating measures and the promise of greater resources tomorrow if the proposals are coupled with political reform of the mechanisms of social decision-making. The former economic advisor of Solidarity argued that 'an indispensable condition for rebuilding the socialist welfare state and its efficient functioning are basic political reforms' (quoted in Kolarska-Bobinska, 1987, p.2)

The Polish contributors to this British–Polish dialogue may have something to learn from the Anglo-Hungarian discussions described above. Equally, there are unique political and economic circumstances and experiences in Poland that can inform a wider East–West dialogue aimed at clarifying what might by the mechanisms for the realization of a future welfare society.

The East–West dialogue at Leeds in April 1988

These Anglo-Hungarian and Anglo-Polish dialogues converged in the conference upon which this volume is based. They were joined and cross cut by older and newer discourses. The contributions from or about the GDR and Bulgaria brought the orthodoxy of the unity of social and economic policy back into focus. The contributions from British feminist scholars of social policy challenged, unsuccessfully, the East Europeans to address centrally and critically the relations between production and social reproduction. The conference, which was jointly organized with the Critical Social Policy[3] Editorial Board also focussed on the racism of Western welfare states and many contributors enjoined the East Europeans to question from this standpoint their vision of a united Europe. The East–West social policy dialogue that also addresses the North–South welfare divide and the associated racism of limited citizenship and welfare rights in Europe has hardly begun. Taylor, (1989) addresses this issue very cogently in a recent article on citizenship and social power.

Some of the actual dialogue that took place at the conference is reported in the next chapter. That chapter consists of three parts. The first part is the opening address by both John Keane from London and Julia Szalai from Budapest. Developing a point made earlier in this chapter, their address attempts to establish as one of the initial premises of the conference that the dialogue can only develop if it breaks out of the language of socialism and starts from a critical approach to certain Marxist categories. The language of socialism is simply unusable by Eastern critics where it has been robbed of all subversive and critical content.

The second part consists of lightly edited extracts from a less structured dialogue session that brought together contributions from the UK, USA, Poland, Hungary, Czechoslovakia, Bulgaria and Yugoslavia. Some fundamental disagreements emerged in this discussion. Some of the UK and US social policy analysts, not heeding the strictures of Keane and Szalai, wished to use a Marxist class analysis to portray working class resistance to aspects of economic and social policy reform in Eastern Europe as justified whereas, for the East Europeans, such resistance stood in the face of changes which were necessary if any economic and social progress was to be made at all. Western Marxists found themselves as the defenders of the equality of social welfare in conditions of poverty and contended with the East Europeans who justified the differentiation and pluralization of welfare as a conditions of improved welfare for all.

The third part consists of several of the contributions to a plenary session on the topic of women and 'socialist' social policy. Several of these consider why feminism had not rooted itself in critical thinking in state socialist societies. This theme reflects and develops upon the chapters in the last part of this book. The first initial poignant reactions from the conference floor are added.

Developments in and analysis of social policy in Eastern Europe: the situation in 1988

In the light of the issues raised during the development of the East–West social policy dialogue it may be interesting to note some of the more salient features of the papers assembled in this volume.

Miroslav Ksiezopolski, borrowing theoretically from the West, applies Titmuss's three models of welfare (residual, achievement performance and institutional redistributive) to the current Polish situation. He finds that a combination of the achievement–performance model and the institutional redistributive model apply with an omnipotent state exercising formally full control over the conditions of living of the population but that, because the level of institutional provision is so low, citizens are forced to meet some of their needs by recourse to the 'socialist market' (bribery, patronage, second economy and so on). The most likely scenario for the future of social policy in Poland is that market-orientated economic reforms would reduce the importance of social policy, regarding it as a burden on the economy, with a consequent widening of inequalities, a privatization of some services and a lowering in the level of social security provided by the state. On the other hand social policy analysts in Poland point to an alternative future within which industrial restructuring would still take place but guided by social policy concerns. Social needs should be the starting point of a restructured economy and social considerations should dominate economic planning. This alternative scenario should still lead to the 'de-monopolization' of the state in social provision and imply a place for markets in the economy and could only be implemented with the active participation by citizens as the subjects of welfare.

Lena Kolarska-Bobinska focusses attention on the increasing role the enterprise is likely to play in Poland in the provision of welfare for its employees if the market reforms are introduced with the state withdrawing from its responsibility for welfare. A differentiation in popular attitudes on the question of economic reforms is also reported. The suggestion is made that Solidarity will divide between those whose interest is the protection of the security (albeit low level) now provided for the poor and those whose interest is the stimulation of the economy in general. A welfare state and not the feudal welfare firm is necessary she argues if the country is to be politically stable during the coming period of economic reform. The poor, protected as they are by feudal employers, may otherwise have no interest in the stimulation of capitalism in Poland.

Magdalena Sokolowska and Andrzej Rychard add to our understanding of Polish welfare by describing the alternative, both formal and informal, ways in which health needs are met. The ambivalent reaction of the authorities to these alternatives is analysed.

Julia Szalai's paper reflects how much more developed is thinking in Hungary about the form welfare policy should take in the wake of the break up of Communist Party control and orthodoxy in Eastern Europe. She provides in the first part a fully rounded critique of the state redistributive system and then makes the case in some detail for a future within which there is a parliament, independent trade unions, a self-financed social security fund that is operated on the basis of employer/employee negotiations (which provides for a well-funded basic pension and benefits, an additional wage-related element, and allows for voluntary additional cover), and democratic elections to local government that is funded from taxes on enterprises. These elected bodies would purchase social services from providers on behalf of their citizens. The separation of democratic control from funding runs counter to the cry of industrialists (no taxation without representation) but is a central part of her strategy to avoid popular and self-interested cuts in service provision for dependent sections of the population.

Zsuzsa Ferge, whose defence in the past of state intervention and of societal policy has been interpreted as just another variant of centralized authoritarian state planning, provides a riveting paper. She, now free to do so, declares herself a parliamentarian, a pluralist and a democrat and then, with all the power of an earlier generation of British social policy writers like Titmuss, she catalogues in distressing detail the damage that is now being done to welfare provision as market forces are given a free reign in Hungary. The market, she argues, may of necessity, had to become the rally cry for all those who believed in freedom of any kind but in its wake it brings the need to put all the old arguments of Galbraith about public squalor and private affluence back on the agenda. More positively, but with little conviction that anybody is listening, she paints a picture of the fourth road to a welfare future – an improved variant on the Swedish model.

By stark contrast Slavka Ivanova's paper about Bulgaria is equally interesting because it represents an earlier phase of analysis and writing about social policy in an Eastern bloc country. Social policy is subsumed as part of economic policy, which from a Marxist standpoint, has the goal of fulfilling all human and welfare needs. Here the account is burdened by reference to the speeches of the now unseated Zivkov and his proclamations about changes in industrial output and wage levels. Detailed empirical investigations of the social division of welfare are conspicuous by their absence. This represents a stage in social policy writing that was superseded in Hungary over twenty years ago. However Slavka goes on to provide an account of the new economic mechanisms which devolve decision-making to enterprises and involve worker participation. It is not clear whether enterprises will have a greater welfare role in future. Out of these reforms may, nonetheless, come the recognition of the need for detailed social accounting. The discipline of social policy may soon emerge in Bulgaria.

Paul Adams analyses critically and cogently the postwar experience of the German Democratic Republic as precisely (like Bulgaria) one in which social and economic policy have been integrated. The chapter demonstrates through the examples of social security and family policy how the welfare objectives of both conflict with the economic and demographic concerns of government so that policy is fraught with contradictory tendencies. He concludes that the more the GDR becomes locked into the world economy the more there must be an abandonment of socialist social policy with its associated concerns with equity and protection and the more there must be a growth in unequal rewards and benefits. It is difficult, he concludes, not to see in the actual evolution of social policy in the GDR, not the logic of the transition to socialism, but the compulsion of world capitalist competition. The future, however, he suggested was not yet written. How right this has proved to be.

Prue Chamberlayne's study, also focussed on the GDR, provides an important insight into the activities of neighbourhood committees and tenants' associations within this united economic and social policy. The wide participation engineered by the party and the National Front in local projects is seen variously as either developing a mature socialism by the established local leaderships or as a 'broom against bureaucratism' by the reform communists. The part they play in the new era will be interesting to observe.

Ivan Svetlik portrays the emergence of a debate about the future of welfare in Yugoslavia which is more akin to the earlier papers on Poland and Hungary in contrast to the accounts of the monolithic unity of economic and social policy perspectives that dominates discourse in GDR and Bulgaria. Here he notes that the state's recent devolving of responsibilities for welfare onto self-managed communities of interests (SCI) represents an abandonment of formal responsibility by the state for an integrative social policy while not actually allowing the SCI the full autonomy they should have. There are some similarities here to the way in which enterprises have had a welfare function put on them in Poland. Svetlik argues the case, following Titmuss and then Johnson, for a welfare pluralism which combines well-funded state services, SCIs, and local autonomy for mutual care and a limited role for market provision.

Chris Corrin surveys the situation of women in Hungarian society and notes that the much reported on childcare grant whereby women are paid for up to three years to care for children at home was a product as much of labour market (economic) policy as a response to the dual burden of women. She describes the absence of an autonomous feminism in Hungary even among the emerging opposition movement at the time she wrote this in 1988. It will be interesting to see whether the future pluralization of politics in Hungary changes things.

Jirina Siklova, in a paper that could not be presented at the conference because permission to travel was not granted, provides a devastating critique of Czech social policy in terms of its treatment of old people. Although focussed on women in old age who are worse off than men, she notes, typically of internal regime critics, 'in such a context (of poverty), the specific problems of women, as opposed to men, loose their importance'. The main thrust of the critique is the absence of index-linking of pensions (making every increase a benevolent act of the Party) and the small degree of wage relatedness which leads to severe drop in income in old age for some. The case for the social security reform proposals articulated by Julia Szalai for Hungary could apply even more strongly in Czechoslovakia – but there was nobody there yet prepared to listen in 1988. The emerging social policy of the Civic Forum and the new government become a matter for urgent study.

Zuzanna Hughes, writing as a Czech exile provides a curiously uncritical history of the ways in which the case of upbringing of children has been seen as an integral part of state policy since 1940 in order to produce a better fit between family needs and the social system. The concern of Czech authors who write of gypsy families that their 'level of socialization and cultural level are inadequate for the needs of socialist society', are reported with little comment. Only at the end does she permit herself the view that only 'when unpleasant and difficult things are ... written about and faced ... will there be information which is vital for assesssing the effectiveness of existing laws and regulations. When there is a genuine interplay between the legislative framework and the need of families will education for parenthood come of age.'

Mary Buckley's chapter which concludes the book, although based on her study of recent developments in the Soviet Union, has some relevance for the future debate on the woman question in Eastern Europe. It indicates that the debate is now more open in the USSR. This more open debate doesn't lead in a simple way to any particular new policy direction, and certainly not yet new theoretical thinking on the issue. Radical views which raise the division of labour in the home coexist with a resurgence of concerns about a woman's main duty being in the home. Issues once clothed in secrecy are more openly discussed – prostitution, infant mortality, but 'Western' feminist explanations for these are not often presented despite the criticism by Larisa Zuznetsova in 1988 of the Soviet state's partriarchal habits.

Future directions and possibilities

Finally some future possibilities will be discussed for the ways in which social policy may develop in Eastern Europe, for the prospect for the eventual realization of an idealized socialist social policy, and for further theoretical and empirical work in the discipline of social policy.

As a result of the several recent conferences[1] and the resulting publications much is now understood about the nature of social policy in East European countries. Some possible directions for future development are also crystallizing. In some countries (notably Albania) there will be for some time the continuation of the doctrine of the unity of economic and social policy. The reality concealed by this doctrine will be the subordination of all aspects of social policy to the economic requirements of the country. The economic requirements will be largely dictated by both world market forces and the interests of outdated heavy industry. In this context, by many social indicators, provision in health care, housing, education and other areas will fall short of West European levels. Nonetheless the economy will continue to carry out a protective welfare function through guaranteeing employment and low prices and will continue to provide for a relatively egalitarian income structure with some social security benefits for some of the working class set at acceptable levels. The omnipotent state welfare system will continue to provide paternalistically for many citizens the egalitarianism of an impoverished welfare system. The citizens of these countries will continue to die prematurely and live in overcrowded conditions.

In other countries, notably Poland and Hungary but recently joined by Czechoslovakia, Bulgaria and the German Democratic Republic, the Bolshevik project is in retreat. The faith in the unity of economic and social policy has been lost. The party either willingly, in the case of Hungary and Bulgaria, or after having been pushed in the case of Poland, Czechoslovakia and the GDR is facilitating the transformation of these countries into ones which are more decentralized in their management, more market-orientated in their economic mechanisms, and more pluralistic in their politics. The future for social welfare in these countries is variously interpreted as bleak or promising. For some leftist Western critics, perhaps wilfully blind to the mortality rates and the overcrowding, the removal of the protective functions of the economy is seen as a tip in the balance of class struggle against sections of the working class in favour of a new emerging bourgeoisie formed in part from the old nomenklatura. For some radical social policy critics within these countries the same changes are viewed as a necessary stage in the modernizing of the economy which alone can provide for the future of welfare. The real issue is whether, in this modernizing and marketization process, a strong independent social policy will evolve with state guarantees, well-funded from taxes on enterprises and, progressively, for social security purposes, on individuals, with flourishing local democratic welfare provision responding to newly, autonomously articulated needs. The hopes may be there but the signs are not good if the analyses of Ferge, Kolarska-Bobinska, Svetlik and Ksiezopolski are accurate. Of crucial important in the unfolding of the future will be the forms of property relations that evolve as the anonymous state and party property is allocated to new 'owners'. If the new owners are private and corporate share holders the fears of Ferge and others will be justified. If the new owners are cooperatives of workers, or democratically accountable local councils and soviets there is hope for the welfare of all. The role, of course, of the IMF and the EEC, every bit as much as the local actors and social forces, will have a central influence here. In this respect we should note with concern the policy commitments the IMF are at this moment (December 1989) extracting from the new Polish and the caretaker (pending the 1990 elections) Hungarian governments. Among the list of requirements for the loans of hard currency being made of and agreed by the Polish government are:

- significant cuts in public expenditure
- dramatic reduction in subsidy on consumer goods
- a wage freeze with a consequential drop in living standards by 20%
- rise in unemployment from 0% to 2.5%.

This is happening in a country with no insurance based unemployment benefit and an antiquated and judgemental social aid system. The choice of social policy responses being canvassed at present seem to be between opening more Red Cross Soup Kitchens to extending vouchers. The communist government would never have got away with it. It remains to be seen if the Solidarity government will.

The theoretically-derived notions of an idealized socialist social policy need to be re-examined in the light of the negative experience of Eastern European state socialist regimes. While the deformations of these regimes into Stalinist-style dictatorships over needs may not be intrinsically bound up with the conception of Socialism that inspired Marx or even Lenin, we have learned enough of the power of an abused socialist ideology in the hands of self-interest to caution against any societal project which proclaims itself the truth. Mihalay Vajda, interviewed in June 1988 (Deacon, B., 1989), recalled the legacy of the Lukacs school of which he was a disciple.

> It was the last representation of the world-redeeming socialist idea ...In the Lukacs school we shared the world-redeeming view but wanted to negate the Bolshevik method.... There was a contradiction in this position ... We can only know what is to be done about the present according to our values ... Yes, I believe in the need for markets here and for democracy and to build self-activity but I can't answer your question [as to what is the best economic and political pre-condition for the emergence of the best democracy].

We may still be allowed to paint a picture of a welfare future that is more egalitarian, whose provisions are not so closely tied to a work ethic, that facilitate forms of care that are not sexist or racist, that is less structured by nationally bound citizenship rights, that allow for variety and difference in the social needs that are articulated and the ways in which they are met, that is more reciprocal and less paternalistic, more enabling and less dependency-creating, more empowering and less stigmatizing. We may still be allowed to argue that the democratic state has a duty to guarantee some territorial justice and that international authority has a duty to guarantee some global justice. We may still be allowed to argue that markets between collectively owned enterprises must operate within a regulating framework that tries to ensure they help achieve democratically agreed ends. What we are not able to do is to engineer or manipulate social development such that we guarantee this welfare future. The faith in the universal interest of the working class as material carriers of this future must give way to a redoubling of commitment and argument at the level of social values as a necessary part of the process of realizing this welfare future.

Of interest given this redefinition of the socialist welfare project – given this new basis for a radical dialogue between East and West – is whether there is likely to a greater adherence to these values in the context of the developing democratization of Hungary, Poland and elsewhere or whether the West provides a better social base for such ideas and practices to flourish. The hope for the fourth road being realized in Hungary rests on the premise that the predominantly socially-owned economy and the legacy of socialist values must tend towards the ready adoption there of those welfare values and their operationalization in the working out of a pluralist democratic future. This is an empirical question the future will answer.

These immediately preceding comments have been couched at a fairly high level of generality based on what we know so far about the recent development of social policy in Eastern Europe. Much more detailed analysis and research is also suggested by these recent developments however. The immense variety of responses within Eastern Europe (and the Soviet Union) to the break-up of the Bolshevik project provides a fascinating natural experiment against which to test theories of social welfare development, against which to evaluate alternative mechanisms for meeting welfare need, and within which, to try out and experiment with untested ways of implementing aspects of social policy.

The next five or ten years provide an ideal opportunity to conduct a cross-national study of welfare policy in Eastern Europe (comparing where appropriate also with West European countries). Such a project should focus in more detail than most of the papers in this volume have been able to do on selected areas of policy in each country (social security, family policy, health provision, housing, etc.), should chart developments in thinking and practice in all of these areas, and address the following issues:

i) The emergence of *social movements* and the content of the social policy needs articulated by them. An attempt could be made to chart the emerging differential access to power of these emerging social and political groupings. This would include both potential users and potential providers of welfare services.

ii) The study could permit the concretization, therefore, of the concept of a pluralist *civil society*. The new ways (if any) found in practice for groupings in civil society to negotiate with various providers the meeting of their needs would be described.

iii) Progress could be made in the elaboration of a pluralistic range of criteria for the *evaluation* of social policy developments in each area of provision. This work could incorporate the earlier conceptualization of an idealized socialist social policy (Deacon, 1983) but this would need to be regarded as one value-based set of criteria contending with others such as those utilized by transnational agencies such as the ILO, WHO and United Nations.

iv) The scope for *social learning* between countries in search of ways of implementing variants on the welfare state in the context of the marketization of the economies, could be a focus of study. The ways in which alternative practices from elsewhere (USA, Sweden, Finland, Britain) become adopted by intellectuals and, in turn, political parties is of interest.

v) The empirical charting of emerging *social inequalities* in access to income, housing, health care and social security and other services would be a large but useful undertaking. If the fears of Ferge and others are realized then evidence of this type will be necessary to support the case for welfare policy developments.

All of these possible foci of study are of interest to social policy analysts in the West for one overriding reason. Will the new politics of Eastern Europe actually generate anything new in the sphere of social welfare policy? Will we learn from these societies new democratic forms of provision, a new and more acceptable mix of service provision, new ways of combining market mechanisms with the concerns of equity, justice and compassion? Or will these societies simply learn from the West?

Notes

1. 1982 Research Committee on Poverty, Social Welfare and Social Policy at the Xth World Congress of Sociology, Mexico.
1983 European Centre for Social Welfare and Training, Vienna Conference entitled 'Can There be a New Welfare State', Baden.
1987 British Academy of Sciences, Polish Academy of Sciences and Suntory Toyota International Centre for Economics and Related Disciplines. British–Polish Conference on 'Social Welfare in Eastern and Western Europe', Warsaw.
1988 Institute of Sociology of the Hungarian Academy of Sciences and International Social Policy Research Unit of Leeds Polytechnic. International Conference on 'Social Policy and Socialism', Leeds (the Conference upon which this volume is based).

2. The research that is reported in part of this paper was financed by the British Economic and Social Research Council under Grant No. G00232229. The research focus is a Comparative Study of Attitudes to State Welfare Policy. The grant is jointly held by B. Deacon, S. Jacobs and F. William and the Hungarian counterparts are J. Szalai, P. Gyori and J. David. The results will be published in Deacon, B., et al forthcoming.

3. *Critical Social Policy* is a journal of social policy, published by Longmans which gives emphasis to the critical analysis of social policy from socialist, feminist and anti-racist standpoints.

Bibliography

Beresford, P. and Croft, S. (1984), 'Welfare Pluralism: the new face of Fabianism', *Critical Social Policy*, 9, pp. 19–34.
Bozoki, A. (1989), 'New Movements – Old Ideologies in Hungary', Paper presented at Conference on *Citizenship in Europe*, Budapest, May.
Brus, W. (1985), 'Socialism – feasible and viable', *New Left Review*, 153, pp. 43–63.
Campbell, B. (1987), 'The Charge of the Light Brigade', *Marxism Today*, Feb.
Deacon, B. (1983), *Social Policy and Socialism*, Pluto.
Deacon, B. (1989), 'State, Market and Civil Society: The Articulation of Welfare Needs'. In: Millard, F., (ed), 1989.
Deacon, B., Williams, F., Jacobs, S., Szalai, J., Gyri, P. and David, J. (forthcoming), *Strategies for Welfare East and West*, Wheatsheaf.
Evers, A., Nowotny, H. and Wintersberger, H. (1987), *The Changing Face of Welfare*, Gower.
Feher, F. and Heller, A. (1986), *Eastern Left. Western Left*, Polity Press.

Feher, F., Heller, A. and Markus, G. (1983), *Dictatorship over Needs*, Basil Blackwell.
Ferge, Z. (1979), *A Society in the Making*, Penguin.
Ferge, Z. (1986), 'The Changing Hungarian Social Policy'. In: Oyen, E. (ed) (1986).
George, N. and Manning, N. (1980), *Socialism, Social Welfare and the Soviet Union*, Routledge and Kegan Paul.
Geras, N. (1985), 'On Marx and Justice', *New Left Review*, 156, pp. 47–85.
Harris, R. and Seldon, A. (1979), *Over-ruled on Welfare*, Institute of Economic Affairs.
Heller, A. (1986) 'The Republican Dimension', *Praxis International*.
Higgins, J. (1986), 'Comparative Social Policy', *Quarterly Journal of Social Affairs* 2, 3, pp. 221–42.
Johnston, N. (1987), *The Welfare State in Transition*, Wheatsheaf.
Kolakowski, L. (1978), *Main Currents of Marxist Thought*, Oxford University Press.
Kolarska-Bobinska, K. (1987), 'Poland Under Crisis: UnreformableSociety or Establishment', Paper presented at International Conference on *Social Policy and Socialism*, Leeds, April.
Ksiezopolski, M. (1987), 'Polish Social Policy in a Situation of Economic Crisis'. In: Evers, A. *et al.* (1987).
Lee, P. and Raban, C. (1988), *Welfare Theory and Social Policy*, Sage.
LeGrand, J. and Okrasa, W. (eds) (1987), *Social Welfare in Britain and Poland*, STICERD.
LeGrand, J. and Robinson, R. (1984), *Privatisation and The Welfare State*, George Allen & Unwin.
Liska, T. (1982), 'Social Dividend and Welfare', manuscript..
Lukes, S. (1985), *Marxism and Morality*, Oxford University Press.
McAuley, A. (1979), *Economic Welfare in the Soviet Union*, George Allen and Unwin.
Millard, F., (ed) (1989), *Social Welfare and the Market*, STICERD.
Mishra, R. (1984), *The Welfare State in Crisis*, Wheatsheaf.
Nove, A. (1983), *The Economics of Feasible Socialism*, George Allen and Unwin.
Oyen, E. (1986), *Comparing Welfare States and Their Future*, Gower.
Polan, A. J. (1984), *Lenin and the End of Politics*, Methuen.
Regulski, J. and Kocon, W. (1987), 'Local government – welfare policy – decentralisation', Paper presented at Conference on Social Welfare East and West, Warsaw, July.
Sik, E. (1987), 'The Welfare System and Its Future in Hungary; Towards the self-welfare society', manuscript.
Soper, K. (1981), *On Human Needs*, Harvester.
Szelenyi, I. and Manchin, R. (eds) (1987), 'Social Policy under State Socialism'. In: Rein, M., Esping-Anderson, G. and Rainwater, L. (eds), *Stagnation and Renewal in Social Policy*, Armonk, New York: ME Sharpe.
Taras, R. (1984), *Poland: Socialist State, Rebellious Nation*, Boulder, Colarado and London: Westview Press.
Taylor-Gooby, P. (1985), *Public Opinion, Ideology and State Welfare*, Routledge and Kegan Paul.
Walker, A. (1984), *Social Planning: A Strategy for Socialist Welfare*, Basil Blackwell.
Wicks, M. (1987), *A Future for All*, Penguin.
Wilding, P. (1986), *In Defence of the Welfare State*, Routledge and Kegan Paul.

Williams, F. (1989), *Social Policy: A Critical Introduction*, Polity Press.
Zavada, P. (1983), 'Economic Reform, Social Reform', manuscript.

2 Social policy and socialism: citizenship, the working class, women and welfare (an East–West dialogue)

Contributors include: John Keane, Julia Szalai, Bob Deacon, Janos David, Ivan Svetlik, Miroslaw Ksiezopolski, Mita Castle, Lena Kolarska-Bobinska, Tom Hickey, Paul Adams, Hilary Rose, Zsuzsa Ferge, Mary Buckley, Maxine Molyneux and Aldona Fraczkiewicz-Wronka.

This chapter, which is divided into three parts, reports edited extracts of three conference sessions. The first reports the main papers at the opening plenary. The second reports a discussion among a number of participants. The third reports a number of panel contributions to a conference session on women and socialist social policy. Some commentary on these extracts is provided in Chapter 1. It has been decided not to update the text of this chapter in the light of the changes in Eastern Europe in the autumn of 1989. These events highlight, of course, the perceptiveness of the main contributors.

Socialism, civil society and social policy

John Keane (Britain)

One of the most important lessons that I've learned from my contacts with Central and Eastern Europe during the past ten years or so is to get rid of the terms pessimism and optimism. I think they have no place actually in the language of democratic politics. I've been told many times over in countries like Czechoslovakia, for instance, that to be optimistic in these times is to be a fool, and to be pessimistic is to be self-paralysing. This lesson which I learned from the other half of Europe about the dangers of optimism and pessimism has come in handy for me during the past decade in this country when as we all know the Western European socialist tradition, including the British socialist tradition, has found itself in very big trouble.

The string of electoral defeats for socialist governments in Britain and France and the Bundesrepublik, for example, the growing public confidence and, I think, in this country the arrogance of neo-conservatism and the increased reactiveness and confusion of socialist parties and governments and intellectuals are all symptomatic of this so-called decline of socialism. This decline has convinced quite a lot of intellectuals and others, of course, of the need to abandon a socialist tradition altogether. I have encountered this pessimistic conclusion a lot just in recent days when announcing that I was coming to Leeds to talk to a conference on socialism and social policy. The very common response was 'God! Not another conference on socialism'. I think this sort of reaction is displayed in its most caustic form in a very interesting book by Alain Tourraine, the French sociologist, who concludes his study *L'Après Socialism* with the following words: 'Socialism is dead; the word lives on in electoral programmes and in the official titles of parties and governments, but it has been emptied altogether of meaning except of course to designate a vast family of authoritarian states.'

In trying to avoid this kind of pessimism and its opposite foolish optimism I have become convinced of the need to rethink socialist politics in a pretty fundamental way. I am, of course, not the only one. Of particular interest to me is the whole issue of democracy, which it seems to me is becoming more and more central and the relationship of democracy to state institutions and non-state institutions. This concern, I think, dovetails with a very fertile debate that's developed in the past few years about the statist image of socialism. I think there is a pretty remarkable consensus in fact, in Western Europe at least, that socialism has become unpopular for at least one reason and that has to do with identification with the centralized bureaucratic state. And one can see the loss of sympathy for, for example, old Fabian models of socialism and one can see this not only in changes within the Fabian society itself in this country but, for example, in Neil Kinnock's talk of the enabling state. This is symptomatic of the shift away from a state-centred socialism. But I wanted briefly to point out what I take to be some weaknesses in this argument about the need to change the image of socialism and to rethink socialist ideas and policies about state and non-state institutions.

The first problem is that the debate about the state and socialism is marked by an excess of vagueness and imprecision, in particular about the kinds of institutional conditions that are necessary for realizing in practice a more democratic socialism. There is, I believe, a strong consensus about the need for a long-term socialist public philosophy which emphasizes less bureaucracy, decentralization and more democracy and yet there seems to be in the present period in Western Europe, at least, an inability to go beyond these general slogans. The consequence, I think, is that for many people there is a sense that socialism is either some vague, future condition that has little relationship to present day capitalist realities or that socialism, for at least some people, means the dismal reality and the harsh reality of state dominated Soviet-type regimes.

The second weakness in this debate about the state and socialism is, and I think it is the more controversial point, the continuing dogmatism of socialist politics; a dogmatism which I think contradicts the goal of making socialism more democratic. Let me briefly try to explain. Many West European socialist groups, unions and parties frequently sense the democratic potential of recent citizens' initiatives, for example, in campaigns against sexism, against racism, against nuclear power and the erosion of civil liberties. Yet, quite often, these initiatives are thought of as either marginal or as non-socialist, and even in some cases, bluntly labelled as anti-socialist on the grounds that they don't conform to the fixed essence of the socialist ideal, namely the abolition of capitalist production and exchange and the institution of a collectively owned and regulated property system. I think in this way the socialist tradition has tended to lose the support of potential allies whose support could have greatly energized and invigorated the socialist tradition. In a way, socialist ideas have become defensive and frozen, cloistered from much that is normal and complex in the world. In this way socialist politics has become incapable of learning from forging new alliances with other potentially democratic institutions, groups and movements. I think the final outcome of this second problem is that Western socialist ideas and politics have become relatively unreceptive to the new critiques of the socialist regimes of Central and Eastern Europe. It is said, for instance, that these regimes have effectively abolished capitalism and in this respect must be, at the very least, halfway houses between capitalism and socialism. These regimes are seen as benign or at least as better than Western capitalist systems, such as Britain, and I think this kind of attitude has a great problem comprehending the view which one hears all the time in the East that in matters of democracy and standards of living and other issues, the East is actually worse than the West. I think this dogmatism also explains why many Western socialists in the present period cannot understand why in the East Gorbachev is not seen as a kind of Russian Kennedy. On the contrary there is a great scepticism; there is a cautiousness and this is not the case, I think, in the West, and so there is a miscomprehension of the different receptions of the Gorbachev phenomenon. I am going to add here, if I may just briefly, one of my favourite jokes which is, I think, a Czech joke but I am sure there is also a Polish and Yugoslav and Hungarian version. A lot of Western socialists simply don't understand the bitter irony underpinning this joke: the joke is 'What is socialism?' Socialism, the answer is, is the dialectical synthesis of all human history, it takes from primitive communism, the method; it takes from the classical antiquity, slavery; it takes from the medieval periods, serfdom; it takes from capitalism, exploitation and it takes from socialism, the name. A great joke which is received differently in the two halves of Europe.

The third problem that I see with this debate about the state and socialism (and more controversial) is that socialists who presently in the West call for less centralized state bureaucracy have often failed to recognize that some things can be learned by studying the new conservatism which took the lead as we all know in Britain, in France and elsewhere from the mid-1970s in popularizing the demand for less state action and in branding the socialist tradition as the guardian of bureaucratic state power. In this respect, in the British context, for instance, I find myself less attracted to the interpretation of Thatcherism by someone like Eric Hobsbawn who to this day still insists that Thatcherism is somehow foreign to British morality. I find myself, on the contrary, much closer to someone like the Bishop of Durham who has been saying for a number of years that it's very important to recognize that Thatcherism has a sort of parasitic relationship to some key elements in British political culture and in particular this whole principle of self-determination and caring for oneself.

This is, I think, an important argument and it's one that I want to make here with some caution, of course. The key point is that neo-conservative ideologists and policy-makers have promoted a discussion successfully about the limits of state-centred socialism and I think that as socialists we have no choice but to engage this kind of argument. In other words, their morals versus ours, Trotsky's phrase, is actually a self-defeating position for socialists to adopt in the struggle against neo-conservatism. I think it concedes too much. It supposes that the rich if histrionic vocabulary of neo-conservatism, i.e. freedom of choice, individual rights, freedom from state bureaucracy and so on, is of little or no interest to the socialist tradition, and in this way, I think it allows the right to inherit and monopolize an old European vocabulary of freedom and plausibly accuse the socialist tradition of, in fact, being in love with state power.

I presuppose that thinking differently about socialism is quite vital and urgent if it is to regain its position as a theoretically credible and practical political and social alternative. I've tried to argue with empirical examples that the counter-productive identification of socialism with centralized state power can be shattered only if the term socialism is redefined in a radical way so that it, in fact, becomes synonymous with greater democracy, by which, I mean at the most general level a differentiated and pluralistic system of power in which decisions of interest to productivities of various sizes are made directly or indirectly by all their members.

More exactly, my argument is that the questions about democracy and socialism can be posed fruitfully only by rethinking the relationship between the state and civil society. To rethink, that is, the relationship between the complex network of political institutions (the military, legal, administrative, productive and cultural organs) of the state on the one hand and the realm of the social, that is privately-owned, market-directed, voluntarily-run, of friendship-based activities which are legally recognized and guaranteed by the state. This relationship between the state and civil society, a term which I'm not using specifically in Gramsci's sense must be rethought in a way that affirms the necessity and desirability of drawing stricter limits upon the scope of state action, while expanding the sphere of independent social life. In my view, socialism that is theoretically viable and worthy of respect and practice must be synonymous with the democratization of society and the state as well as those bodies such as political parties which act as their intermediaries.

From this revised perspective, socialism, in my view, involves maintaining, not as Marx and almost all early socialists thought abolishing, the division between political and social power between the political and social spheres. It means making, on the contrary, state policy more accountable to civil society and it means democratically expanding and re-ordering non-state activities within civil society itself. In short, it involves democratizing the state and creating a post-capitalist non-patriarchal civil society, a kind of civil society which was unthinkable to the early modern liberal tradition. Now, of course, to speak of socialism in this unfamiliar and, I think, rather abstract way, as synonymous with the democratization of social and political power is certainly not uncontroversial. The acceptance of this radically different, and, I think, generally pluralist definition of socialism is bound to be resisted by neo-conservatives who are in fact, as we're finding out more and more each day, statists are also convinced that civil society simply equals market capitalism which it certainly does not in my own view. The acceptance of this revised definition of socialism is also likely to be resisted, I think, by many liberal democrats whose support, in my view, in the British context at the moment for anti-Thatcher policies is very important. Many liberal democrats, in fact, have an allergic reaction to socialism, but what I'm trying to argue in this and in other pieces is in fact that the views which they hold are compatible with the views which I'm holding here. The acceptance of the revised definition of socialism that I'm offering here is, I think, likely to prove also quite painful for many traditional socialists. It requires them to see that they can learn something from the content of neo-conservative ideology and, a not unrelated point, that the severe crisis which affects contemporary socialism is not merely conjunctural. That is to say it's not simply only to do with the restructuring of the global economy or with the fragmentation of the industrial working class but, in fact, the present crisis of socialism is traceable, I think, back to the very origins of the socialist idea itself.

My revised definition of socialism also requires socialists to abandon their deep misgivings about the extension and deepening of democracy. Many socialists still continue to view democracy, in my sense, in purely instrumental terms. In other words, it is good only to the extent that it delivers or promises to deliver socialism itself defined narrowly in terms of economic equality or the less fashionable, state control of civil society. This traditional socialist reticence about greater democracy, I think, is understandable. It stems partly from the correct recognition that the empowerment of previously disadvantaged constituencies within the civil society does not necessarily work in favour of traditional definitions of socialism based as they are in white, male, heterosexual working-class state-centred and ecologically destructive views of the world. One important implication of my proposals is that democratization will, in fact, prove to be something of a Pandora's box for conventionally-minded socialists. The development or strengthening of new democratic mechanisms within the state and civil society does not guarantee approval for traditional socialist ideas, particularly those centred on the collective ownership and state control of the means of production. On the contrary, whereas stable despotisms, as our friends often know in the East, usually bore their subjects rigid and under these regimes it seems as if time stands still, democratic mechanisms, by contrast, invariably produce surprising outcomes. Unexpected outcomes are one of the more fascinating features of democracy whose extension and deepening is likely to increase the frequency of surprises for all groups, parties and governments, socialists included. A genuinely democratic socialism must accept these surprising and sometimes awkward outcomes and it must recognize – and I think this is the bottom line about democracy – it must recognize that democratic procedures are superior to all other types of decision-making, not because they guarantee better results but because, it's an old-fashioned argument, that they offer citizens the right to judge and to reconsider their judgements about the quality of these results.

Why is this approach which I've sketched here important? What would be the advantage of policies based on this general approach? It seems to me that there are a number of them and I want just briefly to mention four of these. First, I think that recasting socialism in the language of state and civil society explicitly recognizes the urgent need to deal with the undesirable effects of the bureaucratic regulations of state surveillance and invisible government, all of which have grown enormously since 1945. This approach is important for a second reason. It suggests ways in which new forms of social solidarity especially among less powerful citizens can be developed against the atomizing effects of the current restructuring of state bureaucracies and private capitalist markets by the neo-conservatives. Policies based on strengthening civil society would acknowledge the contemporary dangers of uprootedness. This is a Simone Weill's term and it reflects the felt need of many citizens to put down roots within civil society through forms of association which preserve memories of the past, a measure of stability in the present and our hopes for the future. Thirdly, the perspective that I've sketched here suggests the strategic importance of local initiatives for empowering less powerful citizens. They renew the old insight that the decentralization of power is sometimes the most effective cure for parochialism, that through participation, in other words in local organizations, citizens overcome their own localism. This is a paradox and, I think, there's much to be said for this. These policy examples, based on a revised definition of socialism, would also help stimulate awareness of a new insight about power which was developed in the early 1970s but has definitely been developed in many recent social policy writings, for example, you can see this in Bill Jordan's work. This insight that large-scale organizations such as state bureaucracies and capitalist operations themselves always rest upon complex molecular networks of everyday power relations among friends, lovers, neighbours, parents and children and others and that the transformation of these molecular powers, necessarily induces effects upon these large-scale organizations. That seems to me to be a really important insight for thinking about democratization. Finally, the redefinition of socialism in terms of the state civil society distinction and policies geared to this new definition could make possible a more fruitful and lasting cooperation between democrats in both halves of Europe.

During the past three decades or so, the other half of Europe virtually disappeared from the maps of Western socialist political thinking. Many Western socialists forgot the old truth that the destruction of democracy in one country represents a blow against democratic liberties of citizens everywhere. As I see it, efforts at recasting the language of socialism in terms of the state–civil society distinction can help us directly engage democratic politics in the other half of Europe. It's my impression that there has been a tremendous growth of interest in this relationship between state and civil. This is partly because of the failure of reformed communism in 1968, but also partly because of the growing sense that socialism in that part of Europe is undergoing an exhaustion and because independent initiatives and independent groups are either suffocated or extirpated by a type of state which in fact is intolerant of a civil society. In other words, there has been a huge development of an awareness about this distinction precisely because in that half of Europe that distinction between civil society and the state does not exist. It seems to me that in the West by recasting the discussion about socialism and democracy in terms of state and civil society we can help, as it were, construct a language in which it's possible to discuss the problems in common. Today I sometimes feel very pessimistic about this because it seems to me that we are in a Europe divided not only by political boundaries but also by a wall of silence, misunderstanding and mutual suspicion and when we talk to each other it seems as if we are strangers who speak different tongues. It seems to me that that's really the most important thing about this conference that perhaps that miscomprehension can be broken down.

Julia Szalai (Hungary)

People in Eastern Europe, have a view on the world that I would not call (as John does) 'pessimistic', instead I would describe it as 'fatalist'. They have good reasons for that way of thinking. We East Europeans feel that all those constraints and frameworks that we have, and that we do not identify with, are just given, are just put on us from above. What I learned here in Britain is precisely a kind of behaviour of challenging that fatalism, of challenging and reacting with alternative forms of questioning, thinking and action. This lesson has left me with a very deep understanding of how *not to accept* institutionalization as the only way of reforming and restructuring society. It has led me to an understanding of the meaning of civil society and civil action.

The rediscovery of the importance of social forces outside the state occurs at a time when radical efforts have to raise the questions of civil society in both halves of Europe, in the East and in the West. The belief in good reforms regarding the state institutions have to be rethought by the left of the West, in a situation when the new Conservatives have challenged the whole of the welfare state. The story is different in the East. After twenty years of experience of the 1968 reforms, of the belief in modernization by a mere marketization of the system, we have arrived at the recognition that the system cannot be modified partially, cannot be transformed just in the fields of economy. Instead, we need general political and social changes to reach the goals of radical transformation. We have had twenty years of experience of partial modernization via restricted liberalization of the market, and we had to raise the question as to what was ultimately meant by the market versus state debate. Did we really mean, that the debate was just about 'institutions', about economic institutions or institutions of distribution and redistribution, or did we have hidden hopes, utopias of democracy that were embraced by concepts of the market? The lesson of that twenty years' experience is bitter: all those hidden utopias of marketization as the means of generating more freedom and more autonomy, as the way of overcoming all the underdeveloped and missing features of the civil society were just false concepts of the market. We now have to raise direct questions on the needs of civil society and speak in a very straightforward way about social and political needs in our countries as well. That is perhaps the most important lesson. And I think, that is not only my personal conclusion, but a quite widely shared experience of many East Europeans.

On the other hand, with that experience, it turns out that the state in itself is not an alternative either. The state is something which is bureaucratic, oppressive, exploitative and so on, and therefore the state at present is associated with all these social meanings. Therefore there is a strong and broad opposition in our countries to everything that has the slightest flavour of 'statism'. It is a long process to get rid of the idea and practice of the totalitarian state and to define a state that is 'ours', that is created and controlled by the democratic processes of the civil society. I think it should be a different state to the states that we have in the East, but perhaps also to the ones of the West. We shouldn't throw away, however, all the concepts of solidarity, public responsibility, less inequality and so on, all those values that have been long associated with the concept and practice of the state. There should be a third way. I think we are speaking about this third way at this conference and this is one of our common interests. We have a wide range of experiences, even if they are as yet scattered, to imagine a social system, where social needs have their own ways of expression, that are less institutionalized and less bureaucratized, and where communities are able to build up their own institutions for sharing and representing power, and controlling more flexibly what should be controlled.

We need to raise all those questions in the European culture which, I think, haven't been raised for 200 years. The whole concept of the state versus the market goes back very much to the enlightened tradition of the late eighteenth century. The heated discourse of our times can be derived from those old days. It is just a radical version of one strand of the enlightened thinking. In the name of enlightenment we have experienced a development, a continuous development, where some people or some institutions have been in the position of defining what is 'best', and the whole of the society had to work towards that 'best'. The welfare state is about that concept of 'good', and the socialist states have tried to gain legitimation on similar grounds. The general crisis of the latter is obvious, and the deep constraints of the former are also undeniable. Therefore the second part of our common interest in the West and in the East, in my view, is to think about a future development based upon the needs, the real needs of the society, upon processes of new definitions of needs of various social groups, upon ways of more democratic representation and of ways of working together with their diverging views on desirable developments, and on what is best for them. If I understand John correctly, it is much the same thing he was arguing for.

I think I have to finish my introductory words with some comments on whether these questions put here, probably in a very personal way, are just the unique ones of my country, Hungary, or whether they can lead us to a better and more accurate understanding of the general crisis in central Eastern Europe. I would argue that we experience a general systemic crisis all over central Eastern Europe. It is a crisis of a system called most frequently 'state socialism', a system that has been functioning in the countries of the region. Although historical divergences and different degrees of 'reform-interventions' have characterized the 40 year stories of the system in different countries, we have to emphasize that it has been the history of the *same* system in *all* the countries, a system of totalitarian 'socialism'. Therefore we have to give up all the hopes of partial economic or marginal political 'reforming', all the hopes of a type of 'reform communism'.

The system has arrived at its crisis for four reasons: ideological, political, social and economic ones. Here I have said some words about only the ideological crisis, that is, a crisis of Marxism. There is a great need now to build up new frameworks, new concepts of development, and a need to understand the role of Marxism in the historical processes of the last 100 years. That analysis is a precondition of rephrasing and radical concepts of a future development.

The roots of the political crisis go back to the Stalinist period, which did not end with the death of Stalin. We have to understand that the whole structure of our political institutions was and is imbued with Stalinism. Although Eastern Europe got rid of Stalinism on the surface, with all the criticisms that were levelled at it, little has really been changed. The key point of suspicion regarding the reforms of Gorbachev (I would speak here only on my own behalf) is the fact that the political system in itself is still based on a one-party system. The whole of the social political order is based on a hierarchical semi-military building up of the system, and if we regard that as the classical Stalinist form, then it can't be reformed just by changes of persons or just by getting rid of the very, very drastic forms of Stalinism. This is the essence of the political crisis. Since these systems can't work any more, partly for social and economic reasons and partly for the lack of legitimation given to them by their societies, the political crisis cannot be resolved within the given framework. The manifestation of the political crisis might be sharper this year and might be less sharp in another year, but it is a common crisis all over Eastern Europe.

What about the social crisis? Here I am a bit more uncertain regarding other East European countries, but quite sure regarding my own country. We can speak about a social crisis in Hungary for at least three reasons. All those achievements which seemed to be expected of the state socialist type of development turned out not to be achieved. First, there were the expectations of reduced inequalities, which were perhaps the main hopes of the system. But we live now with great inequalities and with a steady increase of them in many aspects of our lives; these are a product of the state socialist system. Second, there was a hope for an organic integration of society. That hope also turned out to be false; we experience a deep and dangerous disintegration of our society that can be explained by a number of social facts. I won't speak too much about it here, but the fact has to be stated: there are massive groups who are just drop-outs of society. The manifestation of social disintegration is quite a new, but very marked phenomenon that we can't deny any more. The third aspect where we have lost hope in the social functions of the system, is that it just can't establish a standard of further development for a number of large groups of society. This leads us to the economic crisis which is obvious and much more discussed. What I want to say is that we suffer a general crisis which is rooted very much in the system and in the functioning of the system. Therefore, we have to raise radical questions on the routes out of it. These questions lead us to claim general, radical reforms which are much deeper and much more far-reaching, than just a 'new' relation between the state and the market. These claims lead us to the articulation of a need for new relations between the new state and the emancipated civil society.

Working class interests and economic and social policy reform

Bob Deacon (Britain)

May I open this discussion by raising two points. Firstly let me suggest that a pluralistic model of welfare has been emerging as a possible future for welfare in a number of the East European papers at this conference. This is a model which provides for a mixture of state and market and community and other forms of provision. Is this pluralistic model of welfare and the way it could emerge a way of creating the civil society and its new relationship to the state that John Keane was talking about in the first session and does that have something to offer socialist rethinking about welfare in the West? Alternatively does this version miss what some of the people at this conference would say is the basic point, that this civil society can't be created without a social revolution of the working class against the ruling class of existing state socialist regimes?

Secondly, and connected to this, there has been less discussion, I suspect, than some of us might have liked to have had here on social forces in Eastern Europe. We've heard some of the models of the alternative to state and markets and the way self-managed communities of interests might negotiate with others to provide for welfare. We've heard not so much of the social forces that might lie behind these models, particularly in relation to the reform projects and the push for markets to be part of the future. I think it would be valuable to have a little more discussion about this. Is it the case that the social forces who seem to be resisting the marketization are the unskilled, poorer sections of the working class, who have an interest in maintaining the protection that the state socialist regime provided for them even if it was the low pay, low benefits, low levels of services type of protection? Is it, therefore, being said that a section of the working class in East European countries who have an interest in continuing to be protected by the old regimes are reactionary and are opposed to some progressive movement ushering in marketization and pluralization?

Janos David (Hungary)

I think that what lies behind your first and second questions is the nature of the civil society. We need to ask what kind of autonomous movements or semi-autonomous movements are now legal or half legal and how far they can go in building up a new kind of society. It would be very interesting if we tried at first to be very empirical. We need to show in what form and why, and with what kind of meaning these movements are existing now.

Ivan Svetlik (Yugoslavia)

One question is the role of social science and the role of political movements in changing welfare provision. I think that there has been a shift in our country in terms of this communication between the social science community and the government. The last government proposals contain quite a lot of results and proposals made by social scientists which was not the case before.

This could be understood as a part of the emergence of social movements or political movements which also include other groups like environmentalists, feminists, groups which fight for civil society, for alternative ways of military service and so on and so forth. There are all these groups and they have a very important role in introducing changes and altering the welfare system. I must say they have become, at least in the northern part of Yugoslavia, so strong that politically their demands must be taken into account. I would say this is a process and I see it as a very important one in the discussion about the nature of changes and in discussing possibilities arising from these changes. To answer the question of whether changes should be introduced from above or below, I would say changes are going to be introduced increasingly from below in the sphere of welfare as far as I can see.

I think we can say that the state, however democratically controlled and however organized, is not a sufficient enough instrument or sufficient enough welfare agent (by sufficient I mean economic sufficiency and social sufficiency) to provide for welfare. If you take the economic sufficiency one must take into account a growing bureaucracy which is expensive which tends to grow as an autonomous body and which costs more and more. But also decentralization doesn't help very much because if the logic of the state doesn't change then you would have by decentralizing an increasing number of small centres operating in the same way as the biggest one and tending to increase costs even more. In terms of social efficiency this broad centralized system cannot meet the real needs or original needs the right way and at the right time. It cannot respond to the original needs and if it responds, it responds usually with a time lag because it needs time to be brought into action. Therefore, I think, as far as I'm concerned, there is a logical consequence to look for an alternative and this is, in my opinion, a welfare pluralism or, if you like, a multidimensional welfare system. In this it is my opinion that the state has a very important role but at the same time a very precisely defined role by which I mean that the state must guarantee some universal programmes in order to establish a kind of social integration and to create and carry out some selective programmes in order to establish a minimum of social equality within the society.

Miroslaw Ksiezopolski (Poland)

I think that those changes that have been made up to now are very positive changes. I have mentioned them in my paper (Chapter 4), and they were possible mainly because of Solidarity. But on the other hand, these movements neglect social policy issues in the same way as the government. In my opinion they use social policy issues as a tool, as a political tool to achieve political ends but not to achieve social ends. I think it is very easy to demand better social infrastructure, better wages and so on but used in that way, there is very little thinking about how social policies are to be organized and what would be the design for those social policies. So it's very ambivalent the role of this Solidarity movement. The political goals are much more important for them anyway at this stage in the social change. Concerning your question about low paid workers as an obstacle to the reform, it is true that low paid, low qualified workers will lose a lot. This group of workers is potentially against the economic reforms because, maybe they don't know about it now, but after the reform they have to lose, relatively, in these terms because they have to be paid relatively less than now. The only chance to win their support is to create for them perspectives that their living standards will be improved in real terms but not in relative terms. In relative terms they have to lose. So their position could be very reactionary but it could also be pro-reforms.

Mita Castle (Britain)

I find a central paradox of the East European situation is that very often the defence of egalitarian principles and the defence of the minimum wage or guarantees come from within the conservative Bolsheviks of the state apparatus or the old bureaucracy and that very often reformers try to attack that and therefore by implication, in a way, separate themselves from the ordinary working classes who have to some extent a vested interest in the existing system. In maintaining that egalitarian principle, because that's what they have experienced, that's what really gives them some advantage in the long run. Why should some of the working class go for the uncertainties of the market, why should they go for the differentiations, etc., etc.? This conflict has arisen throughout various reforms in Eastern Europe over a period of time. The classical example of Czechoslovakia is relevant here. The reform sections of the Czech movement were actually attacking, directly attacking the working class as a conservative force. They were actually saying that it is the working class that defends against the reform, that they are really the people who are holding up progress. One has, I think, to step beyond this position because to my mind, not because I'm using Marxist analysis although I think it is important to bring it in, I do believe that it is the ordinary working people that are a much stronger political force in those societies than anybody else and, interestingly enough, they are the ones who can actually hold the state bureaucracy to some account. Bureaucracy cannot go ahead with reforms unless they are actually defending some of the principles of the working class. They are the bureaucracy because of the pledge they've made a long time ago that they are acting on behalf of the working class. They are in a way actually defending the principles. Their legitimacy of power is based on maintaining the egalitarianism. I think the reformers have to come to terms with that and to actually ally themselves with the working population or make that kind of alliance rather than keeping their distances, which has been the case, to my mind, up until now.

Lena Kolarska-Bobinska (Poland)

I just want to say that there is no interest of the working class as a whole. This is why I make this differentiation between the qualified and the unqualified. Other research introduces these different lines of division. What I am saying is that in Poland a qualified part of the working class in the big cities and big industry are in favour of greater wage differentiation. The reformers do have alliances with this part of the workers' councils. These workers' councils are the active ones. The ones formed in the big industries. We consider them as the only real defenders of the reforms. I am saying that it's not true that the reformers are a group of people who just act in a completely abstract way.

The economic reforms help the qualified worker today. They're secure in their jobs, they have high qualifications, they have experience of solidarity among themselves, they have a lot of things, and they are the best earners. Remember they are the most wealthy group in the population. They are very highly qualified workers so their interest is in the reform to earn more, I would say.

Tom Hickey (Britain)

I can't say that I'm in favour of change that unquestionably is going to speed up unemployment, lower wages, further differentiation of the working class, increase income differentials. I think every socialist should be opposed to those and perceive perestroika not as the way of changing society and undermining totalitarianism but as a way of actually defending the interests of the ruling class in a country that has to undergo industrial and economic restructuring just in the same way as is being done in the West.

Mita Castle (Britain)

At the moment, so it seems, heavy industry is putting a stop to any new developments. I mean the heavy industry economy is not in the interests of the bureaucracy, nor is it in the interests of anybody else in the society. It is no longer capable of producing results. It's come to a standstill. It's not in the interests of the bureaucracy because it doesn't give them the opportunity to say, well we have achieved or we have not achieved our plans. It is at a standstill. Nor is it capable of producing consumer goods which would be capable of resolving social unrest. So I think the process of dismantling the heavy industry economy is at the root of social reform and the whole discussion is about where the welfare state is going or where social reform is going or which are the social forces which are actually joining together. I do actually believe that it is the working class that holds the balance of power. The dismantling of the heavy economy at the moment will inevitably have repercussions on the living standards of the working class and it is at that point that some sort of new alliances should be made.

Paul Adams (USA)

I think the world economy is absolutely crucial here. I think we can see this most clearly in the case of Poland. It's not simply a matter that the bureaucracy is concerned with its own legitimacy and its own privileges although I think that is very important. It is also the fact that the Polish economy is thoroughly integrated into the world economy which means that its rulers, whatever their subjective wishes, have to act as the agents of accumulation in the national economy. That's why they have to act as capitalists and therefore why we as Marxists have to oppose them in just the same way we oppose Thatcher in this country.

Women's interests and 'socialist' social policy

Hilary Rose (Britain)

I have been asked to speak a little about the international gender division of labour but I think to do that I have to begin at the beginning which is to say that the old welfare state, certainly as it was conceived of in the West and my remarks will particularly bear on that situation, were achieved by a compromise by two forces and that was capital and male-organized labour. And it was agreed that in return for social peace capital would be allowed to get about its business and that the trade unions and civil society, as that group reflects civil society, would benefit; but that the chief beneficiaries, prime beneficiaries, of the welfare state would be men. Women would only benefit insofar as they had relationships with men, that is they benefited insofar as they were the wives and the daughters of men. Therefore, the old welfare state was set up in a peculiarly nationally-bounded way based on these particular compromises with first class working class citizens and very much as second class (we can argue about whether they were working class or not) their wives.

All of that debate took place, and those conclusions took place, very much within a national economy. It had relationships to other parts of the world and indeed, Britain, my own country above all, had very important relationships created through its imperial past. As a consequence, we saw a sort of second wave of people coming to Britain as the economic boom developed and there was this bringing in of people to the labour sites. Now what's happened in the world is something radically different and it has to alter absolutely dramatically the thinking about the future of welfare and it is this which I think this debate, our discussion, has not yet paid sufficient attention to. That change is that as the pattern of industry itself has moved, the people now are no longer able to move in any simple way. Cotton for example, having been stolen from India to Manchester has now gone back to other Asian parts of the world and so cotton has moved around in its production and that's made an enormous difference to the possibilities of welfare. I think we have to see that in Britain there are very serious problems about the future of employment and that unless those who have employment develop very different attitudes about the number of hours they need to work, then there is really only an exceedingly bleak future for the great majority of the population in Britain. The people who are most likely to be excluded from any share in the welfare future are, of course, women and black people and these are debarred by what we understand as sexism and racism. I don't think that our discussion has sufficiently addressed itself to what is happening at a global level and increasingly we are a global economy. I don't think we've addressed ourselves sufficiently to the very limited utility of the nation state. I find it embarrassing to quote Daniel Bell but I will do so and that is that for all practical purposes the concept of nation is either too big or too small. For a whole lot of purposes we need to use aggregates that are smaller than the nation state because they're more useful, and for other purposes the category of nation state is simply too small. We must talk in terms of Europe, Asia, Africa. I'm really sort of grumbling a bit and saying, what about thinking about the rise of the new social movements? Is feminism truly represented in the papers? I find it's not very much. There are feminist papers but the men's papers seem to be remarkably ungendered with one or two glorious exceptions. There is very little discussion of environmentalism as a new social movement which radically must change our thinking about social policy. There's very little account of the rise of black people either within their own countries driving national liberation movements nor is there very much account of black people and other disadvantaged groups within British or East European society. I start off, I hope controversially, by having a good grumble.

Zsuzsa Ferge (Hungary)

We ended the last session by talking about political movements and the fact that you can read the history of East European societies as a struggle for citizenship against an overwhelming totalitarian state. If this is a context I shall make three points. The first is – why could we not have feminism in those countries? The answer, I think, is very simple. It's just because a movement of this type will prefigure what civil society is about, citizenship is about, political rights are about and that very centralized politics of course do not allow this type of movement to happen or to be created. This is not a complete answer because we could not have a number of things which we actually did have. We didn't have feminism also, and this is my second point, because feminism in the West really developed an agenda around the issues of the personal as political. But this is adverse to everything which is attractive in East European societies. The reality and the danger is that the private becomes political too often and always. Private life we had and we really would try to stick to it and to enlarge it and not let the political into the private. We have an over-politicized life so we want to defend it. Thirdly, shall we have feminism or shall we not have it in the future? I have shown in another paper (referred to in Chapter 12) that the situation of women in Hungary, which at first was really improved through work and other means, was not really solved because as usual some of the original goals of socialism have been formally obtained but not genuinely. Surface results covered the deep problems and what I am suggesting is that we need mobilization as citizens. We should have rights and I thought in this paper that the issue, the inequality of gender, inequality between the genders, the domination of women which was persisting both in private life and in public life, those are issues which should be addressed by this *citizens'* movement. I concluded by saying that whether you will call this movement feminist or not and I think not, because of all the connotations of feminism I have mentioned, this movement, as with all movements which try to articulate particular needs and particular interests, should have a place and I would say will have a place in Hungary in the future.

Mary Buckley (Britain)

I don't actually have anything more to say about women and perestroika other than what I write in my paper (Chapter 15) so what I thought I'd briefly do is just introduce to those who weren't there when I read my paper how we ended that session on socialism and women's interests and discuss the issue of how we in the West can best understand women in Eastern Europe. The question was put 'how can we do this from Western Europe?' and our response, and I think we can speak for you here too, was that firstly, we have to learn the language, secondly, we have to go there, thirdly, we have to read the primary sources and not rely on the secondary sources because they are often misinformed or incorrect. Now this, of course, poses lots of problems which I'll come to in a minute, but this seemed to be **a** starting point for understanding. Also we assume that this works the other way round. If people in Eastern Europe want to understand Great Britain they must really come here and see and read and talk to people. This was the starting point. Once there, of course, there are further problems. Problems of discourse, because we work with certain concepts and these concepts don't always go down well or aren't interpreted in the same way as we use them. Feminism, of course, is such a concept. This morning Chris said she had to drop it when in Hungary because it doesn't help dialogue and this touches a range, I think, of issues that somehow are hurdles to discourse. These include not just feminism but the idea of femininity. This particular concept is differently placed in different contexts and the notion of psycho-physiological characteristics of the sexes is ingrained in some East European literature and we really don't see things in quite the same way. The promotion of motherhood there being a duty to the state has its impact. It is not seen here as a duty to the state in quite the same way. The notion of women's organization is slightly different in the Soviet Union; the newly revived movements are helpers of the party. To a certain extent they take cues from above which isn't to say they don't have the space for initiative but again it's a different form of organization. Of course also, the notion of the personal is political is differently placed and we need to be sensitive to this. Having got this far there are problems because do we then end up with some sort of cultural relativism? In order to understand do we have in a sense to go as native as possible? But if we do that, how do we analyse the data? After all, we are in the business of collecting information, sitting back from it and then analysing it. So, the question becomes what do we do with this? My own response to that is that we should do things that are manageable. Now this isn't a plea for no theory because, I think, we do need the theory but at the same time we can really go overboard on the theory. For example, and this may be provocative for some, the concept of class struggle I found in our discussion yesterday was so frustrating because it really doesn't help me in the work I do. I suppose I plead for middle range theory and in manageable goals such as asking questions like 'how can we compare the implications of policies under Thatcher with the implications of policies under Gorbachev?' To answer this we have to talk to people, read the press and see what's happening. Now, these are, I suppose, quite small projects but, I think, until we can do these it's hard to rejuvenate theory which we also need to do as well.

Maxine Molyneux (Britain)

The socialist states then have not been immune from these trends concerning women's issues but for various reasons they've not been the focus; these various negative aspects of women's position have not been the focus as we've discussed before of political mobilization by women. Female collective action and resistance in these societies is restricted and is diffused in a variety of different ways including the establishment of officially endorsed women's organizations which operate on very narrow definitions of women's interests and a variety of other political constraints that operate against independent action. Yet, as we heard this morning, women's issues are being taken up in these countries and that is a new thing; it's been happening in Cuba, it's been happening certainly in Nicaragua, it's happening, as Mary Buckley has said, in the USSR and in Hungary. In a variety of different sites feminist issues have been raised and feminist critiques of various kinds are being made available. It has been very difficult for their regimes to ignore these various, as it were, feminist critiques – they're not movements but questionings if you like – of the social structure. They've been difficult to ignore, I think, for four reasons. The reason socialist states have had to listen a little bit more are first of all that the internationalization of feminism as a social movement has meant that socialist policy-makers, those academics and individuals who've had to travel around in the UN decade for women, went to international conferences, talked to various people and women from a variety of countries, not just from the West but from the South as well, who were involved in feminist practice so that feminist critiques began to be heard this way. It was possible for a Hungarian to listen to a Cuban feminist perhaps rather than to a North American feminist. There was a dialogue that went on in that decade. For all its limitations there was an internationalization of the debates about women's position. Secondly, the intensification of social contradictions in those countries has put feminist issues on the agenda and governments have their own interest in trying to address them. Thirdly, of course, sociological research has shown quite plainly what is happening to women in those societies and the findings are not good. Finally, there is a sense of growing female discontent. It may always have been there but what we are learning about is that it does actually exist in documented form.

So for those reasons it's very easy to see why these governments are having at least to listen to some of the arguments coming from a broadly-defined feminist position but what impact can this feminist approach or these feminist strands of feminist discourse and critique have on policy? The answer, at least it seems to me, and it seems to quite a few people here, I think, is probably very little; although there is some room for manoeuvre as has been discussed earlier today. There will be some if it coincides with government priorities. Certain measures will have to be taken but there are still a number of obstacles to any fuller realization of demands of the kind that would actually make women's lives easier. It would take a real move to establish much more egalitarian relations between the sexes in the longer term. One of these obstacles is clearly organizational, the absence of any independent feminist movement. Secondly, something that came up this morning in this very important area, the absence of any theoretical debate of women within society and the economy generally, let alone politics. It's also true, incidentally, of socialist feminism in the West, which tends to abdicate any discussion of a theoretical kind about women in socialist states. Thirdly, there is again this problem of the resistance and hostility to feminism, a kind of anti-feminism within national cultures and there are lots of reasons for that which I don't want to go into now. Nonetheless one could pose the question in a slightly different way – what is the threat that feminism is seen to represent? Perhaps more than distaste for women's centred approaches and theory is what feminist politics actually represents and what feminist academic work represents or what a feminist position represents in general. A brief listing of these, I think, shows how dissonant its characters appear in the eyes of more orthodox commentators from the socialist bloc. I will finish then by saying something about perhaps what feminism is; why feminism is seen as something of a threat; the sorts of things that have come up in discussions with socialist policy-makers have led me to think that these are, at least, some of the elements which might explain it – it's not an exhaustive list.

First of all it's clear that feminism does represent a critique of existing social relations and practices but it also interrogates the natural and the normal, something which is incorporated as an explanation or justification of quite a lot of social policies concerning women in the socialist states. I include here the structure and division of labour, which is not interrogated in any serious way in socialist countries and specific family forms and cultural practices around domesticity. Secondly, feminism does have a vision of the alternative form of living which can be described as the humanization of social relations, something which has not been on the agenda or discussed in any sufficient way within the context of socialist countries and is often regarded as too difficult a subject. It's not the right moment, there isn't the money for it, it's a luxury. Thirdly, feminism does attempt to provide some kind of holistic analysis of the situation of women which does give a place to issues like sexuality which has been seen as marginal in conventional approaches to the analysis of social relations. Sexuality is regarded as an important area of discussion and research in feminism and yet in many socialist countries it is regarded as a taboo subject and is not yet regarded as serious and it is not consequently considered important. One of the things to illustrate this point is that sexual violence or rather wife battering in Nicaragua has been very extensive and one of the reasons for this, following some investigations, is that women withdraw sexuality, they don't allow their husbands sexual access as a form of contraception because there is no wide availability of contraception. Contraceptives and abortion are illegal. There is a link in these factors once you open a question up. Fourthly, feminism represents a different methodological approach and it is not exclusive to feminism. Different methodologies can be tried and tested and many of them attempt to get away from positivism and deploy different techniques. Feminism is associated with a different kind of approach which does involve a focus on women and different methodologies to uncover women's interests and beliefs. Fifthly, feminism is associated with a different conception of politics. It's not exactly the point about politicizing daily life or taking politics into the home but actually making clear that within the home there are already politically constituted relations; there are already relations of authority and hierarchy, privilege and of subordination. Feminism is not about, as it were, taking the state into the home but rather removing those kinds of practices or challenging those kind of practices more effectively. And finally, following from that point, feminism does, in common with other strands of social science and theory, actually believe that authority is not just something that emanates from the state but is present in a variety of different sites within the social formation and, therefore, the discussion about how to emancipate any oppressed group must take into account the multiplicity of forms of oppression and materialization of authority relations. I don't want to go on. I've finished really. What I wanted to say was really that in the context of the socialist states feminism, you can see, represents rather a radical and to some minds inappropriate social movement. It does challenge, quite radically, government priorities but at the same time it's clear that, without any kind of a feminist input into existing policies or any debate around crucial issues, women's strategic interests will continue to be displaced and inequality, I think, will probably continue to grow. Any influence feminism might have of a much more direct kind will depend crucially on access to state power and to some degree of popular support or mobilization around feminist issues. Since neither of these is the likely prospect in any of the socialist states at the present time again any improvement in women's socioeconomic position is likely to be rather slow in coming. I'm sorry to end on a pessimistic note but if there are other trends which might contradict that perhaps we could talk about them.

Miroslaw Ksiezopolski (Poland)

I think there is no place for feminism in Poland. The first problem which a woman faces is just to run the house. They have no free time for political movements like feminism. We are all deprived, so the first, the primary movement is to change our situation for both women and men and afterwards, maybe I'm not sure, these feminist issues can arise.

Aldona Fracziewick-Wronka (Poland)

I'm from Poland. I live in Poland. I think that I am able to give my opinion about the feminist movement. I want to say that I completely agree with my colleague [Miroslaw]. I never see my position as a woman in the Polish social stratification as a bad position. I only feel myself to be in the same role and in the same position as men. I'm quite satisfied that I live in Poland and I feel very good as a woman. But I would be in a bad position, really bad position if I were a man.

Zdravka Toneva (Bulgaria)

I have one question for all of the panel. If the social situation of women is so hard, if the work life of the women is longer, why then are men's lives much shorter? This is not only a biological but a social problem.

PART B
HUNGARY AND POLAND:
Economic and political reform and the space for an independent social policy

3 Is social policy a problem in a socialist country?
The case of Poland

MIROSLAW KSIEZOPOLSKI

One can imagine that a socialist country has better possibilities to carry out social policy than other countries; the term social policy seems to be so obviously connected with the notion of socialism that during a certain period in the postwar history of Poland the need of social policy was denied in general, mainly because all policies of the state were treated as social policies and it is still very difficult to make a sharp distinction between what constitutes social policy and what constitutes other state policies.

In his introduction to social policy R. M. Titmuss (1974) has distinguished three models of social policy: residual, achievement–performance and institutional. These models are mainly used with reference to capitalist countries but it could be interesting to identify the most important structural features of contemporary social policy in Poland and compare it with the premises of these three models. One can expect that social policy in a socialist country would have a lot of features in common with the institutional model and nothing to do with the residual one.

In Poland social policy is distinguished in a narrow and in a broad sense. The first one is understood as activities concerned mainly with the satisfaction of basic needs of the population and with compensation for the negative consequences of the economic development. The second one designates activities connected with planned changes of social structure and planned formation of the living conditions in order to eliminate the deep causes of social problems and to achieve social progress. Social policy in a narrow sense is considered to be appropriate to capitalist countries; the second broad sense seems to be naturally characteristic of a socialist country.

In this chapter I would like to consider what social policy has been carried out in our country up to the 1980s and what are the alternative possibilities for its future in the coming years. I would try to find out which model of social policy has been developed in Poland and what functions it has performed. So the central question of this chapter will be what are the possibilities of implementing such a broad or an institutional social policy in a socialist country like Poland?

Polish social policy up to the 1980s

After the Second World War deep changes in the political, social and economic systems were introduced in Poland. Land reform, nationalization of the means of production and the banks created a solid foundation of solving the main social problems and it became possible to set the course for socioeconomic development in the desired direction.

From the end of the 1940s opinions emerged that social policy had become useless in the new socioeconomic system. There were several reasons to declare the end of social policy. Firstly, the notion 'social policy' had very negative ideological connotations in the minds of the new leadership. Another reason was based on the naive conviction that all social problems could be solved very easily, almost automatically, by general transformations of the socioeconomic system. One expected that the planned development of the economy combined with the right to work for everybody and with new 'revolutionary' working-class consciousness, would eliminate all forms of deprivation and all aspects of social pathology. One also believed in efficiency of single ad hoc actions which could solve certain social problems once and for all. The third argument referred to the difficulties in distinguishing between an 'autonomous' social policy and other state policies. In a socialist country all traditional goals of social policy became the most important objectives of the whole state policy, so the separation of social policy from other state activities seemed impossible and unnecessary.

As a result of that argumentation social policy was declared superfluous in a socialist country like Poland. It coincided with the beginning of the period of forced industrialization. Almost all available material and human sources were invested in heavy industry at the cost of all other sectors of the economy and at the cost of the standard of living of the population. Social benefits were treated as an element of production. The right to benefit was inseparably connected with work and all outside the socialized sectors of the economy were denied such a right.

The 'come-back' of social policy took place in the middle of the 1950s. As it turned out social problems had not disappeared. Significant growth of industrial output and elimination of unemployment were not sufficient to restrain people's discontent with the declining living standard and the underdevelopment of the social sphere. Policy-makers had to realize that although the revolution has created new unique possibilities to solve social problems, still general reforms have not guaranteed any automatic solutions to these problems, and that economic growth has not been sufficient to achieve adequate social progress.

This understanding has led to the almost uninterrupted expansion of social policy. The share of social expenditure in the national product increased up to a maximum of about 25% in 1982 from 17.6% in 1979 and 22.7% in 1986. The scope of social benefits has been widened greatly. Benefits and services have been opened to all with few exceptions. In general one may say that a quite well-developed system of social services and social benefits has been established. It conforms in principle to the norms and standards set by ILO's conventions and by various international pacts. The extension of coverage and the amount of benefits is on an average European level. However, taking into account the relatively lower level of GNP per capita, Poland allocates more resources to social policy than has been done by the leading capitalist countries at a similar degree of economic development.

Unfortunately, the almost constant development of social benefits and services has not been accompanied by an adequate rise in the 'prestige' of social policy among other state policies. The development of industry has always had the priority and the social sphere usually obtained what had been left after satisfying needs of the productive sector. Despite many real achievements social policy has failed to go too far beyond a framework of purely social activity; temporary goals have prevailed and social policy could not be liberated from the circle of fragmentary interventionist activities. I would call it an ad hoc social policy, characterized by the absence of a complex approach, undertaking fragmentary, incoherent and casual actions, with variations of the level of benefits due to the lack of revalorization or index-linking mechanisms. What is more important, there has never been any clear vision of the desired model of social policy, of the meaning of the so-called 'social function' of a socialist state or of the mutual relations between social policy and economy.

Characteristic features of the Polish social policy

According to Titmuss the Residual and the Industrial Achievement–Performance models of social policy are based on the premise of market sovereignty. In both models social needs are to be met on the basis of merit and work performance. The role played by state social policy is very limited; it should be targeted towards helping only those individuals which are incapable of meeting their needs properly either through the private market or through the family. The institutional model of social policy holds that the right to a decent standard of living should be separated from work performance and that social policy has to secure the satisfaction of the basic wants of each citizen, providing universalist benefits and services outside the market on the principle of need.

In the following I shall review the degree of development of the Polish social policy by examining three key variables: (a) the principles of distribution, (b) the role of the state, and (c) the degree of solidarity.

The principles of distribution

The distinction between work performance and need as a condition for welfare seems to be quite simple in theory and very unclear in practice. One assumes that during a transitory period on the way to communism, i.e. in a socialist society, the leading principle of distribution should be 'to each according to work', and only after the establishment of the communism, the other principle 'from each according to work, to each according to need' would take precedence. It was obvious already that in the transitory period some kind of public funds would have to be created to serve common purposes. According to Marx those funds should be assigned for satisfying common needs like education, health care etc. or the needs of people unable to work. Marx was convinced that from the very beginning the common funds would constitute the greater part of a national product than in the present (capitalist) society and that they would increase as the new society developed. However, neither the range of human needs to be satisfied by social policy, nor the criteria of eligibility for access to the common funds have ever been clear in practice.

In the Constitution of Poland the following social rights have been set forth: right to work, to education, to health care and to help in case of disease or disability to work, to care for mother and children and right to rest. Only the right to work and to education are unconditional; all other rights are dependent on participation in work. After the war Poland has continued to build its social security system on the foundations of the classical insurance model which assumes that the right to benefits and their amount depends on employment and (or) previous contributions. Except for the right to free education most other benefits are earnings- and work-related. Universal flat rate benefits granted upon citizenship have been virtually unknown, with few minor exceptions.

Since there is no unemployment and since the right to work is inseparably connected with the obligation to work (more moral than legal because work is not compulsory), it is assumed that in a socialist society each citizen is able and ought to support himself with earned income. Hence the very low status of the clients of social assistance. During the first half of the 1950s those outside work were in general denied the right to help. Nowadays social assistance is devoted almost exclusively to help individuals unable to lead an independent life, mainly those in old age and disabled people.

The strict connections between social rights and duties, between work performance and level of satisfaction of individual needs conform with the basic principles of the Achievement–Performance model. On the other hand, however, Polish social policy always has little to do with the traditional self-reliance ideology. It may sound illogical but the pressure to increase individual performance has been connected with quite successful efforts to deprive the same individuals of the responsibility for their security and welfare. It was mainly possible due to the central regulation of wages. During the whole postwar period wages were intentionally kept on a low level. Wage policy assured a decent livelihoood to every employee but made it very difficult to reach a much higher standard of living by an increase of individual work performance.

At the same time low wages left practically no room for individual initiative to contract one's own welfare; it was assumed that the money withheld from the wage fund would finance the social security system and would enable many basic goods and services to be offered free or at a very reduced price to all citizens. This assumption (or promise) has been only partly fulfilled – low wages have first of all made it possible to keep the share of accumulation in the national product on a relatively high level.

Simultaneously the relations between work and 'social wage' have been partly blurred. Although the access to benefits and services has had to be earned, the 'social wage' has been considered primarily to be a gift from the socialist state rather than a citizen's right. So it is the state which ought to be praised for its benevolence, and consequently the state, not the people, is responsible for satisfying the constantly growing number of needs.

The relatively high importance of the 'social wage' in the total consumption of the population could serve as a good argument for the institutional character of Polish social policy. It is far from clear, however, to what extent need has constituted the main principle of distribution of the 'social wage' or to what degree on the other hand that distribution was based on the principles of work performance, achievement and merit. We know, for example, that prices below cost have a social foundation only to some extent, and in many cases subsidies contribute to further inequalities through unequal access to different goods and services. They also to a high degree cover the costs of low performance of both the institutions of social infrastructure and the economy.

The role of the state

In the marginal model the range of human needs that are satisfied by social policy is strictly limited and the primary responsibility for satisfying those needs lies on the individual and on the family. Normally the state would interfere only when individuals are incapable of self-help. The institutional model is based on the premise that the society is primarily responsible for the welfare of the individual, so it's impossible to fix any boundaries for public social commitments.

Common responsibility for the welfare of the citizens has been one of the most fundamental values of socialism and a possibility to 'socialize' a process of meeting basic human needs has always been considered as one of the main advantages of the new system. In such circumstances the institutionalization of social policy seemed to be inevitable. This did indeed happen to excess. The state dominated the process of meeting all major social needs, at the same time depriving people of the responsibility for their welfare. The state was considered to be almost 'omnipotent'; all other subjects were to play only supplementary roles. They mostly did what the state had commissioned them to do; individual or group initiatives were limited either by the lack of resources or by a necessity to have state approval or permission to act, which was very difficult to get. Gradually most people got accustomed to the fact that they had the right to obtain help from the state and the following relationship – the state as a provider of all benefits and services and the people as recipients deprived of any real influence on the shape and quality of benefits – became dominant in social consciousness.

The state monopoly in the social sphere, however, turned out to be more formal than real in many aspects. Firstly, in many cases a family is still held responsible for the satisfaction of basic needs of its members. Secondly, as it turned out, the state was unable to fulfil its duties to the full both as an employer and as a disposer of social wage. Though it has succeeded in maintaining full employment still it has not been enough to secure a satisfactory level of living. The low wage level made it difficult to base individual wages on the principle of 'a fair day's work for a fair day's wage'. In most cases there is no visible connection between the productivity of a single worker and the wage he receives. In many of the cases part of the wage fulfils the function of social benefit rather than the means of a reward for achieved work. So, quite contrary to the original intentions, the right to work has been changed into the right to wage – low, but certain. The wages have got the character of an universal social benefit, something like basic social income or social dividend for all employed in the socialized sectors of economy.

For the majority of the employed the level of living safeguarded by such a wage is unacceptable, hence individual welfare depends often not so much on official earnings from ordinary work but rather on many different additional sources of income. The centrally planned economy has its own, specific free market and its own competition for privileges, fringe benefits, access to scarce goods and services etc. This second or third division of the national product is based on very unclear, discretionary principles; in many cases individual or group standards of living depend more on meritocratic selection than on work performance.

On the other hand, despite a significant development in the social sphere the state has failed to reach a satisfactory level in meeting many major needs. It has forced people to seek other ways to increase the degree of satisfaction of their needs. Reinforcement of family role in meeting these needs was one of the answers. Another was mutual aid. The third one was quasi-privatization of some of the social services. The costs of all such services are covered entirely by the clients. There is no private or public insurance against these costs.

The degree of solidarity – universalism versus selectivity

The marginal social policy tends to be targeted towards the truly needy, hence means-tested benefits predominate and other social programmes are usually organized around occupational groups, mirroring their social status. The institutional social policy prefers universal type of progammes treating uniformly the entire population. Broad solidarity replaces group interests, and a society takes over from an individual the responsibility for financing social programmes.

According to the Polish constitution social rights are granted to every citizen. It's accompanied, however, with the more or less explicitly stated assumption that social programmes would be organized to suit first of all the needs of 'working people' and their families. In principle it was tantamount to an almost universal system of benefits and services, since according to common belief in a socialist society, owing to full employment, there would be no place for 'non-working people'. The interpretation of who belongs to the 'working people' has substantially changed over time. Nowadays the system of benefits covers almost the entire population. The social security system, however, still favours employees in the socialized sectors.

Some important features of residualism have, nevertheless, been preserved. Firstly, those who are not working or have not worked sufficiently long have to rely on their families or on social welfare. As recipients of public assistance they are still being given a stigmatized status. Secondly, many benefits and services are still means-tested and they are granted only to people having incomes below a certain, sometimes very low, level. In recent years, due to the economic crisis, the selectivity of some programmes has been substantially strengthened.

As one can see it's very difficult to classify the Polish model of social policy. Structurally it has many features of both: institutional and achievement–performance models. The strong public sector and the state as a provider of all benefits and services on the one side, and the strict (although sometimes only formal), ties between rights and duties, work performance and individual welfare and relative importance of selective measures on the other side. The state has been able to secure a minimum or a decent standard of living to practically all citizens, but it has failed to achieve the expected and promised level in meeting many major needs. On the one hand the institutionalization of social policy resulted in people being deprived of the responsibility for their welfare, on the other hand the same people were forced to compete with others in order to maintain or to improve their living standard. Consequently a quite unexpected welfare-mix has emerged: the almost 'omnipotent' state exercising formally full control over the conditions of living of the population, and individuals and families with limited possibilities of activity but still substantially dependent on the 'socialist market' force, in meeting their needs.

The prospects of social policy development for the coming years

Since the late 1970s Poland is undergoing a deep economic, political and social crisis. Contrary to the typical crisis in the capitalist countries, the Polish one is not a crisis of over production, it's a crisis of scarcity: scarcity of foodstuffs, manufactured goods, flats, social services and on the other hand scarcity of democracy, motivation for work etc. There is no unemployment but Poland has problems with excessive employment in some sectors of the economy, with the disappearance of an ethos of work, low labour performance or low quality of work.

The crisis puts social policy issues on the agenda with a renewed strength. There is a common feeling concerning the necessity for changing the priorities for further development of this policy, but there is no agreement as to which priorities should take precedence. Before the 1980s there was no debate in Poland about limitation of the social activity of the state. The state responsibility for the welfare and security of the citizens was taken for granted. The economic crisis has changed this situation. The allegation that Poland has become an over-protective state has been given currency by some policy-makers, economists and journalists. The main argument against the present system is that it essentially hampers the process of getting out of the crisis and the introduction of economic reform.

That allegation is strongly denied by Polish social politicians who are trying to prove that in fact the state is not protective enough rather than vice versa. Both the first and the second views have had strong impact on the social policy carried on in the 1980s. One could distinguish some characteristic features of this policy in the last few years, which might be helpful to predict further development.

Firstly, the efforts to restore a visible connection between the productivity of labour of a single worker and the wages he receives have only been partly successful. The wages still fulfil a function of social benefit; strong pressure from the employed have forced policy-makers to accept an increase in wages to compensate for high inflation and there has been not much money left to differentiate earnings according to labour performance.

Secondly, the attempts to limit the protective functions of the state have met very strong opposition from the employed and trade unions and have finally failed. Policy-makers have learned to be very cautious in proposing cuts of social expenditures or in openly taking away social benefits from the people. Social policy, however, somewhat unnoticed by the public opinion, has acquired a more selective character. The provided measures have been concentrated on the protection of the standard of living of the truly needy and the real value of aid to other groups has decreased. This applies also to the expenditures for social services and social infrastructure.

Thirdly, though the pragmatic need of action in crisis superseded clear demands for long-term solutions, still it was possible to introduce some very progressive, systemic measures. The most important of them was automatic revalorization (index-linking) of pensions, introduced in 1986. Simultaneously the amount of an increasing number of benefits is determined in this way. The process to develop a mechanism which could effectively protect beneficiaries from inflation has only begun and still many benefits are not indexed at all.

Fourthly, the unconditional right to a decent standard of living for all citizens, so well-known from the institutional model, is becoming more and more clearly defined and accepted to an increasing degree both by the policy-makers and the people. In the 1980s there has begun regular research on the so-called social minimum level (i.e. poverty level). Gradually, although with many difficulties and reservations, the social minimum level has been taken into account in determining minimum wages, minimum pensions and the amount of other benefits.

The last feature I would like to mention is a beginning of demonopolization of social policy. In the beginning of the 1980s many different social initiatives emerged, as a matter of fact in all spheres of people's activity. These initiatives proved that people want and can take over from the state part of the responsibility for their own welfare. In the following years people's activity in these areas diminished and again it become more controlled, directed and less spontaneous. Recently, however, the policy-makers seem to be more and more aware that the state alone is unable to meet people's needs on a satisfactory level and that better utilization of the existing potential of voluntary activity, including also the charity activity of the Catholic Church, is indispensable. The informal blockade of possibilities of voluntary action outside the official system is becoming less tight, which in the most recent two or three years is resulting in the creation of many new initiatives in voluntary and self-help activities both in the frame of existing institutions as well as outside them.

At the beginning of the 1980s it seemed that social policy in Poland had entered a decisive period of its development. From the above mentioned remarks it's clear that indeed some important changes took place but social policy has retained a narrowly social, passive character. In the year 1988 Poland has begun the so-called second stage of the economic reform. The reform implies deep marketization of the economy – compulsory methods in the management of the economy are to be rejected, firms are to be changed into independent, self-financed and self-governed organizations. At the same time price subsidies have to be greatly reduced and social services are going to be 'economized'.

The programme of the reform is not accompanied by a clear and comprehensive conception of social policy. We only know that policy-makers want to limit state responsibility in the social sphere (less subsidies, some commercialization of public services) and that social protection of the weakest groups in society would be strengthened. It's obvious that a marketization of economy must naturally be in conflict with many social goals, but the nature of that conflict and its possible social implications seem to have marginal importance for the authors of the reform. Once again material growth and economic efficiency are becoming the ultimate goals of state policy and once again economic growth has to secure an automatic solution of all social problems.

It's relatively easy to predict the future development of social policy if the economic reforms are implemented in accordance with the above depicted features. Firstly, social policy will retain its marginal position and in case of conflict economic reasons would have precedence. All available sources will be allocated to the development of industry and social expenditures will still be treated as a burden to the economy.

Secondly, in all probability social inequalities will sharply increase, individual competition will undermine solidarity and the level of social security will diminish. The concentration of social policy on selective measures will be paralleled by a decreasing importance of universal benefits and services. It's uncertain to what extent diminishing consumption from common funds and less security could be compensated by an increase in private consumption. One can expect further 'privatization' of social services that, in connection with increased selectivity of social policy, will reinforce the divisions in society generated by the new market. The individualization of the struggle for survival is already clearly visible; at present such a struggle doesn't contribute too much to an increase in common welfare, it's rather a new division of the national product, the division which has little to do with work performance.

Thirdly, in the programme of reform, irrespective of quite opposite declarations, the welfare and security of an individual appears not as an ultimate goal but rather as an unknown outcome of the economic game. People are again becoming an object of economic and social policy measures, and not the author and subject.

Is there any alternative to this rather gloomy perspective? In the recent prognosis of the Polish Academy of Science a more optimistic scenario was outlined. Its authors, expressing the opinion of a majority of social politicians, have proposed to diametrically change the priorities for further development of the economy. One has to shift the priority from heavy industry onto those branches which directly satisfy people's basic needs. Needs and consumption should constitute the starting point for all economic planning and not production for production's sake. Only in such a scenario could social policy acquire a proper position among other state policies and only by such a change of priorities would it be possible to subordinate economic growth to the achievement of social progress.

Already at first sight it is obvious that this scenario creates real possibilities to carry on on a broad, progress-orientated and institutional social policy. There are some reasons to think so. Firstly, the starting point will be the needs of all citizens which would favour a more universalistic, long-term and complex approach. Selective and temporary measures might well recede into the background.

Secondly, the individual and his needs would become the ultimate goal of both economic and social policy. It would therefore be easier to find solutions aiming simultaneously at economic and social progress. It also creates better possibilities for the people to regain a subjective role in the creation and in the realization of social policy.

Thirdly, at last social policy could cease to be treated as a burden to the economy and policy-makers could treat social expenditures as investments to accomplish socioeconomic goals. In that way social policy could become an important factor of economic growth, and not one of its obstacles.

The last and most important point is that the possible 'materialization' of the above depicted scenario would be impossible without strong will and support from both policy-makers and society. This scenario doesn't assume the preservation of the present status quo. Deep economic reform is absolutely necessary, as well as the restoration of a clear connection between productivity of labour and standard of living. It is also indispensable to demonopolize state social policy which implies, among other things, an increase in the responsibility of many other subjects. All these cannot be done without conflict. There certainly would be losers and all people would have to find their own place in the new socioeconomic conditions. It seems obvious that such a fundamental change of the economy, particularly in a heavily indebted country like Poland, is impossible without a decrease in the standard of living of the population. Poles are not eager to accept any reduction of their welfare and in recent years we have observed how people with great determination have tried to defend and maintain their level of living. Hence the legitimation of the reforms and the willingness to carry the burdens of change would be feasible only when the shape of these reforms would be an outcome of a democratic decision-making process.

This is where I see a great chance for changing the priorities for further development of social policy. The reform, in a form corresponding to the above scenario, opens new possibilities for social activity, but on the other hand such a reform also depends on there being a broad, progress-orientated and 'socialized' social policy. An individual, a family or a social group must become a subject with full rights, and not only or mainly objects of social policy measures. It is the only way to win people's acceptance and support for the proposed reforms. It is also the best way to direct social policy towards awakening a feeling of affiliation with a community, towards promoting mutual aid or social motivations. The 'socialization' of social policy and the creation of conditions enabling people to manage to a greater degree by themselves, in cooperation with the family, other citizens or social organizations, does not imply a release of the state from the primary responsibility for the welfare and security of the citizens. It means only a new division of duties between the state and other subjects. In such a scenario there are no reasons to give up an achievement of basic socialist values like equality, social justice or solidarity. However, one has to clearly define what do these values really mean in the present state of socioeconomic development. And of course it would be naive to think that the co-existence between these values and the market-oriented economy would be easy to establish.

Bibliography

Titmuss, R. (1974), *Social policy. An Introduction,* London.

4 Socialist welfare state in transition: the state, the market and the enterprise in Poland

LENA KOLARSKA-BOBINSKA

A basic feature typical of real socialism is the strong interrelation between the economic, the political and the welfare function of the state. The interrelation leads to the loss of identity of each sphere: their objectives and principles become vague and confused, a fact that results in the poor performance of each of them. Thus, the economy is both an arena of political bargaining and one of the institutions which fulfil welfare principles.

The present economic reform is said to be aimed at changing the existing situation and lending economic sense to phenomena that occur within the economy. Much less is being said or written about what exactly the interrelations between the welfare and the economic sphere should be, whereas those between politics and the economy, e.g., the role of the party in factories, are not mentioned at all.

Speculation about the interrelations between the welfare and the economic sphere is chiefly based on the ideology and objectives of the present reform. According to its mid-1980s version, enterprises should introduce a far-reaching economy into their undertakings and subordinate them to profit-making. Pay levels should also have the same function: instead of securing a moderate standard of living, they ought to provide incentives to more efficient work. The Labour Law is going to be amended to better meet the requirements of the new system. It is likely that the rules which protect employees' rights will be more flexible, even permitting the firing of inefficient workers. Envisaged is the temporary unemployment of the workers of bankrupt enterprises, the national system of social benefits will be selective rather than universal, there will be payments for those benefits, some of which are going to be replaced with less costly equivalents, etc. Much is said in connection with reform about the necessity to decrease the welfare responsibilities of the state, on the one hand, and to diminish the welfare principles within the economy and the enterprise, on the other. The question arises as to whether the introduction of economic mechanisms which are going to reduce the welfare functions of the economy ought to result in, or be accomplished by, a reduction of such functions at the state administration level.

In Western European countries it is the state which is primarily responsible for the welfare of its citizens. The idea of the welfare state is, among other things, to make the inequalities, tensions and conflicts brought about by market mechanisms less severe. However, this is done outside the economy without violating its logic. It can thus be said that the welfare state has been created to safeguard the stability of the market-orientated, politico-economic system.

The welfare state in socialism is supposed to be a model of social order aimed at averting contradictions. This is the reason why its principles have been introduced into the sphere which has been known to generate tensions and conflicts: the economy. This move has, however, failed to head off social tensions caused, among other things, by Poland's poor economic performance. It has become clear in recent years that the introduction of economic mechanisms into the economy will remove these tensions and will protect the stability of the system. This should help shift welfare mechanisms and agencies outside the economy. However, the question is, should it also seriously reduce them at the state administration level? I would say 'no' although the issue is debatable. It seems that during the implementation of reform in Poland, the state is trying to get rid of the welfare responsibilities it finds burdensome. True enough, one can hear an occasional statement that, in implementing reform, the state will take measures to protect the most underprivileged. Such statements, however, are meant to reassure people who are frightened at the prospect of a continuing decline in their living standards and those who are afraid that the identity of socialism will change. In practice, the state is trying to alter the terms of the present social accord. Withdrawing from its responsibilities in the name of the market and reform, the state encourages enterprises to take over some of them.

Reform envisages a separation, although inconsistent and vague, of the social and the economic sphere. I will undertake to prove that, in practice, the opposite is taking place. A simultaneous occurrence of various factors is actually broadening the scope of the social welfare responsibilities of enterprises. In a planned economy, enterprises have always performed such functions. However, instead of disappearing, this phenomenon becomes increasingly common. One of the reasons is that enterprises have to relieve the pressure which unsatisfied social needs generate and act as a buffer to lessen social dissatisfaction caused by the failure on part of the state to fulfil its responsibilities. A cut in the welfare activities of the state in the name of reform results, in this way, in tendencies at the enterprise level which are unfavourable to the reform. The existing legal, organizational and ideological solutions are used by other groups in order to realize their interests and satisfy individual needs. Hence the argument that economic reform itself has been the least important consideration in practice: what the authorities primarily aim at is social peace which they would be happy to secure at a minimal cost; enterprises want to keep their employees and to operate smoothly; employees want to have those of their needs met which they cannot have satisfied outside the enterprise or without its help. Reform comes last because until 1988 it had chiefly existed in verbal declarations, as a symbol rather than as a set of concrete economic mechanisms capable of moulding behaviours of enterprises and people.

Welfare and the interests of the enterprise

The consolidation of the non-economic or welfare functions of the enterprise is a result of both certain permanent features of a planned economy which the present crisis has made extremely conspicuous and the phenomena developed in the past few years of crisis. There are four points that can be elaborated.

(i) Mechanisms typical of a centrally-planned economy

One such mechanism is a shortage in the labour market, caused by a strong tendency to invest combined with inefficiency of such an economy (Kornai, 1985). The shortage has increased in recent years because many employees seek better pay through changing work places. Although a law regulates wage increases in each enterprise, enterprises are in a position to offer substantially different pay. The shortage is also caused by the emergence of the private and the 'Polonian' [1] sector in the economy as a source of capital that can meet society's pay and income expectations. What I primarily have in mind is not only the number of skilled workers and experts seeking employment in the private sector but the very existence of this sector as a point of reference while assessing one's situation. This also is a reason why employees look for more attractive and better paid jobs, not always in the private sector. For many, the entrepreneurial spirit does not mean the opening of one's own business or company, since they have neither the capital nor necessary knowledge, but searching for better paid jobs. So, due to the shortage. which is not counteracted by economic mechanisms, enterprises take whatever measures are available to them to lure workers and keep them satisfied. A very important measure is meeting those welfare demands which employees cannot have satisfied without the assistance of the enterprise.

(ii) Phenomena directly or indirectly brought about by the economic crisis in recent years

Inflation and the lack of stability in various markets decrease the buying power of money and make it impossible to exchange it for goods and services. At the same time, income growth is limited with centrally-imposed regulations. In this situation, enterprises use their 'social funds' – part of the profit the enterprise allocates for providing its employees with some social benefits – to increase wages with cost-of-living payments, on the one hand, and enhance the value of wages by offering their employees various goods and services, on the other. In fact, by doing the latter, enterprises strengthen the buying power of money and make it possible to spend it. Enterprise social funds are therefore used to compensate for the impact of inflation in the economy on the purchasing power of its employees. More generally the withdrawal of the state from its welfare activities has led to a multitude of unsatisfied needs which has created a void and caused the following social reactions. First, the deeper frustration of and increased demands on the part of people who, for various reasons, have to rely solely on social benefits provided by the state. Second the meeting, according to one's possibilities, of one's own needs outside the state sector. Third, the organizing of people whose aspirations and needs are similar in order to help each other or to undertake activities alternative to those carried out by the state. Fourth, and this is the point relevant to my argument, employees begin to use their own organization to satisfy their own needs.

The pressure of unsatisfied social needs the enterprise comes under is not only exerted by its own workforce. It is also caused by the fact that various associations, cultural institutions, children's homes, public libraries, etc., do not have money. Facing growing expenses and limited state subsidies, public and social welfare institutions turn to enterprises for financial and commodity help.

(iii) Laws which encourage the development of social services against the principles of reform

These are mainly laws which regulate the social and housing funds of enterprises. Until 1986, how these funds were raised and spent was regulated by a 1982 law defining the finances of state enterprises. The law established the self-management's independence in this area, and consequently, led to a division of enterprise into the rich, i.e. those which had ample means for the provision of social benefits, and those which were worse off. The free hand to use the social fund resulted in spending it on all kinds of extra payments. In this way enterprises sidestepped the law which curbed pay increases because money paid from the social fund was not subject to high taxation. Thus, the effects the above law produced were in line with the spirit of reform and wage differentiation and incentives. The 1986 law which encourages enterprises to equalize the conditions of workers at the expense of motivation and economy has, however, undermined these practices (Niedbala, 1987). The law also prohibits, with some exceptions, the use of the social fund for extra payments for employees.

The 1986 law is against reform and its close examination confirms the aforementioned opinion that the state is trying to burden enterprises with welfare responsibilities with a view to conveniently easing social tensions rather than effectively reforming the economy.

(iv) An important role in the process in question is played by the image enterprises have created about themselves as friendly and always-ready-to-help institutions

It is hard to tell to what extent the welfare image of enterprises merely legitimizes the interests of enterprises and their productive activities, or how much it is a product of the still existing ideology that enterprises not only undertake production but also educate their employees and are responsible for their well-being. The image has partly been created in anticipation of consequences the reform will produce. As I have said before, there is a growing belief that the state does not want to, or cannot, fulfil its welfare responsibilities. 'If not us, who else will help people?' a director of a big enterprise asked me and answered himself, 'No one. This lands us with certain responsibilities.'

As can be seen from this short presentation of the problem, the chief factors stimulating the social role of enterprises are the small role of the market and money and the diminishing welfare role of the state, i.e., two basic mechanisms which help satisfy needs and interests.

Assuming that the state owns these enterprises and organizations, this could mean, in effect, only a change in the way the state operates and not a change in its welfare function. Thus, it could be argued that the above processes will somehow deconcentrate and decentralize the welfare role of the state instead of becoming a qualitatively new phenomenon. I do not think, however, that this is the case since the taking on of more social responsibilities by enterprises not only affects their operation, but also greatly alters the character of social policy. Social policy as an instrument of the modern state, an element complementary to an efficient economy, vanishes to reappear as an instrument of the policies pursued by various enterprises to realize their own interests, one of them being strict control over the behaviours of employees. At the time when, in accordance with declarations, reform in Poland is being implemented in order to modernize the economy, the reality is that strengthened within this economy are elements of paternalism and feudalism. The small role of the market and the diminishing role of the state will consequently lead to the re-emergence of some feudal-system characteristics in Poland.

The welfare activities of enterprises

I have discussed factors which are inducive to the strengthening or increasing of social responsibilities of enterprises. I now want to outline in a little more detail some aspects of these welfare activities. Some of these responsibilities enterprises have to fulfil as part of their administrative duties. In other words, as the owner and supervisor of enterprises, the state has required them to take over its responsibilities. After carefully examining the role of enterprises in the light of Poland's social insurance law in recent years, Tomasz Mordel showed a gradual burdening of enterprises with responsibilities that used to rest entirely with state insurance companies (Mordel, 1986). At present, as far as social insurance is concerned, enterprises complement state insurance companies, contribute financially to and provide insurance. According to Mordel, ZUS, the national insurance company, has, in a way, incorporated social insurance departments operating in enterprises.

Until 1980, housing cooperatives had had a quota of apartments they had been selling to enterprises. After the total collapse of the national housing programme in the early 1980s, the pressure of social needs in this sphere intensified so much that many enterprises were virtually forced to build their own apartment blocks. Although still in the initial stages the process has already assumed many forms. A few years will, however, have to elapse before the effects are seen. The construction of 'enterprise apartments' is encouraged by from-below interests, but also the state has given its blessing in the form of more relaxed laws and better credits. Equally, or even more important, is the priority enterprises have been granted in the allocation of rationed materials necessary for the construction and equipment of apartments. These priorities are usually taken care of by heads of *voivodships*, Poland's largest local authority administrative units. Although the purchase restrictions placed on most of the allocated materials have been lifted, those which are considered the most necessary for the building of apartments are still rationed. The housing needs of enterprises can easily be justified by their production targets, especially as a failure to meet them can produce dangerous effects, whereas members of housing cooperatives are not in a position to exert such pressure and, therefore, are less dangerous. Thus, the housing programme of enterprises has been given priority in the allocation of building materials, although it is much less effective and economical than cooperative housing.

The thriftiness and entrepreneurial spirit of enterprise managements, workers' self-managements and social organizations which take advantage of various formal relaxations connected with the implementation of reform to meet the needs of their workforce cannot be overlooked. In this sphere, reform does not help develop economic incentives or improve efficiency to satisfy the customer; it helps increase the range of social benefits provided for a small, but in the future increasing, part of the workforce. Thanks to the reform-caused relaxation of regulations, enterprises have developed various new organizational ways of building apartments. Many have set up building companies, e.g., the Warsaw Car Factory and four other enterprises have bought out a large building company that has gone bankrupt to have their own building of apartments. The All-Polish Trade Unions Alliance (OPZZ) came up with an initiative that it would financially sponsor the setting up of a few tens of small construction companies which would build houses for various enterprises. According to information released by the Main Statistical Office (GUS), 28% of all apartments constructed in 1987 were built by enterprises; ten years before the percentage was less than 20. At present, enterprises own and administer over a million apartments (*Zycie Warszawy* 3 Feb. 1988). Enterprises build apartments not only for their employees, but also for local communities, thus helping out the state. According to *Zycie Warszawy* of 2 Feb. 1988, '...area development is a responsibility of the state administration, but lack of means often indefinitely postpones work and without the help of enterprises the construction of many a housing estate would have to be put off'.

Needless to say, only those enterprises which have the money and the technology can afford to undertake these activities. This is a very important statement because many authors write that, due to the crisis and inflation, the financial situation of many enterprises has deteriorated, and consequently, so have their welfare activities. The already existing division into small, weak and poor enterprises and huge, prosperous ones whose bargaining position is strong has been widened. Inflation makes bigger the differences not only between social groups, but organizations as well. Both types of these inequalities are part of the growing economic disparity within Polish society. From the standpoint of social policy, the transfer of control over welfare activities to enterprise does not, for many reasons, appear to have been a move in the right direction. Welfare activities pursued by enterprises are, because of the very nature of these organizations, against the spirit of social policy. For instance, this kind of welfare does not include the most needy – old age and disabled pensioners, single mothers, families with many children, etc., and those categories of employees not connected with strong industrial organizations.

In the social policy literature and in politics there exist two fundamentally opposite standpoints concerning the mutual relations between the economy and welfare. On the one hand, some argue that the two spheres are complementary to each other: the more market-orientated the economy, the broader should be the scope of the state's welfare activities; the lesser the role of the state in the economy, the greater its role in the welfare sphere. On the other hand, others argue that the two spheres are entwined: the more market-orientated the economy, the lesser should be the range of the state's welfare activities. There should be a diminishing role of the state in both spheres.

In Poland a third reality is taking place. The withdrawal of the state from many of its welfare activities and a smaller effectiveness of these activities are not accompanied by any noticeable changes in orientating the economy towards the market. In fact, a reverse process is taking place: the decrease in the state's welfare activities is accompanied by the broadening of the social welfare sphere in the economy through the agency of the enterprises. Below I discuss the opinions of different social groups about these issues.

Social interests and changes in the welfare role of the state

The overlapping of the political, the economic and the social sphere in Polish society results in some basic ambivalences and contradictions in public attitudes towards the different spheres of the state's activity and of the market.

This is expressed through an acceptance of the state's welfare activities and a simultaneous rejection of its efforts to control political and economic behaviours. Pawel Kuczynski writes, 'The ambivalent attitude towards the state is expressed, on the one hand, by demands put forward on it, and on the other, by reluctance to accept the encompassing-all monopoly role of the state. In other words, the slow change of the attitude towards the state is manifested by a belief that the state should "secure" and take care of employees' social security and standard of living but refrain itself from interfering in the liberties of the individual' (Kuczynski, 1986). In this context I am of the opinion that a competitive market is for many people a means of attaining this freedom – the highest value. It is also a means of setting a limit to the undeserved privileges of many people, of basing pay on clear and measurable factors and not on arbitrary administrative decisions, of making abilities rather than political merits a starting point for careers, etc. *Thus the market is I believe perceived as a means of limiting the political and economic functions of the state. However the non-acceptance of the social consequences the market produces is a result of regarding social benefits as something valuable or due as a right.*

Thus when there is a tendency to reduce state control over the economy for political and efficiency reasons this is accompanied by a fear that the welfare-providing state will completely withdraw its welfare function. Such feelings influence society's attitude towards various economic solutions, for instance, towards a free market in prices. Although the state raises prices and constantly declares it necessary, some 75% of those who responded to a questionnaire in 1985 were against a free, uncontrolled by the state, rule of prices (Morawski and Kozek, 1986). How popular and manifested by which groups is the attitude of demanding a broad range of responsibilities from the state remains debatable. In spite of growing dissatisfaction with the state's welfare activities, many groups, especially those with low social status, expect the state to provide social benefits treating them as something society should receive. This type of attitude should be traced back to the basic characteristics of the political and economic system of real socialism. Without going into detail, it has to be noted that the 'I-demand' attitudes are reinforced by the deteriorating living conditions of many groups because of the crisis.

Not without consequence is the way economic reform is presented in the mass media. The media debunk the market and tell society to get ready for hardships that loom ahead. This results in growing fears that living standards will continue to decline; consequently, people are afraid of reform itself. It also produces 'I-can-do-nothing-about-it' attitudes and a feeling of helplessness: people feel the state should provide for them and take care of them, e.g. they want the state to fix prices in order to protect the consumer. This belief is a result of mass media reports about the arbitrary, uncontrolled and unjustifiable raising of prices by enterprises and private producers. Society is repeatedly told that, without state control, enterprises make unjustifiably huge profits at the expense of consumers. Moreover, according to the mass media-created image of the market, producers arbitrarily and without restraint fix prices. Such an image is presented to the public because it only confirms society's hitherto experience: prices in the planned economy have always been fixed arbitrarily and in line with political, ideological or social principles. They never resulted from economic mechanisms or the cost and profit calculus or the laws of demand and supply.

This opinion about the arbitrariness of prices is now imposed on the image of the market economy, the only difference being that, according to many people's opinion, in the market-orientated economy many more people will arbitrarily fix prices. This is where the other reason for supporting state control over prices lies: it is much easier to negotiate prices with one partner, the state, than with a multitude of invisible, anonymous enterprises. Experience has shown that when the state raises prices an effective pressure may be applied, new prices can be protested. In the case of a furniture factory, however, such pressure will neither be possible nor effective.

While writing about the mythological character of the market I am nonetheless aware of the strong and positive associations the term actually evokes in the majority of the population (Kolarska-Bobinska, 1988). For many people they are not a result of a direct contact with a market economy, or of personal experience. I have mentioned before that such associations are a result of identifying the market with efficiency and with freedom. A competitive market is identified also with a high standard of living which the centrally-managed system has failed to ensure. Hence there is a discrepancy between high social acceptance of the term or notion 'market' and the reluctant acceptance of its concrete real consequences.

It has to be noted that the negative opinions about price rises by no means illustrate society's general attitude to far-reaching economic changes: it is just a natural protest against pauperization. In short, although when the economy is reformed the attitudes of expecting help and welfare from the state should transform and diminish, there is a whole range of factors which keep these attitudes alive and which make people develop different attitudes towards the social, political and the economic spheres of the state.

Such ambivalence of feelings to the state and the market could be a source of strong cognitive dissonance. However, it is made less severe, among other things, by the fact that many people treat welfare as a right of citizens and its provision as a duty of the state. According to this belief, social benefits are not just a gesture of goodwill on the part of an 'understanding master', but something that a non-personal law grants society. The cognitive dissonanace is not a common thing also because of the fact that social groups which support welfare the strongest are also the most ardent supporters of the existing political system. This kind of attitude can be attributed mainly to the elderly, the poorly educated, and unskilled workers. The refusal to accept the existing political order in Poland prevails rather among specialists and engineers, persons with higher education, young people and town inhabitants. These groups of people in general accept the principles of a market economy and regard welfare as relatively unimportant.

The situation is complicated by the new reform ideology according to which the state is determined to limit its welfare activities and to support the market, a symbol of freedom and prosperity. The question arises whether this new element will modify the attitudes of different social groups towards the political aspect of state authority. In other words, will the supporters of a market economy back the political authority when it becomes clear that the latter consistently implements its programmes and favours their interests? For instance, will the private sector, which refuses to accept all the aspects of the state in Poland, become one of its allies? Will farmers, old and poorly educated people stop supporting the political authority when the welfare activities of the state are reduced as a result of reform? I think that both groups will polarize their views and interests. Among the market supporters are people who are ready to give their support to the political authority as soon as it has secured them conditions for pursuing their economic interests. In addition there are people who link their support for economic reform with political reforms. For them market reform is to be a road to democracy, not its substitute. On the other hand although people with a low social status link their attitude to the political system with their attitude to the welfare state, the latter is not the only determinant of their general political views either. Of some importance is, for example, higher authoritarianism of older people, rural dwellers and those with poor education (Koralewicz-Zebik, 1986). The higher the authoritarianism, the lower the need for democratic changes.

Another question arises: how, in connection with the implementation of reform that is meant to limit the role of the state in the economy, will the beliefs of respondents who say they belonged to Solidarity change? In 1980, Solidarity members were a little more egalitarian than members of the 'old unions'. In 1984, they were more unegalitarian (Kolarska-Bobinska, 1986). In 1988, their opinions did not differ from those of the rest of society. Solidarity activists, as unionists, should speak strongly in support of employees' rights, whereas market laws will limit them. Thus, in the present situation, Solidarity, a trade union, should oppose market reforms. This is not the case, though, because *market reforms have been perceived as a means of limiting the influence of the political authority, not as a way of limiting employees' rights.* It has to be noted, however, that such thinking is typical of the initial stage of reform when more important was not its essence but the very fact of a change being made. In other words, whenever the basic problem is an impossibility to introduce any change, its supporters set up a reform-minded alliance regardless of their different outlooks and interests. These differences will surface when the alliance has achieved its objective and reform has become a fact. The divisions will be a result of different views or group interests. Revealed will also be interests joined by a common attitude 'towards something', not only 'against something'. It can be assumed that, market reform having been implemented, Solidarity followers will be divided into rightist supporters of the market economy and leftist defenders of employees' rights. Their attitude towards the fundamental social issues rather than towards the political authority will influence their beliefs and self-determination.

When the so-called Round Table talks between the government and the opposition were under way, certain divisions had already appeared within Solidarity. Their source is both the double role of the trade union, an advocate of change and a defender of employees, and its attitude to a future socioeconomic order which should be introduced in Poland. In the latter case, the division is into supporters of a pure market economy and those whose views are more socialist and who prefer a developed welfare state. During the Round Table negotiations the divisions, which affect both Solidarity and the party, were suppressed. It can be assumed that in time the divisions both within the 'banned' trade union and Poland's Communist Party will intensify and manifest themselves. Solidarity faces a choice: it will either precisely define its identity, and consequently, lose several potential allies, or vaguely define its identity and win a multitude of followers who, in time, will cause a break-up of the union into a number of smaller organizations.

The official trade unions are in an equally complicated if different situation. They cooperate with the government and in such capacity are perceived by their members and society. In 1984, members of the official, 'new' as they came to be called, trade unions were, much more than non-unionists, in favour of strengthening the party's role in exercising authority (Rychard, 1986). On the other hand, though, their whole programme is designed to defend the employees' rights of their members and to protect their living standards, including housing. The programme legitimizes their existence but simultaneously puts them in certain opposition towards the government-sponsored reforms and price-increase programme. Discussing a somewhat lukewarm support for the programme of changes presented in the referendum, the government spokesmen pointed to the trade unions' reluctance as a reason behind it.

The above are only speculations. However, I do believe that the early anticipation of changes to come has already generated divisions within groups whose views on the role of the political authority in society and the economy have hitherto been uniform.

Conclusion

In the past few years the role of the state as the economic life regulator and the institution which satisfies various social needs has seriously diminished. What is important here is the fact that the void left by administrative regulators has not yet been filled with a market mechanism, nor has the gap of unsatisfied needs been filled with activities of groups and organizations which are not state controlled. It is hard to tell to what extent this period is temporary, as nothing can yet be said about the system which will emerge as a result of changes within the economy and society. One thing appears to be certain: *the system which is no longer centrally administered, and which is not yet regulated with economic mechanisms, is developing its own methods of solving the emerging social problems.*

The meeting of many social needs with the help of enterprises, or within them to be exact, is one of these mechanisms. From the point of view of employees and enterprises it is a necessary adjustment. From the point of view of the state, it is a stabilizing activity. Whichever the case, it does not solve social problems on a large scale. Nor is it a solution that would help reform. The strong pressure on part of society that the standard and variety of the hitherto provided social benefits be maintained has different sources but similar effects. The poor performance of the social sphere and the giving up by the state of many responsibilities strengthen the feeling of injustice, of being underpaid and exploited: in short, they strengthen the 'I demand' attitudes. In this situation, implementing reform which may produce serious social consequences, the state should pay special attention to the social sphere and its own welfare responsibilities. In its efforts to relieve the economy of such responsibilities, the state ought not to give them up at the level of its administration. On the contrary, in the time of crisis and the implementation of reform, being aware of the expectations of various social groups, the state should improve the performance of the social sphere, should treat it as a factor that is external in relation to the economy, but which helps implement reform and which does not act against it. Instead of this, within Poland's industry solutions which can be described as feudal paternalism are being encouraged and developed.

As I have said before, the welfare state which emerged in many Western European countries in the mid-1940s was meant to ease the social consequences of the market-based system, and by so doing, to stabilize it. Much is being said at present about the crisis the capitalist welfare state is faced with. The welfare state has come to be perceived by some as a self-generated source of the crisis of the capitalist economy, i.e., as a factor which destabilizes it. Such thinking is also present in Poland but in relation to the planned economy: there is a growing body of opinion that the socialist state is over-protective and that there is a basic contradiction between its welfare activities and economic mechanisms. This thesis does not, as I have mentioned before, adequately reflect the relations between solutions in the economic and the social sphere. Its function is political rather than scientific. It is very important at present to define these relations between the economic and social spheres as complementary and stabilizing the system, especially as neither the present economic nor social solutions taking place in Poland will help that stability.

Note

1 This term is used to refer to capital invested by expatriate Poles in Poland.

Bibliography

Kolarska-Bobinska, Lena (1986), 'Pozadany lad spoleczny i polityczny w gospodarce' ('A Desirable Social and Political Order in the Economy'). In: Jasiewicz, K., Rychard, A. and Adamski, W. (eds) *'Polacy 84. Dynamika konfliktu i konsensusu'* (*The Poles of 1984. The Dynamics of Conflict and Consensus*), Warsaw, Warsaw University.

Kolarska-Bobinska, Lena (1988), 'Mitycznosc rynku i realnosc reformy' ('The Myth of the Market and the Reality of the Reform'. In: Gomulka, S. and Polonsky, A. (eds) *Polish Paradoxes* (UK) and *Studia Sociologiczne* 4, (Poland).

Koralewicz-Zebik, Jadwiga (1986), 'Autorytaryzm spoleczenstwa polskiego W 1984' ('Authoritarianism of the Polish Society in 1984'). In: *The Poles of 84*, op.cit.

Kornai, Janos (1985), *Niedobor w gospodarce* (*Economics of Shortage*). Warsaw, PWE.

Kuczynski, Pawel (1986), 'Swiadomosc polityczna robotnikow – pomiedzy modernizacja a "normalizacja"' ('The Political Awareness of Workers: Between Modernization and "Normalization"'). In: Morawski, W. (ed) *Gospodarka i spoleczenstwo. Wartosci i interesy zalog przemyslowych* (*Economy and Society. The Values and Interests of the Factory Workforce*). Warsaw, Warsaw University, Institute of Sociology.

Morawski, Witold and Kozek, Wieslaw (1986), 'Spoleczenstwo polskie wobec Problemow reformy i gospodarki' ('Polish Society and the Problem of Reform and the Economy'). In: *Economy and Society*, op.cit.

Mordel, Tomasz (1986), 'Ewolucja zakladu pracy w polskim prawie ubezpieczen spolecznych' ('The Evolution of the Work Place in the Polish Social Insurance Law'), *Polityka Spoleczna*, (*Social Policy*), no. 5/6, 1986.

Niedbala, Zdzislaw (1987), 'Cele zakladowych funduszy – socjalnego i zakladowego' ('The Objectives of the Social Fund in Enterprises'), *Social Policy*, no. 7, 1987.

Rychard, Andrzej (1986), 'Poglady polityczne: stosunek do zasad i instytucji zycia publicznego' ('Political Views: the Attitude Towards the Principles and Institutions of Public Life'). In: *The Poles of 1984*, op.cit.

'Zakladowe fundusze mieszkaniowe – zasobniejsze' (More Ample Housing Funds of Enterprises'), *Zycie Warszawy* daily, 2 Feb 1988.

'Mieszkanie dla pracownika' ('An Apartment for an Employee'), *Zycie Warszawy* daily, 3 Feb 1988.

5 Alternatives in the health area: Poland in comparative perspective[1]

MAGDALENA SOKOLOWSKA AND ANDRZEJ RYCHARD

The purpose of this chapter is to examine the sphere of health in Polish society and ways of satisfying these needs. The starting point is the thesis of the declining role of the formal ways of satisfying these needs and the increasing role of alternative ways. We shall look at the sources of the process, its forms, and also at certain consequences for the social structure.

There is a rich literature regarding alternative ways of satisfying social needs, or the institution of 'alternativeness' in general, in various Western countries. This type of analysis is particularly strong in the sociology of medicine and in studies of life-styles and economic systems. Our particular interest is alternative mechanisms operating in a system of centralized political power. The system is one of 'officially limited alternativeness' – limited by reason of political doctrine. Yet, these limitations are to a certain degree only formal. For pragmatic reasons the system permits and tolerates various kinds of alternativeness in social, economic, and even, to some extent, political life.

We concentrate, in this chapter, on alternative mechanisms operating in the health field. This is a first attempt to shed some light on this phenomenon, to link alternative mechanisms in health care to the broader societal context. We present a general model of 'alternativeness' in the health area, a model that is relevant for international comparisons. Although we think that our general model of alternativeness is fairly well developed, in our present formulation we have not developed the framework for comparative analysis very fully. Unfortunately, there are virtually no empirical data enabling international comparisons of alternativeness in the health area. Students of health care in

Europe have been rather slow to develop systematic studies of the alternatives, even in Western European countries. In Poland and other Eastern European countries, systematic sociological investigations in the health field are only just beginning to be undertaken; moreover, alternatives to the formal system of health care are only just emerging in Eastern Europe. 'East–East' comparative analyses hardly exist and there are no 'East–West' comparisons. Scholars from the East and West have recently engaged in a pioneer work to compare their welfare systems, but the health element of welfare systems has not thus far been the object of these studies. Even in those Western European countries where such alternatives as self-help groups are far advanced, there has been a general lack of theory and explanation (World Health Organization, 1987).

Two sources of alternativeness

Ineffectiveness of the health system and general conditions

Medical institutions do not fully accomplish their professed goals. Generally speaking, such a goal as 'good societal health' is formulated in a too general and all-encompassing way. It is obvious that expecting these goals to be realized exclusively, or even mainly, in the operations of the official health systems is a misunderstanding. As is well known, health does not result mainly from medical practice. Nonetheless, the expansion of the definition of health has generated excessive expectations with respect to the medical system. The medical system has been unable to meet such expectations. This is, of course, part of the more general process of the 'crisis' of the welfare state. During a meeting of European experts on social development programme, the participants 'saw the growth of new social initiatives in the area of welfare as some kind of response to alleged failures in the operation of welfare states, both in socialist countries and welfare capitalist societies in Western Europe' (*Eurosocial Reports*, 1985, p.7).

This universal process is reflected in Poland. It seems, though, that there are also some other factors at play in Poland, perhaps specific to this country. Empirical data cited below support this thesis. There are findings from international studies on health care utilization carried out in 12 regions of the world, including the Lodz area (Kohn and White, 1976; Rychard, 1984). The need for health care, as measured by infant mortality rates, number of ill persons, chronic severity of illness, and other measures, is greater in Lodz than in many other areas studied. On the other hand, the volume of health care resources is at the median level, and the organization of health care resources makes utilization difficult. A large problem is the shortage of general practitioners. The result is an overloading of the hospital system with its modest resources.

The health system is a part of the larger social, political and economic system. The ineffectiveness of the state health system is not the only factor necessitating the appearance of alternative solutions. For alternative solutions to arise, certain general conditions must exist. Among these general conditions, the most prominent feature of the sociopolitical system, its nominal absence of alternatives, becomes, paradoxically, an additional stimulus to the appearance of alternativeness. This thesis is only a paradox on the surface. It is firmly rooted in the theory of organization, mainly the theory of bureaucracy, which posits that the spontaneous appearance of informal arrangements as an unintended effect of pressure for complete formalization is unavoidable. Here one can also cite analyses by Polish sociologists showing, mainly with respect to the economy, how the tendency toward total control gives rise to effects that lead to the loss of real control (e.g.Staniszkis, 1980).

There is still another reason specific to Poland for the occurrence of alternative solutions in health care. Socialist ideology has created rather high expectations connected with the protective functions of the state. For example, a new health service was one of the most attractive elements of the socialist system introduced in Poland after 1945. A universal, easily accessible, and free health care system was an enticing slogan that immediately found response in a nation exhausted by the recent war, still remembering the pre-1939 conditions when economic barriers made it difficult for most people to avail themselves of health care. The new model was also favoured by many physicians, because, in the Polish historical and cultural traditions, the physician's profession was much less a free profession than in many other countries. It was always strongly marked by elements of vocation, or even mission, and of public service. The new system provided freedom to the physicians in treating their patients, and to the patients, freedom in availing themselves of medical assistance. All this was immensely attractive.

In the early 1950s, Poland entered a period of accelerated industrialization. This led to an expansion of the industrial health service that was to put into effect the principles of a class-based policy, offering to the workers privileges in the sphere of health care. The then minister of health wrote:

> Without refusing to any social group the medical assistance for the preservation of life and avoidance of disabilities, we shall pursue a class-based policy. We have to bear in mind the fact that the large masses of those covered by social insurance are quite heterogenous. We shall concentrate our means and efforts primarily on health care for the working class and its leading groups, namely miners and large-industry workers... The health service, which formerly used to serve mostly the propertied classes, now has the task of shifting the principal focus of its activity and of providing medical assistance to the working classes who are building the better, socialist future of our country, and above all to the leading working class. (Sztachelski,1950, 1951)

The new form of health care elicited needs and demands that industrial workers had never before experienced. The bringing of medical assistance close to the workers taught them to avail themselves of the health service, but also made them feel all of its defects and shortcomings more and more acutely. Where, several years before, people clamoured for a nurse, they now wanted to have a physician; where, not long before, access to a physician seemed to be a final demand, they now felt the need of having several specialists at their disposal. From that point of view, the industrial health service really did carry out its tasks (Sokolowska,1983, pp. 91-2).

The gap between slogans and facts was being more and more clearly felt on a national scale. In sum, 'the socialism which people see is compared with the socialism which they would like to see and of whose rightness they are convinced: the clash between reality and the standard gives rise to highly negative opinions here' (Nowak,1979, p.163).

The final reason for searching for alternative solutions is not universal, to be sure, but neither is it entirely specific to Poland. It is the economic and social crisis that has been going on for several years. It is obvious that this situation has a bearing on the functioning of the health system. We see here a double influence. On one hand, the crisis means continued under-investment in the health system and hence its overloading – which, in and of itself, is conducive to the development of alternative solutions. And, on the other hand, alternatives to the formal health system can be welcomed and even encouraged by the state, because this results in a saving of government expenditures.

We mentioned earlier the universal reasons and those specific to Poland for the appearance and development of alternative solutions in the health field. One of the reasons specific to Poland is the very nature of the Polish sociopolitical system. We devote the next part of this chapter to its brief description.

Nature of the sociopolitical system in Poland: crucial points

Never, at any time, did a system completely without alternatives function in Poland. The government that introduced a new political system after World War II refrained from liquidating such institutions as private ownership of land in agriculture and the Roman Catholic church. In the field of politics as well, even though one political party began to play the dominant role, the government nevertheless decided to retain, at least in form, certain institutions of parliamentary democracy. The first group of deviations from the centralized model, then, are those that make allowances for national historical traditions.

In addition, we must recognize alternative mechanisms that result from the dynamics and transformations of the new system. Some of them are unintended effects of the effort to achieve total control; others, in turn, result from various counterpressures by the society. The informal sphere that has been described as the 'second economy', and also as the 'second system of health care', belongs to this group of phenomena.

The subject of 'alternativeness' in the socio-institutional life of socialist societies has attracted the interest of researchers for several years. For example, Besancon (1984) has applied such a concept to the Soviet economy and Scharlet (1984) has used the notion of the 'contra-system' in analysing several spheres of life. Noteworthy among numerous Polish analyses of this phenomena is Wnuk-Lipinski's (forthcoming) distinguishing of three kinds of 'dualities' – in the political, economic and sociocultural spheres.

The common feature of these conceptions is the thesis that there are a certain variety of ways of satisfying various needs. This diversity comes from the ineffectiveness of official mechanisms in satisfying those needs (Scharlet,1984; Koralewicz-Zebik and Wnuk-Lipinski,1986; Rychard,1986; Adamski,1985).

One of the most promising concepts is Hankiss's idea of the 'second society'. His theory concerns Hungary – which is why it can be useful for analysing the situation not only of Poland but also of socialist countries more generally. According to Hankiss (1986) there are in Hungary now four forms of social organization: a first society, (in both its formal and its informal sphere), a second society, and an alternative society. The main difference between the second society and the alternative society is that the second society is transitory: it retains none of the features of the first society, but it does not yet contain some of the distinctive features of the alternative society.

The problem of alternatives is to some extent universal, not only for Western countries but also for socialist countries, which seem at first glance to have very centralized and hierarchical structures. The difference between Western and Eastern alternativeness is that Western alternative mechanisms can be more readily adapted to the official, established institutions than can Eastern mechanisms. The source of this difference seems to be ideological: it lies in a greater tolerance for pluralism in the official ideology of Western countries.

The attitude of state or official systems to these alternatives varies considerably. Focusing again on Poland, we can say that the official attitude is one of ambivalence. There are conflicting reasons for this: doctrinal and pragmatic. For doctrinal reasons, the state cannot relinquish its aim to attain a monopoly of control over various spheres of life. Hence it should have a rather negative attitude toward alternative solutions. On the other hand, for pragmatic reasons it is necessary to increase the effectiveness of centralized official mechanisms. This gives rise to a tolerant attitude toward some deviations from inflexible rules toward informality. As scholars note (e.g., Staniszkis,1984; Marody,1985), the informalities of, for example, the second economy, perform stabilizing functions for the system. Hence, official tolerance is a rational reaction. Some of the deviations from inflexible rules are even consciously built into the system by the state. Staniszkis calls this a peculiarly 'authoritative system' (see also Iwanowska, Federowicz and Zukowski,1986).

The 1980s are witness to a rapidly changing situation in such socialist countries as Poland, Hungary, China and the Soviet Union. These ongoing changes produce a new type of alternativeness, understood as attempts at democratization and decentralization. This means that the notion of alternativeness may refer not only to informal social forces but also to officially undertaken, but still not really implemented, reforms.

Hence, in sum, reactions of the state to alternative solutions are distributed along a continuum from certain doctrinal obligations to certain necessities of a pragmatic nature. We believe that this duality or ambivalence is one of the characteristic features of the institutional system, not only in Poland but also in other countries.

The argument presented in the first two parts of this chapter makes it possible for us to formulate a general model that describes the conditions under which alternative mechanisms for the satisfaction of health needs arise. We present this model in a diagram that attempts to recapitulate our argument thus far (see Figure 5.1).

The essence of our argument is the thesis that only the combined influence of all of the factors in the diagram can cause the appearance and the development of alternatives in the system of health care. The relative importance of these factors differs from one socialist society to another. For example, in Poland there is a kind of 'institutional tradition' in the area of alternativeness. We mean here the role of private agriculture and the position of the Roman Catholic church. These are independent institutions – quite unique in socialist countries. This tradition certainly contributed to the emergence of mass organization (*Solidarnosc*). Because there was no such tradition in any other socialist country, the emergence of alternativeness in these countries had to rely on initiatives stemming from the system itself. We can mention here the economic reform policy in Hungary, which was implemented by the Communist Party. The only extrasystemic alternativeness in most of the socialist countries were small-scale initiatives in the areas of human rights, ecology and welfare. Poland is the only socialist country in which all the factors of alternativeness are at play: 'the reforms from above', mass movements 'from below', and the importance of historical and cultural heritage. Nevertheless, whatever the local specificities, the main processes occurring in the Eastern European countries are similar. All of them point to the opening up of the system.

A preliminary typology of the alternatives in Poland

According to our analyses thus far, the mechanisms of alternativeness are not specific to Poland. Thus we must develop a theoretical rationale for studying this phenomenon cross-nationally. According to Swinnen (1986, p.13), it is possible to analyse alternativeness in the economic area from three perspectives: segmentation theories, (dual labour market theories), dual economy theories,

```
┌─────────────────────────────────┐
│ Universal medical factors       │
└─────────────────────────────────┘
                             ╲
                              ╲
┌─────────────────────────────────┐
│ Universal and specific economic │
│ factors                         │
└─────────────────────────────────┘
                              ╲     ┌──────────┐
                               ↘    │Alternatives
                                    │in health
                                    │care
                                    └──────────┘
┌─────────────────────────────────┐   ↗
│General sociopolitical and cultural│
│conditions specific to the socialist│
│countries:                       │
│– unintended effects of          │
│  centralization                 │
│– deviations from the dogmatic model│
│  of socialism: the role of the private│
│  economy, the role of Churches, │
│  democratization, pluralization of social│
│  life, and economic reforms.    │
└─────────────────────────────────┘
```

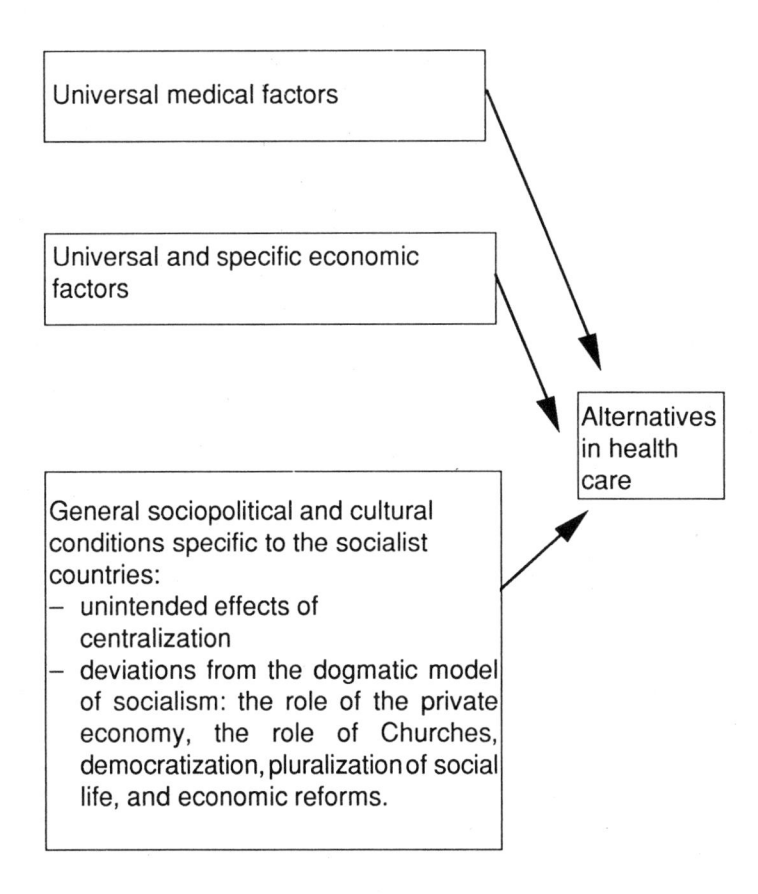

Figure 5.1 Factors influencing the development of alternatives in health care in the socialist countries

(distinguishing the formal and informal parts of the economy), and 'the democratic socialist alternative' (with the idea of 'useful work' as a central concept). Other theoretical typologies are also possibly useful for specific types of alternatives, for example, the concept of the 'patron–client relationship' in the area of political life or the theories of alternatives life-styles in the area of 'everyday life'. There are two important features of all these theories:

1 They are limited to specific social spheres: the economy, politics, and so on.
2 These theories are at the same time universal in the sense that they can be

adapted for interpreting alternativeness both in socialist and in capitalist societies.

Among many typologies of the 'new social initiatives', that is, alternative ways of coping with social problems, the most interesting seem to be those in which the authors explicitly define the theoretical criteria for their typologies. For example, Swinnen (1986) asserts that one of the most important dimensions of the new Dutch initiatives in local economic development is their horizontal versus vertical policy. The main difference between these two forms seems to be the emphasis on self-help ideology in the first versus the emphasis against 'bureaucracy' in the second. In this typology, internal structures and modes of activity are the main factors. In our schema, other factors are more important: these are the relations of the alternative mechanisms with the official, state-owned health system.

It does seem though that Swinnen's approach is relevant to our purposes, albeit from a slightly different point of view. In Poland we have to approach the issues more broadly than he does, because we must deal with the general question of highly centralized and bureaucratic power, as against local, democratic power. The issues here have been addressed systematically for the first time by *Solidarnosc*. Of course, these issues relate to health. Otherwise, slogans like 'community health', 'community participation', and the like make no sense.

Our analysis here is not addressed to the detailed description, or to the characteristics of the specific forms, of alternatives in the health area in Poland. Our intention instead is to formulate some more general questions. We should first define the types of alternatives that we are discussing. We have in mind here mechanisms alternative to the official health system, which predominates in Poland. Briefly, however, let us mention that according to data obtained by Sokolowska and Moskalewicz, the official health system of Poland includes 95% of the country's health personnel, resources and services. This 95% 'contains' within it, however, many alternatives and informalities. There are alternatives that are accessible to citizens in general. In addition, there are alternatives of another kind. There is an official system of health care for persons in certain positions on the so-called nomenclature list. There are also separate health care systems for employees of particular branches of the economy. These are the counterparts of special sectors of the economy (e.g. Besancon,1984; Wnuk-Lipinski,1988). We omit them from our analysis because of their elitist character. They are extremely important as a feature of the system, but they are not alternatives available to society as a whole, which is the subject of our analysis. Nor do we deal with the family, which in all societies is a major source of care for the chronically ill, the aged, and disabled family members.

The typology of alternative ways of satisfying health needs that we suggest here is based on two criteria. First, the criterion of formality versus informality of a given solution. By 'formal' we mean such solutions, which although different from state health care, are nevertheless recognized and legitimized by the state. Second, the criterion distinguishing alternative solutions within the system from those outside the system. The first type consists of officially recognized private medical cooperatives; the second type consists of self-help groups, healers or activities under the auspices of the Roman Catholic church. Such activity is specific to Poland. Unfortunately, we do not know how the Polish situation compares to that of the other socialist countries. Empirical comparative studies are badly needed. We present our typology in Figure 5.2.

We have provided typical examples for each category. Our typology is a simplification of the phenomena in the sense that, in principle, mixed types of solutions are the most frequent. More important than including certain phenomena of particular types is to consider the relationships among the four types and between all four types and the official health system. We can assume that all four types are required by each other and by the society. We have no empirical data, but it is safe to assume that there are certain links between all four types of alternative institutions, as well as between each of them and the official system. This four-part whole is dynamic: in certain periods some solutions are informal and beyond the system; at other times, they are incorporated within the system.

It is safe to say that each of the four types has its own relationship with the official health system. There is a continuum of the 'involvement' of them with the official system. Some of them penetrate the system almost completely (private medical practice). Others have far-reaching independence.

When analysing the relations between alternative mechanisms and official systems, we face the problem of delineating the main structural differences between these entities. According to some Western authors, the main differences between formal services and the new informal initiatives should be analysed in the following terms: explicitness of definition of functions; universality (formal services are more universal); limits of period of activity (formal services are unlimited); hierarchical organizations; and based on taxation versus other sources of financing (*Eurosocial Reports,* 1985, p.17).

The usefulness of our typology is that it enables us to define more precisely the attitude of the state toward alternative solutions. This depends on which of the four alternatives we are dealing with, and on the political and economic situation. We can hypothesize that in periods of economic crisis combined with relative political stability, the state tends to tolerate external solutions – both formal and informal. During a period of political tension with economic crisis, however, tolerance of alternativeness declines. Under these circumstances, the authorities do not believe that the economic gains from acceptance of alternativeness provide adequate compensation for the political costs – a certain loss of monopoly of control. It seems than in Poland we still have the former situation: the state has to tolerate various kinds of alternatives, although it uses a specific strategy towards them, namely, attempting to

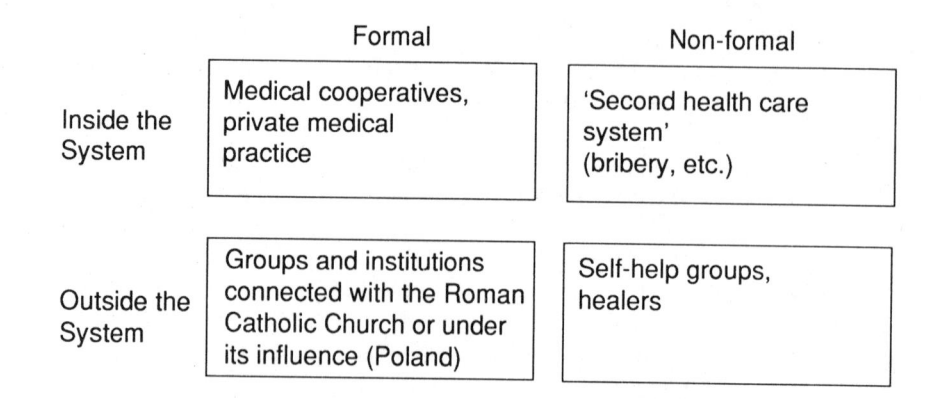

	Formal	Non-formal
Inside the System	Medical cooperatives, private medical practice	'Second health care system' (bribery, etc.)
Outside the System	Groups and institutions connected with the Roman Catholic Church or under its influence (Poland)	Self-help groups, healers

Figure 5.2 A typology of alternative ways of satisfying health needs: the case of the socialist countries

exercise control without bearing any financial responsibility. Sometimes, promises of financial help can be a way of making these alternatives dependent on state structures. This is a well-known phenomenon, not only in Poland.

We should initially distinguish the following types of relations between the state-owned health system and alternative solutions: antagonism, coexistence, cooperation and containment (partly based on Scharlet, 1984, p.145). We believe that the relations between the state system and alternative solutions within the system are part of the process of cooperation or of 'sponging', but relations with external solutions are more often antagonistic. The antagonism of these relations is influenced, in an important way, by conflicts of this type being more probable the greater the extent to which alternative solutions become a substitute for 'old' solutions. Conflict is avoided when alternative solutions are complementary to the existing ones (*Eurosocial Reports*, 1985, p.28). We believe, however, that this postulate can be fulfilled only in the case of 'controlled alternatives', that is, alternatives that are in a certain sense created by the state. The alternatives that seem to be dominant in Poland are often of a substitute character.

From this point of view, it is useful to compare some Polish and Hungarian institutions. There is a new type of monoprofit cooperative in Hungary, created to cope with some everyday problems of the elderly, children and families 'which cannot be dealt with either by the families themselves or by the established services' (*Eurosocial Reports*, 1985, p.25). These cooperatives (called 'LARES') do work that is essentially non-professional. As the authors of the report stress: 'Enterprises like LARES cannot and should not be seen as potential substitutes for state services provided by paid, professional staff' (*Eurosocial Reports*, 1985, p.26); We do not know how widespread the use of this complementary and non-substituting mechanism of activity is in Hungary. Nor do we have systematic knowledge about such mechanisms in Poland. Nevertheless, it is possible to hypothesize that, in Poland, alternative institutions are more often a kind of substitute for the 'official' institutions than is the case in Hungary. Differences in the effectiveness of economic and social welfare systems between Poland and Hungary seem to be one of the explanatory factors.

The situation in Poland with respect to the 'opening up' of the formal system, however, is far from stable. Especially in the recent years (if not months), we are witnessing rapid changes in all areas. These changes involve politics, the economy, culture, education and also health.

Most analyses of these issues have been addressed to the economy (Rychard,1987a). We think, though, that there are types of alternatives in health care that are similar to those in the economy. It can be observed generally that our political system more readily tolerates alternative solutions that are located in the peripheries of the system, while the nature of the system itself remains intact. Staniszkis (1987) asserts that these 'peripheric' changes stabilize the 'core' of the system and that privatization outside the state system is easier than privatization inside the system. In our opinion, all types of changes at the peripheries or outside of the system are more tolerable for the power elite than are changes of the system itself. For example, it is much easier to establish small private firms than to reform the state-owned economic sector in any basic way. We cannot rule out, however, the possibility that in the future the growing number, diversity and quality of the 'peripheral' institutions will change the nature of the core of the system. The influence of extrasystemic changes on the core of the system is not exclusively a Polish phenomenon. Such processes are present also in the other socialist countries. The most important process is that many innovative forms are located outside the state-owned economic sector but have an impact on that sector (Iwanowska,1988). The 'innovation' consists not only in the location of these industries but also in the type of industry – which is often electronics.

There have recently been interesting events occurring in the Polish economy, which signify the growing importance of an individualistic, market orientation resembling – we would say – early capitalistic values. At the same time, there has been some decrease in a 'socialized' orientation, such as workers' councils, cooperatives and self-governments. It is striking that these changes stem from such disparate sources as the government and some independent oppositional circles (Rychard, 1987a).

In the area of welfare and health, new slogans have emerged, slogans such as 'reprivatization'. These slogans correspond precisely to those used in Western European countries. For example, there are more and more advertisements in the daily press offering private (paid for out of pocket) home visits of medical specialists, home nursing care, and even special examinations, such as EKG. There are also, however, powerful hindrances to getting approval for foundations that could alleviate the health burden of the society. This is a good illustration of the thesis that our political system tolerates changes on the peripheries more readily than at the 'core' and – paradoxically – changes that are more liberal–conservative (privatization) than those that are 'socially orientated'.

Changes in the socialist countries are occurring very rapidly. Our typology (Figure 5.2) distinguishes four elements and emphasizes the borderlines between them, but the borderlines are becoming less accentuated and the interconnections among all four elements are increasing rapidly. These changes, of course, are not only occurring in Poland. The dominant role of the state sector is decreasing in the socialist countries, while the role of nonstate institutions is increasing. According to Szalai (1988), who describes the situation in Hungary, one can say that we are witnessing the 'dead end' of the postwar period in real socialism. Szalai also stresses the role of emerging civic initiatives around health services.

Conclusion

Do alternative solutions in health care have an elitist or egalitarian influence on the society? Bednarski (1984) addressed this problem with respect to the 'second economy' in Poland. He tends to believe that the second economy has an elitist function, because not everyone can take advantage of it. We believe that, in the case of alternative ways of satisfying health needs, the matter is somewhat different. Most alternatives result from the inefficiency of the state health system. Can we assume that these largely social reactions will have exclusively elitist effects on the society? The diversity of these forms is so great that it would be hard to find a family in Poland that does not have recourse to at least one of these alternatives. To be sure, not all of the alternatives are equally accessible to everyone, but let us not forget that the official health system itself often intensifies social inequalities. Hence, one can hardly speak of alternative ways of satisfying health needs as unequivocally and uniquely elitist. This, of course, does not mean that alternative solutions are always free from limitations and weaknesses of several types. Although the quoted opinion was written specifically with respect to self-help groups, we think that it is pertinent to all alternatives in the health area. Above all, alternative mechanisms concentrate mainly on individual health and do not cover health at various levels, from micro to macro. The development of these mechanisms cannot reduce the responsibility of national governments in the West and in the East for the health of their societies.

Note

1 First published in *Cross-National Research in Sociology* edited by Melvin Kohn, Sage Publications, Inc. USA, 1989.

Bibliography

Adamski, Wladyslaw (1985), 'Aspiracje-interesy-konflikt' ('Aspirations-Interests-Conflict'), *Studia Socjologiczne* 2.

Bednarski, M. (1984), 'Drugi obieg' ('Second Economy'), *Zycie Gospodarcze* 35.

Besancon, Alain (1984), *Anatomia widma/Anatomy of Specter*. Warszawa: Krag.

Eurosocial Reports. (1985), 'European Experts Meeting on Established Social Services Versus New Social Initiatives', no. 25.

Hankiss, Elmer (1986), *Pulapki spoleczne (Social Traps)*. Warsaw.

Iwanowska, Anna (1988), 'Prywatni modernizatorzy panstwowego sektora gospodarki' ('Private Modernizers of the State Economy'). Paper presented to the Polish Sociological Association Conference 'Reform and Alternatives', Warsaw, June 9–10.

Iwanowska, Anna, Federowicz, M. and Zukowski, T. (1986), *Rynek-demokracja-swiadczenia wzajemne (Market-Democracy-Reciprocal Services)*. Mimeo.

Kohn, Robert and White, L. (1976), *Health Care – An International Study*. Oxford: Pergamon.

Koralewicz-Zebik, Jadwiga and Wnuk-Lipinski, Edmund (1986), 'Wizje spoleczenstwa, zroznicowan i nierownosci w swiadomosci spolecznej' ('Visions of Society, Social Differences and Inequalities in Social Conciousness'). Mimeo.

Marody, Miroslawa (1985), 'Sens zbiorowy a stabilnosc ladu spolecznego' ('Collective Sense and Stability of Social Order'.) Mimeo.

Mrela, Kazimierz (1984), 'Lad spoleczny i tozamosc organizacji: rzeczywistosc organizacyjna socjalizmu realnego' ('Society and the Identity of Organizations: Organizational Reality of the Real Socialism'). Mimeo.

Munday, Brian (1984), 'European Meeting on Established Social Services Versus New Social Initiatives – Conflict, Change and Cooperation.' *Eurosocial Reports*. Vienna, no.25.

Nowak, Stefan (1979), 'System wartosci spoleczenstwa polskiego' ('Value System of the Polish Society'), *Studia Socjologiczne* 4.

Nowak, Stefan (1984), 'Postawy wartosci i aspiracje spoleczenstwa polskiego' ('Attitudes, Values, and Aspirations of the Polish Society'). In: *Spoleczenstwo polskie czasu kryzysu*. University of Warsaw, Instytut Socjolgii.

Rychard, Andrzej (1984), 'The Health Care System in Poland: The Case of Lodz as Compared with Foreign Regions: A Secondary Analysis', *Social Science and Medicine*, 19, 8, Pergamon.

Rychard, Andrzej (1986), 'Poza legitymizacja systemu: Procesy przystosowawcze w Polsce lat 80' ('Beyond the System's Legitimacy: Adaptation Process in the Poland of 80's'). Mimeo.

Rychard, Andrzej (1987a), *Wladza i interesy w gospodarce polskiej u progu lat 80 (Power and Interests in Polish Economy in the Beginning of the 80's)*. Warszawa: Uniwesytet Warszawski.

Rychard, Andrzej (1987b), 'Granice reform gospodarki' ('Limits to Economic Reforms'). Mimeo.

Scharlet, R. (1984), 'Dissent and the "Contra-System" in the Soviet Union'. In: *The Soviet Union in the 80's,* vol.35, no.3, edited by E.P. Hoffman. New York: Academy of Political Sciences.

Sicinski, Andrzej (1983), *Styl zycia, obyczaje, ethos w Polsce lat 70 z perspektywy roku 1981 (Life Styles, Customs Ethos in Poland in the 70's from the Perspective of 1981)*. Instytut Filozofii i Socjologii, Polska Akademia Nauk.

Sicinski, Andrzej (1985) 'Style zycia miejskiego w Polsce' ('Urban Life in Poland'). Mimeo.

Sokolowska, Magdalena. (1983), 'Health as an Issue in the Workers' Campaign', *Sisyphus,* 3.

Sokolowska, Magdalena and Moskalewicz, Bozena (1987), 'Health Sector Structures: The Case of Poland', *Social Science and Medicine* 14/9.

Staniszkis, Jadwiga (1980), 'Systemowe uwarunkowania funkcjonowania przedsiebiorstwa przemyslowego' ('The System Determinants of the Functioning of the Industrial Enterprise'), *Przeglad Socjologiczny* 32.

Staniszkis, Jadwiga (1984), 'Racjonalnosc-wlasnosc-dynamika' ('Rationality-Property-Dynamic'). In: *Przyjaciel Nauk 1-2*.

Staniszkis, Jadwiga (1987), 'Dynamika uzaleznienia' ('Dynamics of Dependency'), *Kontakt* 65/September.

Swinnen, Hugo (1986), 'Dutch Situation of LEIs: Theoretical Background for Local Economic Development', *Eurosocial Reports* nos. 43–44.

Szalai, Julia (1988), 'Social Crisis and Reform Alternatives'. Paper prepared for the *International Conference "Social Policy and Socialism"*, Leeds, UK., April 11–14. (Published in this volume.)

Sztachelski, Jerzy (1950), 'Plan 6-letni w sluzbie zdrowia' ('The 6-year Plan in the Service of Public Health'), *Zdrowie Publiczne* 9/12.

Sztachelski, Jerzy (1951), 'Wytyczne pracy sluzby zdrowia na 1951 rok' ('Guidelines for the Functioning of the Health Service in 1951'), *Sluzba Zdrowia* 11/12.

Turski, Ryszard (1983), 'Kryzys struktury spolecznej' ('Crisis of the Social Structure'). In: *Polityka spoleczna a struktury spoleczenstwa polskiego*. Polskie Towarzystwo Ekonomiczne.

Wnuk-Lipinski, Edmund (1988)), 'Inequalities and Social Crisis', *Sisyphus* 5.

World Health Organization (1987), 'Self-Help and Chronic Disease', *Report on a Workshop*. Leuven: WHO.

6 Outline for the radical reforms of social policy in Hungary

JULIA SZALAI

In the reform conceptions that have emerged in recent years in Hungary everywhere crops up the thought that even the most urgent economic reforms cannot be implemented successfully today without the reform of social policy and of the system of political institutions. From the analyses it turns out, of course, that very different notions of society, of value-choices and of intentions of change are hidden behind the almost 'slogan-like' demands asserted many times grammatically practically in the same way. In spite of the diversity of notions and ideas, however, when reading the vast majority of writings on general principles of the reforms, the reader is convinced that the reform of social policy cannot in fact be neglected any more. Some steps should be taken towards reform at least, since the effective functioning of the market unavoidably goes hand in hand with the strong differentiation of incomes and with the increase of social inequalities. So that the extent of these differentiations and tensions remains endurable, a separate corrective system is required: and this is the system which is called 'social policy' by most of the authors . Thus, the functions of social policy (and reforms are required to ensure these functions) are on the one hand to 'leave the economy alone', not to shackle the economy's free and normal organization and to counterbalance and correct the unavoidable and 'undesired' side effects of the functioning of the 'liberated economy' on the other.

I would not start from this rather general point in this chapter however. Instead, I would like to follow a different pattern. What I try to argue for is that it is naturally necessary to make social policy independent and to radically reform it, but not (or not primarily) in the interest of the success of the economic reform, but 'for its own sake'.

The reason behind the above statement is that social policy is in crisis – the necessity of its radical reform is stemming primarily from this fact. It should be emphasized that it is not the ending of the increase of the national income or the unfavourable economic processes that cause its crisis (these factors may only deepen it and make it more visible). The crisis stems first of all from the fact that the 'traditional' social policy of the 'ideal' planned economy that had been elaborated for the classical central redistributive system of state socialism has fulfilled its mission; it has outlived its usefulness and has increasingly become an obstacle in fulfilling the social tasks aimed at by its institutional and distributional forms and its services. Its survival has been a source of dysfunctions and social troubles for decades contributing to the unstoppable increase of social inequalities instead of diminishing them. What social policy today gives to its subjects are the many irritating, humiliating and painful experiences of unfairness, defencelessness and chronic shortage. Social policy has come to be associated with widely unsatisfied needs, of understandable bureaucratic regulations, of haphazard solutions of services of more and more unacceptable levels. Thus, the classical social political system has become the reason for and source of crisis, not because of the increasing problems in the economy or still less because of some kind of reforms of it, but simply 'in its own right'.

The essence can be expressed in a different and clearer way, in saying that the crisis phenomena emerging in the fields of social policy and economy derive from the same source. What can be seen very clearly in the confusions of both spheres is the internal crisis of the central redistribution system. Although it has been modified and repaired many times during the past decades, it has to be seen that with regard to its basic structure and power relations, the system has been functioning *without any change* from the beginning of the planned economy up to the present day. In this sense it is better and more precise to speak of a *social* crisis of which the crisis of the economy of social polices just a *part*. Hence, radical reforms should touch the sources of the entire system's crisis and the fundamental structure of central redistribution – both in the fields of economy and social policy.

The above-mentioned fundamental structure is the structure of power; therefore the issue of the reform is none other than the issue of *power*. What the reform must mean in the case of the economy is the separation of the state and market, in the case of social policy the separation of the state and civil society. Furthermore the autonomy of the state and its citizens and the independent self-organization of the society are the basic prerequisites upon which the elimination of the crisis, any positive perspectives of the society and the Europeanism of the country depend.

It is because of these ultimately decisive characteristics of power that a political turn is required in order to have any actual reforms in social policy.

The present state donation system based on the principle of distributing the residues (once other economic 'needs' are met) must be transformed into a social self-defence system controlled by the population. The political guarantees of such a turn in the system of social policy are not different from those in any other fields of economic and social life: they lie in a truly elected parliament representing the people, in the independent trade unions, in local autonomy and in the strict separation of the legislative and executive power.

Even if it follows from my argument that I consider the 'sectoral reform' of social policy impossible *in principle*, it is yet to be explained what have been the purposes and real functions of the traditional social policy of central redistribution. In what sense can we say that this system 'has fulfilled its historical mission'? I also have to answer the question whether (in addition to the mere desire for democratic institutions) there are any social conditions in social life today for changing social policy in the above sense of a real self-defence system? If such social conditions do exist, what are they? Can it be a realistic goal nowadays to argue for institutions guaranteeing the normal living standards for all citizens, diminishing mass poverty and meeting needs for the generally better satisfaction of the population? Are these aims not pure dreams amid the grave indebtedness and economic crisis of the country? I will try to examine these questions one by one in the following.

State socialist central redistribution and social policy

As it is commonly known, in the period of building the socialist planned economy, the new system abolished social policy in general. All of its traditional institutions were cast away as the requisites of overthrown capitalism. At the same time – and it is the essence of its self-contradiction – the planned economy was regarded to be the main trustee of social rationality and the social good. It followed that each and every segment of economy and society, of private and public life, became imbued with social considerations as the central intention. In this sense we can say that the elimination of social policy was accompanied by 'injecting social policy' into the entire system. All this happened not as an ideological mistake or because of the 'encroachment' of the Stalinist voluntarism, but because it all belonged to the essence of the totalitarian system.

After 1945 the new system began as a grandiose modernization programne, which, in the social historical sense, carried the denial of and a promise to finally solve the two interrelated decade-long burdens of earlier Hungarian social development. One burden was the partial (unsuccessful) integration of the society between the two wars. And the other cardinal question was closely connected to it. It seemed to be an unquestionable necessity to overcome absolute poverty of a non-European scale. (see Szalai, 1988).

The cessation of social policy and its identification with the centralized planned economy itself obtain a meaning and become an organic part of the grandiose programne in the above context of social prehistory. The planned method of economic control, the associated political processes, full employment forced by the devaluation of the labour force and – in parallel with this – the redefinition of social membership by binding it to employment, quantitatively satisfactory health services defined as 'allowances in addition to wages' and the established system of social security degraded to a 'budgetary branch' and subordinated to the all-time political objectives have all been meshing as inseparable gears and have been serving the social transformation programne intended and controlled by the central power.

Thus, the essence of this programne and its main feature was that it saw the solutions of the two basic problems, i.e. the former bifurcatedness of the society and that of mass poverty, in executing a radical integration experiment. The concrete realization of the integration experiment was expected from the total restructuring of social relationships. For this purpose and in the hope of building up a radically new society, existing social relations were regarded to be 'conservative' and 'non-socialist', and they had to be destroyed and reorganized, down to the very private level of family life.

The programne for the radical reorganization of the society was aimed at a well-controllable building principle arranged into a single-centred, tight, military hierarchy as an *integration* formation. As a *modernization* programme it proclaimed the transformation of the one-time agricultural country into an industrial society, the rapid economic development surpassing all previous developments and the ideal of social justice. All this rested fundamentally on two pillars: the feasibility of the programme was to be guaranteed by the supremacy of state ownership and by the omnipotence of the centrally planned economy organized on that ownership basis. The great illusion of the totalitarian system of the classical planned economy was that these two institutional pillars would guarantee the birth of an economy and society which would be more harmonic than any previous ones and in which the outcomes of rapid development could be distributed in the most just manner, in the spirit of equality. All this was thought to be realistic since the waste resulting from the unplanned functioning of the market and from the struggles of conflicting social interests seemed to be automatically and structurally eliminated by the new system.

From the point of view of today's discourse on the situation and on alternative solutions, it is very important to emphasize that in this system it is not the 'unsuccessful' economic policy, the 'control mechanisms' of production and distribution, the 'arbitrary political act of will' or the social rights defined 'too widely' which constitute the problem. It is the most fundamental feature of the system that ideologically, economically, politically and in its social consequences this programme is *coherent*. Its elements cannot be separated as 'correct' ideological and 'distorted' economic and social processes.

Accordingly, the crisis today is the crisis of the *system* and not the crisis of its individual elements.

The social historical validity of the central redistribution system of state socialism stemmed just from its double purpose. It had created a single-principle integration (even it was an unorganic one) and it had eliminated the absolute poverty of large masses. The historical barrier to its validity and the deepening crisis of the system stem from the fact that it was founded on an 'inorganic integration'. The unifying principle of the central dictates has begun disintegrating with the depletion of the sources of extensive growth and upon reaching the level of full employment (i.e. upon the depletion of the usable labour reserves). On the other hand, the relative security offered by the system previously has diminished. It means that in the end the system has not proved capable of integrating the society, making the economy prosper, making the country catch up with the most developed part of the world and of eliminating poverty for ever. Today we already know that the society of central redistribution is not the society of economic rationality and common good, but it is the system of the priority and superiority of politics above all.

The political aim of forced economic development has reduced the satisfaction of social needs to simply a means i.e. to the means of maintaining the artificially low level of wages which represent the most important and most durable source of centralized surplus. The 'principle of residues' of the social objectives comes from this fact. It directly follows from the logic of the centrally controlled planned economy that it seemed sufficient to decree administratively the equality of access to the social remunerations. In the system of the all-embracing 'planned control' the declaration of rights seemed to be identical with the automatic guarantees for their realization. The most important counterpoise to the still artificially depressed wages are the so-called free social benefits in kind and the central redistribution system of social security remunerations covering the entire society.

The most important function of the machinery of centralized redistribution in everyday reality is, however, to operate and finance the economy because of the daily reproduced state dependency of its institutions. Nearly 60% of the national budget concentrating some 80% of the Gross Domestic Product (GDP) flows through the economy again – in the form of donations, subsidies and supports – to keep it alive. In this way it becomes understandable that the 'social budget' (the source of health services, culture, education, etc. defined as 'free' state benefits and the source of the entire social security) – in spite of all goodwill – gets again and again into a hopeless residue position for structural reasons. In such a situation the functioning of the social sphere is controlled not by the needs but by the scarcities: available money, means, investment and labour force must be concentrated where they are needed most. As a result of the several decades-long residue position the most general characteristics of the social services today are almost hopelessly lagging behind others elsewhere, their institutions are chronically over-used and, because of serious over-use, their general standard is steadily deteriorating. Chronic shortages are accompanied by permanent troubles of supply and functioning, while increasing inequalities of access have been created and reproduced on this decreasing bases. That is the explanation why social policy once regarded as one of the most important achievements of socialism is regarded from a budgetary point of view, a paralysing item of expenditure, while at the same time, it has become the main source of poverty, poor services and defencelessness in the everyday experience of the population. It is perhaps needless to repeat in the light of the above, that all this is not simply a matter of resources. In the given system of state socialism, economy and central distribution keep each other captured. It is this mutual captivity, where social policy can only be a resource-draining ballast, and the livelihood of its subjects, i.e. the citizens, is just a 'burden' of distribution policy, unless they help themselves 'on their own'.

Social policy on a different basis

I hope that from what I have written so far the main thesis of my conception of a real reform of social policy has become clear. It is necessary to break with the habits and procedures of haphazard repairing solutions and supplementary resource-creating juggleries, and, instead, a radical re-evaluation and re-interpretation of the entire role, purpose and function of social policy is required. So that this 'reinterpretation' becomes reality, social policy must serve the society rather than the central state's will. Its institutions must become the institutions of social self-defence which are to fulfil the citizens' needs. This process, however, cannot be carried out without the self-organization of society, its separation from the centre, and without a newly-built, legally-regulated relationship between the state and civil society, permitting the latter to create institutions functioning in the interests of the independent and autonomous members, groups and communities of the society.

In representing citizens and their social needs, *trade unions* and *self-governing* institutions of *public administration* have a salient role. The 're-interpretation' of social policy cannot be imagined, on the other hand, without establishing independent trade unions safeguarding the interests of employees taking part not only in the first, but in the second economy, and, on the other, without placing the institutions of administration – through free elections – under control of the citizens. Only in this way will social policy get out of the distribution–political trap of the budget's all-time restrictedness, and will its main own institution – the social security system – become self-financing and self-governing, independent of the state budget, and will a network of social services, adapting itself flexibly to the emerging needs, be born and prosper.

Let us examine the question of social security first. Social security – as it has briefly been mentioned above – is the fastest growing expenditure item of the national budget in the traditional system. By now we are faced with the paradoxical situation where the budgetary spiral is further spun in an uncheckable manner by full employment and the nominal increase of wages, while the real value of its benefits is dropping day by day. This situation is contributing considerably to the fact that those social groups (the pensioners, the sick, the disabled and families with several children), in the resources of which social security remunerations play a decisive role, fall in large numbers below the subsistence level and their means of life is at stake. The reform of social security is one of the most burning questions of social policy.

There is, however, one important question. Is it possible at all amid the general crisis of the economy to make social policy independent and eliminate its basis of functioning which is the principle of residues? Is not the demand that social security must guarantee the reasonable living of all citizens (children, old people, disabled, sick and unemployed persons) illusory, when the chronic lack of resources is endangering the maintenance of even the minimum of traditional services? It is clear that it would have been easier to carry out the steps to be outlined below and the smooth transition into a self-financing system in the years of economic prosperity, than today. In spite of all this, what my answer to the questions raised expresses is not hopelessness, but the urgency of change-over . The irrational functioning of social security is generated not by shortage of money, but by the structural processes of the budgetary redistribution system.

Putting it in another way: it is possible to make social security independent and self-financing today, but the precondition for it is that the control of social security should gradually be given over by the state to its maintainers (to the employees and employers) and to its users, i.e. to the citizens, and that the state should respect the autonomy of social security under all circumstances. In order for it to become independent it is only one of the conditions that social security separates from the national budget and becomes an independent economic unit. Equally important preconditions are the autonomy in decision-making and the guarantee for the right of control. Without self-governing control financial independence would simply mean that the budgetary burdens would be pushed back to the companies, the employees and to the population. Independence should be gained in such a manner that the 'new' social security can form its regulation system and its decisions in negotiations and bargains between the independent trade unions (and their associations) protecting the interests of the employees, and the interest-protecting groupings (chambers) of the employers. That kind of bargaining procedure should arrive at decisions on the extent and share of contributions of employees and employers (which would probably be remarkably different from those applied today), on the most expedient types and methods of investment, etc. Therefore, the consequence of this change-over would probably be, in practice, that for a long period two different systems, organized and operated according to different principles and rules, would have to coexist.

The new system should utilize the contributions by the newcomers entering the labour market and/or the contributions paid by the employers for them. Only in this way can we imagine the just introduction of the funding principle of self-financing, i.e. the introduction of the long-term pledging of the contributions to pensions. This is so because in the past the contributions of the pensioners of today and tomorrow 'served' the concentration and redistribution of resources within the state budget, and therefore it follows that the state has an undisputable obligation to provide for their pensions. It must finance these 'old-type' pensions – although as an expenditure item decreasing year by year – invariably from its central budget.

As a result of this dual system the scarcity of sources of social insurance payments would be moderated within a few years, as the newcomers to the new system would begin to utilize what they pay as a contribution to pensions today only after several decades. It is not an unreal dream, but it may become a reality under the above conditions, that the interest-bearing capital of the 'newly' created retirement funds would gradually ensure enough money for raising other social security remunerations (family allowance, childcare benefit, sickness benefit, etc.) on the one hand, and for introducing new services, first of all various forms of allowances for children and the old-aged *on the basis of citizen's right*. In addition, one of its first tasks should be the introduction of a reasonable unemployment dole and the index-linking of pensions paid according to the 'old system'. Since, due to the crisis of the existing system of social policy, it is primarily the responsibility already of the employed middle-generation and the old people themselves to provide for the livelihood of the children, sick people and the old age persons (if they can) through extra work, overstraining themselves by overtime and through their activities in the second economy, one can well argue, that the above objectives would probably be given general social support. All these financial objectives are important enough for the people to be prepared to sacrifice for them a certain part of their actual incomes in the interest of their future and all-time security. Actually, the most obvious and most understandable forms of the 'personal income taxation' are the social security contributions that are repaid in the personal income utilization according to needs, and, in addition, that can be best controlled even by the *individual* citizen.

According to what has been written so far, the financial bases of social security services of a reasonable level can be established without a considerable rise in the individual (and the entrepreneurial) social security contributions. The reform of social security is not an illusion. But I have to emphasize again that the elementary condition for the legitimacy of this objective is that social security be in fact the financial security net and self-defence system of the society. This cannot be imagined without the self-governing form of its administration and without the public control of the legality of its functioning. It is the self-governing administration of social security that has to decide about the basic social priorities of the system as well as about its financial development and the sequence of needs satisfaction.

In fact, and to put it more precisely, social security is not necessarily a single system, but the federation of self-governing social securities dealing with the satisfaction of different needs. There may be an argument in favour of separated 'family', 'sickness', 'old age', etc. social securities adjusting their own self-governing policy, economic investments, etc. more naturally and with less transmissions to the needs of people represented by them. For example, the section dealing with sick people would place an emphasis on making health services prosper, and the 'unemployment banking institution' would consider the investment and credit policy adjusted to create more jobs as the main course of its market activity.

In addition to those mentioned so far, there are two further conditions for the safe functioning of this social–political financial system.

One condition is *parliamentary law-making* relating to the basic principles of the services and permitting only rare modifications. The social self-defence nature and the integrative force of social security can be undermined if the individual groups of the society are turned against one another by the frequently changing, more favourable or unfavourable laws on family allowances, unemployment or pension. This latter one is an especially sensitive problem. The reason for it is that the people are 'paying a tax' for decades for their pension, and the very meaning of their investments can be queried if the conditions and rules for the right to have a pension are changing as frequently as they do nowadays.

The other precondition for the safe functioning is that the *(benefit-delivering) payment obligations and the (fund-raising) economic activities* of the social security must be strictly separated. However, the former should legally be guaranteed and from the financial point of view – even in the case of full independence – the state budget would be responsible for it. As regarding the latter (economic activity) the self-government should have a free hand. And from this point of view social security can in the same way as anyone else be a market contractor (either a 'credit bank' or a 'capital investor'). It will probably be one of the most important political decisions of the self-government of the independent social security to make a balance between the risk of 'becoming rich' – which might result in a failure – and the temptation of bigger remunerations that can be paid from the accumulated incomes.

Let me now write a few words about the other large field of social policy, namely social services. The reforming of social policy should embrace an extension of the variety of public services in kind with ensured quality as well as keeping them free of charge or at least at a moderate price level. How can that all be done given the present conditions of scarcity, over-use, hidden payments and deteriorating quality?

I have written above that the institutional location of these social services should be basically the system of public administration responsible to its electors. So that the administration works in fact for the welfare of the people and for the achieving of social objectives, it is necessary to clearly separate its representative and bureaucratic nature, to strongly weaken the latter one (and make it 'functional') and to represent the people through free elections . But what is also needed in addition to these political and legal conditions is *money*. The bases for the financial functioning of public administration (on all its levels) are the *taxes*: personal ones and the taxes paid by the enterprises, contractors, institutions. In my view (as I have already written) personal income taxation has a place and role first of all in social security, in guaranteeing general financial security and material well-being through it, and, in addition, in strengthening people's self-confidence of citizenship.

Beside that, personal income taxes collected by the local administration may serve to accomplish important local objectives and the common aims of the local people's representation. The services of the administration, however, should basically not be built on personal taxes but on taxes of the *enterprises* and those of *institutions*. The rationale of my argument is that due to the nature of services , the financial interrelations between delivery and coverage of the services of the representative state and the resources for financing them are so indirect and complex, that they are not easily understood by the citizens. Therefore it seems to be illusory, that they can control those services and their most adequate financing through their *taxes*. The forms of the *general and proportionate sharing of social costs and those of social control* must be clearly separated: the former one is a matter of incomes and redistribution, while the latter is a political issue. And only their separation can ensure that the burden of taxes would not be the means for limiting the state objectives and that the representative control would not be attached to any financial census. The institutions and enterprises should be taxed but the people should control the local services.

The tax assessment of the representative state must be approved by the legislation, i .e. the parliament. It also requires a parliamentary decision and social publicity as to what should be the share in the redistribution of tax incomes between the local, regional and central levels; as to what and according to what principles are monies used by the society for health care, education, for the direct redistribution aimed at compensating for the inequalities of services among settlements, etc. Thereafter, the tax-based money (which, according to my conception are not direct tax incomes, but redistributive incomes originating from tax sources) is handled by the public administration system. This system 'purchases' education, teachers and schools, health – doctors, medical consultation rooms, assistants and hypodermic needles – roads, kindergartens, social workers and services supporting the families, etc. If the objective is very important, then it is entirely the public administration which buys the services (and in this case these services will be free to the customer), or, if the objective is not so important from the social point of view, then perhaps the buyer, is only partly the administration. In this way it could be ensured that the services 'can sell' on the market (and that it would be an equally useful thing to undertake the care of old aged people as to invest in making fashionable clothes or dresses) such that the level of services becomes higher and 'more elite' and that, in spite of this, customers or users could utilize them not according to direct market principles or to the extent of their purchasing power but because the democratic public administration system has purchased them on their behalf.

Naturally, in addition to purchasing services the local public administration probably need not rule out the possibility that in the case of certain aims it finances not the institutions, but the (potential) customers. This means that through its supplementary benefits, the administration would make 'able to buy' those who on the basis of their own capacities are unable to buy the services offered at a market price. In spite of this, the basic strategy in my opinion should be a financial policy of the administration aiming at not the individuals, but at the services. The reasons are manifold. Partly this seems to be the only way of avoiding the formation of a dual system of services (the disintegrating forms of the 'poor' and the 'middle-class' health care system and education). Secondly, supplementary benefits are always personalized and humiliating, while service financing is impersonal and activity-oriented. Thirdly, general income security – as I have already written – is basically the business of social security. The mixture of its principles with methods of taxation would in the end make actual control very difficult and it is not certain that actual control could even be vindicated. On top of this, this kind of 'mixing' could well become the starting point of quarrels between the two systems – the self-governing social security and that of public administration – and it also might create shifting and problems of smooth functioning in both spheres. Besides, the general, widespread provision of supplementary benefits substituting the purchase of services could result in the citizens 'using up' tax resources against each other instead of strengthening solidarity and integration.

The further task of social self-governing is to facilitate and ensure the economic security and prosperity of its electors. In this sense we must also think of the system of social services from the point of view of economic processes. A community having general well-being without having economic activity, a wide choice of jobs and prospering enterprises can only be imagined as an exception. And if we think of these relationships not only in connection with the micro-communities but with regard to the entire national economy and social welfare, then we have returned to the starting statement of this paper: namely, that real radical reforms of the economy and social policy can only be imagined together. And the basic condition for their joint success is the radical change of the entire political system. It means that the society having *served* the state should become a *civil society* organized, independently of the state, coexisting with it in legally regulated circumstances.

Bibliography

Szalai, J. (1988), 'Social Crisis and Reform Alternatives,' *Medvetanc*, 1987/2; Appendix; Budapest, 1988.

7 The fourth road: the future for Hungarian social policy

ZSUZSA FERGE

The necessity of a fourth road

The 'third' road of Sweden has meant a deliberate break with the ideology and practice of liberal capitalism and Bolshevik communism (Meidner, 1979). The current outcome is a parliamentary democracy operating with popular control, a highly-developed, essentially market economy, and one of the world's most developed systems of social (and societal) policy. Hungary is now in crisis and is in search of a way out. Liberal market-based capitalism is not an attractive alternative for many. The road followed up to now (i.e. a variant of Bolshevism) is a blind alley. The third road of Sweden seems to be a desirable choice, but because of the difference in the historical context and conditions this model is hard to follow. Hence the necessity to explore the possibilities of a 'fourth road'. Before drafting its outlines, however, one has to have a closer look at the present situation.

The economic reform and social policy

Issue of a theoretical nature

The economic reform programmes which have been proliferating in Hungary since the early 1980s[1] have been infused with various latent and manifest political implications. So much so that up to 1987 many of them have been considered by the central power as hostile. The *latent* political message was incorporated in various economic categories proposed by the reformers such as deregulation, self-regulating markets, autonomous decisions of economic agents, the interests of the (individual or collective) owners of the means of production, and so forth. Explicitly or not, these categories are menacing the existing party, or state, or economic powers. The *manifest* political implications have surfaced when the conditions of the market reform have been spelt out. A civilized market cannot function without legal protection of the contracts, or without legal guarantees against the erratic or arbitrary intervention of the state. These requirements unavoidably strengthen the role of parliament and weaken not only that of the government, but also that of the Party – at least in all cases which can be administered by law. An important corollary has been the demand for more openness and a more overt public life. Without this condition the participation and control of the citizens remains illusory both inside and outside of the market.

The political significance of the reform projects explains the oddities of the scholarly debates over them. The *academic* or professional critique of the *economic* reform ideas was for long handicapped by the fact that the political power did not allow until very recently the overt surfacing of *political* reform views. It was only in the guise of economic projects that the citizens could express their will to regain control over civil society, and could fight for more freedom and more rights. One cannot over-estimate the role of the economic reformers in triggering a new way of thinking. At the same time, the consequence of this situation was that *freedom* and the *market* have become synonymous. Any apprehension or reservation about the market could be interpreted as an attack on the fight for freedom, or the arguments expressing such qualms could be used for this assault. Therefore if one did not want to be identified with, or become a tool of Stalinist forces, one had to formulate one's critique with the utmost caution, and even then misunderstandings have been frequent.

In the latest period (the second half of 1988) the situation has improved: political reform projects can be now formulated in their own right, without any camouflage. Hence it has become possible to discuss separately the issues related to the economic reform and those connected with the political reform. This allows one to speak clearly, or rather, this allows me to state that I fully endorse the demands of the political reformers concerning the necessity of a democratic, multiparty parliamentary system. As for the economic reform projects, I may agree with the major part of the proposed changes without accepting all of its theoretical components and its practical implications.

As far as the market is concerned I always accepted Karl Polanyi's assumption that the market was, and ought to be, present in all (economically relatively developed) societies. However, I have always doubted (following once more Polanyi's lead) that the market has to *integrate (by means of money) all the factors of production including land and labour,* and has to cover all possible needs. Such an extensive market means (at least in my understanding) that society becomes again subordinated to a monolithic power which is dictating, together with the ways and means of need satisfaction, a special value system. Hayek is certainly right in affirming that the dictatorship of the market is more acceptable than political dictatorship because it operates in an impersonal way. But it is still a dictatorship.

As for the integrative role of the market, I have argued both on logical and empirical grounds that 'the various markets might operate with different conditions and rules, because ultimately this is not an economic but a political issue' (Ferge, 1986). The most important matter in this respect is the relationship between the market and the labour force. Labour power is no ordinary commodity: human beings are at stake. By the same token wages and salaries are not simply the market price of the labour power. They form the basis of livelihood, and they constitute a system of distribution shaped by social forces. Thus (in my view) the market has to be influenced to the extent which allows the protection of people, the prevention of their being at the mercy of the market.

One of the worst types of vulnerability is unemployment. Yet practically all economic reform projects affirm that in the medium run 'albeit this is not desirable, it is unavoidable to accept not only structural, but also global unemployment'. In my understanding this price is too high to endorse. I therefore think that an active labour market policy is an indispensable prerequisite of the reform. Genuine structural reform is unthinkable and unfeasible without it. The other main form of vulnerability is a wage which is not sufficient to assure a minimum livelihood. The market left to itself may or may not secure a decent minimum wage.

In a democratic market society organized interests are imperative to exert pressure in favour of active employment policy or of an acceptable, legitimate wage system. The intervention of the state in such matters cannot become legitimate either without mass pressure. Incidentally, because of the relationship between social forces and outcomes on the market, one has to doubt the validity of an often heard – but not disinterested – cliché. Nowadays it is frequently affirmed in Hungary that wages are too levelled and have no stimulating impact on productivity. Henceforth an essential prerequisite of the reform is the significant increase in wage differentiation. The catch is that if proper wage bargaining occurs, there is no way of knowing in advance whether the outcome will be a more levelled or a more differentiated system. But the wage system will become 'efficacious' only if it is based on a consensus reached by wage bargaining.

A second question connected with the limits of the market is related to need satisfaction in and outside the market. In all economic reform projects there is a recurrent demand, according to which the systems which allocate services free or in a non-market way have to be abolished: 'the subsidization of the institution ought to be replaced by the support of the individual citizens' ('Fordulat es reform', p.39, or Kopatsy, 1988) The arguments sustaining this claim are manifold. The most frequently mentioned reason is that allegedly state redistribution has increased inequalities. Freedom of choice and the greater efficiency of the market are also invoked.

Sociologists (in Hungary as elsewhere) have repeatedly refuted these contentions. In their view it is more appropriate to finance institutions than individuals. Otherwise 'the dual systems of the allocation of services will inevitably emerge, leading to a middle class and a 'poor' service in the health service or in schools, producing disintegration (Szalai,1987). They refer to extensive statistical evidence showing that the inequalities of redistribution tend to decrease when the quality and quantity of the 'free' services are improved. They mention the humiliating aspects of social assistance. The compatibility of free services with freedom of choice (an explicit objective of the reform of Finnish social policy) (Wiman, 1987) is also invoked. Indeed, if services are decentralized and democratized, the local councils may finance non-state agents in a number of fields (even if there are important reservations about this solution). These non-profit institutions[2] may promote a variety of innovations in the social sphere and may increase the flexibility of the system. In the case of the health service the alleged efficacy of the market is seriously questioned on the grounds which are mentioned by Glennerster (1985). On the whole, sociologists share the conviction that if the character of central power changes, if the state would operate with more participation and control of the citizens, then many adverse or harmful aspects of state redistribution could be remedied.

A further debate focuses on the residual character of social policy. Practically each variant of the economic reform projects mentions the necessity of a social 'safety net' for the most needy to counterbalance the additional difficulties created by the reform (Antal,1982, 1988). No doubt, there is a need for a safety net, and sociologists were among the first to direct attention to the deficiencies of this net. However, *the safety net cannot be more than a last resort.* If too many fall into it, it will *collapse*. The basic objective of social and societal policy is to prevent the fall of people into the net (by means of employment policy, wage policy, social security etc.).

All the above issues – the limits of the market, the respective roles of the market and welfare redistribution, those of the state and the citizens in shaping the contours of social policy – have been proposed for debate by some sociologists for a long time. Yet, they have not been recognized as vital, and no professional or public debate has developed around them. At the same time, however, a number of steps are being prepared and occasionally taken which, (according to the previous arguments) threaten with socially harmful consequences.

It has to be added that it took time and intellectual effort until the sociologists dealing with social welfare succeeded in rejecting the traditionally accepted pattern of thought according to which social policy is 'state responsibility' both in a capitalist 'welfare state' and in a 'socialist caring state'. The cumulation of adverse social experiences and a radical change in the political conditions have been necessary to openly formulate a basic query. And this is as follows: *if in East European socialist societies social policy has often operated in an inhuman and inequitable ways, why should the central power change this state of affairs, why should it decide, merely on the basis of some rational arguments, to move into a direction which does not offer any advantages for itself?* Once, however, the question is asked, the only answer is that such a change cannot occur without a democratic political system. In such a system it *may* happen that an autonomous and (nearly) self-regulating economy, i.e the market, is counteracted and controlled by another autonomous and (nearly) self-regulating sphere, that of social and societal policy. '*The sphere would be motivated not by market, but by social interests, and activated not by market mechanisms, but those of social movements.* If both spheres operate adequately, then their confrontation could produce the legal, non-arbitrary limitation of the market' (Ferge,1988).

The practical reform steps of the recent past

The economic situation did not ameliorate in the last year. The reason lies not only in the brevity of time. Many important reform steps have been shunned if they threatened prominent political or economic interests. In what follows I deal only with those aspects of the implementation of the reform which affect adversely either the situation of the citizens or the chances of a sound social (societal) policy.

Up to now the interests of the state budget have dominated all other economic or social interests. Elements of the reform package have been taken out of context and implemented in an isolated way, if the financial equilibrium was served in this manner. This explains the introduction of an excessively severe income tax system *without* the wage reform and the price reform, or the acceptance of unemployment without previously implementing an active employment policy and a decent unemployment benefit. Most notably, this explains the shift of the burdens of the crisis on the shoulders of the population, and more specifically on its weakest groups. As a consequence poverty is rapidly increasing, hitting by now about one third of families. New forms of insecurity and hardships are emerging, with downward spirals of fatal impoverishment, leading to cuts of gas or electricity, the accumulation of heavy debts, excessive deficiencies of the diet especially of the elderly and so forth. Discontent is growing because meanwhile the economy is not progressing, but income inequalities are spectacularly increasing, partly because of the rise of a new, to some extent, parasite group of pseudo-entrepreneurs (such as tax experts).

Marketization has followed up to now the path of least resistance. In the sphere of the economy, where the market would have a genuine role, anti-market lobbies, state subsidies and haphazard or autocratic state intervention proliferate. In the sphere of welfare redistribution, though, where need satisfaction should occur – by definition, as it were – outside the market, there is no way of stopping the progress of the 'market', i.e. the load-shedding of the state, placing increasing financial burdens on the population in the name of a market ideology. The examples abound, from the price increase of school meals (outpricing many children) to the outrageous price increase of the shelters for the homeless.

In short, market forces are gaining in the sphere where they had nothing to do, while lingering in fields where they should flourish.

Centrally planning economic policy made practically a fetish of so-called productive branches. Thus the 'non-productive' sectors and activities – from education to telecommunication services – have been disastrously neglected. Some of the economic damage caused by this error have been recognized by now, and the ideologically-loaded expression itself has been abandoned. A new category has taken its place, though. It does not cover the whole of the former non-productive sphere, but only part of it. The activities and institutions which are sacrificed by the current monetarist etc. ideologies are those the utility of which cannot be measured in money terms, or which do not promise high profitability or rapid rates of return. The state is rapidly withdrawing from many fields of culture or education, threatening thereby the survival of the widely recognized opera house, the production of records, or some ensembles. The same fate menaces irreplaceable public collections, museums, archives and libraries. University faculties and chairs teaching subjects or preparing for professions of no visible economic value are more or less handled as private hobbies unworthy of public support. This miserly treatment hits not only such sciences as classical philology and aesthetics but also social policy and adult education. The whole educational system is underfinanced from the primary schools onwards, which are increasingly overcrowded and lack elementary facilities. Cultural homes and even schools are forced to make money which is possible only at the expense of their basic activities. Social workers and social work centres are more needed than ever before, but there are not enough funds either for social work education or for expanding the services at the necessary rate. Social and cultural activities increasingly seek the generosity of Hungarian or foreign charities.

In short, non-profit activities are increasingly delegitimated, and the future is threatened by the parsimoniousness of the present.

There are endeavours to introduce market elements into the traditional large welfare institutions like the health system, the school system or social security, which are also cause for concern. These systems certainly operate at present with innumerable deficiencies and flaws. Still, I doubt that the only way for their improvement leads through marketization and privatization, implying a segmented voluntary insurance system and the rejection of free and universal access in the case of health and school.

As far as the reform plans of social security are known, it is likely, on the one hand, that it will be soon separated from the budget and become an autonomous body. With proper state guarantees (which are projected) and genuine self-governing bodies (which are projected, but only in a more distant future) this move could be beneficial. It can lead to a more responsible system which is 'counting' its incomes and outlays, without necessarily 'calculating' with profits,[3] i.e. without accepting the values of the market. However, there are powerful efforts promoting the market logic within social insurance. They are related to the idea of a 'three-tier' system. The *first* tier would consist of universal, flat rate benefits financed by taxation, such as a basic pension or the childcare grant as citizen's right. This would be an important step forward, because up to now truly universal benefits offered as of right have been the exception rather than the rule in Hungary. The *second* tier would cover the earnings related benefits, i.e. pensions and sick pay financed by contributions. The principles of classic insurance, i.e. the equivalence principle or risk-sharing among the insured would strengthen, and solidaristic or redistributive components would weaken in this tier. The *third* tier would be built up of voluntary insurance schemes, contracted individually or in a corporative way (e.g. in the form of pension schemes organized by individual firms).

Whether these changes would improve the social security of the citizens or not, i.e. whether they would assure both elementary, basic security and protect to a predefined extent the standards already reached, depends essentially on the quality and organization of the first and the third tier. If the first tier were to be generous enough, it would assure basic security for all, and even the absence of solidaristic and redistributive elements in the second tier would not seriously matter: decent and properly indexed minimum levels would be guaranteed by the first tier. And if the role of the third tier were to remain limited, i.e. were it to be a genuine option for those who want additional security, it would be no more than an innocent expression of freedom of choice. However, strong interest groups seem to operate against this optimistic scenario. My forebodings are based on the observation of the operation of new interest groups, especially of the newly built up insurance market, and of the new, monetarist tendencies defending at all costs the interests of the state budget. The main problems to be foreseen are the following:

– The standards of the first tier may not be generous enough owing to an alleged or genuine shortage of funds.
– The compulsory earnings related scheme is likely to define a low ceiling over which it will not cover the earnings. Thereby the third tier will have an important role. This means that the groups which have relatively high incomes and relatively great social strength will become uninterested in the compulsory systems, the quality of which would fatally dwindle down.
– The bigger firms are likely to organize their own pension schemes. Those working at smaller firms, those having occasional or temporary jobs, all

the relatively low-paid earners who have no money to be spent on optional extra insurance, plus all those who are not considered important enough by the firms to be included in a favourable scheme will be left out of the third tier. If however, it is made compulsory to join the corporative pension schemes, then one has to face the contradiction spelt out long ago by the International Labour Office. If firms are allowed to build up compulsory schemes but the overall scheme is not, then the debate is no more about the merits or demerits of compulsion, but about the acceptance or rejection of social solidarity.[4]

– In case of financial difficulties or the bankruptcy of the firm, either the state has to finance the losses of a group, or the insured persons will suffer.

Other apprehensions may also be spelt out about the increased role of 'private' i.e. optional insurance schemes. The crux of the matter is that if voluntary insurance plays a central instead of a residual role, then two consequences are hard to avoid. One is central state redistribution in favour of the better-off groups. The other, and more important, consequence is the increase of inequalities among the elderly (Kohl, 1988) or, more precisely, the emergence of a *segmented security market*,[5] strengthening the inequalities occurring within the economically active groups.

The switch from a public health system (introduced in Hungary in 1978) to an insurance-based health system is also controversial. The arguments in favour of health insurance invoke freedom of choice, more efficiency and economy, increased financial interest of doctors and hospitals. Unfortunately, they do not take into account a number of foreign experiences.

It is for instance known that insurance schemes usually do not cover geriatric patients, mental patients, mentally or physically handicapped people and, sometimes, lasting and incurable diseases. The groups involved, which are usually weak and not vocal, have to fall back on the public service, or they might stay unprovided for. A similar fate threatens those who are unable to pay the insurance fees or can buy only a cheap or partial insurance.

A British analyst questions the economic arguments in these terms:

> As the dominant provider of health care and major employer of medical staff and purchaser of drugs, governments can be held accountable for rising medical costs and have an incentive to control them. The containment of medical prices and dubiously effective and expensive treatments have been more successful in Britain than in almost any other country. Insurance schemes on a fee-for-service basis are, by contrast, very ineffective in containing costs. The consumer is not faced with the true price, he merely passes the bill on to the insurance company... The demand for medical care is unusual. It is not made by the consumer but by the suppliers, the doctors, who have a monopoly of knowledge and diagnose our need for care. Insurance companies find it very difficult to argue with the diagnosis. Escalating medical fees and insurance

premiums have been the result in most countries that finance their health schemes this way. (Abel-Smith, 1976)

The administrative costs in private insurance schemes are high because of the extra cost of handling claims. (Glennerster, 1985, p. 142.)

An additional problem arises because in a *democratic* state the citizens may find some means of controlling the standards and priorities of the public health system, but they have much less voice and less possibility of participation and control in the case of insurance schemes. My contention is that the Hungarian public health system has been substandard and defective in many respects not because it was public, but because it was run by an undemocratic state (i.e. totally lacking public participation and control), and because it has been heavily underfinanced.[6]

I don't suggest that the Hungarian social security and health systems will be necessarily worse 'on average' after the proposed changes are introduced than they are now. This is unlikely. However, I am practically sure that there will be a more pronounced differentiation whereby the stronger groups are likely to gain, and the weaker ones will most certainly lose. (The same is likely to happen to education if the school system also becomes segmented.) It is therefore open to doubt whether it is worth while – for society as a whole – to introduce these risky steps, or whether it would not be more rewarding to experiment with decentralization, democratization and, in the case of social security, self-government, without giving up the state's, or, rather, society's responsibility in these matters. This implies a radical change of the state instead of the individual institutions, which is no doubt a taller order.

I suspect, though, that the institutional changes described above are almost inevitable. Not only are they in the interest of the stronger groups who have been particularly frustrated by the bad public systems and who expect relatively rapid gains from the changes. There is no mass opposition on the part of the potential losers either. In the absence of widespread debates it was relatively easy to make the majority believe that the market will correct what the state has spoilt. And the losers will not realize the damage done to them before it is too late to change the new, fragmented institutions.

– Increasing insecurity and poverty have revived with incredible speed the traditions of the age-old 'politics of poverty', including relief offered to the 'deserving, truly needy'. Social assistance has changed in the last years inasmuch as a growing number of individuals and families having a regular and legal income from pensions or wages are now becoming 'truly needy'. In other words, wages and pensions are increasingly inadequate to assure a minimum livelihood. The social assistance given to active earners and their families is not only tragic. From the point of view of the economic reform it is also controversial. One of the objectives of the economic reform is the withdrawal of state subsidies to production. But assistance given to low-wage earners is nothing else but *indirect subsidy offered by the budget to ineffective production, unable to assure living wages to workers*. If the firm were to pay acceptable wages, its costs would be higher. It would then need either higher state subsidies – or it would go bankrupt. Seen from this angle, assisting active earners means that economic restructuring is slowed down, i.e. it is *bad economic policy* (Myles,1988).

It has to be added that the current regulations in social assistance are inadmissibly obsolete. The Hungarian system of social assistance has remained fully discretionary. No social assistance is based on rights. It has to be applied for. Its accordance depends on whether the applicant is deemed deserving by the administrator in charge, and whether the local council has available funds. In fact and this is the second major problem – because assistance does not constitute a right, its financing is not first priority of the local councils. Thus the councils may run out of funds and deny assistance even if they find the case fully justified. In addition, because of the humiliating aspects of the discretionary procedure many individuals and families in genuine need do not apply at all for the help of the local council.

Experience and logic suggest that a system of social assistance cannot be effective (i.e. cannot reach those in need)[1] cannot be rational (i.e. devoid of prejudices), and civilized (i.e free from humiliating aspect), if it does not operate with rights and norms. This elementary axiom did not as yet affect officialdom. *There is a widespread illusion that a safety net can be created without adequate wages, pensions and social benefits as of right, if only the truly needy would be properly identified.* Therefore the current discretionary practice of social assistance is expanding, which is divisive, expensive and, with high taxation, less and less legitimate. Concurrently, the administrators are increasingly uncertain about having found the 'most needy' among all those in genuine need. The pressure is growing to 'improve' means-testing and control, to develop better methods of registering the poor; in short, to combine lawlessness with an ineffectual and costly bureaucracy.

No doubt, crisis management is a necessity. But it should not endanger either the present or the future. The solutions due to necessity should not render more difficult the transition to a society which allows more equity and more autonomy to its citizens. The 'fourth road' tries to describe such a society in some detail.

The contents of the 'fourth road'

The fourth road is neither a paradise on earth, nor a remote utopia, nor again the 'Marxist' idea of an 'historically necessary future'. It is a possibility.

Whether some of its elements will come true or not under the conditions of a new political democracy will depend, hopefully, on the will and strength of its citizens. Indeed, I do not believe in a coming age of equality, liberty and solidarity. But it is worth working for less inequality, inequity, unfreedom and anti-solidarity. I do not believe that work could become a need (in the Marxist sense) in the foreseeable future. But it might be possible to create a society in which work is available for those who want it, and where jobs are less harmful both mentally and physically. I do not believe in 'distribution according to work', partly because this nice idea cannot be translated into practice, and partly because it has lost its validity when Hungarian society accepted income from capital and entrepreneurship as legitimate. It should be possible, however, to arrive at wages which assure a livelihood in line with the general conditions of society, and the differentiation of which is legitimated by democratic wage bargaining. I do not think that 'distribution according to need' is a maxim which can be applied in practice in a relatively developed and sophisticated society. The citizens of a society might nevertheless opt for some needs to be taken out of the competence of the market and made independent of the purchasing power of the consumer, i.e. they might decide which needs should be satisfied in the non-market sector. These decisions are not necessarily harmful for the economy. Damage may be avoided if the agents of production who are eminently motivated by market forces (i.e. entrepreneurs, managers) can compromise over these issues with the workers, or if decisions concerning production are shaped in a participatory way.

The *political* context of the 'fourth road' is, then, a pluralist, multiparty parliamentary democracy, allowing for democratic will-formation. This is a necessary, albeit not a sufficient condition. (Currently quite a few Hungarian political scientists and jurists, for instance Mihaly Bihari, Peter Schmidt, Istvan Kukorelli, Gabor Halmai, Bela Pokol, Laszlo Solyom are working on the outlines of such a political system and on the feasibility of the project.)

The *economic* context is a variant of what is called 'socialist market economy' as described by authors such as Alec Nove abroad, or Tamas Bauer and Pal Juhasz in Hungary. Some of the main ingredients of the system are multiple forms of private and collective ownership, but (if parliament so decides) with an upper limit or private ownership; a majority of small cooperative or other productive units which render possible genuine participation; entrepreneurship, competition and a veritable market, which does not, however, dominate society as a whole.

The *social* context is partly defined by the political and the economic conditions, and partly by a strong non-market sector with its own values and mechanisms. This sector which constitutes the field of social and societal policy is of central importance in my approach. It depends on the strength of this field to what extent will market and money dominate society and whether it would be possible to curb market interests for the sake of labour, for instance. The non-market forces will determine whether the values of the market will permeate all social relationships, or whether there will be a place for a truly multifold value-system. It will depend also on them how far non-profit activities will be accepted and legitimated. Even if this sounds rather pompous, I presume that the non-market sphere should also be the soil of an integrative and solidaristic morality.

Issues arising on the boundary of the market and the non-market sphere

The dynamics of the system are generated, among other things, by the continuous confrontation of the forces and interests of the market and the non-market sphere. The stakes of the bargains may be manifold. They may range from working conditions to the alternatives of technological development, from job creation to distributional issues on the macro- or micro-level. The following economic issues are of paramount importance in relation to the societal policy of the 'fourth road':

- How is it possible to approach as closely as possible to full employment without solutions implying compulsion, or the criminalization of unemployment, or only formal, sometimes sham results?[7] Up to now the best way seems to have been worked out by the active labour market policy of Sweden. This policy is realizing by and large what it promises because it is not a single piece of legislation, but related to other arrangements.
- How can sufficient resources be obtained for the coverage of needs entrusted to the non-market sphere? The first (necessary, but not sufficient) condition is, obviously, an economy which 'delivers the goods'. The socially acceptable allocation and utilization of these resources is the responsibility of parliament and also that of the self-government of social security.
- How can income inequality be contained within limits which might gain consensus? The main instruments seem to be the legal limitation of private property; a solidaristic wage policy (akin again to that of Sweden) which restrains high earnings in order to assure decent minimum wages; and, finally the tax system. In this context it seems worth while to recall some of Galbraith's warnings:

> For promoting equality, a reasonable equal distribution of income is much superior to an unequal distribution which is then remedied by taxation. Once people have income, they have a not wholly surprising resistance to action, however righteously inspired, to remove it. And their ingenuity in defending possession is great. (Galbraith, 1974, p.287)

The proposed 'fourth road' is in many respects a copy of the Swedish third road. There are nonetheless significant differences. One is that Hungary nationalized all private property in 1948 and 1949. While the excesses of nationalization are now withdrawn and limited private or non-state ownership is encouraged, at least up to now no social group has wanted to go back to unlimited private ownership. The scenario described here is based on limited ownership. A second major difference is in the conception of the non-market sphere. In Sweden the role of the state was more legitimate in this field than it is nowadays in Hungary. Also when Swedish social democrats conceptualized the 'third road', alternative movements and the struggle for personal autonomy were weak or non-existent. In present day Hungary they cannot be ignored. This means that the stages which in Sweden followed each other (Hedborg and Meidner,1984) are overlapping or superimposed in Hungary.

Needs having priority in the non-market sphere

As for all other needs assigned to the non-market sphere, it is again up to the bargaining procedures of social groups having different commitments to agree upon their range, standards and the ways of access to need satisfaction. The approach to these needs may be varied.

My assumption is that *existential security* is one of the basic needs, in two different senses. *Elementary security* is essential in guaranteeing that no one will fall under the threshold of minimal livelihood as agreed upon by society. The apparently simplest way to achieve existential security is the unconditional acceptance of the 'right to existence', i.e. a basic income on citizen's right. Several technical solutions are proposed to serve this aim, from negative income tax through tax credits up to the social dividend or the 'universal allocation' advocated by the French anti-utilitarian movement (Collective Charles Fourier, 1987). While these solutions seem to be simple and efficient, in reality they are either disintegrative and counter-incentive (like the negative income tax), or hardly realistic under the present conditions. I tend to think therefore, even if this sounds rather old-fashioned, that near full employment, decent wages and adequate minima in social security benefits offer the most realistic solution.

The other important component of security is the possibility to maintain as nearly as possible the standards of living already arrived at in case of sudden changes or crises in the life situations. The main instrument in this case is offered by earnings related social insurance benefits. Pensions, sick pay and, in Hungary at least, a childcare benefit already serve this purpose, but other 'risks' may also be covered in the future. These benefits are funded by contributions, and handled by social insurance schemes.

In a second approach I consider the basic conditions which promote the reduction of *inequalities in the physical and social life chances of individuals and social groups* (Ferge, 1982). This view is quite close to the ideas of Len Doyal and Ian Gough. In their conception the basic goal is human liberation from all forms of exploitation and domination. They are searching for the preconditions of liberation in the realm of need satisfaction. They assume –

and endeavour to prove logically – that *health and autonomy* are the two most basic and most essential needs, covering a number of other, more 'commonplace' needs as well.

> It is health rather than survival – both physical and mental health – which is the most basic human need and the one which it will be in the interest of individuals to satisfy before any others... .We know now that physical health will always require a minimum level of nutrition and liquid, varying amounts of sleep, exercise, warmth and so on. Mental health will similarly require an empirical minimum of human contact, emotional support, opportunity for emotional expression and privacy...The second set of basic needs which must be met for actions to be successful relates to individual identity and autonomy – the private and public sense of 'self'. Our second basic need for autonomy translates into the basic need for *creative consciousness* – the ability in theory to formulate both goals and strategies for achieving them. (Doyal and Gough, 1986, pp. 47–50)

Among the objectives of the 'fourth road', then, an important place is assigned to the autonomous and free choice of 'life' of individuals, together with assuring the conditions of autonomous options in a consensual way, by market and non-market means. This objective can be approached only if there is a multiplicity of actors in the various fields entailing a pluralism of agents, instruments and value systems. In the shaping of the non-market, or welfare sphere there should be room for all the alternative groupings and movements venting new needs, and assuring the flexibility of the system. The traditional 'corporative forces', the unions of labour and of employers should continue to assume an important role and despite the not unjustified fears from a state which is constantly threatened by tendencies of bureaucratism, paternalism or over-centralization, let alone dictatorship, the state has to retain momentous responsibilities in guaranteeing political, economic and social rights. Only the nature of the state has to change because of genuine democratic control and participation. 'The question is not whether or not there should be a state. It is what sort of a state it should be, and how it could meet the needs and rights of those it should serve rather than dominate' (Doyal and Gough, 1986, p. 59).

Arriving at the end of this essay, I have to reaffirm that I did not want to engage in utopian thinking. I am not naive enough to think that the programme described above is on the agenda of the near future. But if some of us agree that these are not unrealistic objectives for a not too distant future, then one might start to discuss them, to make them adaptable, and to find ways to start to implement them. A set of such objectives may help to get out of the present social and value crisis.

Notes

1. One should talk about the economic reform plans of the 'first' and the 'second generation'. The first period lasted from the early 1950s up to the implementation of the economic reform in 1968. 'Second generation plans' have been elaborated since the early 1980s. The most important document of the 'new wave' is the document 'Fordulat es reform' written by prominent reform economists, among others, L. Antal, T.Bauer, L. Lengyel and M. Tardos.
2. Absurdly enough, the non-profit sector is not yet fully recognized in Hungary. Human services may be as heavily taxed as any economic activity.
3. About the distinction between 'counting' and 'calculating', i.e. between counting with resources on the one hand and calculating in order to make profit on the other see Bourdieu, 1977.
4. See the report of the ILO: *'Towards the twenty-first century*, 1984.
5. I have to thank my colleague, Dr Laszlo Szucs for this expression.
6. The share of the health system has amounted for the last decades to 3 or 4 per cent of the GDP, which is one of the lowest rates both in Eastern and Western Europe (Gacs, 1985, 1987).
7. The problems mentioned here are familiar in Hungary. Full employment was achieved from around 1965. However, it was flawed on several accounts. Formal full employment was assured by means of within wall unemployment. As soon as this was questioned on the grounds of efficiency and rationalty, punitive measures were introduced in order to force people to accept substandard jobs.

Bibliography

Abel-Smith, Brian (1976), *Value for Money in Health Services*. Heinemann.

Antal, Laszlo (1982), 'Gondolatok gazdasagi mechanizmusunk reformjarol' ('On the reform of the economic mechanism'), *Medvetanc*.

Antal, Laszlo (1988), *A reform uj szakasza: A szocialista piacgazdasag megteremtese. (The new period of the reform: the creation of a socialist market economy)* Tezisek. Sokszorositas.

Collective Charles Fourier (1987), 'L'allocation universelle.' *Bulletin du MAUSS* (Mouvement Anti-Utilitarista dans les Sciences Sociales), Septembre.

Doyal, Len and Ian Gough (1986), 'Human needs and socialist welfare,' *Praxis International*, vol. 1. no. 6.

Ferge, Zsuzsa (1982), *Tarsadalmi ujratermeles es tarsadalompolitika (Social reproduction and social policy)*. Kozgazdasagi es Jogi Konyvkiado.

Ferge, Zsuzsa (1986), 'Gazasagi reform, szocialpolitika es legitimacio' ('Legitimation by market and by social policy'), *Valosag*, 10.

Ferge, Zsuzsa (1988), 'Gazdasagi es szocialis erdekek es politikak' ('Social interests and the economy'), *Gazdasag*, 1. szam.

'Fordulat es reform' ('Change and reform') (1987), *Medvetanc*, 2. szam melleklete.

Galbraith, J.K. (1974), *Economic and the Public Purpose*. Penguin.

Glennerster, Howard (1985), *Paying for Welfare*. Basil Blackwell.

Kohl, Jurgen (1988), *Public/private Mixes in Pension Politics*. copyright IPSA.

Kopatsy, Sandor (1988), 'A koltsegvetes tundoklese es bukasa' (The rise and fall of the budget'), *Valosag*, no. 11.

Meidner, Rudolf (1979), 'Unsere Vorstellungen vom dritten Weg.' In: Wirtschaft und

Gesellschaft. Kritik und Alternativen (ed. U. Gartner and Jiri Kosta). Duncker und Humblot, Berlin.

Myles, John (1988), 'Decline or Impasses? The Current State of the Welfare State.' Studies in Political Economy, Summer.

Nove, Alec (1983), *The Economics of Feasible Socialism.* George Allen and Unwin.

Polanyi, Karl (1944), *The Great Transformation.* Beacon Press.

Szalai, Julia (1987), 'Tarsadalmi valsag es reformalternativak,' *Medvetanc*, 2. szam melleklete.

Wiman, Ronald (1987), *From the Welfare State to a Welfare Society.* National Board of Social Welfare, Helsinki.

PART C
BULGARIA, THE GERMAN DEMOCRATIC REPUBLIC AND YUGOSLAVIA:

Different realities; different interpretations

8 The social policy of the People's Republic of Bulgaria and the problem of welfare in socialism

SLAVKA IVANOVA

The focus of the attention of all people and the whole social policy of Bulgaria since 1956 (The April Plenary Session of the Bulgarian Communist Party) has been the problem of the social and economic development of the country. This global problem is of great importance for the development and application of the limited human resources in the overall development of socialist society.

The welfare of the socialist society means the welfare in the society as a whole. The welfare of every man, of every family, is like an inner engine responsible for the development and welfare of the society as a whole. This is the dialectical principle which must be followed and observed all the time.

The theoretical concept of welfare

There is harmony and unity between the theoretical and political concept of the social policy pursued in our country. The basic precepts of this theory develop on the basis of the Marxist theory of the development of socialist society. The social welfare is seen as a material prerequisite for social development. According to the Marxist concept

> wealth is on the one hand a material thing, ... and it is realized in material goods, material products to which Man is opposed as a subject; on the other hand as a value, the wealth is simply using human labour and this is not done with the purpose to govern and oppress, but rather for personal consumption of the riches of this labor... In all its forms wealth finds expression as a material product which is outside the individual or accidentally is to be found together along with him. (Marx, 1968)

The conclusions of Karl Marx, made more than a century ago, revealed the relations and the laws, governing the creation of welfare in the different social orders. 'In the ancient world wealth was not the aim of production but in the modern world of powerful industrial development production turns into an aim of Man and wealth is an aim of production' (Marx).

This regularity is valid for the modern socialist society: people achieve their welfare by the production of material products and goods and the development and improvement of production has turned into an aim of the whole society. The introduction of the results of the modern technological revolution in the production process is one of the most important tasks of the Party and the government, of all work teams and collective bodies.

By elevating production on the highest technological level and by applying new methods and means of using the socialist property, are carried out the plans and projects, designed for the growth of national income as well as for the increase of the social welfare and multilateral development of Man.

The modern concepts of wealth and welfare in our society are connected with the problem of meeting the constantly growing needs and requirements of the people. A number of party congresses and national party conferences were dedicated to the problems of the social policy in Bulgaria as well as to the problem of improving people's welfare. (Zivkov,1986a, 1986b, 1988). The basic directions in the development of social policy may be summarized in the following way:

- following an economic strategy in production which leads to a 'qualitatively new growth' as a new stage in the formation of a developed socialist society (Zivkov,1986a) in the conditions of constant technological innovation, and of decreasing the share of the state budget in investments in the economy as the links between the producers and the domestic and foreign market are widened and extended;
- formation of new concepts about the further advance of socialism in Bulgaria (the so-called July concept) which placed 'the problems of change in the very nature of socialism, and not only in the forms, the results and the phenomena in which this nature finds expression' (Zivkov,13/9/1987);
- delegation of new rights to the work teams about the lending of socialist property and its use, in which property must be turned from anonymous into a property of work teams, enterprises and self-managing economic organization;
- development of a whole variety of forms of socialist property – cooperative, state, community, mixed, personal, group property and others – at the same time following the principle of self-management and economic autonomy of the producers;
- development of the social policy in the conditions of a consistent system of reforms and economic measures designed to extend the domestic market and the purchasing power of the population and to raise the wages

and incomes of people simultaneously with the total reorganization of the system.

The characteristic features of the latest strategic decisions about socialist development and the increase of people's welfare are determined by a number of objective prerequisites and by the development of a new theoretical trend in the field of the social and economic regulation and reconstruction. The impact of the reconstruction process in the economy and in social life taking place in the Soviet Union can be felt in Bulgaria as well. Also the changes in the production resources and in the economic results, in the basis and superstructure of society, in the industrial relations, imposed a total re-evaluation of the ways of developing and pursuing the social policy. The social policy must be dynamic; it should not be an outcome of the economy, but on the contrary, it should go ahead and be a decisive factor in the process of planning and developing the society and the work teams. The general aim of the people and the scientists is to raise and put the social policy on a high level and to surmount 'the contradictions' of the technological revolution (Kostov, 1987) and to carry out 'the overall production process, whose ultimate result goes back to the Man himself' (Staikov *et al.*,1987) in order to achieve the growth of 'social welfare' with its basic components – the way of living and living standard (Velikov *et al.*,1986).

In the last few years the development of the new trends in social policy brought about a new way of presenting the crucial aspects of social policy in our country: the people's welfare and achievement of social equality. The people's welfare is seen as 'a unity of the way of life and the standard of living' (Velikov,1986). The social equality is connected with the overcoming of the differences between the physical (manual) and mental work, between the town and the village, between the incomes and their dependence on the quantity and quality on work, on work results, on the abilities and needs of the people, on the solution of the problems connected with the socially weak people etc.

The socialist work and the new social relations based on it, prefigure freedom of individual development to the extent of 'universality of the needs, abilities, production forces etc.' – as Karl Marx pointed out. In this development of the needs of the individuals and the conditions of gratification of these needs there exists a great possibility for turning into an end itself the overall development of all human resources as an objective process. People develop according to the rules and laws of the overall production process in all its aspects and areas – in the area of the reproduction of the means of production, in the area of the reproduction of consumer goods, the reproduction of the population and the work force, the reproduction of land and the natural environment. People do not reproduce by any definite model. They strive to be what they have become, to be in absolute motion, to subject natural forces and to use them for their own needs, and to multiply their abilities and life opportunities. People see wealth and welfare as a prerequisite for the complete extension of their inner nature, for the realization and fulfilment of their aims, for the transformation of the time for compulsory work into a time for a free choice of work (free time) – all these things are an expression of welfare and wealth in socialism. The biggest asset for the society is its members and the possibilities for their overall and free development.

There are still differences between the theoretical concepts and reality, due to the contradictions in the development of life, to the transition from one level of production into another, to the imperfections of the offered models of social management, as well as to a number of external factors, connected with the inequalities of the international markets, with the differences in the development of the production forces and industrial relations in the countries taking part in this international market.

Practical trends in the development of social policy

The problem of achieving 'an efficient level of social policy' (Gorbachev,1986a) in Bulgaria as well as in the Soviet Union and the other socialist countries assumed particular significance when the strategy for a deep perestroika and qualitative changes in the social sphere was adopted. The social sphere includes several aspects:

- the interests of the classes, communities, social groups, nations, the society as a whole;
- the relations between society and the individual, between the work teams and between these teams and society;
- the working and living conditions, employment, purchasing construction of houses, transport etc.;
- people's health;
- the services for the population;
- the free time of the people.

The determination of those aspects is a complex theoretical and practical problem, which had not yet been finally solved (Zdravomislov,1986; Velikov et al.,1986). Each of these aspects of the social sphere develops according to the adopted strategy in the field of social policy. In our country this policy is connected with the fulfilment of the so called 'tasks of primary importance' which are solved and carried out annually and in five-year plans. These important tasks and problems are the following as defined and adopted at the National Party Conference in 1978:

1 stablizing and extending the domestic market and improving the living standard of the population;
2 improvement of the purchasing power of the population by raising their incomes and by increasing their wages and salaries;
3 the extension of the service system for the population and the total reconstruction of this system;

4   preserving and restoring the living environment;
5   increasing the quality of education and the culture of the population;
6   solving problems connected with the health of the population;
7   the overcoming of the alienation of labour and of the alienation of the socialist property, and creating a scope for expression and development of the interests of the individuals, of the work teams, of society as a whole, as well as the combination of these interests;
8   the creation of prerequisities for the development of self-management.

The real results of the social policy in the area of each of these tasks can be traced in the statistical accountancy and in the various sociological studies, carried out on a macro- and micro-level. To be more precise in our conclusions, we offer some of these results to the attention of the eminent experts from the leading countries of the world in the field of the social policy and people's welfare.

In the first task – that of the field of the stabilization and the expansion of the domestic market there are proposed measures to increase the commodity funds by 9% in 1988, and the purchasing power of the population by 5.8%. This rate of increase of the commodity funds, which has begun to exceed and get ahead of purchasing power, will be kept up by the end of the five-year plan. Also, according to the plan, by 1990 the production of food products will increase twofold and the supply for the population of durable goods will increase too: now per 100 households there are 39 cars, 45 telephones, 96 refrigerators, 96 television sets. The problem is to increase the number of colour television sets and, in 1989, 120,000 colour television sets will be manufactured in our country and another 40,000 will be imported. The problem connected with the import of cars will be generally solved and by the end of the five-year term 120,000–140,000 cars will be imported.

The stabilization of the domestic market and the increase of the living standard of the population depend also on the ratio between imports and exports. The import of various consumer goods will increase as well as the import of industrial products. Cooperation with the other socialist countries and some capitalist countries will be extended. There will be more prerequisites for the creation of joint ventures on an international level with favourable terms for the foreign companies and with the creation of duty-free areas in the country.

Regarding the second task connected with the increase of the purchasing power of the population, new decisions have been taken concerning the increase of nominal and real pay as well as the increase of the minimum pay up to 140 levs in 1988. Also in the present year the minimum salaries of the three main categories of working people will be increased as follows: blue-collar workers – 140 levs, higher education specialists – 230 levs, managers and executives – 350 levs. There will be introduced three qualification levels for each of these categories and there will be determined a minimum of pay for each one of them – for the blue-collar workers 140, 200 and 300 levs; for the specialists with higher education – 230, 350 and 450 levs; for the manager and executives – 350, 450 and 550 levs. Conditions are being created for the increase of pay in accordance with work performance. This can rise to 80% or more of basic pay. The increase of pay over 80% will be taxed in a progressive way. The average annual pay of the blue-collar workers reached a level of 2657 levs per year in 1986. The average annual work pay of the workers and employees as a whole reached a level of 2682 levs per year in 1986. (*Statistical Reference Book,*1987).

Nominal pay has a quickly growing index and this process began in 1983. Real pay also began to increase with a higher index after 1984. In the next five years an even faster increase in the real and nominal incomes of the working people is expected. The allowances, grants and pensions also increased in the period 1980–1986. The average annual pension reached a level of 1188 levs in 1986, but disability pensions and professional and occupational accidents pensions are the ones that are being increased in the most dynamic way – 2173.9 million levs for 1986. The sum total of the paid pensions in 1986 is 2249 in number and in the next few years they will increase because of the ageing of the population and because of guaranteed pension rights for women over 55 years and for men over 60 years.

The allowances also increased in three directions – for indemnities for temporary disablement, for monthly payments for children added to the salary of one of the parents, for looking after little children. Grants and scholarships remain relatively stable because of the relative stability of admissions to higher institutes during the last few years, but it is expected that they will increase in the years to come.

The purchasing power of the population is expected to gradually increase but it will be affected by the inflation process and the orientation of the country towards levelling the commodity prices with the international commodity prices towards the end of the five-year term. The high level of consumption now is due to the following factors: nominal pay, real pay, real income per head of population, and the social funds of consumption (including the renumerations during the annual leave and some additional leave). The social funds of consumption have the highest index of growth for the period 1960–1986.

The improvement of the living standard of the population is a phenomenon which must be observed and examined over a long time period for a given country. In the conditions existing in socialist Bulgaria the social funds of consumption per head of population determine the living standards and constitute a big part of the opportunities for extending people's cultural development and for meeting their growing cultural and social needs.

The third task, the expansion of the service system in the present year, has been turned into a subject of complete reconstruction. The chief criterion for this reconstruction is the meeting of the needs of the market (Labour Code, 1986). The commodity producers will bear the main responsibility for the gratification of the needs of the population. In this connection new prerogatives and rights are being delegated to the enterprises and economic organizations in light industry and the competition between domestic and foreign markets is been encouraged. Conditions are being created for enterprises to set up their own shopping centres and chains of such centres. All forms of property are being fostered and have the right to develop on an equal basis.

The new criterion for applying a given form of ownership is its 'flexibility and effectiveness in meeting the needs of the population' (Labour Code,1986). A flexible commercial policy will be pursued for ensuring the population of different commodities and services. Cooperation with other countries and firms is being stimulated and different kinds of international joint ventures have been created. In connection with tourism many commercial centres will be founded with the cooperation of leading world companies, working with catalogues and delivering goods at the addresses etc. Each territorial community has the possibility to follow its own economic and commercial policy. A special commercial chamber is expected to be founded as well as a stock market, constantly functioning auctions, consultation bureaux and others. The function of commercial and industrial fairs, exhibitions, advertising agencies – all this is being improved rapidly.

Now the population of Bulgaria has at its disposal 41,354 shops and refreshments stalls, 26,611 public places and restaurants. There are $0.42 m^2$ commercial area and $0.50 m^2$ in eating places per head of population. There are 46 enterprises and catering centres per each 10,000 people. In the enterprises and the educational centres are founded many canteens – there are already over 6,586. A vast service net for the population is being organized. The towns are water supplied and 98.6% of them are supplied with electricity. The supply with telephone posts is particularly increasing: there are now 231.8 telephone posts per each 1,000 people of the population.

Significant attention is now being paid to the development of transport, of a number of public services such as laundries, barber shops and hairdressers, public swimming pools and baths, parks and gardens, hotels and recreational centres. A big part of the public services are concentrated in the towns and in their centres in particular, but for more than 20 years, new forms and ways have been looked for to ensure the development of complex services attached to enterprises and new housing complexes.

There exists a direct relationship between the organizations of the system of public services and the time allotted to housework: the growth of the public services leads to the decrease of the housework work load, and to the creation of time reserves which help women take part in economic life and stand on an equal social and economic ground with men. The educational system is developing in an analogical way. The same thing goes for the way of bringing up the younger generation. A principally new culture of the way of life is emerging and the character of labour is changing on a public and social scale.

The fourth task, the preservation and restoration of the living environment, is a comparatively new field of development in the social sphere in our country, imposed by the rapid industrialization and urbanization. In the country there exist old and new plants, and enterprises built in accordance with technologies which are detrimental to the people and the natural environment, as well as with technologies which are in keeping with the requirements of the people and with the laws of the natural environment. The riches and beauty of nature in the central part of the Balkans must be preserved, considering the impact of the technological revolution on the natural environment. A number of scientists in our country have put forward the question of regarding land and nature as basic elements, taking part in the reproduction process: people must restore the balance and equilibria in nature and multiply its riches as well as put in a lot of efforts for its enrichment. This is not an easy thing to do. The capital investments designed for preservation and restoration of the natural environment reached 2 billion levs in 1984 and 1.6 billion levs in 1986, the focus being on the investments for the introduction of technologies for preserving and purifying water and its sources, for minimizing noise, for preservation of the air etc.

The fifth task, the raising of the educational and cultural level of the population, is a basic problem of the overall social policy as well as an important prerequisite for the further development of the country. By enhancing the intellectual potential, which is a specific trend in the development of our country, are laid out the directions of the overall economic, social and cultural development of the country. In 1970–71 in Bulgaria there were 4,933 educational schools and institutes in which 81,402 teachers and lecturers taught 1,554,306 students and pupils. In 1986–87 the educational schools and institutes were 4,187 in number, the teachers 109,339 and the students and pupils 1,616,727. One teacher works with an average number of 15 students, and 34 pupils study in one schoolroom on average. Various new forms and ways of education are being experimented with and eventually applied. In this respect it must be said that computer education is gaining new ground and special computer clubs are being founded, designed to get the younger generation familiar with the new technologies. There have been improvements in the forms of the different sorts of education – full-time, extramural, evening. There have also been developments in combining the educational process with work in practice and with the new opportunities for doing some extra work, created for the students in their free time. The functions of education and culture are manifold and numerous. The basic functions are those of the mass media – television, radio, theatre and cinema, and the libraries are all accessible to the whole population. The culture has its own material values, its own adherents and makers – eminent writers, composers, artists, scientists etc. – but it has also its dynamic and ideological trait: it is accessible and open to all people and through its various forms and means of expression, it attracts people of all generations and seeks contacts with the other countries and peoples, and what is more it is being constantly enriched.

The sixth task, the solution of problems connected with health services, has been stressed and emphasized within the overall social policy. The new requirements of the people and society are connected with 'the need of enhancing the role and the responsibility of doctors and of raising their material reward' (Zivkov, 1988). Our health services are free of charge and financed wholly by the state, but their extension is limited because of the numerous social policies pursued and followed in accordance with this manner of financing. Now new forms of financing health services are being looked for, and in this respect the most favoured idea is to link health services with the industrial enterprises. The near future will show which of all these models will win recognition. Each citizen of the country is entitled to services in this field and is entitled to a free choice of doctors and health institutions. The free reception of people by doctors is allowed at definite hours and teams are formed for a voluntary additional work in their free time.

The seventh and eighth tasks concern the overcoming of alienation and the introduction of self-management. The labour and the equal labour right in the socialist society is a 'sacred' right, which is a subject not only of economic, but of social policy as well. The factors which play the main role for the protection of labour in the enterprises are the following: the equal labour right irrespective of sex, age and the national and ethnic peculiarities of the population; a uniform legal regulation of the forms of employment, of labour contract terms, of the duration of working time, of the rights and obligations of the work teams and their members; the stimuli for retraining; of equal labour as far as its complexity, strain and working conditions are concerned.

All these rights of the working people were updated and laid out in a new way in the new Labour Code (1986). With the new Labour Code have been created prerequisites for improvement of industrial relations in our socialist society on the basis of the improvement of the relations existing in the collective way of working. Prerequisites have been created for the normal functioning of the primary work team and of the basic team (of the enterprise) under conditions of the complete extension of democracy and self-management. New rights and obligations were delegated to the general assemblies and to the meetings of representatives responsible for taking decisions, to the team boards of the teams and to the executives by means of open voting of the members. The economic board of the enterprise consists of between seven and 21 members, of which half at least are workers directly employed in the production process. All managers and executives are appointed in the enterprises by means of a competitive examination or by being selected by a committee of experts. The competition basis has begun to expand thus comprising a constantly growing number of jobs.

The trade unions were given new rights: the right of a professional organization, the right of legal initiative and participation in the preparation and ratification of new provisions, the right to participate in the process of economic planning, the right to protect and increase the working activities of workers and work teams, the right to cooperate and to take part in the technological innovation and the quality improvement process, the right to participate in the collective management bodies and institutions, the right to organize general meetings and to elect collective management bodies, the right to organize and be responsible for the holidays and recreation of workers and others.

There have been created conditions for the improvement of the collective bargains in the enterprises and among them for placing the socialist property at the disposal of the work teams with the help of a special decree of the people's Assembly, made in 1987. This marked the beginning of the application of a principally new model of socialist management under the conditions of direct responsibility on the part of work teams and not on the part of the state, for its preservation, multiplication and improvement. In this way an atmosphere was created for enhancing the economic, social and political interests of workers and their work teams in the organization and management of labour and their labour in particular.

The centralized and monopolized forms of state management of the socialist property were critically reconsidered, since they do not bring about the improvement of the interests of the people in labour any longer, but rather have brought about the alienation of a great part of the workers from the means of production, from the final products, and from the process of their commercial realization on the markets, from the distribution process. The process of alienation from labour and production conditions is connected with the transformation of the property into an 'anonymous', 'state' property, 'opposing' the worker. In the present period the work teams make contracts about the property placed at their disposal and along this line of bargaining accept the legal directions and provisions concerning its use and management as well as the amount of work in their enterprises.

The process of transition from administrative management to economic management through the active participation of the self-management bodies in the work team as well as of all participants in the production, exchange and distribution processes, is not easy. It requires a high level of competence, culture, increased social activity, decisive actions designed to surmount the influence of the bureaucratic administrative machine on the decisions in the field of the social and economic policy. In this connection the reform in the whole superstructure of society was included and completed successfully and its link with the basis became closer, as well as its link with the processes connected with the development of our society. The main factors for the development of the interests of the people about improving the social welfare are now being concentrated and centred in the work teams and in the primary groups:

- the social nature of man is realized through the systematic unification of the people for a joint activity and through the property itself, which

preserves its social character, but becomes concrete under the concrete conditions and circumstances and is turned into a real bearer of the objective value relations;
- each member of society is linked with the gross reproduction process and endeavours to improve his welfare and entrusted property by means of dedicated and selfless labour and various life activities in favour and for the benefit of society, along the path of collective and joint labour;
- the work team is already a central integrator in the joint work and life activities of the people, as well as the educational staff, the creative staff etc. – in general this central integrator is the group of people which is formed on the basis of common interests, aims, needs, and which has the quality of a reorganizer in the relations between the people and the social groups and communities.

The typical condition for the emergence of the alienation of labour, that is the transformation of human activities into a power which is alien and dominates over the people, is eliminated when the level of team spirit is very high and when the welfare of the society is constantly on the rise. From this point of view it must be pointed out that the importance is increasing of the individuals, of the groups and communities, of the work teams as well as of the state. These interests are dependently functioning social relations which are in constant interaction, opposition, agreement and harmony.

Bibliography

'Basic Trends in the Reconstruction of the inner trade and Services', (1988), *Rabotnichesko Delo*, N.62, 2.03, S.
Evgeniev, G., Ivanova, S. and Ivanov, B. (1988), 'Culture of Labour', *Profizdat*, Sofia.
Gorbachev, M. (1986a), 'Political report of the Central Committee of the Soviet Communist Party at the 27th Party Congress, Sofia', *Partizdat*, p. 65.
Gorbachev, M. (1986b), 'Of the perestroika of the cadre policy of the Party', *Partizdat*, p. 20.
Kostov, G. (1987), 'Social Policy in the People's Republic of Bulgaria and the Advance in Science and Technique'. In: Social Problems of Labour in the conditions of the Technological Revolution, Sofia, V. II "*Karl Marx*", pp. 121–6.
Labour Code (1986), *Nauka i Izkustvo*, Sofia.
Marx, K. and Engels, F. (nd), *Selected works*, vol. 46, p. II, p. 411.
Marx, K. and Engels, F. (nd), *Selected works*, vol. 46.
Nuikin, A. (1988), 'Ideals or Interests?' *Novoi Mir*, no. 1–2.
Program of the Communist Party of the Soviet Union (1986), Sofia, *Partizdat*, p. 44.
Staikov, Z., Ivanova, S. et al. (1987), *The Interests and the Reproduction Process*, Institute in Propaganda of Marxism and Leninism, 1987.
Statistical Reference Book (1987), ZSU, Sofia.
Tchangli, I. (1973), 'Labour, Izd', *Nauka*, Moscow.

Velikov, N. (1986), 'The new quality and character of social policy', in 'Social Problems of Labour in the conditions of the Technological Revolution', Sofia, VII. *"Karl Marx"*, pp. 5–17.

Zdravomislov, G. (1986), 'Needs, Interests, Values', *Politizdat*, Moscow.

Zivkov, T. (1986a), Opening Speech and Closing Speech at the 13th Party Congress, *Partizdat*, Sofia.

Zivkov, T. (1986b), Report of the Central Committee of the Bulgaria Communist Party at the 13th Party Congress, Sofia, *Partizdat*, p. 27.

Zivkov, T. (1988), 'Of the reconstruction process and the further development of socialism in Bulgaria', *Rabotnichesko Delo*, 21.01.

9 The unity of economic and social policy in the German Democratic Republic

PAUL ADAMS

If we look at what the advocates of perestroika in the Soviet Union propose in the area of social policy, we find much to be said for the official East German position to the effect that the German Democratic Republic (GDR) had already been following that policy years ago. We might then conclude that, at least in this area, the influence of Gorbachev's reforms on the GDR has been negligible, or even that the real influence is in the other direction – the GDR provides a proven model for Soviet reform. This chapter will examine the strength of this argument and suggest some problems with it.

Restructuring national economies in the face of falling profit rates, reduced growth, and increased international integration and competition has in many countries included efforts to reshape the welfare state. More important than attempts to reduce total social spending, which have not been very successful, have been shifts in social policy intended to restructure incentives to work and save, to use tax and other measures to increase inequality and reward successful economic performance. The process has required renegotiating the terms of the social contract between labour and capital, or imposing new terms on the former. Workers lose a certain amount of the security that social policy affords, while their living standards are tied more closely to their direct wage and less to benefits provided in cash or in kind by the state (the social wage).

Perestroika and social policy

In the Soviet Union, the leading advocates of restructuring (e.g., Aganbegyan,

1988, pp. 15–20) argue that productivity cannot be raised by the old method of continually squeezing living standards and treating social policy as a residual category, a sphere of public expenditure to be considered only after industrial and military demands have been satisfied. On the contrary, raising living standards for some groups is seen as essential to an efficient and motivated workforce, and hence to productivity growth. The problem is to restructure both wage and social wage income so as to strengthen work incentives, reward workers whose skills are most needed, and increase the income of the intelligentsia absolutely and in comparison with that of workers.[1]

Perestroika has meant a new attention to social problems and social policy, with plans for major improvements in housing, pensions, and family policy. At the same time, as Abel Aganbegyan (1988, p. 19), Gorbachev's leading economic adviser, explains, 'Putting the social policy into effect goes hand in hand with the principle of social justice in modifying the former unjustifiable levelling out of salaries'. 'Social justice' here means increasing inequality. It requires widening differentials between workers, and between workers and technical and scientific personnel. Pay is being increased so as to reward qualifications and on the basis of the unit's final output, that is, to reward efficiency and quality. At the same time, enforcement of quality control standards means pay cuts for some workers. One implication of this is that wage-based consumption (including wages and earnings-related social benefits) will rise as a proportion of total household consumption.

The East German precedent

If all this seems familiar to an observer of social policy in the GDR, it is because the same themes have characterized its development there since at least the eighth party congress of the ruling Socialist Unity Party (SED) in 1971. For the GDR's first two decades from its founding in 1949, social policy was in practice aimed at providing a minimum and relatively homogeneous level of security and health, and was in theory rejected before 1967 as a concept inapplicable to a socialist country. A new approach was adopted in the 1970s. Social policy achieved acceptance, even prominence, as a concept under the rubric of the 'unity of economic and social policy,' and social welfare spending expanded.

The shape and direction of post-1971 social policy in the GDR are strikingly similar to current developments in the Soviet Union. After more than twenty years of neglect at the expense of industrial investment, housing has been given priority since the early 1970s in the GDR. An ambitious programme of housing construction and renovation (averaging some 200,000 dwellings per year in the 1980s) is under way, which is intended to solve by 1990 what had become a severe housing problem and major cause of popular discontent. Private housing construction is encouraged (Childs, 1987, pp. 12–13; Michalsky, 1984).

Compared with the Soviet system, East German social insurance has always been relatively simple and universal in coverage. It has, however, become more generous and more differentiated according to occupation and earnings, with the goals of rewarding performance and steering the economy. The GDR pension reforms anticipated Soviet proposals in the sense that they upgraded benefits and tied them more closely to performance. Soviet plans to increase benefits, introduce an element of regular adjustment of benefits to current wage levels, and to base the initial benefit more realistically on previous earnings (as opposed to basing it on an artificially boosted last year's earnings) are moves in the same direction – higher pensions linked to economic contribution – as that already travelled in the GDR.

The GDR also anticipated Soviet plans by developing a series of measures which substantially improved the position of women and facilitated the combining of employment and parenting roles. Since the mid-1970s, the GDR has had in place, and has continually upgraded, a strongly pro-natalist family policy, including a year's paid maternity leave with job protection, birth grants, housing loans to new couples (which are given in proportion as they bear children), preference for housing, social security credits for child-rearing, and family allowances (Adams, 1989a; Helwig, 1987; Speigner, 1987).

Social policy and economic development

Although the GDR's rulers rejected social policy as a concept until the late 1960s, the social policy they pursued in practice, then as now, was oriented to the demands of industrial production and the need to raise productivity. But in the state's first two decades, this meant holding working class living standards, comprising both wage and social wage, at low levels. The drive to speed up work, while living standards were squeezed, was a recipe for rapid industrial development in Stalin's Russia, and became the model for the GDR, but it has tended to prove increasingly counterproductive as centrally directed economies have aged and growth rates declined. The limits on a social policy that is designed above all to restrict and control consumption, and to subordinate it to accumulation, are set in the first place by the demands of modern production, which requires workers with a rising minimum level of education, nutrition, and housing. They are also determined in part by internal working class resistance, whether in the form of the 'negative control' (Arnot, 1988) exercised by workers in conditions of labour shortage or in the form of open revolt, as in the uprising of June, 1953 in East Germany.

Attempts by Russian leaders, beginning with Stalin's first successor Malenkov, in 1953, to expand consumption were continually thwarted by the inability of the Soviet economy to afford a big enough carrot, and by the pressure of military competition on investment priorities (Nove, 1982, pp. 324–34).

In 1971, the GDR faced a different situation. On the one hand, economic prospects appeared good and on the other, contrary to earlier expectations and promises, living standards were falling further behind those of the Federal Republic. Social policy developed and expanded as a key focus of state activity. Its official goal was to shape the development of society, moving simultaneously toward social homogenization *and* differentiation according to occupational achievement, meeting basic human needs *and* stimulating work performance.

It seems reasonable, then, to conclude that Gorbachev's perestroika in the field of social policy is unlikely to have any influence on the GDR, since its main tendencies are already much more developed there. Not only do we find the same emphasis on housing, on improving pensions, and policies aimed at facilitating the combination of maternal and work roles. We also find a social policy adapted to the economic exigencies of an advanced industrial country that must compete in a world capitalist economy, one aimed at reinforcing rather than undermining work incentives. For example, the earnings-related pension system acts as a concealed multiplier of occupational success, perpetuating into old age the differentials established in working life. As such, it provides an amplified reward for work performance. Family policy is geared to the meeting of both immediate and long term labour force requirements.

Bradley Scharf (1987, p. 14; 1988) has pointed to some other characteristics of GDR social policy which suggest themes associated with the restructuring of social policy in the West, and which, we might add, are also in the spirit of Gorbachev's perestroika. One such theme is the encouragement of church, voluntary, and local initiatives and responsibility in a wide area of special welfare needs and direct social service provision. (At least a thousand points of light, as George Bush might put it, can be identified in the Evangelical and Catholic social services alone.) Another theme found in the GDR, as in Britain, the United States, or the Soviet Union, is a strong emphasis on the need to increase differential rewards, and to decrease universal non-contributory social provision as a proportion of household consumption.

Perils of perestroika

Despite the similarities between Soviet plans and East German accomplishments, it would be a mistake to conclude that perestroika has had, or at least that it will have, no influence on social policy in the GDR. The impact of events in one country on the formation of social policy in another cannot be reduced to a matter of what measures or ideas one set of policymakers borrows from another, important as this process of policy diffusion sometimes is.

The extent to which the GDR may be pushed in the direction of more fundamental reforms, in social policy as elsewhere, must depend on the effects of perestroika, and still more, glasnost, in the Soviet Union and in Eastern Europe as a whole, and cannot be divined from present Soviet policy proposals. These effects may include changed economic circumstances (making it harder or easier simultaneously to raise and differentiate living standards), political ferment within the communist parties (including the SED), and working class revolt. Here we must necessarily be more speculative, but the experience of earlier restructuring attempts is instructive.

The need for restructuring is not unique to centrally directed national economies. It is continually forced on large firms in the West, especially when years of stagnation, waste, inefficiency, and resistance to innovation begin to render them uncompetitive despite their earlier monopolistic position. Management structures and pricing policy have to be reorganized, and investment redirected to raise labour productivity. Resulting conflicts within management, sometimes involving boardroom coups and campaigns in the press, more readily assume a political character the larger the firm and the closer the merger between control of industry and control of the state.

In the Soviet Union and Eastern Europe, where that merger is farthest advanced, attempts at major restructuring have always involved political conflicts, and often social convulsions. As the cases of Hungary in 1956 and Czechoslovakia in 1968 remind us, such conflicts within the party leadership can produce a crisis of legitimacy within the rest of the party and the state apparatus; a loss of confidence and direction that can be paralysing. In these circumstances, one section of the leadership, in order to win its argument, may appeal to wider sections of the population, especially the intelligentsia. The risk for the regime is that it may lose control of society, as other classes, above all the workers, take advantage of the situation to mobilize on their own behalf (Harman and Zebrowski, 1988, pp. 12–17).

Stability and reform in the GDR

The experience of the GDR, however, may seem to challenge this scenario. Here is a case of a state-directed economy which has undergone reform without political upheaval (notwithstanding Ulbricht's ouster in 1971, which may be attributed more to detente and Soviet–West German relations than to economic policy). The GDR is clearly Eastern Europe's more successful economy (Childs, 1987, p. 16; *New York Times*, May 15, 1989). Economic reforms are in place or under way. They include the *Kombinate*, or vertically integrated state corporations, the more efficient use of resources in production ('socialist intensification'), and the utilization of the special relationship with the Federal Republic (Jeffries and Melzer, 1987). The social policy reforms proposed by the advocates of perestroika have already been accomplished, efficiently and without fuss. Far from being a problem for the regime, social policy is a major source of regime legitimation and stability. Since reform carries a risk of political destabilization, is not needed, and is not demonstrably successful elsewhere, the SED has no incentive to embark on the course taken by states in much more serious economic trouble.

This is certainly the message that the SED leadership has been conveying to its rank and file, as well as to Gorbachev himself when he attended the party's 1986 congress. But the confidence with which it is put forward may be misplaced.

The GDR economy, despite its relative strength in Eastern Europe, has serious problems. Its debt, its trade deficit with the USSR, its dependence on the Federal Republic for meeting its technological and financial needs, its technological backwardness compared with the West in the areas (especially computers) where it most strives to be competitive, its low level and relative ineffectiveness of investment, and its declining competitive position in relation to the newly industrialized countries all suggest a highly vulnerable economy, even without world recession or other external shocks. Its lack of room to manoeuvre may preclude either a significant further increase in living standards or, without serious repercussions, a major or sustained austerity programme (Childs, 1987; Francisco, 1986; Poznanski, 1986; *Studies in Comparative Communism*, 1988; *DIW Wochenbericht*, 1988, 1989).

The way in which the growing integration of the world economy limits the room to manoeuvre of national states and has vitiated state-directed autarky as an economic strategy, is a growing concern of East German economists (Parsons, 1988). As one aspect of state efforts at economic organization, social policy reflects the possibilities of state management of capital and labour, and of within-state solutions to problems of economic and social development. Those possibilities, which only recently provided the strategy for parties of all hues, East and West, seem to have shrunk in the face of growing integration of the global economy (Harris, 1983, p. 237).

But the GDR depends, more than most states, on its capacity to provide its population, in return for their quiescence, a secure and rising standard of living. As Lovenduski and Woodall (1987, p. 428) put it, 'With little alternative, the GDR leadership has based its claim to legitimacy not on state institutions themselves but on their output. Achievements of economic prosperity and social policy underpin the stability of the GDR.' The capacity of the GDR to ensure economic security and rising living standards in face of its own, as well as the whole of Eastern Europe's, integration into the world economy – and that in a prolonged period of crisis, low profit rates, slow growth, and intensified competition – must be a matter of considerable doubt, even to the country's officially confident leaders. The hard winter of 1987 exposed and exacerbated the GDR's economic vulnerability, and the difficulties persisted throughout the year. Economic performance did not improve in 1988 despite a mild winter (*DIW Wochenbericht*, 1988, 1989). The East German economy looks strong by the standards of the countries of the Council for Mutual Economic Assistance (CMEA), but it must compete and earn hard currency in a global economy. A hard winter in the world economy may quickly convince a section of the party leadership of the need for further economic reforms.

The GDR may be pushed in the direction of further restructuring not only by its own economic difficulties, but also by the pressure of the Soviet Union, whence we may expect persistent demands for higher quality manufactured goods in exchange for its oil, closer integration of the CMEA, and even informal contacts with, and support for, reform-minded SED leaders by members of the Soviet politburo. This latter process may have been initiated by Gorbachev's 1986 visit to the SED party conference, when the Soviet leader met individually with all the members of the SED politburo. To the extent that it is complemented by similar international contacts between opponents of reform, differences of emphasis among SED leaders may widen into serious divisions.

Insofar as perestroika proceeds in the Soviet Union, and economic and political pressures mount in the GDR, we may expect some of the problems of the already restructured East German social policy to become more visible and pronounced. As many writers on Western welfare states have pointed out, social policy may be a source of conflict and controversy as well as of legitimation, of increased, even unmeetable, expectations as well as secure and content citizens, of conflicts between economic and political goals, and of economically or politically functional programmes that become dysfunctional but difficult to change over time (Adams, 1985; Bell, 1976, pp. 230–36; O'Connor, 1973). Even a brief examination of East German social policy reveals problems and contradictions which suggest that it may be unable to sustain a stabilizing role under conditions of heightened economic crisis or social conflict. This is the case even for areas of undoubted and substantial success, such as housing and family policy.

Economic and social policy: unity or contradiction?

Economic goals have always provided the driving force of social policy in the GDR, but the achievement of a functional adaptation of one to the other has proved elusive. The use of social policy to hold down consumption, so that industrial and military investment could receive priority, we have seen, created a barrier to increased labour productivity. But raising living standards while differentiating rewards according to performance produced difficulties of its own.

Efforts to increase inequalities in the wage system, as well as in employment-related social benefits, typically run into the problem of ensuring that the resulting differentials reflect performance, whether according to the individual or production unit, or that they have the steering function that was intended. Policy outcomes reflect class struggle and the balance of class forces as well as the calculations of planners. Thus efforts to differentiate wages on the basis of performance led in the 1960s, in the face of worker resistance and management indifference, to what Jürgen Strassburger (1984, p. 125) has called a 'completely unplanned differentiation of the entire wage system' which no more fulfilled the function of stimulating individual performance (a role it was increasingly expected to fulfil) than any of the other economic functions of wages (the allocation function, qualification incentives and so on).'

Housing, despite being an area of great progress in the GDR, is also a focus of discontent (Scharf, 1984, p. 112). Although rents are very low and housing, after years of neglect, has high priority, the shortage, low quality, and regional and urban–rural inequalities in housing that persist are seen to be, not the outcomes of an automatic process of allocation such as the market, but of conscious political choice. The processes through which the housing is allocated to individuals, including the criteria based on need, work proximity, and special service to the state, as well as their application in particular cases, depend on bureaucratic decisions. The result, according to Helga Michalsky (1984, p. 254), is that 'Complaints that arrangements are inflexible and bureaucratic and that decisions, especially the extent to which persons or groups are favoured, are inscrutable are the norm.'

Michalsky (1984, p. 252) makes a similar point about the special pension schemes. They are resented, she argues, because of the lack of demonstrable connection between their award and any merit or need of their recipients. These special schemes represent a mixture of political reward and economic steering, rather than an effort to meet special needs. In practice, however, they have costs in terms of legitimation without clearly advancing economic goals.

The relative paucity of the basic pension has for years been an unfavourable point of comparison with the Federal Republic. Retirees could leave the GDR with ease, in contrast with members of the present or future workforce, and, if they settled in the Federal Republic, were entitled under West German law to a pension based on what they would have earned in the West. The ideological effect is to present the East German welfare state, not as an expression of a caring society which provides for all its citizens from cradle to grave, but as a mechanism whereby a state-directed economy geared to production for production's sake organizes its population to ensure the maximum availability of its labour power at minimal cost.

The provision of an earnings-related tier of old age insurance makes it possible for workers to achieve greater protection against loss of income in retirement, but also widens and perpetuates inequalities based on differential earnings which may or may not be regarded as justified. An earnings-related system, despite its economic advantages in terms of rewarding occupational achievement, may also limit the state's ability to articulate social with economic policy. In part this reflects the contradictory nature of social insurance itself. To the extent that its insurance aspects are emphasized, so that it is seen as a semi-contractual, contribution-based arrangement, the state's capacity to adapt the programme to changing economic circumstances without undermining its credibility is limited. In rewarding occupational achievement through relating benefits to earnings, the old age insurance system builds up enormous long run obligations which may be impossible to guarantee in face of economic depression or unfavourable old age dependency ratios.

The battery of family policy measures designed to ease the combining of work and motherhood has undoubtedly improved the lives of East German women and is a substantial achievement of the regime. But since the large majority of women (90%) take the full year of *Babyjahr* leave rather than the statutory six months' maternity leave, the measure is extremely costly. Generous family policy measures of this kind inevitably compete with other economic priorities such as debt repayment and capital investment (Adams, 1989a).

There is also a conflict between the long term need to replace the labour force through childbirth, which requires measures to offset the costs, in terms of leisure and money, of motherhood, and the immediate need for female labour. Pregnancy is, for the employer, relatively unpredictable, and in industries that employ a high proportion of women of childbearing age, such as textiles, the obligation to provide for an unknown number of year-long leaves, with the right to return afterwards, is burdensome. Apart from the immediate problems and costs, the effectiveness of East German family policy as a pro-natalist programme is unclear, and seems in any case insufficient to prevent a major demographic problem for the old age insurance system in the next century (Adams, 1989a; Büttner *et al.*, 1987;' Speigner, 1987; Vortmann, 1978).

Ideologically, there is also a contradiction between on the one hand the emphasis on the equality of the sexes and the liberating power of work outside the home, which supports the very high level of female labour force participation, and on the other hand the high valuation of motherhood and the virtues of the three-child family. The gender-specific form of such measures as the *Babyjahr* extended maternity leave (which is in most circumstances available only to the mother) has been criticized in both East and West Germany as reinforcing traditional sex roles in the home, contrary to the GDR's basic family law (Adams, forthcoming, 1989a; Dölling, 1988).

In short, although economic goals have always provided the driving force of social policy, and although the latter has adapted to meet changed economic requirements (the need to raise living standards, differentiate incomes, encourage childbearing and female labour force participation), the achievement of a unity of economic and social policy is not unproblematic. In terms of legitimation and the putative social contract, social policy is two-edged. On the one hand it offers a degree of security and protection from such Western (and, increasingly, Eastern) evils as unemployment, homelessness, and destitution. But on the other, it assigns control over a large part of consumption to the state, and holds it responsible for its policy choices and their outcomes. The state, however, has limited room to manoeuvre, given the exigencies imposed on it, not only by the given level of development, but also by its integration into the world economy and need to be competitive. In present conditions, this means for the GDR as for other East European countries, a dangerous conjuncture of growing aspirations and a diminishing capacity to satisfy them.

Conclusion

The view is widespread among East German intellectuals (as it is among reformers in the Soviet Union and conservatives in the West) that social policy, far from being the handmaiden of economic policy, is an obstacle to its proper functioning. From this perspective, workers are too much protected from the need to be productive, by job security and by wage and social wage income that is unrelated to performance. On the other hand, they argue, intellectuals, specialists, and technicians are too little rewarded for developing and using their abilities. The political and economic pressures of perestroika in the USSR can be expected to give increased weight to such views. The authority of the Soviet leadership, together with the direct economic pressures on the GDR to restructure, will push the regime to try to renegotiate the social contract, in which relatively lax labour discipline, welfare state protections against poverty and unemployment, and stable or rising living standards have bought political quiescence, but at the additional price of weak and vulnerable economic performance. Insofar as economic reform runs into obstruction from party leaders and industrial managers, reformers will need to deploy glasnost against them. The danger of such a process is that it may produce ferment in the party, confusion among the censors and security forces, and the space in which wider opposition, reaching deep into the working class, can develop. Perestroika may not constitute a concrete programme in the Soviet Union or have produced any fundamental change in the economy there, but it has involved an attack on workers in the form of speed-up, increased job insecurity, wage cuts and price rises, and has simultaneously allowed them the opening to protest and resist. Glasnost and perestroika have, in this sense, raised expectations of change and granted the opportunity to complain, while also giving workers much more to complain about.

The conditions appear to exist for revolutionary convulsions in Eastern Europe and the Soviet Union in the next few years. They may be more likely to begin in other countries (including the Soviet Union) than in the GDR, but there is no good reason to believe that the GDR will be able to insulate itself from their effects, to erect its own 'iron curtain' against its neighbours and allies. Even economic and political changes of a much less drastic nature will transform the internal as well as the external environment in which the leaders of the GDR operate. Since social policy is not simply a technical device for managing domestic consumption, but also a response to external and internal threats, to pressures from outside and below (Adams, 1988), it cannot remain unaffected by the processes at work in the Soviet Union.

Note

1. There is no need to provide incentives to save, of course. The problem is rather to increase production of consumer goods so that already high personal savings can be absorbed in an even slightly desubsidized economy without producing massive inflation.

Bibliography

Adams, P. (1985), 'Social Policy and the Working Class', *Social Service Review*, vol. 59, no. 3, pp. 387–402.
Adams, P. (1988), 'Social Democracy, War, and the Welfare State', *Journal of Sociology and Social Welfare*, vol. 15, no. 2, pp. 27–45.
Adams, P. (1989a), 'Family Policy and Labour Migration in East and West Germany', *Social Service Review*.
Adams, P. (1989b), 'State Capitalism and Social Policy: The Unity of Economic and Social Policy in the German Democratic Republic', *Research in Social Policy*.
Aganbegyan, A. (1988), *The Economic Challenge of Perestroika*. Indiana University Press, Bloomington and Indianapolis.
Arnot, B. (1988), *Controlling Soviet Labour*. Sharpe, Armonk, NY.
Bell, D., (1976), *The Cultural Contradictions of Capitalism*. Basic Books, New York.
Büttner, T. *et al.*, (1987), 'Some Demographic Aspects of Aging in the German Democratic Republic', International Institute for Applied Systems Analysis, WP-87–116, Laxenburg, Austria, November.
Childs, D. (1987), *East Germany to the 1990s: Can It Resist Glasnost?* Special Report No. 1118, Economist Intelligence Unit, December.
DIW Wochenbericht, Deutsches Institut für Wirtschaftsforschung, West Berlin, vol. 55, no. 5, February 4; and vol. 56, no. 5, February 2.
Dölling, I. (1988), 'Culture and Gender'. In: Rueschemeyer, M. and Lemke, C. *The Quality of Life in the German Democratic Republic*, Sharpe, Armonk, NY.
Fransciso, R.A., (1986), 'The Foreign Economic Policy of the GDR and the USSR: The End of Autarky?' Presented at a conference on the German Democratic Republic in the Socialist World, Racine, Wisconsin, September.
Harman, C. and Zebrowski, A. (1988), 'Glasnost – Before the Storm', *International Socialism*, no. 39, Summer, pp. 3–54.
Harris, N., (1983), *Of Bread and Guns*. Penguin, Harmondsworth.
Helwig, G., (1987), *Frau und Familie: Bundesrepublik Deutschland DDR*. Verlag Wissenschaft und Politik, Berend von Nottbeck, Cologne.
Jeffries, I. and Melzer, M. (eds), (1987), *The East German Economy*. Croom Helm, London.

Lovenduski, J. and Woodall, J. (1987), *Politics and Society in Eastern Europe*, Macmillan Education, London.

Michalsky, H. (1984), 'Social Policy and the Transformation of Society'. In: K. von Beyme and H. Zimmermann, *Policymaking in the German Democratic Republic*, St. Martin's Press, New York.

New York Times (1989), May 15.

Nove, A. (1982), *An Economic History of the USSR*. Penguin, Harmondsworth.

O'Connor, J. (1973), *The Fiscal Crisis of the State*. St Martin's Press, New York.

Parsons, J.E. (1988), 'Which Road to Oz? "New Thinking" in East Germany about the World Economy and the Course of Socialism', Working Paper no. 2045–88, Alfred P. Sloan School of Management, Massachusetts Institute of Technology, Cambridge, Mass.

Poznanski, K. (1986), 'Competition Between Eastern Europe and Developing Countries in the Western Market for Manufactured Goods'. In: US Congress, Joint Economic Committee, *East European Economies in the 1980s*, vol. 2, Government Printing Office, Washington, DC.

Scharf, C.B. (1984), *Politics and Change in East Germany: An Evaluation of Socialist Democracy*. Westview, Boulder, and Pinter, London.

Scharf, C.B. (1987), 'Private and Public in East German Social Services', Paper presented at annual meeting of American Association for the Advancement of Slavic Studies, Boston, November.

Scharf, C.B. (1988), 'Social Policy and Social Conditions in the GDR' in Rueschemeyer, M. and Lemke, C., *The Quality of Life in the German Democratic Republic*. Sharpe, Armonk, NY.

Speigner, W. (1987), *Kind und Gesellschaft*, Akademie-Verlag, Berlin (GDR).

Strassburger, J. (1984), 'Economic System and Economic Policy: The Challenge of the 1970s', In: von Beyme, K. and Zimmermann, H. *Policymaking in the German Democratic Republic*. St. Martin's Press, New York.

Studies in Comparative Communism, (1988), special issue on the GDR economy, vol. 20, no. 1.

Vortmann, H. (1978), 'Geburtenzunahme in der DDR – Folge des "Babyjahrs"', *Vierteljahrshefte zur Wirtschaftsforschung*, vol. 3, pp. 210–32.

10 Neighbourhood and tenant participation in the GDR

PRUE CHAMBERLAYNE

Until the events of October 1989 the GDR appeared exceptional in the Eastern bloc. One of the most stable countries in Europe, it enjoys relative economic success, comprehensive welfare provision and vigorous forms of participation in the workplace and the community. Moreover its critical intellectuals, even those who insist on the separation of party and state, are overwhelmingly 'loyal' reform communists who seek to realize the democratic potential they see within existing state structures. In contrast, the 'post-Marxist' dissidents who predominate in Hungary and Poland have 'turned' their attention from state–party relations to society itself and seek the building of an independent civil society (Rupnik, 1988, p.284).

The reform communist view, while prevalent among academics, was only one approach encountered in the course of brief research into neighbourhood and tenant participation in the GDR in 1987.[1] Reform communists see a potential and indeed an inevitable dynamic in society towards a real politicization of decentralized forms. Sceptics, however, view participatory mechanisms as a futile attempt to counteract the atomization and privatization of society, tendencies which are only exacerbated by the state's own policies, its housing designs, for example. In this view 'real' life for the majority centres on the private *dacha* and future generations will lack the political will to sustain grassroots collectivism. Some sceptics also regard 'participation' as a cynical attempt by the state to extort free labour. 'Citizen initiatives – it's citizen exploitation!' was one response. For officials at local government level, however, participatory forms constitute and legitimize the seamless web of state–party–people. Proud of their *bürgernah* (face-to-face) approach,

145

officials see participation as a mechanism for convincing local people of the state's sincere and unstinting efforts to overcome difficulties, to engender civic support and cooperation.

The research consisted of interviews with local officials in two localities, discussions with academics, and searches of GDR sociological literature, particularly Journal articles.[2] The purpose was to investigate the mechanics, scope and extent of participation in tenants' associations and neighbourhood organizations, and evaluate its political significance, placing centre-stage GDR definitions of the situation.[3] The views of tenants themselves could only be gauged by informal discussions and inference. The first part of this chapter contextualizes and details these decentralized local government systems. The second part tackles questions of interpretation, considering the three main GDR standpoints encountered in the light of some wider Western and Eastern European literature.

The two most commonly used frameworks in discussing political phenomena in Eastern bloc countries are those of totalitarianism and a pluralist version of structural-functionalism. These frameworks offer quite different insights into the political significance of participation, although both lay stress on the tensions between authoritarian and democratizing or liberating tendencies in such policies and practices. Bahro also focuses on the struggle in Eastern European societies between bureaucratism and emancipation, but for him the contradictory forms of consciousness lie in individuals (Bahro, 1977).

Apart from contributing to the appreciation of diversity in Eastern Europe the chapter aims to interest those in Western societies now grappling with the debureaucratizing of state welfare services. For the fostering of social responsibility and mutual self-help through decentralized management and monitoring structures has a much longer history in the GDR than in Britain.

Local government structures and participation

Local government in the GDR is a three-tier system subject to democratic centralism, that is central leadership, planning and control.

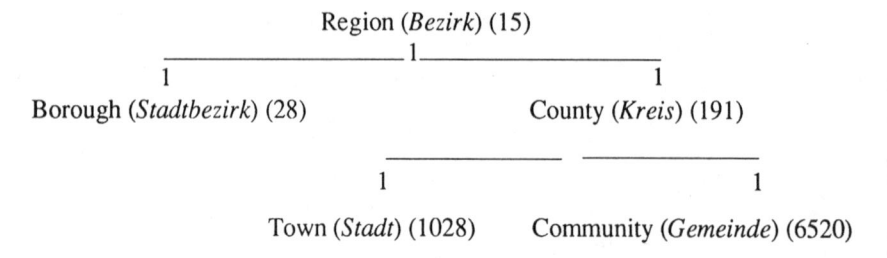

```
                        Region (Bezirk) (15)
        _____1_____
        1                                            1
Borough (Stadtbezirk) (28)                  County (Kreis) (191)
                                    _____
                                    1                   1
                            Town (Stadt) (1028)   Community (Gemeinde) (6520)
```

Figure 10.1 Levels of local government (*Statistiches Jahrbuch*, **1986**)

This research was carried out in a second-tier borough of Berlin, Treptow, and a third-tier southern steel town, Riesa (Figure 10.1). Treptow, with a population of 110,000, enjoys elegant previously bourgeois areas, historically working-class districts and a good share of south Berlin's lovely parks and waterways. Its housing stock falls desperately short of its employment needs, and it is soon to acquire the last of Berlin's massive, new high-density residential areas, to the delight of its planners. Riesa, with a population of 49,000 and severe pollution, extends from its old industrial centre across cornfields to deteriorating high-rise satellite settlements. There is a housing waiting list of 3,000 and widespread frustration about transport and inadequate provisions.

Local government in the GDR is responsible for planning, coordinating and directly running a number of sectors in the local economy which extend far beyond the brief of even the most comprehensive welfare system in the West. Food supplies, household repair services and building works are mostly separate enterprises (VEB – *Volkseigene Betriebe*) or cooperatives (*PHG – Produktionsgenossenschaften*), accountable to but not directly administered by local government. Organized on the principles of centralism and self-responsibility they maintain a balanced budget, operate their own incentives and deploy their own profits, but tend, apparently, to become a law unto themselves.

Since the declaration of 'the unity of economic and social policy' in 1971, industry and local government have been exhorted to work closely together (Gothe, 1983). Industries are asked to draw up annual 'community contracts' in which they pledge to run creches, provide school meals, renovate and build housing and sports facilities (*Kommunalvertrag*, 1987). Such cooperation was easier to achieve in Riesa with its close, small-town links between council and industrial chiefs and its excess labour in antiquated industries than in metropolitan Treptow with its dire labour shortages. All workplaces are also called on to sponsor neighbourhoods, give annual donations, provide meeting rooms, and tools and materials for community projects.

Another distinctive feature of local government in the GDR is the degree of pluralization provided by the 'alliance politics' *(Bündnispolitik)* organized by the National Front. The five parties[4] and several mass organizations,[5] which must accept in advance the 'binding role of the SED (*Sozialistische Einheitspartei Deutschlands*), nominate candidates to a common slate for elections, are represented on executive bodies at all levels of the state, and have their own newspapers. Started in the 1940s as a means of Integrating 'non-proletarian' class forces into the political life of the state, this system does allow party identities representing different social forces and cultures. Moreover the SED's long concentration on the sphere of production 'left' local government to the National Front, creating a space enthusiastically used by the other parties. Since the SED must outshine the other parties, increased attention to reproduction through the policy of 'the unity of economic and social policy' has led to a certain vigour in local affairs.

Three parallel structures link local government to the grassroots in the GDR: (1) the councillors, commissions and people's assembly; (2) the executive (*Rat*) and council administration, and (3) the National Front which organizes elections, the neighbourhood committees and tenants' associations. Councillors, mandated by their own parties, are ratified by and accountable to their own workplaces and allocated to a neighbourhood (*Wohnbezirk*) by the National Front.

	Assembly		*National Front*
	─── 1 ───		1
1		1	
commissions		*Executive*	
councillors		ward committees state delegates building committees inspection system	neighbourhood committees social committee order and security
			tenants' associations
		petitions	

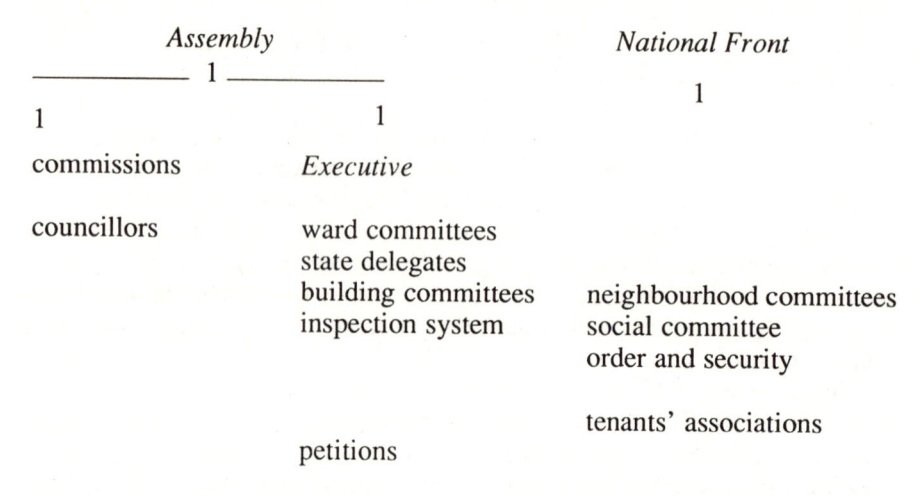

Figure 10.2 **Decentralized structures in local government**

From three to five neighbourhoods, each approximately 800 households, form a ward (*Wahlkreis*). The full people's assembly of 277 councillors in Treptow, 153 in Riesa, meets quarterly.[6] Councillors belong to commissions, one corresponding to each department. They monitor the implementation of assembly decisions and the functioning of local services, and often visit local facilities. Commission meetings focus on particular problems such as shoe repairs or hygiene, as do assembly meetings. Councillors conduct surgeries and receive and follow up petitions (*Gesetz*, 1985; *Arbeitsgrundlagen*, 1984; *Handbuch*, 1984).

Executive members are also councillors, elected as full-time directors of departments by the assembly. The key figures are deputies to the Mayor, who combines the role of leader and chief executive in the British system. While all parties are represented on the executive, an inner cabinet of SED members, a 'gang of three' (*dreier Gremium*) consisting of the mayor, the secretary of the of the SED and the secretary of the National Front, is said to constitute the real leadership in local affairs. The mayor's immediate superior is the SED secretary at the next tier of government, a woman in the case of Riesa.[7]

The executives endeavour to decentralize their work 'away from the green table' in the town hall. They often hold open executive meetings In the localities, chair monthly ward committees of 60 to 80 persons from a wide variety of agencies, and also chair building committees (*Bauaktive*) in areas of major renovation. In such ways direct communication is established between a range of officials and local representatives, progress and problems are discussed, and work is monitored by those directly concerned. Tenants, for instance, sign completion documents in the case of building works.

'State delegates' (*Staatliche Beauftragte*) the 'long arm of the mayor', are another means of reaching out from the town hall. These are full-time employees from the central administration, handpicked by the mayor, meeting under the chairmanship of the executive secretary, who 'voluntarily' attend neighbourhood committees. In this way complaints and problems can be transmitted directly to the relevant functionaries, avoiding delays and red tape.

While ward committees and state delegates are recent innovations, the petition system stems from the Soviet Union. However the GDR has tightened its operation, so that any request or criticism must be responded to within a month and in a personal manner (*Eingabengesetz*, 1975; Schulze, 1985). In Treptow 50–60% of petitions, about ten a day, are addressed to the mayor.

Both councillors and National Front activists, while welcoming measures to shortcut bureaucracy, were chary of executive bypassing of the political system, and particularly of the system of state delegates. Complaints of high turnover and inadequate calibre among councillors were not surprising given the dismissiveness of the executive towards them and the frustrations of their arduous but residual watchdog function. This is not to belittle monitoring, which receives all too little attention in the West. But the domination of the SED and the executive seems such that the people's assembly and commissions fail to constitute a forum in which real debate can take place.

The National Front organizes the political life of the area.[8] Its secretarial meets fortnightly and includes the executive secretary of the council, the secretary of agitation and propaganda of the SED, and the secretaries of of all the parties and mass organizations, which in Treptow are all full-time posts. In Riesa the chairman, the director of planning from the steel plant, conducted business with impressive swiftness and directness.

The National Front plans and is responsible for implementing the programme of citizen initiatives (*Bürgerinitiativen*). These community self-help projects renovate old people's flats, build and maintain playgrounds, open spaces and other communal facilities and collect secondary raw materials like scrap iron, glass and paper. The proceeds contribute to the local authority budget and very specific targets are set each year (*Konzeption*, 1987; *Kommunalpolitisches Programm*, 1987.)

The neighbourhood committees (WBA–*Wohnbezirksausschüsse*) mobilize and organize the community projects, and their chairpersons are crucial to successful local political work. Formerly mainly pensioners, they are now likely to be young, middle-aged industrial managers, by no means all in the SED.[9] The chairperson, probably a man given the demands of the position, 'leads, initiates, inspires the political life of the area, and must be able to face a lot of challenges' such as angry residents, disaffected youth, and obstructive council bureaucracy, said one academic.[10] Needs and resources in neighbourhoods vary according to their demographic profile, physical condition and the generosity and character of the sponsoring workplace.[11]

A major task for the neighbourhood committees, in conjunction with the housing department, is to promote, coordinate and activate their 50 to 80 tenants' association leaderships (HGL – *Hausgemeinschaftsleitungen*), each consisting of 10 to 12 households. Larger blocks with several entrances, and tower blocks subdivided into sets of floors, have stewards (*Vertrauensmänner*) who attend meetings and act as the main contact with the neighbourhood chairperson. In the case of new buildings a provisional leadership is established at a ceremonial handing over of keys attended by representatives of the housing department, the executive, the domestic insurance agency, the police and the neighbourhood committee.

Tenants' associations meet two or three times a year and organize their own repair plan system. Two lists are drawn up, one, including general maintenance, which the tenants undertake to carry out themselves, individually or collectively, the second repairs pledged by the housing department. Tools can be borrowed free of charge from support centres (*Stützpunkte*). The tenants' association is also authorized to call in registered craftsmen for emergency repairs up to a certain level of payment, a sum paid direct by the council. In Riesa only 30% of tenants' associations contract such repair plans, compared with 80% in Treptow. Most in Riesa still operate the older 'cooperation contract' whereby individual tenants take on small repair and maintenance jobs. Many green spaces are maintained by such individual contracts. Tenants are paid 50% of the standard value of work they carry out and 80% of the value of their stair cleaning, according to details specified in a manual.

Tenants' associations can accumulate substantial sums of money from repair and maintenance work and from collecting materials for recycling. Such funds are spent on social events, house improvements (such as creating a meeting room or workshop in the basement, or buying communal sports or household equipment), or on rebates to members, which is what one association which had saved about £3000 did. Occasions for parties and outings are numerous: Mayday, Children's Day (June 1), the Day of the Republic (October 17), Christmas, the Spring or Autumn cleanup, birthdays of elderly members.

Estimates of the proportion of such thriving tenants' associations varied wildly, from 15–40%. Many felt anonymity reigned in the newer districts. Yet over half of Treptow's tenants' associations had entered the golden house number competition.[12] Moreover the material value of the 'citizen's initiatives' organized by the National Front is impressive and has increased enormously in the last few years:

Table 10.1   Value of 'Citizen's Initiatives' by year in Riesa and Treptow

Riesa	1972: 1mM	1986:	1.9mM	1987:	3.2mM	1988:	4.5mM
	£330,000		£630,000		£1.6m		£1.5m[13]
Treptow	1971: 1.9mM	1981:	33.6mM	1985:	41mM	1987:	29.5mM
	£630,000		£11.2m		£13.6m		£9.8m
					(Volkswirtschaftsplan, 1987)		

Note: Figures at current rate, £1=3M, not adjusted over time.

Since 50% of the value of work undertaken was paid for, as were materials, the support centres and the administration of monitoring and reimbursing, little may have been saved. Without this voluntary effort, however, many tasks would have remained undone, due to shortages, particularly in parks and buildings departments. Opinions varied on the feasibility and necessity of such voluntary activity in the future. Party members find the commitment they are expected to make to social organizations burdensome and new technology will free up labour, especially for heavier work on public facilities and open spaces. A specialist in care of the elderly insisted on the need to professionalize the voluntary home care system.[14] But no one questioned the effectiveness of the tenant repair system or the value of promoting sociability and social responsibility through tenants' associations. Moreover the encouragement of do-it-yourself furthers skills and saves on craftsmen.

Those in the West concerned with decentralization of services, efficiency and accountability in the public sector, involvement of industry in community provision, and the promotion of voluntary activity, social responsibility and community networks might well have something to learn from experiences in the GDR. Practices which could be examined include: financial incentives in fostering mutual and communal self-help; the very small size of neighbourhood units and tenants associations (800 and 10–12 households respectively); the monitoring of building work and management of repairs by tenants; the widespread system of grassroots monitoring bodies; the use of independent book-balancing enterprises and craftsmen cooperatives in local government.

Perhaps the GDR has created in the public sector a sense of personal investment which is associated with owner occupation and the private market in the West and with informal exchanges involved in self-provisioning. In

Britain open spaces on estates have been fenced off into individual plots and flats sold off to promote individual responsibility. Tenant self-management through cooperatives, as in Glasgow, is a newer development, though that outdistances the GDR in terms of consumer control.

The political meaning of participation

High levels of participation in the GDR are proudly attributed to the political system, although small-scale organization is also diversely and deeply rooted in German culture. The communal staircleaning tradition is one example. 'Voluntary work' (*ehrenamtliche Arbeit*) originated in the 19th century Eberfelder system in which ratepayers were obliged to supervise ten or so poor families in a particular district. At the turn of the century grassroots associational life (*Vereinsmeierei*) abounded, and was deplored by the socialist movement. Nazism used the highly decentralized Blockhelfer and Gauleiter systems and in the postwar period material and ideological struggles focused on the smallest neighbourhood level. Among the ruins 'We helped each other, we had to. And we have continued to nurture that system among our children. We've used it really well', said a tenant leader. During the mass exodus and 'ideological class war' of the 1950s the National Front set up local 'enlightenment' offices (*Aufklärungslokale*) to talk to people face-to-face about their doubts and worries.

There are two main approaches to participation in Eastern European societies in academic literature, pluralist and totalitarian. The latter, predominant In the West during the Cold War, became fertile ground for Eastern European thinking in the period of pessimism following the Czech débâcle of 1968 (Rupnik, 1988; Kagarlitsky, 1988). This writing has explored subjective and cultural aspects of political experience. Meanwhile a more pluralistic approach developed among Western academics in response to the evident loosening of Stalinist monopoly power and in recognition of the engagement of populations to an extent denied by the 'puppet' models of structural functionalism and social control. More recent Western writing has argued the need to consider political values and culture, and greater accessibility begins to make such empirical studies possible and to reveal the diversity of political currents in Eastern European societies (Brown, 1984; White, 1979, p. 15).

Official ideology in Eastern Europe is inherently functionalist in its belief in the identity of interest between the individual, the party and the state, and the official task of sociology is to further social integration (Gouldner, 1971, pp. 447–77). This policy orientation has undoubtedly played into the functionalism of the Western political systems approach to Soviet-type societies. Yet, while the greater recognition of social differentiation since the 1960s has only slowly shaken official functionalist assumptions, Western academics have increasingly observed the destabilizing contradictions surrounding systems of participation. Eastern European writers of the totalitarian school also point to the instability of official strategies, whether of incorporation into or exclusion from politics.

Baylis has compiled a comprehensive list of the political, economic and managerial functions of participation in the GDR; political socialization and moral education; stimulation of production and technological innovation; providing a source of new managerial and technological personnel; facilitating communication between the intelligentsia and manual workers and between higher officials and ordinary citizens; providing a sounding board and safety valve for grievances; creating a system for dealing with miscreants and unresponsive and inefficient manual workers – (Baylis, 1976, p.33). In contrast with earlier models of 'directed society' and 'oligarchic petrification', such a system of 'institutionalized pluralism', in which 'all manner of influences – recommendations, problems and complaints' flow upwards is relatively flexible (Adams, 1980, p.122). Zimmerman also points to the stress on bottom-up communication in literature on the GDR's 'mature socialism'. Social organizations are deemed to make an independent contribution to stability and efficiency, by providing correctives on policy, feeding in expertise, and acting as an instrument for criticism and self-criticism. Making a reality of participation will allegedly enhance talents arnd positive engagement in a highly educated population, giving rein to the 'driving forces of socialism'.

Zimmerman underlines the contradiction between the scope of such aims and the limitations on participation in practice: the individualization of complaints, the lack of open discussion of choices between proposals, and party control over all interest organizations. For Friedgut, 'participation' in the Soviet system involves citizens in problem-solving and in the responsibilities and burdens of power rather than in power itself. 'Mobilized public activism' involves little citizen initiative; it is intended to induce conformity through purposive activity and organized persuasion (Friedgut, 1979, p.323).

For several writers the contradictions surrounding participation are dynamic. Churchward considers that mobilization or legitimation models fail to explain the scale of active participation in Soviet society. He maintains that the revolutionary traditions to which socialist regimes claim heritage still engender expectations and commitments (Churchward, 1983). Krisch likewise recalls the radical, libertarian and social democratic traditions of Berlin and Saxony, which existed alongside the authoritarianism of Prussia, and claims that GDR citizens have achieved a shift from subject to participant status. However the regime is in a dilemma. It aims to evoke legitimacy through participation, yet is unwilling to risk a genuine political response (Krisch, 1982, pp. 120, 113). For Zimmermann too, finely balanced participation solves nothing. 'The urgency and social power' of interests cannot find expression within the light grip of democratic centralism and conflict remains concealed. When it does manifest itself it will be widespread and outside the political system. On the other hand, if the limitations are accepted enthusiasm rapidly transmutes to wearisome and routinistic duty. Meanwhile the party, preoccupied with the orchestration of 'participation', neglects its strategic tasks (Zimmermann, 1982, pp.79, 77).

Those writing in the 'totalitarian' tradition offer different but equally varied insights into participation. In the 1950s, Western interest focused on 'total' aspects of the Soviet system. At that time Lefort defined totalitarianism as 'a form of society ... in which all activities are linked to one another, deliberately presented as modalities of a single world' (Lefort, 1986, p.75). More recent Eastern European writers have focused on either the 'essence' of totalitarianism or its mechanisms of power (Rupnik, 1988, p.268). The passivity engendered by the system is stressed in most accounts. 'One is not required to believe the lie; it is enough to accept life with it and within it. In so doing one confirms the system, gives it meaning, creates it ... and merges with it', writes Havel (Rupnik, 1988, p.271). And politics has become so depersonalized through technology and rationality that human conscience is destroyed (Havel, 1984). In fact, Soviet-style regimes now typically demand 'moral torpor, mediocrity, and an exclusive concern with minding one's own business and cultivating one's personal career, family life and other "private" concerns' (Keane, 1988, p.4).

If Nazism was totalitarianism from above, says Zinoviev, mature communism is totalitarianism from below, with the workplace cell key to the formation and manipulation of the 'new man'. Yet Eastern European writers, like their Western pluralist counterparts, insist on the instability of these regimes. Channelling all activity into the private sphere holds dangers; human conscience will reassert itself, and the state's very attempts to prevent genuine pluralism catalyses independent initiatives (Keane, 1988, p.4).

For Bahro the contradictory aspects of society, bureaucratic and emancipatory, coexist in the minds of individuals. Social consciousness comprises four elements. One involves the functions of production and reproduction, another the hierarchically organized knowledge which maintains the tutelage of the state. These two functions constitute 'absorbed expertise'. But history has reached a stage where only part of creative energy is absorbed in daily living. There remains a mass of 'surplus consciousness', some of which is channelled into such compensations for the stunting effects of society as possessions, consumption and striving for power, but some of which strives to overcome subalternity. Excess creative energies exist in all strata of society, and the revolutionary strategy necessary to bring about cultural revolution and a self-managed society must centre on the balance of forces between surplus and absorbed consciousness. The daily contradictions confronting bureaucrats force even their thinking along emancipatory paths and many wear impenetrable disguises (Bahro, 1978, pp.253–348).

Each of these frameworks is helpful in 'mapping' and interpreting the different viewpoints encountered in the research on tenant and neighbourhood participation in the GDR. The concerns of political philosophers, lawyers and social policy specialists with structural relationships between individuals, groups and the party or state naturally lie within the parameters of pluralist debates, whereas the urban sociologists' concern with micro-level social engagement speaks to the totalitarian perspective. Since local government officials are concerned with macro-, intermediate- and micro-level relationships in politics, their views find resonance in both frameworks. Within whichever group is being considered, a divergence between more 'open' or more 'closed' views is to be found. In the case of the local government leaders this highlighted a cleavage within official ideology, rather than as among academics, a conflict between establishment and reform communist ideas.[16] The views of each of these three groups are now considered, beginning with the political philosophers, lawyers and social policy specialists.

Although social differentiation began to be recognized in Eastern Europe in the 1960s, the debates still appear coded even in academic journals, and are virtually excluded from newspapers. A.-J. Heuer's work of the mid-1960s, much criticized at the time, was celebrated in the law journal *Staadt und Recht* (State and Law) on the occasion of his sixtieth birthday in 1987. He had urged the fuller expression of conflicts between workers, their work collectives, and the state; every collective and individual must develop their particular interests in their own terms in order to become a driving force of action. Engels is cited on the struggle for human interests and needs as the dynamic of history (Quilitzsch et al., 1987, p.657; Mand and Schulze, 1985). The legal historian, Schöneburg advocates more flexible political forms in order to integrate the prevailing range of interests in society. The political system should ensure that 'the widest range of conscious, partly non-organisational and also spontaneous activities ... can be incorporated nto the general context of political power by the party' (Schöneburg, 1981, p.261).

Such views implicitly challenge the form and substance of party control, although journal articles ritualistically affirm ultimate party leadership and the eventual absorption of the whole of society into the state (rather than vice versa!) . In 1985 an article in *Wissenschaftlicher Kommunismus* surveyed proposals for greater autonomy of local government in other Soviet bloc countries, for making local assemblies real forums for debate, strengthening their power relative to executives and delegating decision-making powers to committees (Heuer and Schönefeld, 1985, p.8). Soviet discussion has subsequently encompassed independent, elected 'organs of public self-government' (*Moscow News 14*, 1989, p.14). But 'self-government' is conspicuously absent in GDR discourse in favour of 'participation', 'co-operation' and 'democratic centralism'.

The role of citizenship rights in building socialist democracy is also a recurrent theme in *Staat und Recht* "It is in the individual that potential can be found to extend the creative, active participation of the citizen, to discover "driving forces"', and the exercise of individual legal rights, and the assurance of due process promote social engagement (Thiele, 1987; Pohl,1982). In fact workplace rights are more developed and utilized than 'citizen rights'. In a residential area survey only 34% had attempted to influence community decisions, whereas 81% had done so at work (Kahl et al., 1984).

Citizen rights were a concern of academics rather than local government officials, though even academics were hesitant about their full realization.[17] As the basis of political development and legitimacy, rights are constantly expanded. It is specified, for instance, that creches should lie within 600 metres of any user's home, and services for the elderly in no way meet declared 'rights'. Academics were also nervous of opening up of discussion of such policy issues as housing design, allocations or raising rents, all topical and urgent in their own circles, to the wider public. 'What would people make of such discussions?' asked one social policy 'radical'.

Among these academics there appeared, therefore, the very dilemmas of participation explored by such pluralist writers as Zimmermann and Friedgut. While advocating the expression of a greater plurality of interests and the exercise of individual rights, they also clung to a gradualist, controlled approach, in negation of their declared intentions.

Debate among urban sociologists centred on the processes by which the 'socialist way of life' develops.[18] According to one view, communal practices must be fostered by the state against modern tendencies to anomie and individualism; they do not flow naturally from socialism. Informal relations, the starting point of normative and interpersonal integration, may be shaped through the sensitive organization of democratic participation, although any surveillance function by grassroots organizations would jeopardize social relations between residents and with the authorities (Kahl, 1984). The 'targeted influencing' of individual and collective ways of life also requires finely-tuned information about neighbourhood differentiation (Niederländer, 1985). Another view insists on allowing spontaneity. 'I consider it wrong that everybody should be led by the state or an organization. People group themselves together with their interests. That should be supported. They have many sensible ideas.' This sociologist considered free and vigorous informal organization, often of 'uncertain and dubious' origin, to be the source of social norms and control and the means of avoiding anomie.

These views 'speak' most to the totalitarian perspective, although both organized' and 'spontaneous' approaches are a far cry from Havel's impersonal rational politics (Havel, 1984). The idea of 'engineering' the 'socialist way of life' through community participation may be thought to exemplify Zinoviev's cell structure, totalitarianism from below, as may the emphasis on getting people to 'join in', and holding 'house' discussions.

The stress on a sensitive, personalized approach and the careful avoidance of surveillance functions seems to run counter to this, however, as does evidence of a great deal of spontaneous community activity, none of it mentioned in the press. Protests by mothers in the DFD in Riesa at shortages of children's clothes and shoes had gained local official support and brought promises of immediate action by central government. Academics frequently mentioned personal involvement in such successful campaigns as changing a planned carpark into a playground, preventing the demolition of flats to make way for a road and stopping the building of a satellite town in favour of inner city renovation. Agendas are not simply set from above, nor is the population passive in the face of frustration.

Local officials, in striking contrast to academics, made no mention of conflicting interests, of citizen rights, or of the value of spontaneous activity. Their purpose in participation was integration, usually by convincing the population of the good offices of the party and the state, occasionally by shaking up the complacency and inefficiency of the bureaucracy. Petitions draw attention to problem areas and provide opportunities for face-to-face links, 'so that the people of Treptow know that there is a mayor in there who cares for them personally'. Through a personalized approach, people can be convinced of the state's difficulties and even persuaded to help in finding solutions (Pohl and Schulze, 1984; Lehmann and Pohl, 1986). Neighbourhood chairmen, their finger on the pulse, 'tell us about the political situation, the problems, what we should be worrying about'. 'Frank discussions' in tenants' associations and house meetings are defined as the heart of neighbourhood work: 'Satisfied needs awaken new desires which must be discussed and which must correspond to actual possibilities' (*mach mit*, 1987).

Local leaders showed no sign of fearing or resenting participation. They said it was a natural maturing process in socialism that people should want and need to engage in decisions affecting their lives and to use their creative and critical abilities more widely. Proposals and petitions should be respected and responded to, and they anticipated more vigorous participation as conditions improved. Motivation was most difficult in rundown areas. Officious forms of control were carefully avoided and relaxed personalities sought out to serve on neighbourhood law and order committees responsible for such matters as late night noise. 'Nothing works on command', said the mayor of Treptow.

The paternalistic, placatory approach contradicted official rhetoric about participation under mature socialism, and there were signs of extreme frustration with it. This was illustrated at a National Front meeting in Riesa, when, on roadwork problems, the familiar argument was made for explaining the difficulties, persuading people that progress was underway. In retort, the chairman, a young technocrat from the steelworks, insisted on the need for results, since a mature and critical population would not be trifled with. Factory workers, clocking on at 6am, were annoyed by the permanent state of disrepair of the road network and by lax timekeeping and work discipline among roadworkers. Similarly, at a neighbourhood committee meeting in Treptow, bitter anger was directed at a housing official for continued delays over housing repairs for elderly people. Councillors were also frustrated at their restricted role. 'Bleating' was ruled out, criticisms must be 'realistic' and pose 'a solution', yet there was no forum for working out counterproposals.

Conflicting views of participations appeared among local leaders, as among academics. In practice the 'placatory' view seemed predominant, despite fluency in a more open interpretation and the avoidance of flagrantly authoritarian methods. The 'action' approach, closer to official rhetoric, seemed to be gaining ground, pressed by the newly injected industrial cadre, in representative rather than executive positions. Their appointment, on National Front committees and as neighbourhood chairmen may result from party determination to shake up local bureaucratism and sensitize the handling of a frustrated public. Quick housing repairs, for example, are deemed to affect the local political climate (Markovits, 1986, p.725). Yet the action approach fell short of the 'reform communist' advocacy of independent representation of interests and development of citizen rights, which was common among academics. Nor did it meet official claims for participation as 'leading and planning' society or 'the exercise of power' (Ritter, 1972, p. 7). Nor was the argument convincing, that having been started in limited aspects of housing environment, participation would be spread to more weighty policy issues.

Conclusions

Cutting across the views of such academics as political philosophers, social policy specialists and urban sociologists, and local government leaders are two distinct approaches to participation. On the one hand is the 'establishment' view of those who want to organize it from above, whether as placation and as a more active driving force for existing 'mature' socialism. The conflict between placatory and more action-oriented approaches indicates that the shift from subject to participant status (Krisch, 1982, p.120) is still contended within the establishment. On the other hand is the 'reform communist' view of those who believe in spontaneous participation, the freer expression of group interests, as a broom against bureaucratism, and in the wider formulation of policy. In this spectrum of more open and closed attitudes, neither 'end' is extreme. For despite 'totalitarian' features in the 'establishment' view, and a more restricted approach to participation in local government than official ideology of 'mature socialism' would allow, neither impersonality nor passivity, as hallmarks of totalitarianism, pertain in the GDR.[19] But neither do the 'reform communist' views encountered among academics amount to a vision of emancipatory democracy, since even the most radical clung to cautious gradualism and overall party control, even when they advocated a transformed party and separation of party and state. No one was proposing an independent civil society as is widely advocated in Hungary and Poland.

Both establishment and reform communist views were confidently held, and envisaged further developments, gradual and radical respectively. The reform communist view considered that the combination of democratic, decentralized structures, government rhetoric and a highly educated and politically acute population would produce an inevitable dynamic for further change, in the manner suggested by Bahro with his notion of 'surplus consciousness'. Presumably the GDR regime has been sufficiently flexible for this view to retain credibility, in contrast to other Eastern European countries where so many critics have abandoned reform communism.[20] If reform communism is to continue to hold in the GDR, the gap between the policy and practice of participation will have to close and its official claims be realized. That may give rein to more emancipatory energies, the very dilemma at the heart of participation in an essentially authoritarian regime. The events in October 1989 suggest that the reform communists achieved too little too slowly. Now the people have participated in overthrowing the old regime, the reform communists are fighting a rearguard action to rescue some credibility for the Communist Party in the run up to the May 1990 elections.

Afterword

At the time of writing, December 1989, as the GDR awaits free elections and is opened up to Western economic pressures, its future is uncertain. But the revolution of November 1989 has brought a new focus to local government. The physical and infrastructural decay in towns and villages is seen as a major cause of the mass exodus of population to West Germany and of the breakdown of confidence in the party and the state. It is proposed that local areas assume much greater economic and political responsibility for their own affairs and that they are radically democratized. The Socialist Unity Party (SED) has abandoned its 'leading role' and regional party secretaries have mostly resigned or committed suicide. The mayors of both Treptow and Riesa have been ousted, the former accused of overriding executive colleagues, especially in the distribution of housing.

In many areas civic committees (*Bürgerkomitees*) have been established by the new opposition groups such as New Forum, Democratic Awakening and the Green Party, and joined by the mushrooming new community organizations such as the autonomous women's groups. Acting somewhat as shadow councils, these civic committees have set about maintaining law and order and the functioning of services and have pushed forward investigations into the state security service (*Stasi*). The *Volkskammer* (Parliamentary) committee investigating corruption and the abuse of office was so overwhelmed with petitions that they have been redirected to the local level. Formal changes will await the outcome of the elections in May 1990, but proposals are afoot to transform the National Front into a 'civic movement' (*Bürgerbewegung*) with constitutional rights, incorporating the new civic committees. Neighbourhood committees, associated with prying, are unlikely to survive, but ward level representation and organization are likely to be strengthened. In terms of political will, prospects for the radical democratization of local affairs look bright, although economic constraints are likely to be severe, giving rise to sharp conflicts.

Notes

An earlier version of this chapter was published in *East Central Europe*, 1987–1988, vols. 14-15, pp. 81–116.

1 A three-week visit organized by the British Academy and the Institute for Sociology and Social Policy at the Academy of Sciences in Berlin. This was my third visit to the Institute.
2 In Treptow interviews were conducted with the mayor, a councillor, the secretary of the National Front, the planning chief and a tenants' association chairman, all but one men, and I attended a neighbourhood committee meeting. In the southern town of Riesa, I interviewed the mayor, the council secretary, the chairman of the health commission, a group of commission chairmen, a neighbourhood committee chairman and a state delegate, all but one of these women. I also attended the town National Front committee. Interviews with academics were mainly organized at the Institute for Sociology and Social Policy with a number of researchers with personal experience or a research interest in local government.
3 Levels of participation in public activity are high in the GDR (*Statistisches Jahrbuch*; Starrels and Mallinckrodt, 1975; Schulze et al., 1985).
4 The SED (*Sozialistische Einheitspartei Deutschlands*), formed in 1946 from an amalgamation of the KPD and the SPD, is commonly referred to as 'the party'. The CDU representing Christians and the LDPD (Liberal Democratic Party) craftsmen and small traders were both refounded in 1945, whereas the NDPD (National Democratic Party) was formed after the war, primarily for petit bourgeois nationalists including former Nazis. The fifth is the Peasants Party (BP).
5 The main mass organizations are the trade union, the FDGB (*Freier Deutscher Gewerkschaftsbund*), the women's organization, the DFD (*Demokratischer Frauenbund Deutschlands*), the youth organization, the FDJ (*Freie Deutsche Jugend*) and the pensioners organization, *Volksolidarität*. There are a number of others to do with sport, culture, Soviet friendship, consumer cooperatives, gardeners, the Red Cross, technology and children (Zimmermann, 1984, p. 65).
6 An area of comparable population density to Treptow in Britain would return about 34 councillors, each representing c.3000. The councillor to population ratio in the GDR is about 1:500.
7 Both mayor and executive secretary were women in Riesa. The fifteen commission chairmen at a group interview with me were also all women, mostly in their 30s. Nationally 37% of councillors and 25% of mayors are women, although the proportions in leading positions are much lower (Meyer, 1986, p. 307).
8 The National Front coordinates the 'block politics', whereby parties and mass organizations share a common slate at elections, are each represented on executive bodies at all levels of the state and have their own newspapers. There is no membership of the National Front as such. Voting must be unanimous.
9 Party membership is workplace-based. Neighbourhood branches mainly consist of pensioners (WPO – *Wohnbezirkparteiorganisation*), since 91% of women of working age are in employment.
10 The Treptow neighbourhood committee agenda: (1) Report on self-help projects Jan–June

1987; (2) Preparations for Day of the Republic festivities including conferring of awards; (3) Subcommittee and social organizations reports, e.g. order and security; social commission; supplies committee; DFD. Contention arose over a new one-way system, summer shop closure schedules, housing repair delays, a confused elderly woman who refused to go into a home. Training for a new watchdog committee on shop supplies, services and repairs (*Versorgungsaktiv*) was being planned.

11 The Riesa steel plant gave its neighbourhoods about 1000M, about £330.
12 Berlin, as part of its 750th anniversary facelift, organized a 'golden house number' competition. Treptow organized river trips for its most active tenants' associations and gave sculptures to those with the most attractive garden areas. There was a heated discussion at the Treptow neighbourhood meeting as to whether a house which had done wonderful repair work but which had a crumbling old facade could be given the prize.
13 Figures given verbally.
14 As part of its social activities, *Volkssolidarität* organizes the younger elderly to care for the housebound.
15 Baylis (1976) examines the inappropriateness of Western assumptions about democracy and participation in studies of Soviet-type political culture.
16 The academics were more likely to express personal opinions since I had met them before, whereas local government interviewees gave formal replies. However, I did get to know some local government interviewees informally, and furthermore the differences between academic and local government attitudes were clear from journal articles.
17 Workers rights are seen as shackling labour discipline and rationalizatlon. Unoccupied flats were cited as another 'abuse' of rights, against which the state is impotent. Tenants retain unused flats for future use and/or subletting.
18 Much sociological work in the GDR centres on the 'way-of-life' model. (Kahl, 1984, pp. 20–34).
19 As was mentioned earlier, many viewed the GDR as a privatized 'niche' society of weekend houses, gardens and cars, and saw the vast housing estates as atomized and alienated. To establish whether privatism equates with social passivity would require further study.
20 This is all the more surprising given that the Gorbachev reforms are still officially rejected as irrelevant to the GDR. However, democratizing processes elsewhere in Eastern Europe inevitably strengthen reform communist and even more oppositional views in the GDR.

Bibliography

Adams, J. (1980) 'Political Participation in the USSR – The Public Inspector' In: *Nelson, D.* (ed.), ibid.

Arbeitsgrundlagen für Abgeordnete der örtlichen Volksvertretungen (1984), Staatsverlag der DDR, Berlin (East) 112 pp.

Bahro, R. (1978), *The Alternative in Eastern Europe* London: New Left Books, 463 pp.

Bayliss, T.A. (1976), 'Participation Without Conflict: Socialist Democracy in the GDR', *East Central Europe*, vol. 3, no. 1, pp. 30–43.

Brown, A. (1984), *Political Culture and Communist Studies*. London: Macmillan, 211 pp.

Churchward, L.G. (1983), 'Public Participation in the USSR'. In: Jacobs, E.M. (ed.), *Soviet Local Politics and Government*. Unwin Hyman, 225 pp.

Edwards, G. (1985), *GDR Society and Social Institutions*. London: Macmillan, 188 pp.

Friedgut, T.H. (1979), *Political Participation in the USSR*. Princeton, New Jersey, 353 pp.

Gesetz über die örtlichen Volksvertretungen (1985), Staatsverlag der DDR, Berlin (East) 44 pp.

Gothe, R. (1983), *Zusammenwirken von örtlichen Staatsorganen und Kombinaten.* Staatsverlag der DDR, Berlin (East) 90 pp.

Gouldner, A. (1971), *The Coming Crisis of Western Sociology.* London: Heinemann, 528 pp.

Handbuch für den Abgeordneten (1984), Staatsverlag der DDR, Berlin (East), 220 pp.

Havel, V. (1984), 'Anti-Political Politics'. In: Keane J. (ed.) ibid., pp. 381–98.

Heuer, U.-J. and Schönefeld, R. (1985), 'Politische Organisation und Sozialistische Demokratie', *Wissenschaftlicher Kommunismus*, no. 3, pp. 8-10.

Kagarlitsky, B. (1988), *The Thinking Reed – Intellectuals and the Soviet State from 1917 to the Present.* London: Verso, 374 pp.

Kahl, A., Wilsdorf, S. and Wolf, H., (1984), *Kollektivbexiehungen und Lebensweise.* Dietz Verlag, Berlin (East).

Keane, J. (ed.) (1988), *Civil Society and the State: New European Perspectives.* London: Verso, 426 pp.

Kommunalpolitisches Programm des Stadtbexirks Berlin-Treptow für das Jahr 1987, 73 pp.

Kommunalvertrag 1987 zwischen dem Rat der Stadt Riesa und dem VEB Rohrkombinat Stahl- und Walzwerk Riesa und der Zentralen Betriebsgewerkschaftsleiting des VEB Rohrkombinat, 30 Jan 1987.

Konzeption des Stadtbezirks Berlin-Treptow zur Weiterführung der Burgerinitiative 1987, 12 pp.

Krisch, H. (1982), 'Political Legitimation in the GDR'. In: Rigby, T. and Feher, F. (eds.), *Political Legitimation in Communist States*, London: Macmillan, 177 pp.

Lefort, C. (1986), *The Political Forms of Modern Society: Bureaucracy, Democracy and Totalitarianism*, Oxford: Polity Press, 352 pp.

Lehmann, H. and Pohl, H. (1986), 'Eingaben der Bürger und weitere Vervolkommnung der sozialistischen Demokratie', *Staat und Recht*, vol. 35, no 1, pp. 11–19.

mach mit (Zeitschrift für die Ausschüsse der Nationalen Front der DDR), 1987, no. 3, 44 pp.

Mand, R. and Schulze, C. (1985), 'Gesellschaftliche Organisationen, Interessen und Grundrechtsverwirklichung', *Staat und Recht*, vol. 34, no. 2, pp. 124–31.

Markovits, I. (1986), 'Pursuing One's Rights Under Socialism', *Stanford Law Review*, vol. 38, no. 3, pp. 689–761.

Melzer, M. (1984), 'The GDR Housing Construction Programme: Problems and Successes', *East Central Europe*, vol. 11, nos. 1–2, pp. 87–96.

Meyer, G. (1986), 'Frauen in der Machthierarchie der DDR oder: Der lange Weg zur Paritat', *Deutschland Archiv*, vol. 19, no. 3, pp. 294–311.

Nelson, D. (1980), *Local Politics in Communist Countries.* Kentucky, Lexington 230 pp..

Niederlander, L. (1985), 'Fragen zur Leitung und Planung sozialer Prozesse in territorialen Einheiten der Grossstadt', *Wissenschaftliche Zeitschrift der Humboldt-Universitat zu Berlin, Gesellschaftswissenschaft*, vol. 34, no. 8, pp. 698–701.

Pohl, H. and Schulze, G. (1982), 'Die Verantwortung der Organe des Staatsapparates für die Verwirklichung der Rechte und Pflichten der Bürger', *Staat und Recht*, vol. 32, no. 7, pp. 608–19.

Pohl, H. and Schulze, G. (1984), *Anliegen der Burger – wie werden sie bearbeitet?* Staatsverlag der DDR, Berlin (East).

Quilitzsch, G. *et al.* (1987), 'Interessenwidersprüche und politisches System', *Staat und Recht,* vol. 36, no. 8, pp. 656–63.

Ritter, T. (1972), *Eingabenarbeit – Grundsätze und Erfahrungen,* Staatsverlag der DDR, Berlin (East), 52 pp.

Rupnik, J. (1988), 'Totalitarianism Revisited'. In: Keane J. (ed.), ibid., pp. 263–89.

Schöneburg, K.-H. (1981), 'Methodologie staatstheoretischer Forschungen über politische Systeme sozialistischer Macht', *Staat und Recht,* vol. 30, no. 3, pp. 254–8.

Schulze, G., Muller, K. and Pohl, H., (1985), *Bürgeranliegen – Bürgerinitiative,* Staatsverlag der DDR, Berlin (East) p. 121.

Statistisches Jahrbuch der DDR, Staatsverlag der DDR, Berlin (East), annual.

Starrels, J. and Mallinckrodt, A., (1975), *Politics in the GDR.* New York: Praeger, 397 pp.

Thiele, F. (1987), 'Individualisierende Rechtsanwendung und ihr Einfluss auf die Entfaltung der Triebkräfte des Sozialismus', *Staat und Recht,* vol. 36, no. 4, pp. 335-7.

Volkswirtschaftsplan 1987 des Stadtbezirks Berlin-Treptow, 77 pp.

White, S. (1979), *Political Culture and Soviet Politics,* 234 pp.

Zimmermann, H. (1984), 'Power distribution and opportunities for participation: aspects of the socio-political system of the GDR'. In: Beyme K. von *et al.*, (eds.), *Policymaking in the GDR.* Aldershot: Gower, 401 pp.

11 From a one-dimensional to a multidimensional welfare system

IVAN SVETLIK

Introduction

The period since the beginning of the 1980s has been marked by a severe crisis of the welfare state, or speaking broadly, of the welfare systems. It was caused primarily by the internal contradictions of welfare systems themselves of which the productivity gap has been the most important one (Gershuny, 1983, pp. 12–13). The attempts to raise productivity of the production of services by means of new technologies and new means of rationalizations following the principles of industrial production (Toffler, 1981) have jeopardized the quality of services rather than solved the problem of the rising costs. The external constraints stemming out of the economic slowdown and the fall of the Keynesian economic model has been of secondary importance, although not insignificant for the crisis of welfare systems. They have speeded it up.

Socialist countries entered the crisis of their welfare systems a bit later than their capitalist counterparts. This does not mean that they may overcome it sooner or easier. Quite the contrary. The crisis of the socialist welfare systems could be much deeper and longer due to some additional factors of which we would like to mention two. The first one has been slow technological change which will influence a very modest economic growth compared to Western countries. The second and most important one has been the one-dimensional structure of the socialist welfare systems.

The purpose of this article is to present the analysis of the one-dimensional structure of welfare system with special reference to Yugoslavia, and to show that this characteristic has deepened its crisis by sweeping away various alternative forms of services provision. The crisis has become so acute that it demands reconsideration of some basic postulates on which the welfare system has been grounded. This is also the starting point for the discussion about the future of welfare in Yugoslavia which could be relevant also for some other Eastern and Western countries.

Before beginning the analysis we would like to make a terminological clarification. Instead of welfare state we use the concept welfare system. This concept embraces not only the institutions, measures and programmes which have been developed, financed and controlled by the state, but also those which have evolved and have been preserved outside, i.e. in the domain of civil society. This approach will help us to present the problem of the one-dimensional structure of the welfare system more clearly. It could be particularly useful in Eastern countries where the concept of welfare state has not been used frequently (Sik and Svetlik, 1988, pp. 273–4).

Production of services

Production or provision of services serves the satisfaction of individual or socially recognized needs. In principle there could be as many ways for the production of services as there are for the production of goods. By production we mean different types of work that could be found in different social settings. Thus wage labour is by no means the only generator of services.

Following the authors like Pahl (1984), Melvyn (1986), Gershuny (1983), Sik (1984), Toffler (1981), Robertson (1985), some French authors (La documentation Française, 1983) and Svetlik (Svetlik *et al.*, 1988), we can disaggregate work into several types on three levels. On the first level work can be split into formal and informal. On the second level a distinction can be made between two types of formal work, i.e. employment and self-employment, and also between two types of informal work, i.e. work for exchange and self-production. On the third level one can find different types of employment in private and state-owned organizations, and also two types of self-employment: individual and cooperative. Informal work for exchange can be either reciprocal, i.e. black market work and grey work in households and in groups of relatives and friends, or non-reciprocal, i.e. altruistic work. Self-production can be also split into individual and mutual or a community production.

The types of work enumerated above represent the complete variety of possibilities that have been evolved and preserved in a society in order to produce goods and services needed. The question is how many of these possibilities have been actually used and to what extent? To answer this question precisely one would have to conduct special research. Here we will present some results from partial analyses.

As far as Yugoslavia is concerned we can firmly claim that the only legal production of services like personal care, social security, health, education and others takes place in socially-owned and state-controlled organizations. These organizations are formally autonomous and self-managed but in fact controlled by state institutions. Private schools, private hospitals, private daycare centres and other private social service-producing organizations are forbidden. The only legal form of work for production of services is thus employment or wage labour. Only in 1989 it is expected that private service provision will be allowed in some marginal areas.

The situation is even worse regarding self-employment. This type of work has been limited to some traditional artisans, craftsmen and professionals like lawyers. Private dentists are allowed only in some republics. Childcare as self-employment is possible only if controlled by childcare centres. Production of services on the basis of individual self-employment is thus very marginal. Self-employment in the form of cooperatives practically does not exist and some attempts to establish cooperatives e.g. for childcaring have faced enormous legal barriers and opposition of socially owned institutions. Although a liberalization is expected in this area one can not hope for fast changes.

Moving to the informal area the picture has become less clear. We presume that black market work is quite widespread especially in those sectors where public services are insufficient and private practice is not allowed. This is the case with dentistry, childcare and teaching of musical instruments, languages and some other subjects. Although illegal, this production has been widely tolerated. Black market work has turned into grey work.

The extent of individual altruistic work is difficult to estimate. It represents an irregular activity which depends on responsiveness to the needs of people living in the surrounding area by those who are ready and able to render some free services. On the local level some groups of older people, especially women, and youth groups could be found. They try to find dependent people who would need some help and organize and provide various types of service for them (Svetlik *et al.*, 1988a). They usually work as members of voluntary organizations like the Red Cross, the Association of the Friends of Youth and others. However, they have not been generously supported by the state or social institutions either financially or organizationally. The official policy has been rather to control those who participate in these organizations rather than to provide additional services to those in need.

Reciprocal exchange of labour has been widespread, aiming especially at solving housing problems. Nowadays more than half of the new housing units in Yugoslavia are built privately, which means that people build houses for their own use. They organize building, they work themselves physically and they are helped by their relatives, friends and neighbours. Concerning social services, reciprocal exchange of labour has been limited primarily to kin groups.

Self-production of individuals and families has been widespread also. According to research results (Svetlik, 1988), Yugoslav adults weekly spend 32.8 hours on household activities, bringing up their children and gardening.

Activities like self-education and recreation are not counted. Mutual production has been practised up to now mainly for the construction of some commonly-used facilities within villages or other local communities e.g. for paving roads, constructing waterworks and telephone or cable TV networks. Mutual service activities aiming at providing childcare services and various types of self-help groups have not been found frequently.

A general picture about the production of services in Yugoslavia would be as follows. There is a formal production limited exclusively to the services rendered by socially-owned and state-controlled organizations. On the other hand there exists also the informal production of services which has survived as part of the traditional way of life and as part of traditional institutions. Quite often it has grown because of the insufficiencies of services rendered by formal institutions. The official policy has been to invest money and knowledge into formal service producing facilities, and to leave informal ways of service rendering on the margins of the welfare system expecting them to become obsolete. The aim has been to put children in daycare centres, the elderly in old age homes, the disabled in the institutions for disabled etc. The informal sector has been treated as a disappearing sector which does not merit any special attention and support. Such a policy towards production of services can doubtlessly be described as one-dimensional.

Apart from some positive consequences of one-dimensional service production like easier control of service-producing organizations, more simple systems of money allocation and service distribution, there have certainly been quite a few negative ones. Several potential service producers, formal and informal, have been prevented from rendering services which has caused a great waste of human resources and knowledge. Scarce public resources could be supplemented by money, knowledge and the free time of individuals. In many cases a modest financial, organizational or counselling support to volunteer organizations and groups, to self-help groups, families or individuals would result in larger quantities and in better quality of services than in the case of the spending of these resources by the formal service institutions. Having all formal production of services concentrated in socially-owned organizations, one loses the criteria for their cost-efficiency and for the quality of services. Competition has been eliminated. Instead we have got a monopoly of welfare bureaucrats and professionals. They are not stimulated enough for cost reduction, quality improvements and innovation. In the case of crisis there is no safety boat to jump in.

Needs and their recognition

When talking about social services, Titmuss takes as a starting point the concept of needs which he divides into social and individual (Titmuss, 1987, p.43). The question now is how the matching between various individual and social needs for services and the variety of ways of their production, i.e. the variety of types of work that we have described above, is being achieved.

One can satisfy one's needs alone or in the group on the basis of mutual production. However, in order to satisfy their needs most people depend on others. Those who have time, ability and knowledge can enter the networks of reciprocal exchange of labour. Most dependent individuals who are lucky to live in a surrounding where there are volunteers, can be assisted this way. Some may have money to buy services on the market, regular or black. In all these cases the satisfaction of individual needs is the main question. People know what they want and look for ways how to get the adequate services. Some need the same services and coordinate their searching activities. They organize mutual aid or self-help groups or they approach volunteer organizations.

In order to meet socially recognized needs there have been special mechanisms called welfare programmes developed within welfare systems. They aim at satisfying those needs shared by a larger number of individuals. This system is rather complicated for at least two reasons. First, there is a question of how can people communicate their original needs to the level of the institutions that create programmes and to the organizations that render services? Secondly, there is the question of how to find a common denominator for the different needs of large numbers of individuals? It is an extremely demanding task to elaborate a procedure that would enable a continuous and authentic transfer of individuals' needs to the higher social levels and to prevent various social institutions from determining socially recognized needs with no respect to individual specifics. Here lies one of the most important questions of our welfare systems namely, how to establish the acceptable balance between autonomously expressed and heteronomously recognized human needs.

The nature of a one-dimensional system of service production in which the socially-owned service organizations dominate is such that these organizations sell their services on the free market only exceptionally. Therefore there are very few services that can be bought directly by individuals. Most services are rendered according to programmes determined by the state, by the enterprises, or by self-managed communities of interests (SCI) of a certain republic or commune (Svetlik *et al.*, 1988). There is a high probability that these programmes are created by the administration and professionals of the state, SCI and enterprises without a sufficient respect for the real needs of individuals. Heteronomously defined needs thus dominate the autonomously defined ones. Paraphrasing Gorz, these could be averaged needs representing the real needs of nobody (Gorz, 1980). This situation cannot be outbalanced by the satisfaction of autonomous needs in the informal sector.

The above described situation is completely congruent with the prevailing norms, values and ideology of those socialist countries where communist parties hold the power. The party always knows best and so does also the state which it controls. State officials who are in charge of welfare programmes are supposed to know the needs of individuals better than individuals themselves. They are expected to judge which needs should be satisfied to what extent and by what means.

If such a situation lasts for a long time it can have a great impact on the structure of the welfare system as well as on the behaviour of the individuals. They become increasingly passive. They expect the state to give them employment, to orient their children into the right educational programmes, to take care of their health and of their economic security. Increasing passivity lowers their abilities for self-education, for job seeking, for judgements about their physical and mental status, etc. Their dependence on institutions increases. Bureaucrats and professionals define who is ill, who is insane, who needs a certain sort of knowledge, who is disabled, who is economically deprived or dependent, etc.

The contradiction of autonomously versus heteronomously determined needs has been tackled in Western countries by means of tri-partite managing bodies in which representatives of the state, of the capital and of the labour participate. It has also been tackled by organizing special clients' organizations and by the direct and participative involvement of clients into service-rendering processes. However, professionals and financial experts of the state administration still play a decisive role.

In Yugoslavia there has recently been an attempt to eliminate the state as a service-providing agency determining what is needed, and to enable direct contacts and direct bargaining between services and consumers, i.e. between enterprises and local communities whose members need certain services and pay for them, and service providing organizations, i.e. schools, daycare centres, health centres, etc. Service consumers and service providers should bargain for the quality and quantity of services as well as for their allocation and costs. So-called self-managed communities of interests have been established. Their structure and functioning are described elsewhere (Svetlik *et al.*, 1988a).

The core ideal of SCIs has been to make a shift from welfare state to welfare society. Unfortunately a great mistake was made by the attempts to give the SCIs all the functions carried out previously by the state. There is no sense in replacing the state as the exclusive official subject in charge of creating and carrying out welfare programmes by another equally exclusive formal structure, i.e. SCIs, without a necessary functional differentiation. What has happened in fact is that the state has informally retained a financial and institutional control over the welfare system without any formal responsibility for overall social policy. We have hundreds of SCIs in different welfare areas, from the community to the republic level, of which each deals only with its specific problem. The welfare system has remained non-differentiated while social policy has become partialized.

Returning to the one-dimensional nature of the welfare system we can now complete the picture. There is only one legal type of work, i.e. employment in the socially-owned organizations, for the production of services. Providing services on the basis of informal work has become marginalized. Heteronomous needs increasingly dominate autonomous ones. The influence of individual service consumers on welfare programmes is small and their possibilities to choose from among different services are not great either. The organizational structure, financing and management of welfare systems including service-producing organizations are not differentiated. The state retains control over welfare systems regardless of institutional changes. At the same time it does not bear responsibility for the integral development of social policy as a whole. These are in our opinion more important reasons for a deep and longlasting crisis of our welfare system than the productivity gap and slow economic growth.

The equality problem

The bottom line of Titmuss's argument for welfare programmes is undoubtedly the attainment of greater social equality and the improvement of the social and economic position of socially deprived and marginalized groups. In this respect Titmuss's philosophy of welfare (Titmuss, 1987) does not differ from the one developed in socialist countries. Classless society, abolishment of social privileges and relatively equal distribution of goods and services among workers have been the most accentuated political goals. The ways for the achievement of these goals, however, differ considerably.

It seems that the endeavours for social equality in socialist countries have been assumed to be closely connected with the one-dimensional welfare systems. There has been an assumption that only socially-defined welfare programmes, socially-controlled welfare organizations with the prescribed structure of activities, determined management procedures and standardized services for standardized types of clients could prevent unacceptable social differentiation. It has been feared that private and cooperative service producers might exploit clients or the labour force, select clients according to socially unacceptable criteria and exert their ideological influence over them, e.g. in the field of education. Market distribution of services has been abolished to prevent the differentiation of people between those who can and those who cannot pay for certain services. Enterprise-specific and local welfare programmes have been in a somewhat better position although not particularly favoured because of different economic power of enterprises and localities. Informal and semi-formal service production has not been supported because the outcomes have been unpredictable and informal activities out of control.

The attempts to maintain social equality by means of one-dimensional welfare systems bring about quite high internal costs. If the production of services takes place primarily in socially-owned welfare organizations there is no doubt that several human and material resources that could be possibly utilized for service rendering have been wasted or totally neglected. We have in mind the knowledge and money of those individuals who would like to render services privately or in cooperatives on a commercial basis or as service providers of various welfare programmes. We have in mind also spare and free time of those individuals who would render services informally as members of local networks or semi-formally as members of volunteer organizations. We have in mind decreasing costs and increasing quality of services that would be an outcome of competition between various service providing subjects. We have in mind also synergetic effects of mutual support between a welfare mix of formal, informal and other sectors, (Evers and Wintersberger, 1988). All these examples illustrate the variety of possibilities for the development of welfare. Neglecting them and sticking to the one-dimensional structure of the welfare system can guarantee only one type of equality, it is equality in poverty. Such a welfare system tends towards redistribution of a decreasing amount of services.

Tracing the future of welfare system

We have emphasized at the beginning of this article that the structure, the development and the future of welfare cannot be understood properly if it is limited to the concept of the welfare state. Our considerations about the future welfare must therefore develop this point. On the other hand, however, the state must not be excluded from these considerations irrespective of such intentions mentioned already in the case of Yugoslavia.

As far as the role of the state is concerned, we think that Titmuss's 'institutional-redistributive model of social welfare' (Titmuss, 1987, p.263) could be a good starting point. He argues that

> different societies at different stages of development and with different cultural contexts have to determine a particular infrastructure of universalist services within and around which to develop selective or positively discriminating services provided as social rights, on criteria of the needs of specific disadvantaged categories, groups and territorial areas. The fundamental problem which this model sets for government is to find the 'right' balance between the integrative role of universalist services and the social equality role of selective (or priority) developments. (Titmuss, 1987, p. 264)

The role of the state is thus to integrate a society by means of universal programmes and to reach a certain level of social equality by means of selective ones. It is important to note that social equality generally cannot be achieved by universal programmes of which middle classes benefit more than lower ones (Titmuss, 1987, p. 71). It is equally important to know that up to now only the state has been able to formulate and to lead a holistic social policy. In the case of Yugoslavia the state has to bear responsibility for the attainment of social consensus about the basic needs to be met by means of universal services, and about the groups which need a special aid by means of selective ones. It means that the state is responsible for the elaboration of these programmes, for financing them and for the organization of services to carry them out. Taking into account different stages of development and different cultural contexts, universal as well as selective programmes should differ with respect to republics and regions.

Seeking the ways for the development of welfare must not be limited too much by the possibilities of the welfare state. There are also the resources of so-called civil society which have not been utilized enough or have been left idle. This is especially true for the socialist countries where only recently the problem of separation of the state from civil society has been discussed seriously and widely (Družboslovne razprave, 1988). The best example from the welfare area are the already mentioned SCIs in Yugoslavia. This institution has been conceived as a civil society instituion which would enable a direct meeting of independent and self-managed service-producing organizations on one hand, and individuals and self-organized collective consumers of services like enterprises or local consumers' organizations on the other. Their direct meeting and bargaining without state interference should be established. In fact and unfortunately, the state has not resigned, it has just cowered behind this institution.

The lesson to be learned out of this experience is very important. The SCIs have a viable future only if they are independent of the state. It means that workers of certain enterprises or people of certain localities or neighbourhoods could agree that they would have some services rendered in common, according to the agreed programmes and including criteria of entitlement. On this basis they would make an agreement about the sum of money to be paid by each individual, family or enterprise. They would also try to find a service organization that would be able and ready to render desired services of high quality and by acceptable prices. This way people would obtain those services that would not be given by the universal or selective programmes of the state. They would be able to satisfy their needs beyond the point that is guaranteed to everybody. Let us call these services the intermediary services and SCIs the intermediary structure of the welfare system.

In the domain of civil society there exist a great variety of other forms like self-help and mutual aid groups, voluntary organizations, neighbourhood groups, friendships and kinships which must not be neglected. In fact they already play an indispensable role in the production of services in the informal sector. People participate by giving their share in the form of time, housing, equipment and other facilities, knowledge and also money. It would be a great mistake to interfere with this subtle structure directly by some state measures. Also it may probably be a very risky feature to try to legalize all of them. What these forms of service production need is a kind of supportive environment.

It is difficult to define it precisely; however, it could have a form of modest financial support to cover some direct costs and counselling, assistance in establishing networks, some facilities, etc. given by service organizations. These services could be called welfare mix services. They merit special attention because they could substitute some labour intensive phases of service production in service organizations and thus help in solving the problem of the productivity gap. Home care of sick people, open universities and study circles known in Sweden could serve as examples.

Proceeding from the state to SCI and welfare mix services we have got a continuum of highly programmed and organized services on one end, and loosely organized and rather casual services on the other. Yet we would have to find in this continuum a place for one more type of services, marketable services. To some extent this type of service would be rendered by means of SCI programmes that we mentioned above. However, in this case services would be paid by the enterprises or other institutions and distributed later according to the criteria accepted within a certain enterprise, commune, etc. The market for services means a possibility for every individual to buy services on the market and a condition that these services are available. Nowadays it happens quite often that some individuals are not entitled to certain services or that those services are not in great enough supply for those entitled. Some would like to have more services than they are entitled to. On the other hand service organizations are not always allowed to sell services on the free market. Marketable services would mean the enrichment of welfare, they would be treated as additional to the state, intermediary and welfare mix services.

Whatever services there are in question: state, intermediary or marketable, a monopoly over their production by the state or socially-owned service organizations could be only an exception. It means that individuals, private organizations and cooperatives would be allowed to carry out all sorts of welfare programmes under the same conditions as the existing service organizations. This is unavoidable in order to establish the competition between service-producing organizations, to lower the costs and to increase the choice of services.

The question of social equality must be raised again. Would intermediary, welfare mix and marketable services increase social inequality to an unacceptable level? There exist several options on which the answer to this question depends. If the state universal and selective services were rich enough, the development of other types of services would not pose inequality problems. If they are poor, unacceptable social differences would become visible and would serve as a pressure for more either state or intermediary services. Inequalities caused by service consumption nowadays exist in a hidden form, e.g. avoiding the queue when waiting for a specialist's examination which is seldom possible for individuals of the lowest class. Anyhow, the state must achieve a certain level of social integration and social equality by means of its universal and selective programmes. All the other programmes and services would help to implement the concept of organic equality as well as to make the state's services cheaper and better. They can only enrich welfare. By organic equality we mean the development of human needs and ways for their satisfaction in accordance with one's own and his community's cultural and economic context. It includes also a defined minimum welfare standard below which nobody is allowed to fall.

All in all, we see a viable and desirable future for welfare in socialist countries by making a shift from one-dimensional to multidimensional welfare systems. It means the development of a variety of welfare programmes, engagement of a variety of service-producing agents, the development of new organizational forms and accentuating autonomous needs for services to be met on the basis of organic equality principle. We come thus to the concept of welfare pluralism (Johnson, 1987) for which the core question is how to achieve a viable balance between various sectors and modes of service provision. The alternative: either state or market has become irrelevant.

Bibliography

Družboslovne razprave (1988), no. 5, *Review of The Institute for Sociology*, Ljubljana.
Evers, A. and Wintersberger, H. (ed.), (1988), *Shifts in the Welfare Mix*. Vienna: European Centre for Social Welfare Training and Research.
Gershuny, J. (1983), *Social Innovation and the Division of Labour*. Oxford: Oxford University Press.
Gorz, A. (1980), *Adieu au proletariat*, Paris: Seuil.
Johnson, N. (1987), *The Welfare State in Transition*. Sussex: Wheatsheaf Books.
La documentation Francaise, (1983), *Comment vivrons-nous demain?*, Rapport du Groupe longterme, Commissariat général du plan, Paris.
Melvyn, P. (1986), 'Local Initiatives, experiments in economic and social innovation'. In: *Planning the Welfare Mix*. Eurosocial Vienna and Ministry for Health and Welfare Canada, Montreal.
Phal, R. (1984), *Divisions of Labour*. Oxford: Basil Blackwell.
Robertson, J. (1985), *Future Work*. Gower Publishing Company.
Sik, E. (1984), *Reciprocal Exchange of Labour in Contemporary Hungary*, Papers on Labour Economics. Budapest: Karl Marx University of Economics.
Sik, E. and Svetlik, I. (1988), 'Shifts in the Welfare Mix: Significant Features in Countries with Planned Economy; Similarities and Differences'. In: Evers, A. and Wintersberger, H. *Shifts in the Welfare Mix*. Vienna: European Centre for Social Welfare Training and Research.
Svetlik, I. (1988), *Kvaliteta delovnega življenja (The Quality of Working Life)*. Report on Quality of Life in Yugoslavia, Institute for Sociology, Ljubljana.
Svetlik, I. et al. (1988), 'Neformalno delo' ('Informal Work'), *Delavska enotnost*, Ljubljana.
Svetlik, I. et al. (1988a), 'Yugoslavia: Three Ways of Welfare System Restructuring'.

In: Evers, A. and Wintersberger, H. *Shifts in the Welfare Mix*. Vienna: European Centre for Social Welfare Training and Research.
Titmuss, R. (1987), *The Philosophy of Welfare*, B. Abel-Smith and K. Titmuss eds. London: Allen & Unwin.
Toffler, A. (1981), *The Third Wave*. London: Pan Books.

PART D
WOMEN, THE FAMILY AND EAST EUROPEAN SOCIAL POLICY

12 The situation of women in Hungarian society

CHRIS CORRIN

Introduction

This chapter will cover four main areas of thinking which highlight different aspects of the situation of women in Hungary. Initially I will outline something of what life is like for women in Hungary in terms of the gain and losses they have experienced since the Communist government gained dominance after 1948. Essentially we can ask what effect have the changes made by socialist policy had on the women's situation. Next we turn to consider the ideological setting of this social policy and the differences between radical intellectuals and official policy-makers. The MNOT (*Magyar Nok Orszagos Tanacs*) (National Council of Hungarian Women) plays a certain role in this context in terms of representation/non-representation of women's interests. In turn this leads to a consideration of the nature of the debate about women's equality in Hungary, and the anti-feminist backlash. What colours this debate? What are its historical and ideological roots – where is this debate going, where can it go? As is often the case, we end with a consideration of future change. What are the possibilities for women to organize autonomously? Do women in Hungary have a desire, see a need so to do? There are obvious dangers here for analysts in imposing Western prescriptions onto different cultures. Feminism is an excellent body of writing from which to make a critique of social policy, but the values of a largely white, Western feminism cannot be neatly transposed into other situations with different historical, economic and cultural backgrounds and a different prioritizing of needs and desires.

Changes in women's situation

In starting with a balance sheet of gains/losses over the last 40 years for women in Hungary, it is evident that the gains are impressive. These include political emancipation, roughly equivalent opportunities to education, protected maternity rights and childcare leave within the labour market, provision of creches and kindergartens, father's ability to claim childcare benefit and to spend time with sick children. All of this was unimaginable 40 years ago.

Yet, looking beneath the surface impression of these gains, we can see that many 'secondary' problems have become actual practical losses for many women. In terms of paid work, we see that the average number of men in better qualified and higher-paying jobs is higher than that of women, the sexual segregation in jobs is strong and men get more money for their work. Partly as a consequence of this higher earning power, and partly because of the dominance of biological arguments concerning motherhood, plus the low value accorded to work in the home, very few men take the childcare allowance and choose to remain in the home caring for children. There are not enough creche places available so many women have little choice as to whether they remain in their homes with children or continue to work outside the home as well.

So far as the world of work and family are concerned these remain separated from each other and are primarily dictated by 'economics'. Attitudes to work and family, in their broadest senses, lie at the heart of the questions concerning the value and direction of change through socialist social policy.

The period of concern here is that from the 1960s onwards. We need to acknowledge the importance of the economic background for our analysis of the social policy measures aimed at easing the 'double burden' of women and the difficult financial situation of large families (those with three or more children).

The general economic situation in the 1960s was one which the previous rapid growth of national income was slowing down and economists were beginning to note the end of extensive growth (based on the establishment of new workplaces involving large numbers of those previously not employed – that is, women). Hungarian economists were urging structural change in the economy towards intensification of production. This began to be realized in the system of new economic management introduced in 1968. Essentially this system was designed to give greater autonomy to the enterprise in deciding the details of its activities within the framework of national planning so orientating it towards more efficient production and better utilization of labour power and capital, by applying only indirect regulators.

Of great importance in understanding the atmosphere in which welfare policy was being made at this time we need to recognize the fear of unemployment which was beginning to be felt. Some economists thought the results of NEM would be unemployment, and as full employment *was* a principal socialist value, several safeguards were introduced to avoid unemployment. These included regulations on the employment and income policy of the enterprise, incentives for on-the-job training, several forms of helping adult education, and one of the minimum guarantees, the right to free choice among workplaces (Vajna, 1982). So far as the childcare allowance is concerned this overall threat of unemployment is an important context which has to be kept in mind.

Coupled with this was the recognition of the stressful conditions within which working mothers had to live and work, so there was a perceived need to make policies which would ease the 'double burden' on women. In this context certain aspects of what is entailed in housework in Hungary need to be spelled out. Labour-saving equipment is not readily available to the 'average' Hungarian woman. By this is meant that such necessities (certainly in households with young children) as modern, *reliable,* washing machines are expensive and difficult to obtain. Whilst many households have some form of washing machine, it is a commonplace that more time has to be spent trying to fix them or attempting to obtain some sort of part for them. They cannot be viewed in the same light as their counterparts in Western countries. Such equipment as tumble dryers are almost unheard of in most households. In terms of stocking-up on food and other household goods, the norm in many Western countries is of a household shop once a week, or even once a month, with such things as milk, eggs and even yoghurt and fruit juice being delivered by milk deliveries. Such a situation is a long way off for Hungarian shoppers. Although the fact that much of the food and drink sold in Hungary contains very few, if any, preservatives means that a more healthy diet could be achieved, this also has the effect of short shelf-lives for much produce. Such foodstuffs as milk, cheese, yoghurt and bread needs to be bought daily. This entails queueing not only to pay for one's goods but sometimes be able to use a trolley, as many supermarkets in Budapest and other cities are almost always fairly crowded. The other negative feature of this daily shopping requirement is that even in the larger supermarkets it is not always possible to get everything that is required. Sometimes one shop will run out of yoghurt, or another will run out of bread and so on. It must be remembered that it is women who do the majority of this extremely stressful queueing and carrying home of goods. Even carrying shopping bags home on crowded trams (especially when also caring for young children) can be difficult as the packaging of foodstuffs in Hungary is remarkably poor. The milk, which is sold in very flimsy polythene bags often leaks out onto the rest of the shopping or the shopping bags (not readily available in many shops) given to hold the groceries often split or break altogether. Also there are the inevitable shortages, though in Hungary these are not generally as severe as in other parts of Central and Eastern Europe. Still, when a shopper wants a packet of tissues, tampons or their usual brand of shampoo it can become a tiring business wandering from shop to shop because there is a shortage. These small incidents become a surprisingly major irritant when overlaid onto the end of a busy day at the factory/office/school.

In terms of household work, jobs are not made easier by handy equipment such as squeezy mops or spray cleansers. Most floor cleaning in Hungary is done with a form of headless brush around which a cloth is draped, and most of the cleaning products available are of below average quality in terms of speed cleaning. The same problems which are apparent with washing machines also apply to the few different makes of vacuum cleaners available in Hungary at present. Of the two main types available, the model from Czechoslovakia is very difficult to obtain spare parts for, whilst the Soviet model although less reliable is relatively easier to repair. If someone in the home does not become a good fix-it person the costs of sending equipment into workshops would definitely be prohibitive for most people. In addition, especially if the man in the home has a second job, the task of helping children understand what is required of them at school (rather than actually executing homework tasks) often falls to women as an extra home job.

All the indicators which were pointing towards a situation of surplus labour together with the hardships of the double burden on women formed the basis on which the childcare allowance policy was created. These factors combined with the knowledge that creches and preschools are expensive to build, so it could be seen that paying women to stay at home to care for children, was not only less expensive than investing in the provision of more services but had the added bonus of flexibility – removing sections of women from the workforce for certain periods of time.

In its positive aspect, the childcare allowance, which provides income-related benefit for three years after the expiry of maternity leave, offered a guarantee for young, often skilled or semi-skilled women, to withdraw from the labour force without losing their jobs. This safeguarded them from suffering disadvantages in the competition for workplaces because they were caring for young children.

Since May 1982 the childcare allowance has been available to fathers yet the proportion of fathers taking up this allowance is miniscule (less than 1%). Reasons for this are primarily ideological and concern attitudes to (and within) the family, and the fact that women are regarded basically as the 'carers'. Because of many various attitudinal assumptions, women's earning power is less than men's, so families would suffer financially if men were to claim the allowance, even though it is wage related, as men have higher earning potential within the second economy. Whilst many women view their role primarily in terms of wife/mother, and girls are generally socialized within this framework, attitudes towards the value of work in the home and childbearing remain generally 'condescending'.

It is indicative that employment in areas such as childcare assistance in crèches and kindergartens is extremely lowly-paid, seen to be low-status, and as such, few women actually aspire to it. Yet, when the same job is carried out in the home, without any pay but with extra duties of caring for the home, shopping and cooking for the children, as well as an older parent, perhaps, then this is certainly viewed by society generally as a job that women *should* aspire to.

Much academic debate has centred on the 'ideal' family (socialist family – democratic decision-making, equal gender division of tasks, etc.) yet what is expected of the 'ideal' woman in Hungary is more easily understood in terms of superwomen. Women in Hungary are expected to be reliable workers, wonderful mothers, cooks and cleaners, then to be teachers in the early evening, plus suitable social partners and/or adorable sex creatures at night. This theme of over-expectation crops up in many different ways and it seems that for many women in Hungary such a complex set of social expectations acts as a massive pressure on them – ways in which this can find release are manifold, including decisions about not having more children, getting divorced and strains in women's health.

Maria Markus (1973) aptly pinpoints the dilemma for women:

> All this leads to a situation where there no longer exists any 'natural' behaviour for women, and everything has to be 'explained'. When she is staying at home, she has to explain why she is not working and contributing to the welfare of her family; when she is working, but has no family, it is the latter that has to be 'explained'. In the case where she is trying to fulfil both functions, she may have a sense of bad conscience about not being a good mother (when she is not at work) and not being good worker (when she is not at home – say with a sick child). The existence of this 'bad conscience' can be verified in almost all sociological investigations dealing with the problem of motivation to work, and life satisfaction.

Ideology, social policy and women's interests

We turn now to the ideological framework in which these debates are situated, and our starting point concerns the teleological nature of socialist social policy. A fundamental stumbling block to any emergent social change is this teleological aspect of policy in Hungary. That is, what are the reasons for attempting to institute such change? What are the desired goals? Within this, the ideological framework of policy choice is a major factor. Questions concerning the overall aims of policy-makers are vital in terms of whether benefits/programmes are 'applicable' to all areas of social policy.

Concerned as 'planners' are with the 'overall' picture then full employment is an obvious element in social policy decisions. However, views of what full employment means and on what *terms* this can be achieved, are coloured very much by prioritizing of desired goals, by the criteria of which means suit which ends as well as which 'ends' are the most important.

In terms of its aims there was a definite split in Hungarian thought with an oppositionalist tendency that some argue has been apparent in Hungarian writing since the late 19th century (Huszar, 1981). Throughout the 1960s and early 1970s a group of radical philosophers and sociologists loosely referred to as the Budapest School criticized what they saw as the tendency within Soviet-type sociology to consider only the surface of society in terms of collecting statistics, rather than actually analysing concrete problems by facing theory with reality.

The crux of the difference in outlook between these scholars and the official views in Hungary was that rather than believing that the problem lay in correcting outdated prejudices, the critical sociologists saw the problem as part of the contradictions in the actual conditions of life in Hungary (and other such societies). So a radical, revolutionary change was proposed in such areas as the family and socialization, in order to change society rather than to reform it. The work of Heller and Vajda concerning the possibility of living communist life-styles and the benefits this would have concerning the socialization of future generations (according to democracy not authority) not to mention the context in which women would become equal sexual partners in the manner in which Kollantai once proposed, was part of this radical oppositional strand. The childcare benefits/childcare programmes debate was therefore only a part of a broader official/radical dialogue. However, it has to be said that the 'Budapest School' is now a thing of the past and that in many ways its ideas were taken as much from the Western left of 1968 and the early 1970s in terms of communalism so that these ideas can't be said to have flowed from the experiences of people in Hungary.

In practical terms we can see that in her contribution to *The Humanisation of Socialism* Maria Markus resisted any policy initiatives which narrowed choice (such as enforced maternity benefits) whilst encouraging any measures that seek to extend choice (such as increase socialization of domestic labour, more collective forms of mutual help, greater emphasis on the need for both sexes to participate in housework and learn the skills involved). In terms of socialization and the family, Agnes Heller and Mihaly Vajda wrote of the potential within communist policies for creating new styles of living. Whilst these writers accepted that the family would continue to exist for some time, they did not see the 'socialist family' as the base unit of society, but rather that:

> ...the family will persist as long as it compensates for the alienation and powerlessness of the individual elsewhere. The emancipation of women, the development of more communal ways of living and the extension of democracy must take place alongside an overall humanization of social relations. (Women's Collective)

When we talk of ends, such as the emancipation of women, or even women's liberation, we need to ask what has the National Council of Hungarian Women done, or is it doing, to achieve the emancipation/liberation of women? This Council is one of the main sources of propaganda about women's position in Hungarian society. It is currently in its third phase of existence. Phase 1 was the Democratic Association of Hungarian Women formed in 1945 to help orphans and fight against epidemics and disease. After 1956 this council was reorganized with local councils representing women's interests throughout Hungary. In 1970 there was an HSWP decision to close down these local councils. One reason given was that at most women work in paid employment, women's policy should be within the workplace, so this leaves no need for a separate organization. As 90% of women of working age either learn, or work, so the argument goes, then the protection of women's rights is the task of local youth organizations, trades unions or party organizations. In interviews with officials from the council it was difficult to pin them down as to what the Council actually did in terms of organizing for women. The women volunteers (suggested from their workplace) meet three or four times a year to discuss basic social problems and bring the opinions of women from their workplaces with them. Of the women in the praesidium, most are Party members, elected for four years. Generally, there is a big Women's Conference every four years.

One aspect of this organization which is to some extent influential is its weekly paper *Nok Lapja* (*Women's Journal*) which, as the only authorized women's paper in Hungary has a circulation of up to 1,200,000 (so could be read by up to 5 million people). Whilst this paper does publish articles about women earning less than men in the same jobs, and about husbands who are prepared to help their working wives in the home, it does not attempt to suggest any remedies or to propose any appropriate courses of action. There is very much the air of reading about the 'little women' in it, with reporting of important women's gatherings in terms of 'what the ladies were wearing' or recipes and patterns for clothing always outnumber any articles on women's lives or problems.

So far as Hungarian women themselves are concerned, this organization which is supposed to exist for, and to be made up of, them, is just a 'paper organization'. One young mother in an interview (1986) explained to me that:

> I don't think it does anything for women's liberation. It is only a paper organization. I've never met anybody who has been in it, I don't even know where it is and I've no idea what sort of help I could ask from them ... I think it may have some sort of negative role, because the initiatives might just be put aside saying that 'We have this Nok Tanacs which takes care of such things' or 'You go there and ask them about it'.

This pinpoints one problem for the automous organization of women in Hungary – the fact that this organization exists (on paper or otherwise) means that any other grouping of women wishing to organize around issues affecting women becomes *de facto* illegal. This was the case when some women attempted to organize against the passing of the legislation in the Council of Ministers in 1973 restricting abortion rights. A group of women (some of whom were students) wrote a letter to members of Parliament about the disastrous effects of these restrictions. In a petition, the women argued against the outlawing of abortion for certain women, pointing to the harmful psychological effects of this and saying that this was not a means which would encourage women and men to have children. Not only would unwanted births increase, but so too would illegal abortions. These women did not argue for abortion as a preferred method of birth control. Suggestions made by them as to how to create suitable conditions for stimulating births included resolving the housing shortage, building more creches and kindergartens, in addition to implementing the equal legislation concerning women and making men legally responsible for sharing in childcare tasks. One of the organizers pointed out that the collection of signatures for this petition (1553 were collected – an unprecedented number in Hungary), proved to be as important as writing of it (Korosi, 1984). Whilst the proposed bill was revoked from the agenda of Parliament, it was, in unchanged form, put into force by a decree of the Ministry of Health in September of that year.

This event did show the possibilities of women organizing around women's demands and forming an active women's movement.

The alleged organizers of the 1973 campaign were excluded from Budapest University and unable to finish their studies. Since 1973 until the time of writing (1987) there has been no similar women's organization in Hungary.

The anti-feminist backlash in Hungary

The reasons for the absence today (1987) of any autonomous or feminist women's organization are manifold. The word 'feminism' itself is problematic in the Hungarian context (and within Soviet-type societies generally). This debate is complicated by the role of women within the 'socialist project' (in terms of workers being in Marxism the 'agents' of social change so that women remain something 'other') and by the fact that in Hungary certainly, women's suffrage has been written out of history.

In terms of the more recent ideological setting to this debate we can see that in Hungary there was an awareness of the American swing to the right. Hanak Katalin (1984) gives the example of:

> The western neo-conservative trends, which started to strengthen from the mid-1970s and attack at the beginning of 1980 – while generally questioning the values of the 1960s – considered the women's movement one of their targets. In the USA the so-called 'silent majority' condemned the legal possibility of abortion based on individual decision ...
> According to other conservative trends, the reference given to minorities in a disadvantage position and to women in the labour market was interpreted as a discrimination against whites and men.

As we know, it was this 'silent majority' which went on to become the very vocal 'moral majority', attacking the positive views on the changing social roles of women, defending the traditional views on the family and biblical morals. As Hanak rightly points out, speeding up of legal, economic, cultural and family equality for women caused a form of, open or concealed, anti-women campaign in the everyday political and scientific thinking. This anti-women lobby in Hungary was primarily concerned for the interests and indeed existence of the life of men. This debate in Hungary began in early 1982 with the work of David Biro (1982) which was followed up by several 'dramatic' writings in similar vein. Basically, what these authors were arguing is that the situation of men is worse than that of women.

According to this view, this can be proved by the increasing trends showing middle-aged men dying in a higher number than women in Hungary and at a faster rate. The responsibility for this worsening situation is to a small extent placed within society (environmental damages and overworking) but the primary blame attaches to women. Women, it is claimed, over-use and abuse their emancipation and they use it for having children, then they leave the men – they know only rights, they do not know duties. A subdivision of men's rebellion concerns maintenance payments – some men think it is contemptuous to make contributions (voluntary or forced) to their ex-wives who are looking after the children.

The very nature of this group of writings gives cause for concern in terms of the validity of the statements made. Many of them show examples of wrongly understood statistics, shabby or misunderstood psychological reasons, or in some extreme cases there are sweeping generalizations made. Rather than understanding, they search for a scapegoat making a basic problem of society into a problem of personal life. It is possible that within some of these writings there was the intention to shock. An unfortunate occurrence, in terms of adding weight to the anti-equality group, was that Biro was interviewed on New Years Eve 1982 by a woman who was both assertive and to an extent aggressive in her style of questioning. Biro was only able to get a few (incoherent) words in here and there, and so he was in a strange way 'vindicated' in terms of his theme concerning the misuse of women's liberation. Over the course of this debate Biro became the leading Hungarian expert on the woman question in the public's mind. Rather than dismissing these writings as narrow-minded and ill-researched, it has been recognized in Hungary that it must be accepted that such work, even indirectly, points to the belief that men's rights have been injured by women's liberation.

Within all this debate, in terms of whether the positive effects for women and men have still resulted in the creation of a relationship in which equality and partnership are imbalanced, there is a very mixed ideology. In her work, Sas Judit[1] has argued that the 'blind feminism' which turns against men (she argued that this never had any real foundation and representation in Hungary) did not take men's problems into consideration at all. This probably hinders men in forming new roles. However, the men's rebellion is similarly short-sighted in that it is unable to recognize that women's emancipation is not only of interest to women but it has great advantages from the men's point of view. This would accord with the *Humanisation of Socialism* viewpoint in terms of the socialization of future generations.

Re-opening the feminist debate

The feminist debate has, however re-emerged more recently in Hungary. An article 'Where has Hungarian feminism gone?' published in *Life and Literature* in May 1987 (Pal, 1987) by socialist Pal Tamas begins with a student discussion attempting to define feminism. For the boys it was a rather dangerous and barely conceivable women's aspiration for power, whereas for the girls, whilst not classifying themselves as feminist as this would mean something unwomanly, feminism was not viewed as an aggressive phenomenon. Still, the girls viewed successful women and feminists as contradictory roles. Various interview researches have shown that many women in Hungary do view feminism as a negative, somewhat embittered movement, rather than a positive force for change and development. Many of the women with whom I spoke said that the only propaganda they saw about Western feminism was of a crude or bizarre nature leading them to see feminists in a negative light.

Tamas points out that none of the feminist literature of the 1960s has been published in Hungary,[2] and he notes that amongst the 'educated' few social scientists and journalists who are aware of the existence of ecological movements, alternative movements, and the New Left, they 'do not even know the names of the most disputed feminist ideologists'. Despite the difficulties of getting started in terms of various movements in Hungary, Tamas asserts that of all the 'foreign' intellectual movements only feminism has been missed by Hungarians. There are some standard 'reasons' given for this which, Tamas notes, include the fact that feminism has never existed in Hungary, even the suffragettes at the turn of the century were isolated in Hungary, and as soon as Hungarian bourgeois radicalism slipped out of intellectual life, so Hungarian feminism also disappeared. The second version proposed that no 'isms' of any kind exist within Hungarian society, so that an autonomous women's movement is bound to have problems, given women's experience in public affairs. Yet another 'answer' is that the basic aims of the Western feminist movement have been fulfilled in Hungary, so that feminist movements would only serve to increase women's problems in Hungary.

In this final version – probably the most common – the argument goes that 'have we not got trouble enough without problematizing the female/male relationship?' In this view other things are more important, so that if feminism in concentrated upon, 'real conflicts' are avoided.

In his concluding remarks Tamas (1987) notes the discrimination apparent for women workers in Hungary and states that: 'At the same time a group of highly educated, self respecting well-to-do women with a lot of leisure time, is missing in Hungary, which is the basis of the Scandinavian and American upper middle class feminism.'

In terms of reform however Tamas concludes with the cautionary note that 'reforms cannot be stopped at people's doorsteps' – that is, that the conservative model of private life which is publicized in Hungary at present, forms a barrier to a modernization process. In contradiction to this, an article published at the same time by Zsuzsa Ferge (1987) basically argues that feminism is not 'timely' in Hungary under the present generally bad economic conditions and she notes the increasing attractiveness of the traditional division of labour in terms of:

> The attractiveness of the duality of the 'hardworking man' and the woman staying at home and taking care of her family, has increased over the last few years, because of the growing difficulties in providing a livelihood, more and more men spend more and more hours on extra work on the basis of the new possibilities.

Ferge proposes that none of the 'women's liberation movements' would be followed in Hungary, because these movements are the product of a different social context and they seek answers to different questions.

Conclusion

The duality between oppositionist and official views here is blurred or non-existent. In this context one can get into the realm of transposing Western feminist values onto the situation. We have to decide where our critique comes from and where it can go. Gail Lapidus notes (1978) that in Soviet-type societies the ideology:

> has concentrated on the more superficial economic aspects of women's roles, leaving intact the fundamental family structures, authority relations, and socialization patterns crucial to personality formation and sex-role differentiation. Only a genuine sexual revolution could have shattered these patterns and made possible the real emancipation of women.

Here it might be pertinent to point out that a genuine sexual revolution has not occurred in the history of humanity so is this what feminists worldwide should now be working towards?

In conclusion, as to the possibilities of women's autonomous organization in Hungary at the present there are a couple of major barriers to this (in addition to those above) which come under the headings of ideology and decision-making.

Alena Heitlinger sums up this aspect (1980):

> It must be recognized that the continuing lack of funds for organizations in the consumer sector in Eastern Europe has resulted less from objective economic necessity than from political decisions by Communist bureaucracies that funds would be better spent elsewhere. We must also recognize, in this respect, that the lack of an autonomous feminist power base has influenced official perceptions of economic possibilities.

So Heitlinger points to the needs for women's involvement in decision-making if decisions concerning women are to change. In many senses the future for an automous women's movement in Hungary does not look promising at present. Women in Hungary are living with the burdens of the unrealistic expectations placed on them whilst their 'problems' are being defined and 'solved' by men, in a male-dominant, production-orientated society. It would seem that until women can at least have some significant input into the male-orientated perspective of decision-making and thereby influence work priorities, re-evaluating the 'important' areas and including some of the hitherto undervalued areas, then those attitudes which engender sexism will continue to thrive in Hungary.

A final area of struggle to which observers might look for openings for an emphasis to be placed on women's interests is that of the radical opposition groupings in Hungary. However, the experiences of the past few years seem to confirm that the comment made by Piri Markus (1982) still applies.

> There is no general understanding about women being oppressed, and the subject is laughed at. There are hardly any samizdat books written by women, and extremely few women are involved in the decision-making leadership of the intellectual 'opposition'.

In the fascinating and far-reaching publication *The Social Contract: Prerequisites for Resolving the Political Crisis* (Beszelo, 1987) little mention is made of women's automous interests (Section 3:4 mentions the needs for an association representing the interests of unskilled women). Women's interests in terms of family are represented to some extent, but here we touch upon the whole debate surrounding the family as a site of resistance within Soviet-styled societies which could be the subject of another paper!

Notes

1 Personal interview with author (May 1986).
2 It is the case that much of the feminist literature available in Hungary is of German or Dutch origin and tends to be more concerned with aspects of radical feminism than socialist feminism. As such, it tends to be rejected by some of the small section of people who read it.

Bibliography

Beszelo (The Talker) no. 20 June 1987 or the English translation of *The Social Contract* from Hungarian October Freepress Information Centre, 24D Little Russell Street, London WC1 (Spec. 6/1987/E/).

Biro, David (1982), 'A "teremtes koronai" es a "gyengebb nem"' ('The "masterpiece of creation" and the "weaker sex"'), *Valosag*, no. 9.

Ferge, Zsuzsa (1987), 'Kell-e Magyarorszagon feminizmus?' ('Does Hungary need feminism?'), *Ifuysag Szaamle*, May 1st, p. 3.

Hanak, Katalin (1984), 'Male and Female Communicators on the Screen'. In: *Jel Kep (Symbol)*, Special Edition, Mass Communication Research Centre, p. 160.

Heitlinger, Alena (1980), 'Marxism, Feminism and Equality'. In: Yedlin, Tova, *Women in Eastern Europe and the Soviet Union*. Praeger.

Huszar, Tibor (1981), 'Sociography – The Emergence of a Discipline', *New Hungarian Quarterly*, no. 3, 83, Autumn, pp. 83–96.

Korosi, Suzanne (1984), 'The Non-existence of Women's Emancipation'. In: Morgan, R. (ed.), *Sisterhood is Global*. Penguin, p. 295.

Lapidus, Gail (1978), *Women in Soviet Society: Equality, Development and Social Change*. London: University of California Press.

Markus, Maria (1973), 'Factors Influencing the Fertility of Women: The Case of Hungary' *International Journal of Sociology of the Family*, no. 2.

Markus, Piri (1982), 'Labour Focus Fills me with Greyness', *Labour Focus on Eastern Europe*, Autumn, London.

Tamas, Pal (1987), 'Hova lett a Magyar feminizmus?' ('Where has Hungarian feminism gone?'), *Elet es Irodalom (Life and Literature)*, May 1st.

Vajna, T. (1982), 'Problems and trends in the development of the Hungarian new economic mechanism: a balance sheet of the 1970's'. In: Nove, A. *et al.*, *East European Economies in the 1970's*. Butterworth.

Women's Collective (1984), *Labour Focus on Eastern Europe*. Special Issue on Women, p. 22

13 Women and ageing under real socialism

JIRINA SIKLOVA

In contrast to the recent past, the so-called capitalist and socialist countries are no longer separated by a really 'iron curtain'. Nowadays we do seem to know much more about each other. Still, we often tend to hope, deep down in our hearts, that those on the 'other side' have solved some of the problems which we seem to have in common. One such problem is doubtlessly the rapid ageing of the population in the industrially-developed countries of Europe and the adequate integration of these senior citizens into society, as well as providing them with adequate social welfare.

Perhaps I will disappoint some of you, but in Czechoslovakia both of these problems have not been adequately solved, in spite of the fact that we assured ourselves and the world already 25 years ago, according to our constitution – that we have already created a socialist society. This is true in spite of the fact that the solution of social problems was one of the fundamental demands of socialists in all countries. Yet the situation of old people in our country is very far from resolved. Senior citizens, and among them above all women, of whom there are twice as many as men, are also in my country 'second class' citizens; economically they are on average the worst off age group. This is testimony to a high level of ingratitude on the part of society, because it is the present generation of retired people who had built socialism in our country; these people worked and became old as the workers, farmers and employees of a country where the Communist Party and socialist government have ruled for a full 40 years. 'Ageism' in our country is not based on economic relations; so far old people are not competing with the younger as far as jobs are concerned (until very recently there has been a labour shortage), nor do they have large bank accounts or own property. Just the opposite is true, they are the poorest people in society. Nevertheless, a great deal of aversion against them exists, especially in interpersonal relationships at work and in public places. They are often deemed a 'burden', they 'hold things up', and their income is often looked upon as a burden to society. Negative attitudes toward old parents are relatively frequent in families and are aggravated by a chronic housing shortage and the forced living together of three generations. What was previously the traditional intergenerational bond formed by common family property (land or small businesses) has ceased to exist due to nationalization of all productive assets and the factual loss of land by its integration into cooperatives, and this has been compounded by migration to urban areas due to too rapid industrialization (Kasalova, *et al.,* 1982). The creation of a new hierarchy of values and priorities takes time and has certainly not yet been stabilized. Moreover, the high level of employment among women (almost 96% of all women capable of working are employed), makes it physically impossible to provide the required care to old and/or ill parents or grandparents in the family (*Statistical Yearbook,*1986, Parts 3 & 4). Now a generation is retiring which for 40 years has worked for only a single employer – which in Czechoslovakia is the state – and therefore we cannot be surprised when the adult children of today's pensioners assume that it is the direct obligation of society to care for their old mothers and fathers and to provide for them both financially and from a social welfare point of view.

But society is not capable of providing such care, nor does it consider it to be a prime priority. Ten years ago when a study was made the situation was such, that in terms of the requirements of that time, a full 94% of the required housing units in houses providing services to the aged were lacking; in other words only 6% of the needed number were available. The number of inhabitants in retired person's homes, at that time should have been increased by one-third and the number of social workers who visit the homes of old persons unable to care for themselves on a daily basis should have been doubled (*Statistical Yearbook* 1986, Part 24, Schimmerlingova, 1980). Since then the situation is probably worse; it is especially difficult in large towns, where an accumulation of senior citizens exists. In Prague alone, 28% of the population is of retirement age and now the waiting period for gaining access to a retired person's home is 2 years and three months. It can be done in a shorter time by bribing the officials and physicians (which is of course against the law, but still done) or by submitting an official document about the resistance activities during World War II of the old or ill person, or a written petition by other tenants in the house where the person lives, saying that he or she are so confused that they hamper 'socialist common life' in the house. Also very effective for this purpose is a certificate from an enterprise or local Communist Party organization saying that the person's adult children are so politically committed, that they have no time to care for an ill or old mother or father. In this way a person accumulates more 'points' and the hope for more rapid admission. And because the number of people over 80 years of age has substantially grown (to almost one quarter of a million) during the last five years, appeals are being made to the emotions, filial affection and responsibility of children for their parents and their obligation to care for them. What until recently was looked upon as an indignant situation of reliance upon charity which was considered unacceptable for human beings and typical for capitalism, is now preached as a new and typical characteristic of socialist morality. After decades of teaching that ethics are derived from the material interests and values of human beings as producers, this merely verbal stress on 'honouring the aged' is not very effective.

In my opinion a positive trait of the present situation is the fact that it is now possible to speak and write about the fact that our social welfare measures are inadequate. Defining the problem and putting it on society's agenda are the first prerequisites for solving it.

As in other European countries, so Czechoslovakia is ageing in the demographic sense of the word. Of the 15.5 million inhabitants of Czechoslovakia, approximately 3 million, that is 19.8%, are in the postproductive age group, or of retirement age (*Statistical Book*1986, Part 3). Since the natality of the population is low from a long-term point of view and in some years (for instance in 1986) not even reproduction is taking place, in 1985 we found the ratio of the number of children (0–14 years) and the number of people in a postproductive age to be 24% to 19.4%; in 1990 both groups will be equally large . Forecasts assume that in the year 2010, old people will represent more than a quarter of the population (Malicka, 1986, p. 111) .

But in this sense we do not differ too much from other countries in Central Europe . Only the life expectancy of men is low – only 67.7 years, while in the developed countries of Europe it approaches 74 years. The relation between men and women in the postproductive age group is 34.8% men and 65.7% women; in the age group above 70 years, the predominance of women is even higher (Vigocka, 1987, pp. 46–54).

The age at which women retire is 55 years (if a woman has had 2 children; it is 54 years if she had three or more children, 56 if she had one child and 57 for childless women) and 60 years for men. Doubtlessly, one of the advantages of socialism is that all citizens who have worked either for 20 years are eligible for retirement pensions, or whose husband had or would have had a pension or who had an invalid's pension.

Because the retirement age is not mandatory, people can if their health permits it and if they wish to do so, continue to work and thereby either increase the pension they will receive once they do retire (by about 7% annually), or they can receive part of their pension and continue to earn full wages or they can receive a full pension and work for a limited income (i.e. part-time or not a full year). Those who work in blue-collar occupations or other jobs which people do not like to do, can receive their full pension and full wage (for instance in raw material extraction, some occupations in the construction industry, seasonal work in agriculture etc.). In some of these occupations people in a postproductive age represent sometimes as many as 43% of all employees. Enterprises hire them for such jobs regardless of whether they are suitable or not from the point of view of the pensioner's health (Malicka, 1986, p. 5). The enterprise physician will only point out the inadequacy of the job in question in view of the applicant's age or health, but that is all.

Almost 60% of all pensioners work during the first five years after retirement; during the subsequent five years their employment decreases by one-fifth (Schimmerlingova, 1980, pp. 36-9). Employed pensioners mostly agree (as the findings of a microcensus and other surveys have indicated) that they 'do not work for personal satisfaction, but for financial reasons' (Federalni statisticky urad, 1982). In a socialist country that should not be the main motivation for work in old age.

As I have already mentioned, all employees and cooperative members in our country participate in mandatory national old age and health care insurance. Various previously existing forms of old age benefits (private insurance, various associations or insurance schemes for the self-employed) were annulled after 1948 and the large-scale nationalization of that period. After the collectivization of agriculture and the founding of agricultural cooperatives (approximately around 1952) all citizens received old age pensions (*Survey of Development of Retirement Pensions since 1948*, 1987). The introduction of this pension system was a necessity, especially since the postwar inflation took away the savings of the generation then becoming old, private insurance companies were abolished and the nationalization of all private ownership, including small-scale business and the expropriation of land, deprived everybody of the opportunity to provide for their own old age. These first postwar social old age pensions were really minimal and also a 'class' approach was reflected in their size. The lowest pensions – regardless of the duration for which a person had been insured for old age – were given to former private entrepreneurs, owners of factories or small businesses and richer farmers (*kulaks*). Only after the most excessive atmosphere of the first period of the dictatorship of the proletariat had passed, was the 'class' discrimination of pensions abolished and differentiation according to length of employment and according to three categories of employees was introduced. These categories were determined according to the social significance of the work done (for instance the first and highest category includes miners, airplane pilots, employees in metallurgy and the chemical industry).

At present, retirement (as well as invalid) pensions are based on average monthly earnings for the last 5 or 10 years of employment, which are then subtracted by 50%, up to a ceiling of 24.000 Cz. crowns annually. Anything over this sum is included in the calculations only by one-third. (Beginning with the autumn of 1988 this basic sum is to be increased to 32,000 Cz. crowns annually). By this type of calculation, all pensions are greatly levelled and those who retire suffer a sudden and large drop in their income and living standard. Those with relatively high incomes (for instance over 60,000 Cz. crowns annually), in their old age receive less than a third of their former wage, while those without qualifications and a relatively low wage, receive 70% to 80% or their previous wage. No wonder then, that senior citizens are not satisfied with their pensions and blame society, or simply 'young people' for their low living standard. Only a group of people which is small in terms of percentages differs from the majority, because they receive a 'personal pension' for their 'merits'; they are awarded individually by the staff of the district, regional, municipal or central committees of the Communist Party of Czechoslovakia and include Party Officers and staff, national artists, academicians, high military staff, officers of the police and security forces etc. These people are not included in the statistics, so they do not influence the figures I am citing.

In 1970 the average size of a retirement pension was less than 53% of the average net wage of employees. By 1975 this figure had decreased to 49.4% and at present it is again equal to around 52% (Andel, 1980). The average retirement pension in 1985 was 1,265 Cz. crowns, which was 53.4% of average net wages in that year.

In spite of the fact that we have equality between the sexes, women have on the average 5.6% lower pensions than men under the same conditions, i.e. when they were in the same wage group. This is because women retire at 55 years (see above) and once they attain that age, they less frequently continue to be employed in order to increase their pension as men do, because they are called upon to help with the grandchildren in the families of their children. The high death rate among men and the relatively high number of divorces after 25 to 30 years of marriage (which also in our country seem to have become a 'fashion'), leads to a situation where women, more frequently than men, live alone and have less available financial resources. In 1982 (the last year for which figures are available), a so-called socially acceptable minimum pension (880, - Cz. crowns for individuals and 1,500, - Cz. crowns for a couple) was received by 15.3% of all pensioners and of this figure, 89% were women, this represented 380,000 persons (Malicka, 1986, p. 47). Thus we see that poor and socially needy pensioners in Czechoslovakia are above all women! On the average, they live longer than men, they receive their pensions for longer periods of time and because in Czechoslovakia so far there is no automatic cost-of-living indexing for pensions, the real value of their pension is constantly declining. According to official statistics (which here, just as in most countries, tend to rather overstate the situation), living costs in Czechoslovakia during the last 15 years have increased by 26.5% (*Historical Statistical Yearbook*), 1983, p. 210). This has been especially negative for pensioners, and the more so for so-called old-time pensioners, who had retired long ago. For this reason in 1979 all pensions were increased at a stroke by 30 Cz. crowns monthly, and minimum pensions by 70 Cz. crowns monthly. But to get some idea of what this sum represents, I might add that for this sum you can buy approximately one and a half pounds of butter, or 4 ounces of coffee or one and a half pounds of beef or you can travel 85 kilometres by bus. Because a local telephone call costs 1,-Cz. crown, a joke among pensioners at that time ran: 'Pensions have been raised by 30,- Cz. crowns per month so that we can call the national committee (i.e. the local government which administers social welfare) everyday, to report that we are still alive.'

But I do not wish to stress only negative aspects. A number of recipients of minimum pensions receive once a year, free of charge, coal for heating; they can also receive special sums for buying clothing, they receive free or greatly reduced tickets for cinema performances and special allowances when they have a diet for reasons of disease (for instance diabetes). Medical care is free of charge, as well as all drugs and various aids, such as crutches, canes, wheelchairs, etc.

According to official studies carried out by the Institute for the Study of Social Welfare attached to the Ministry of Labour and Social Welfare (Hirsl, 1983, p. 184; 1986, pp. 17–31), in this country we consider a socially acceptable minimum income to be equal to 56% of the average per capita income of a person living in a specific type of household (single person, two persons or more persons in a household). A subsistence minimum income is equal to less than 42% of this income per household member. In 1980, 8.15% of the population lived in households with a less than minimum income, that is approximately 1,233,000 people (*Historical Statistical Yearbook*, 1983, p. 147) of these, 77.45% persons were over 65 years of age. As a consequence of inflation (which until recently had not been acknowledged to exist), the value of pensions continues to decrease, so the older a person is, the lower his real income. In the 80- to 84-year-old group, 38.82% had minimum pensions and in the group of 85-year-olds and older it was already 59% (Hirsl, 1983, pp. 25–6). And in these categories, women were seven times as frequent as men.

The recipients of minimum pensions in 1985 spent 81.42% of their income on basic needs (food, housing, heat). All other expenditures, including leisure time, foods other than basics, drinks, smoking, travelling, etc. were represented by only 18% of their income (*Statistics of Household Living Standards*, 1985). One of the studies carried out by the above cited Institute, attached to the Ministry of Labour and Social Welfare, cited that 86.2% of old age pensioners questioned had never left their homes during the summer for the purpose of recreation (Schimmerlingova, 1980, p. 48) and 41% live in housing of the lowest (IVth) category, without a bathroom or separate WC, where rent is also very low (Schimmerlingova, 1980, p. 51).

In spite of the fact that specialists for the study of social welfare as early as 1980 pointed to the unacceptable decline in the real value of retirement pensions and recommended various measures which would automatically and continually adapt the level of pensions to inflationary processes and bring them somewhat closer to real wages, nothing has yet been done in this direction. Perhaps some improvements will be introduced in the autumn of this year (1988), when new legislation on retirement and pensions is expected.

The Communist Party of Czechoslovakia (at its Central Committee meetings and its 14th, 15th and 16th Party Congresses), as well as the Czechoslovak government, have in recent years accepted a number of programmes of the type 'The Year of Honour to old Age', or 'A Programme for preparing for Old Age', etc., but so far have not introduced any specific measure for increasing pensions by indexing. Perhaps this is also because that would mean officially admitting to the public that inflation exists in our economy and that price increases are not merely 'price adjustments' or the result of 'innovated' products or better quality products on the market. The existing method of unsystematic, occasional, ad hoc, once and for all types of increasing pensions, or providing 'single stroke' aid to individuals is only an advantage for the decision-making central authority. Financial sums which otherwise might be used for increasing pensions are now freely used by the authorities according to momentary economic situations, and/or utilized for political propaganda and manipulation. Single one-stroke increases are always announced with much ado, as evidence of an increased 'expression of care' provided by a socialist society to old people; what should be a matter of course is interpreted as a charitable gift, which is 'given' to our senior citizens. Such an interpretation is also reflected in the attitudes of the middle and younger generation towards pensioners and leads to a negative image of old age throughout society. For old people themselves, such a policy leads to a lack of security, a feeling of dependence, inferiority and bitterness. They do not know what their rights are in this respect, they cannot plan their future, make decisions about themselves, they can only wait on what the powerful – that is the young and healthy – will be willing to 'allocate' to them.

For propaganda reasons, retirement pensions are interpreted as 'an expression of the care which a socialist society bestows on old people', and not as part of the wages which were not paid during the person's working life, which was withheld and in effect 'borrowed' by society and now, after a period of time are 'repaid' to the creditor. If retirement pensions were interpreted in this manner and substantially differentiated in size according to preceding merits (as reflected in wages), this would of course greatly increase the self-esteem and self-assessment of old people. This would retroactively make an impact upon the attitude of the younger generations towards old people, as well as towards their own future, that is their own old age. It would certainly contribute to a decrease in the neurotic nature of intergeneration relations.

Social welfare and especially retirement benefits are not acts of charity, but the outcome of an agreement concluded between the individual and society, which in our country is represented by the state.

When we compare capitalist and socialist countries we often stress that under capitalism the productivity of labour is higher, living standards are higher, there are more per capita cars and computers and what not. I acknowledge that, but it is not something which I consider to be very impressive. A high level of consumption is not only a source of positive influence and achieving a very high living standard is probably not a socialist country's strong point. I personally have no intention of criticizing our socialist system for the fact that our living standard is not high enough. What I do wish to criticize and reject is the fact that real socialism in our country has, during the 40 years of its duration, not been able to solve problems which are supposed to be its strong point, where socialism is supposed to have clearcut advantages. And those are problems of social welfare policy, where providing for people in their old age with dignity has a primary place. All socialists had this in their programmes already 150 years ago! Beginning with Campanella, through Saint Simone and Owen and Fourier, and of course Karl Marx and Engels, right up to Lenin.

I find that we do not even have our own socialist theory, adequate to our conditions, or a working concept of social security for old age. We often think that pension schemes which exist in the capitalist countries are superior and would like to copy them, if we could. The negative aspects of our pension system and social welfare are not discussed with our citizens or with those who are directly concerned; discussion is replaced by cliches and demagogy about the advantages of social welfare and security under real socialism. In such a context, the specific problems of women, as opposed to men, lose their importance.

I would like to conclude by saying that the situation and social welfare of old people under our real socialism is clearly insufficient. If we do not realize the seriousness of the situation and do not do something about it, the welfare of the next generation in their old age will be even worse. And so we see that in a totalitarian state, such as the real socialist system in Czechoslovakia is, even the size of the pensions our senior citizens receive, as well as the number of places, equipment and personnel available in hospitals and many other aspects of care of the old, become ideological and political problems.

Bibliography

Andel, V., Brestovska, E. (1980), 'Prijmy a spotreba starych lidi v CSSR' ('Income and Consumption of Senior Citizens in Czechoslovakia'), *Informator*, CSVUPSV, Prague, pp. 5–9.

Federalni statisticky urad, Prague (1982), 'Obvyatelstvo v poproduktivnim veku podle udaju scitani lidu, dom a bytu' ('Population in Postproductive Age, According to Census of Population, Houses and Apartments'), Findings of microcensus from 1981.

Hirsl, M. (1983), 'Analyza skupin obyvatelstva s omezenou moxnosti spotreby' ('An Analysis of Population Groups with Limited Opportunity to Consume'). *CSVUPSV pai minister stvu prace* – series B, no. 98, Prague.

Hirsl, M. (1986), 'Pocet, prijem a kupni sila minimalnich duchodu', ('The Number,

Size and Buying Capacity of Minimum Pensions'), *Informacni zpravodaj No. 5–6* – Vyzkumny ustav rozvoje a prace, Prague.

Historicka statisticka rocenka (Historical Statistical Yearbook) (1983), CSSR – FSU, Prague.

Kasalova, H., Douchova, J. and Jungmann, B. (1982) 'Vyzkum zivotni situace starych obcanu' ('A Study of the Life Situation of Senior Citizens'), *Zaverecna zprava 1. etapy dileiho vyzkuma, Vyzkumny ustav socialniho rozvoje a prace* / VUSRP /, Prague, Report no. 904 305 03.

Malicka, L. (1986), 'Zpusob sivota v poproduktivnim veku v CSSR' ('Way of Life in a Postproductive Age in Czechoslovakia'), *Vyzjumna zprava – Ustav pro filozofii a socialogii CSAV*, Praha, HU-IX-3-6 SPZU.

Schimmerlingova, V. (1980), 'Vyzkum zivota a potreb starych obcanu z hlediska sluzeb socialni pece' ('A Study of the Lives and Requirements of Senior Citizens from the Point of View of the Social Services'), *Vyzmumna zprava No. SPEV VI-3/3.1.2*, Ceskolovensky vyzkumny ustav prace a socialnich veci, Prague.

Statisticka rocenka CSSR (Statistical Yearbook of Czechoslovakia) (1986), SNTL Praha – part 24: Socialni zabexpeceni, tab. 24–4, 24–6, 24–9.

Statisticka rocenka CSSR (Statistical Yearbook of Czechoslovakia) (1986), SNTL, Praha – part 3: Obyvatelstvo, part 4: Prace, tab. 4.2 and 4.4: Bilance pracovnich sil.

Statisticka rocenka CSSR (Statistical Yearbook of Czechoslovakia) (1986), SNTR Prague, B part 3: Obyvatelstvo, Federalni statisticky unad. (Projection of population by the year 2000. For every 100 persons at a productive age there are 77 who are economically dependent: 43 children and 34 of retirement age.)

Statistics of Household Living Standards – Volume III : The Income, Expenditures, Consumption and Equipment in Households of Retired Persons in 1985 (*Statistika zivotni urovne domacnosti – dil III*: Prijmy, vydaje, spotreba a vybavenost domacnosti duchodcu za rok 1985), FSU - Ceskoslovenska statistika, 1986, rada: Zivotni uroven.

Survey of Development of Retirement Benefits Since 1948 (Prehled o vyvoji duchodoveho zabezpeceni od roku 1948), *Informacni zpravadaj No. 2*, Prague 1987 – Vyzkumny ustav rozvoje prace pri ministerstvu prace a socialnich veci – pp. 37–51.

Vigocka, M. (1987), 'K rozdilum ve stredni delce zivota mezi muzi a zenami ve bybranych zemich' ('On Differences in the Expectation of Life Between Men and Women in Selected Countries'), *Demografie*, vol. 29, no. 1, pp. 46–54.

Mean after lifetime at birth/expectation of life in Czechoslovakia:

year	men	women
1960	67.67	73.12
1980	66.78	73.96

14 Education for parenthood in Czechoslovakia

ZUZANA HUGHES

In Czechoslovakia the parental role comprises individual and social aspects. Families are perceived as 'basic cells of society', important to social development; the state, accordingly, has a well-defined, highly-formalized family policy intended to help state and family to interact in the upbringing of children, future citizens of a socialist republic. To this end, families in Czechoslovakia are supported by the state through constitutional provisions, laws and regulations and a complex administrative system[1] that delivers a wide range of social support.

State help to families is not only a facet of a pronatalist family policy, but stems from a much wider social policy, aimed at creating a dialogue and relationship between the Czechoslovak state and its citizens. This dialogue shows that both parties are interested in children, as individuals and as future citizens.

In 1988 children remain the focus of social and family policies because the birthrate has declined and families have fewer children in them. Children have become a prized possession of parents, to be loved and cherished but also to be used in bargaining with the state, in order to gain material and other advantages for the family. Czechoslovak social welfare legislation since 1945 reflects this interaction. Education for parenthood, aimed at giving guidance as to the type of upbringing deemed appropriate and desirable in a socialist society, is only the latest expression of this 'dialogue' between the Czechoslovak state and Czechoslovak families.

Education for parenthood is a firm part of Czechoslovak social policy. Guidance has been channelled through state institutions such as schools, clinics, local authorities, army units etc. Lately, a new approach has been introduced: professional guidance, via the media, on modern, responsible childcare. This is based on recent longitudinal research. The new Abortion Act of 1 January 1987 (replacing Act no. 68/1957 Sb.) reflects the change. The new Act firmly declares that (Rotta, 1987):

1. The development of Czechoslovak society has reached a level permitting women to decide freely whether or not they want to have a child;
2. The Czechoslovak National Health system is sufficiently developed to cope with any demand for termination of pregnancy;
3. Longitudinal research (Marhovnova, 1987) has shown that unwanted children are psychologically and emotionally unstable and that they suffer a range of deprivations which adversely influence their future development.

Education for parenthood is considered in Czechoslovakia to be a vitally important factor in developing the 'socialist family', as a specific, creative element in Czechoslovak society (Machova, 1975).

Such education is not a new concept in Czechoslovakia. It can be traced back to the 17th century, to Jan Amos Komensky (Comenius, 1592–1670). He is perhaps best known for his plans for nursery schools (Komensky, 1968) which are very close to what is today considered a good nursery school or kindergarten, including visual aids and learning through play. The idea of purposeful guidance and appropriate instruction of children by their parents was discussed in another famous work by Komensky, *The School of Infancy* published in 1633, where he says that children should not be removed from their mothers and handed over to preceptors before their sixth year of age (Komensky, 1930). At the same time he presented a plan for the guidance of mothers on how to care for their children and how to instruct them, in order 'to plant in a man the seeds of all knowledge with which we wish him to be equipped in his journey through life' (Rusk, 1933).

In our century, in the 1920s, several publications by various authors appeared in Prague, all concerned with education for parenthood (Hynie, 1975). These were largely medically orientated and their primary purpose was to disseminate information on sex, to warn against sexually transmitted diseases, sexual indulgence, unwanted pregnancies. Before the Second World War, a group of doctors and teachers set up a special commission in Prague to elaborate principles of education for marriage and parenthood.

Similar efforts continued after the War, some of them deriving from attempts to define the role of women in the postwar society (Popelova, 1947). This culminated in the 1960s in the establishment of groups concerned with promoting marriage, family and children. Of particular importance were the State Population Commission (*Vladni Populacni Komise*) and a Group of Consultants in Education for Marriage and Parenthood, attached to the Ministry of Education and to the Ministry of Labour and Social Affairs. Only gradually did the emphasis shift from sexual education to other aspects of marriage and parenthood, particularly the care of children, knowledge of child development, home economics etc. As the first statistics indicating an increasing divorce rate and a decreasing birthrate became known in the late 1960s, education for parenthood came up for review and representation, in less personal and more ideological terms, on a markedly pronatalist basis. Only in the late 1970s and early 1980s did concern, aroused by research findings (Machova, 1975; Matejcek and Langmeier, 1981; Matejcek, 1986), about the quality of parenting and the quality of family relationships start to overcome the bias toward population growth:

> Education for parenthood is certainly not a one-time action; it is not a mere instruction about the sex life of a man and woman, and it is not interchangeable with sex education. It is, above all, an essential and inseparable part of the whole education of an all-round developed person, a truly harmonious personality... Education for parenthood which is truly creative is above all a moral matter. It represents an attitude towards the world and life, which does not place my own 'I' in the first place. (Fiser, 1981, pp. 116-17)

This attitude to parenting has been echoed in a number of Czechoslovak sociological studies on the family published since the mid-1970s (Solcova, 1976; Machova, 1979). Continuing the view of pre-1939 Czechoslovak sociologists, present-day scholars such as Otakar Machotka, A. Blaha, F. Uhlir, and Emanuel Chalupny consider the family to be a basic element of social structure, entitled to the protection of society and the state. This view has been based on relevant *legislation* and has been broadened and developed by numerous *field studies* on various aspects of family life and family problems carried out by the Czechoslovak Research Institute of Labour and Social Affairs and the Palacky University at Olomonc (Wynnyczuk and Srach, 1975; Wynnyczuk and Sracek, 1977; Bartosova, 1979; Schimmerlingova et al.,1977; Rollova,1983; Vitek (ed) 1983, 1987).

Particular attention must be paid to relevant legislation – a prominent feature in all the CPEA countries, where Soviet experience is taken into account: by the mid-1930s, Soviet officialdom recognized that social institutions such as law, family and property were after all not likely to 'wither away' – at least not in the foreseeable future. 'Therefore an attempt would be made to re-establish them on a new, socialist basis... it was re-discovered that law is not a luxury but a necessity...' (Schur, 1968).

There is a 'ripple effect' typical of East European countries, largely due to their shared ideology. The view cited above applies not to the Soviet situation alone but can also embrace Czechoslovakia and other CMEA countries.

Another point to bear in mind is the paramountcy of Party control in all aspects of life in these countries, including legal systems. This overwhelming and pertinent factor requires separate study; for our present purpose it will suffice to refer to official documents and statements on social policy.

Use of law as a device of organized social action directed towards achieving social change is widespread and growing in modern society (Dror, 1969), not least in Soviet Russia which 'uses law extensively to bring about and regulate social change...' (Dror, 1969, p. 92) and therefore, '...law plays an important indirect role in regard to social change by shaping various social institutions, which in turn have a direct impact on society...' (ibid.).

'Law' and 'Welfare' both loom large in Czechoslovak family policy and its implementation. The mix, the emphases and the changing balance of these elements illuminate the mechanism of 'fit' between family and society on a general level. Considered in a more specific context, such as that of the role of women or of preschool provision, possible modifications in practice between partners are apparent. Social welfare legislation exemplifies this process of barter and exchange, evident in Czechoslovakia ever since 1948. If we examine particular periods since 1948 we should note the following points.

1948–1950

- The Law on Comprehensive Education of 21 April 1948 (95/1948 Sb.) for the first time made kindergartens an inseparable part of an integrated Czechoslovak educational system. Kindergarten attendance was to be voluntary. Creches were not covered by this Law.
- The Czechoslovak Constitution of 9 May 1948 stipulated equal rights and duties for all citizens and equal access to education and work for both sexes. By implication it was necessary to provide substitute care for infants and young children, together with other forms of substitute provision for families. The Constitution stipulated that motherhood, marriage and family would be protected by the State.

As a result of this legislation, the dual role of women in Czechoslovakia, as workers and mothers, was confirmed. Although the inclusion of kindergartens in the comprehensive educational system underlined the ideological commitment of the Czechoslovak state to collective upbringing of children, the limitations of the Law of 1948 have meant in practice that the Czechoslovak Government has never yet attempted 100% preschool coverage. The growth and development of kindergartens have been much more vigorous than those of creches. Child-bearing has not been separated from child-rearing.

1950–1970

- The Law on Family Law, 1949 (265/1949 Sb.), usually known as the Family Code, which came into force on 1/1/1950, elaborated many points of the 1948 Constitution. It again underlined the dual role of women and featured all the principles summarized by A. Kloskowska (1964) in *Propaganda Model*.[1]

The Family Code enjoined, above all, strict subordination of the family to the wider group. It was directed towards overcoming the inequality of relationships *within* the family but the wider aspects of the family's relationship to society at large were neglected. The assumption seems to have been that the relationship of the family and the newly established socialist society was still at an early and rudimentary stage.

- A Government Population Commission was appointed in 1958, to investigate the falling birthrate, to inform the Government of demographic problems and trends and to advise it on population policy and measures to be adopted.
- A new Socialist Constitution came into force in July 1960. This Constitution officially marked the end of the transition from 'people's democracy' to 'socialism'. It stated that the most important social function of the family, involving both parents equally, was the upbringing of children. It specified the basic means necessary for realization of family equality. In this it mirrored aspects of Kloskowska's (1964) *Propaganda Model*.[2]
- The Law on the System of Upbringing and Education of 15 December 1960 (186/1960 Sb.) broadened the concept of preschool education to embrace the whole period of infancy and early childhood, from birth until entry to primary school. This led to publication in 1967 of a programme of education in creches and kindergartens, for general use.
- The Law on the Family of 4 December 1963 (94/1963 Sb.) stated that motherhood is the most honourable mission of women and that society renders to motherhood not only its protection but also every care, particularly material support to mothers and children and assistance with their health care and education.
- The upbringing of children was entrusted primarily to the family but the Communist Party of Czechoslovakia felt it necessary to specify in this 1963 Law the principles of socialist upbringing which would ensure that child-rearing conformed to the criteria and objectives formulated by the party.
- Civil Law, 1964 (40/1964 Sb.) and the Labour Law, 1965 (65/1965 Sb.) included further measures protecting women from work likely to be harmful to them as potential mothers. An increase in family allowances and lengthening of paid maternity leave followed.
- In 1964 a conference of the Czechoslovak Sociological Association at Hrezany concluded that 'the position of women in contemporary society is characterized by a contradiction between their emancipation and economic activity on the one hand and their biological and social function on the other' (Berent, 1970).

Following on this, there was a further commitment by the State to better and more integrated preschool provision, with explicitly stated ideological objectives for child-rearing in socialist Czechoslovakia. The potential effect was modified by a greater emphasis on the mother-role of women and the reproductive role of families. The fact that, despite its ideological commitment, the State had still not created a comprehensive preschool system with 100% coverage of the eligible age group compounded the ambiguity.

1970 onwards

- In July 1970 a maternity allowance was introduced, promptly dubbed 'mother's wage'. From the ideological point of view this measure represented recognition of motherhood as a socially and economically necessary activity, which must be remunerated. Motherhood acquired a new 'professional' status but the distinction between child-bearing and child-rearing was further blurred.
- On 5 May 1972 the Czechoslovak Government issued Proclamation No. 137/1972 which suggested and outlined plans for promoting the family and parenthood.
- Also in 1972, the respective Ministries of Education (CSR and SSR) published a methodological report on Education for parenthood, for the basic school system generally (Wynnyczuk, 1980).
- In 1973, Proclamation No. 267/1973 laid down guidelines on setting up marriage guidance clinics, to help failing marriages, to cut down the number of divorces, and to help young parents in bringing up their children.
- In July 1976, the Central Committee of the Communist Party of Czechoslovakia approved the important document 'On further development of the Czechoslovak educational system of upbringing', with a section on preschool, which led to adoption of a new concept of preschool education, including among its concerns

    a) development of ideological concepts for preschool education
    b) regular contact between preschool institutions and parents

- In 1976, the Czechoslovak Government decided to introduce a new type of preschool provision requiring less capital and capable of operating in smaller premises with fewer staff. This led to inception of the micro-creche.
- In October 1979, the Czechoslovak Federal Assembly dedicated one whole session to problems of education for marriage and parenthood
- A new Family Code was published in 1982 (132/1982 Sb., with a final version published as 66/1983 Sb.) which comments on widespread changes

in Czechoslovak society in general and in families and family relationships in particular. Its seven articles present a social 'snapshot' of present-day Czechoslovak society, and specify what is considered to be 'a socialist family' and how the State is prepared to support and maintain such a family in a number of practical ways.

It points out that in a socialist society upbringing of children is shared by the family and by the society through its various institutions, namely through preschool education, after-school clubs, the Socialist Union of Youth (SSM), Pioneers etc. It stresses the importance of society's control over children's upbringing and underlines the strengthened role and competence of National Committees (*Narodni Vybory*) in this respect. These committees now have the right to introduce certain upbringing arrangements, so far limited to Court jurisdiction. The whole problem of socio-legal protection of young people and children and the roles and duties of the national committees in the upbringing of children are now firmly anchored in this latest Family Code.

When one considers a legislation such as this new Family Code, one is considering a societal or structural policy. Ferge (1979) has argued that in socialist societies 'a dramatic change' is emerging, due to the fact that social policy can no longer be limited merely to counteracting the deficiencies of basic economic mechanisms. Social policy, construed in Ferge's terms, may be seen as a tool of societal or structural policy, an important element of social planning, and a vital cue for balancing the mutual relationship between the socialist state and the family. Societal policy is 'a normative rather than a palliative instrument' (Ferge,1979).

The Czechoslovak Government Decree no. 71/1966 on the goals of education for parenthood, has a broad mandate, including as it does sex education, contraceptive knowledge, marital counselling, child development, home economics and pronatalist policies. In this form it has been introduced gradually into schools (Fiser, 1979). Teachers, together with medical practitioners, were thought to be the 'best qualified professionals to promote it'. At this stage the campaign was accompanied by a mass media effort to influence public attitudes, in order to bring about an increase in the birthrate (Heitlinger, 1987). Efforts in the sphere or marital or premarital counselling were dominated by the medical profession (Plzak, 1970).

The increase in divorce since 1970 further widened the scope of the education for parenthood campaign. The quality of relationships in marriage became an important concern, because of problems identified by research on various aspects of divorce (Vitek, 1983). Certain types of family were identified as particularly vulnerable:

a) families where both partners have only basic education (without apprenticeship). One group within this category has partners who are *older*, particularly women. Divorce and second, even third marriages are common, as are cohabitation or widowhood. Single parent families abound. (Rollova, l983, pp. 3–4)

The other group belonging to this category is *younger*; at least one partner was a minor at marriage. As with the previous group they have only basic education and lack skills.

Both groups enjoy a reasonable material standard of living but their housing situation is worse than that of other families. Their children lack privacy at home and get little stimulation there. They do not share leisure time with their parents because in the main their parents prefer passive leisure, including spending vacations at home. Such parents are fairly conservative in the upbringing of their children: 'What was good enough for us, is good enough for them' is their motto.

This category also includes a small proportion of families with additional complicating factors, e.g. single-parent families of under-age girls, ethnic minority families (especially gipsy families), where 'the level of socialization and cultural level are inadequate for the needs of socialist society,' (Rollova, 1983, pp. 12–13) and where there is a 'social threat' that children of such parents will inherit their limitations and will perpetuate in their own new families the negative features of their families of origin.

Research showed that members of this group are often clients of social workers, whose help they need on a regular basis in order to survive, or 'in order to fulfil their expected social roles and tasks at an appropriate level'. Effective help in such cases was identified as 'help which meets the need both of parents and children... a complex system of help, involving both the clients and the helpers, including institutions of various kinds' (Rollova, 1983, p.14).

  b) people with a university education constitute a category in which there is a significant number of childless couples and also a fairly high incidence of divorce (Rollova, 1983, pp. 339–57).

Children born to such couples are more likely to face an only child situation', without siblings in a marginally unstable family. Their care will be more often entrusted to other people; quite a significant number of women with university educations forfeit their maternity leave entitlement and use creches, grandmothers and private nannies as substitute carers (Hughes, 1983). Although a high incidence of divorce has been noted, most of these families succeed in coping with their problems for a number of years and manage outward appearances. In divorce proceedings their children are the most passionately disputed 'possession' and veritable battles are fought over custody and access. It is no surprise to find that education for parenthood aimed at such families includes preparation of *both* partners for dual roles, advocates introduction of maternity leave for *both* partners, and stresses the need to teach partners with university education 'how to divorce' with the least detrimental effect on their children.

  c) families with physically and mentally handicapped children.

Research on educational, health and social problems of such families was started by the Federal Ministry of Labour and Social Affairs in 1978 (Vesela, 1978, 1981, 1982). This culminated in a special programme of education for parenthood in 1981 and 1982. Handicapped teenagers living at home, in residential-care establishments or special boarding schools were sampled and interviewed. Some of the questionnaires were printed in Braille, to enable blind young people to take part, and to ensure confidentiality.

Families with disabled children were found to be more frequently incomplete than is the case with families with healthy children. The research conclusion was that the possibilities of education for parenthood for this group and of improvement of their life-styles, have barely been touched upon so far.

One unusual document stands out. It consists of the edited minutes of the working seminar of writers, literary critics and publishing house editors on the theme: 'Today's child through the eyes of paediatrician, psychiatrist and lawyer'.[2]

This seminar was organized by the Union of Czechoslovak Writers in February 1987. The professionals taking part in the seminar illuminate the characteristics of Czechoslovak children in the 1980s, their family life or lack of it, their problems of adapting to and communicating with their particular environment and circumstances.

Special attention was given to families with disabled children. As a general rule, these children are not integrated in society, despite the available network of care and support services. This is because of negative attitudes on the part of a large number of people in society. The seminar sounded a clear warning against intolerance of imperfection and insisted on the right of disabled children to life and dignity.

Problems of child abuse and how such problems should be portrayed in the mass media and literature were also discussed. Perhaps as a consequence, a Czech film about an abused 10-year-old boy was recently shown on TV.

Problems of fostering and adoption in general, and of gipsy children in particular, were discussed at some length and examples of intolerance by society at large towards people who are willing to care for gipsy children as foster parents were brought to light.

There was no talk at the Union of Czechoslovak Writers' seminar of socialist morality as such but many ideas were expressed as to how everybody in Czechoslovakia, including those with any type of disability or handicap, should be able to live. Attempts to give practical expression to such humanitarian ideas are being made. Several participants voiced an important principle: that unpleasant and difficult things must be talked about, written about, and faced. Only that will provide information which is vital for assessing the effectiveness of the existing laws and regulations. When there is genuine interplay between the legislative framework and the needs of families, the education for parenthood in Czechoslovakia will truly come of age.

Notes

1. For statistical data see CSSR (1987), 'Federalni statisticky urad'. *Statisticka rocenka* 1987 *(Statistical Yearbook* 1987), Praha, SNTL.
2. These minutes were published by the Albatros Publishing House, Prague, in 1987 as a 'not for sale' publication, intended for the use and guidance of its employees.

Bibliography

Bartosova, M. (1978), 'Populacni politika v CSSR, 1945–1975' ('Population policy in Czechoslovakia, 1945–1975'), *Vykumne prace*, rada B, 76.

Bartosova, M. (1979), 'Situace rodin s prvym ditetem do veku 3 let' ('The situation of families with a first child under the age of 3'), *Vyzkumne prace*, rada B, 79.

Berent, Jerzy (1970), 'Some demographic aspects of female employment in Eastern Europe and USSR', *International Labour Review* (Geneva), 101(2), February, pp. 175–192.

Dror, Yehezkel (1969), 'Law and social change'. In: Aubert, Vilhelm (ed.) *Sociology of law: selected readings.* Harmondsworth, Mx.: Penguin Books, pp. 90–9.

Ferge, Zsuzsa (1979), *A society in the making: Hungarian social and societal policy 1945–1975.* Harmondsworth, Mx.: Penguin Books, p. 55.

Fiser, Jan (1981), *Od okouzleni k odpovednemu rodicovstvi (From enchantment to responsible parenthood)*, Praha, SNP, pp. 116–17.

Fiser, Jiri (1979), 'System vychovy K manzelstvi a rodicovstvi na skolach' ('System of education for marriage and parenthood at schools'). In: Horak, K. and others, *Hovorime s rodici (Talking to parents)*, Praha, SPN, pp. 157–64.

Heitlinger, Alena (1987), *Reproduction, medicine and the socialist state.* Basingstoke and London: Macmillan Press, p. 42.

Hughes, Zuzana (1983), 'Pre-School childcare and education in present-day Czechoslovakia: Contribution of family and society'. PhD thesis, University of Lancaster, 1983.

Hynie, Josef (1975), 'Vychova k rodicovstvi a jeji vysledky' ('Parental education and its results'), *Populacni zpravy*, 4, pp. 19–20.

Kloskowska, A. (1964). In: Chombart de Lauwe, P.-H. (ed.), *Images de la femme dans la société*, Paris, Editions ouvrières, pp. 115–16.

Komensky, J.A. (1968), 'Pampaedia'. In: Capkova, Dagmar, *Predskolni vychova v dile J.A.Komenskeho, jeho predchudcu a pokracovatelu (Pre-School education in the work of J.A.Komensky, his predecessors and followers)*, Praha, SPN, 6.

Komensky, J.A., 'Rodicum' ('For parents'), Tabor: Skryte poklady, 1930 (An edition of *Information skoly materske*, published 've prospech Detskeho Domova Komenskeho v Tabore').

Machova, Jirina (1975), *Hodnoty spolecnosti (Values of society)*, Praha, Mlada Fronta, p. 49.

Machova, Jirina (1979), *Uloha rodiny v socialisticke spolecnosti (The role of family in a socialist society)*, Praha, SNP.

Marhovnova, J. (1987), 'Nechtene dite a jeho prognoza' ('The unwanted child and his prognosis'), *Deti a my* (Praha), 17(4), 16.

Matejcek, Z. (1986), *Rodice a deti (Parents and children)*. Praha: Avicenum.
Matejcek, Z. and Langmeier, J. (1981), *Vypravy za clovekem (Investigating man)*. Praha: Odeon.
Plzak, M. (1967), *Prvni pomoc pri nehodach manzelskych (First aid in marital accidents)*. Praha: Mlada Fronta.
Plzak, M. (1970), *Taktika a strategie v lasce (Tactics and strategy in love)*. Praha: Mlada Fronta.
Popelova, J., Dymmer, O., Pelantova, R., Solnarova, B., Krchova, B. and Bednarikova, R. (1947), *Politicky bevir moderni zeny (Political breviary of a modern woman)*. Praha: Vladimir Zikes, pp. 21–37.
Rollova, V. (1983), 'Vybrane skupiny rodin z hlediska zvysene potreby pece spolecnosti' ('Selected groups of families in great need of support by society'), *Vyzkumne prace*, rada B, 99.
Rotta, Lubomir (1987), 'Novy zakon o umelem preruseni tehotenstvi' ('New law on abortion'), *Deti a my* (Praha), 17(2), 6.
Rusk, Robert R. (1933), *A history of infant education*. London: ULP, p. 14.
Schimmerlingova, V. et al. (1977), 'Analyza vybranych problemu zivota a potreb neuplnych rodin' ('Analysis of selected problems of lives and needs in incomplete families'), *Vyzkumne prace*, rada B, 72.
Schur, Edwin M. (1968), *Law and society: A sociological view*. New York: Random House, pp. 117–18.
Solcova, Miroslava (1976), *Rodina a jeji funkce v socialisticke spolecnosti (The family and its function in a socialist society)*. Praha: Horizont.
Solcova, Mirolslava (1979), *Socialististicky zpusob zitova a jeho formovani v rodine (The socialist way of life and its formation in the family)*. Praha: Horizont.
Vesela, J. (1978), 'Situace rodin se zdrovotne postizenymi detmi' ('Situation of families with disabled children'), Praha, *Vyzkumne prace*, rada B, 80.
Vesela, J. (1981), 'Vychova k rodicovstvi pro zdravotne postizene, cast 1', ('Parental education for the disabled, Part 1'), Praha, *Vyzkumne prace*, rada B, 91.
Vesela, J. (1982), 'Vychova k rodicovstvi pro zdravotne postizene, cast 2' ('Parental education for the disabled, Part 2'), Praha, *Vyzkumne prace*, rada B. 94.
Vitek, Karel (ed.) (1983), 'Stabilita dnesni rodiny: sbornik referatu z celostatniho vedeckeho seminare' ('Stability of the present-day family: a collection of papers from national seminar'), Olomouc, Universita Palackeho.
Vitek, Karel (ed.) (1987), 'Podil rodinneho prostredi na vzniku socialne patologickhcy jevu: sbornik referatu z celostatniho vedeckeho seminare s mezinarodni ucasti' ('The contribution of family environment to socially pathological phenomena: A collection of papers from an international academic seminar'). Olomouc, Universita Palackeho.
Wynnyczuk, V. (1980), 'Uvod do studia systemu vychovy k manzelstvi a rodicovstvi' ('Introduction to study of the system of education for marriage and parenthood'), *Vyzkumne prace*, rada B, 90, 130.
Wynnyczuk, V. and Sracek, J. (1977), 'Mlada rodina v zemedelske oblasti' ('The young family in an agricultural area'), *Vyzkumne prace*, rada B, 73.
Wynnyczuk, V. and Srach, J. (1975), 'Mlada rodina v prumsylove oblaski' ('The young family in an industrial area') *Vyzkumne prace*, rada B, 65.

15 Perestroika and the woman question

MARY BUCKLEY

Since Mikhall Gorbachev became General Secretary of the CPSU in March 1985 there have been numerous articles in the Soviet press and in academic journals on different aspects of the 'woman question' (*zhensklii vopros*). Perestroika ('reconstruction' or 'restructuring') and its companion glasnost ('publicity' or 'openness') have promoted more frank discussions about problems faced by women at home and in the labour force, and the *zhensovety* (*zhenskie sovety*), or women's councils, have been revived with a view to tackling them.[1] Women's issues have remained on political agendas and have been referred to in the new Party Programme, in speeches delivered in 1986 at the 27th party Congress and in 1988 at the 19th Conference of the CPSU. An All-Union Conference of Women was convened in 1987 in Moscow to discuss what perestroika meant for women. Thus, the 'woman question' in contemporary Soviet society is a visible one.

But what is its significance? Does perestroika entail a radical re-examination of the position of women in the USSR accompanied by calls for changes in gender roles? Or does it mean a reinforcement of traditional gender stereotypes and attempts to entice women out of the labour force and back into the home to soften the impact of future unemployment and to meet demographic goals? Or will it inevitably lead to a widespread debate about women's lives under socialism and to an eclectic mix of policy recommendations? The object of this chapter is to present evidence which backs up each of these three interpretations.

Perestroika and the radical re-examination of the woman question

Some aspects of the woman question that were explored in the late 1980s, such as prostitution, rape, the self-immolation of Muslim women and high infant mortality were not even mentioned as recently as 1984. These and other topics were ignored during the heated debates about female roles of the late 1960s and 1970s. Although some issues affecting women were opened up under Brezhnev when falling economic productivity and declining birthrates caused policy-makers to debate the significance of the female 'double burden', discussions about women's lives have become more extensive under Gorbachev. A range of topics that were previously taboo are now legitimate.

Prostitution

In the past prostitution officially did not exist. It was argued that under socialism the social conditions which gave rise to it were lacking. Now articles in a large number of newspapers deplore its existence and point out its links to a growing number of cases of syphilis, gonorrhea and AIDS. The role of pimps has been condemned and the corruption surrounding prostitution – such as thefts from clients and currency transactions with foreign sailors – exposed (*Sovetskaia Rossiia*, 12 March, 1987, p. 4; *Sovetskaia Rossiia*, 19 March, 1987, p. 4; *Komsomol'skaia Pravda*, 19 September, 1987, p. 2). Nina Mikhailovna, the Madame of Moscow, was criticized for running a team of girls in rented apartments. Apparently men paid from 100 to 150 roubles for an evening's entertainment. Taxi drivers and a director of a local food store helped in the organization of the show. In 1987 Nina Mikhailovna went on trial behind closed doors (*Nedelia*, No. 12, 1987, p. 15).

So the practice of prostitution is now regularly mentioned in the press. What is lacking, however, is rigorous analysis of why it arises. Passing remarks refer to moral degradation, the boredom of youth and the need to rear children with care. But as yet, no attempt has been made at the level of theory to suggest how prostitution is relevant to the woman question. Kollontai moved in this direction in the 1920s, linking it to the New Economic Policy, unemployment among women and a growing business community (Holt, 1977). The relationship between prostitution and socialist development in the 1980s and 1990s awaits analysis.

Infant mortality rates

In the recent Soviet past infant mortality rates were not revealed. Now official Soviet sources point out that in the countryside they are increasing. In 1970 in rural areas 26.2 Soviet children per 1,000 births had died before reaching the age of one. By 1985 this figure had increased to 32.0 deaths per 1,000 in the first year of life. Urban rates have remained high too, with just minor improvement from 23.4 deaths per 1,000 births in 1970, falling to 21.7 deaths per 1,000 up to the age of one in 1985 (*Vestnik Statistiki*, No. 12, 1986, p. 71). Although these increases could, in part, be due to more honest reporting on the part of hospital administrations, they nevertheless reflect a greater openness about infant mortality and a willingness to discuss a topic which was previously cloaked in silence.

Valentina Tereshkova, as outgoing chair of the Soviet Women's Committee, regretted high infant mortality rates at the All-Union Conference of Women: 'To talk of this is painful, but necessary...The death of children up to one year of age is higher here than in capitalist countries' (*Izvestiia*, 1 February, 1987). Tereshkova did not pander to the notion that socialism is always better, as had been so common in the past. Instead, she itemized the various reasons behind infant mortality, including 'the weak material technical base' of some maternity homes, and the 'low level of qualifications of many doctors' (*Izvestiia*, 1 February, 1987). Numerous articles in the press have also blamed: the lack of oxygen and hot water in some maternity homes; staphylococcus infections; anaemia among pregnant women due to poor prenatal care; heavy work loads for doctors (in Chechen-Ingushia one gynaecologist was taking care of 700 pregnant women, instead of the standard ceiling of 150); and the poor quality doctors, some of whom were criticized for not being able to give injections (*Nedelia*, 13–19 April, p. 18; *Izvestiia*, 28 February, 1987, p. 2; *Current Digest of the Soviet Press*, March 11 1987, Vol. 39, No. 6, p. 21). Like prostitution, high infant mortality rates are acknowledged to exist. Moreover, reasons are given for their high incidence.

Domestic labour

A topic which was aired in the 1920s and which has a more obvious place in Marxist theorizing about women is domestic labour. Recall that Engels and Lenin condemned it as narrow, stultifying and petty work and Kollontai advocated that workers should be paid to come round and clean flats, thereby removing responsibility from women to the state. As a topic it was not debated in the 1930s, 1940s or 1950s, but was returned to by sociologists in the late 1960s and 1970s. In a heated debate about female roles, various recommendations were put forward about how best to ease the female 'double burden' or 'double shift' (Buckley, 1986). Part-time labour for women, the mechanization of housework and more kindergartens were the main suggestions. In the early 1980s, before Gorbachev, some female sociologists and economists, such as Elena Gruzdeva and Svetlana Turchaninova, were arguing that men and children should take a more active role in housework (Gruzdeva and Chertkhina, 1983; Novikova, Sidorova and Turchaninova, 1984). In the late 1980s, this cry became louder. The Soviet philosopher Ol'ga Voronina went so far as to argue that a restructuring of domestic life was essential to the spiritual future of the USSR. Unless male 'patriarchal attitudes' towards women ceased, socialism would not flourish (Voronina, 1988). Up until now it has been out of ideological bounds to suggest that male patriarchy is a problem in the USSR.

Sociological research into the domestic division of labour has also increased in volume and is taking new approaches. Bozhkov and Golofast, for instance, advocate comparative analysis across Soviet republics (Bozhkov and Golofast, 1986). Their own work on Russia, Latvia and Tadzhikistan has led them to conclude that 'male' and 'female' domestic roles vary according to a range of variables. Their findings back the thesis that there are no fixed 'men's chores' or 'women's chores' in the home. Instead, they argue that the nature of the domestic division of labour reflects the socioeconomic position of husband and wife as well as other ideological and cultural factors. Their research is much more rigorous than much of the sociological literature of the 1970s. They are sensitive to the complexities of domestic interactions and to the need for multivariate explanations. They also ignore the old Soviet assertion that women are kind and gentle and men are strong and determined, and that these different qualities fit the sexes for different chores.

Working in a similar vein, Dzhunus"aev uses the concept 'egalitarian families' and examines the extent to which contemporary families fall into this category. Dzhunus"aev concludes that those men who do not favour 'equality in daily life' (*ravenstvo v bytu*) harbour stereotypes of male and female chores. These are anachronistic 'in the changing historical conditions of modern family life'. Moreover, such inequalities persist because husbands fail to meet the 'norms and ideals of socialist relations towards women' (Dzhunus"aev, 1985, p. 109). This is closer to the arguments of Fourier and Marx that the degree of humanity of any given society can best be gauged by men's relations with women, than to many Soviet writings of the past which dwelt on female weakness and softness and male strength and assertiveness. While not all articles on family life are in this mould, there is evidence that the relevance of domestic labour to equality of the sexes is an issue that is re-emerging. At the Women's Conference it was announced that. 'We strive to achieve the situation in which husband and wife carry out household chores equally and take responsibility for childrearing' (*Izvestiia*, 1 February, 1987).

Promotion

The promotion of women to top jobs was another aspect of equality of the sexes that was raised at the Women's Conference. Tereshkova lamented the poor promotion records of women, as had Khrushchev in 1956 at the 20th Party Congress and Gorbachev in 1986 at the 27th. Tereshkova pointedly commented 'for every 12 engineers and other important specialists, only 1 is a woman. Even in those branches of industry where women are in the overwhelming majority, they hold few directorships' (*Izvestiia*, 1 February, 1987).

By citing comparative statistics rather than aggregate ones, Tereshkova indicated the precise extent to which equality of result had not obtained. One dominant Soviet tendency has been to avoid stark contrasts between male and female achievements, and to play up the successes of both sexes. The ideological tradition has generally emphasized equality of opportunity and ignored inequality of result.

Tereshkova went further to suggest that leaders were not very interested in promoting equality of opportunity, especially regarding the distribution of mechanized labour. In rural areas as much as 98% of unmechanized work was still done by women. She added that the Soviet Women's Committee had received letters of complaint that sacks of animal feed weighing 50 to 60 kilos were being carried by women. Earlier recommendations of the Council of Ministers were being ignored; women were not being encouraged into mechanized work; leaders did not care about the health of women workers.

Hitherto ideology had suggested that as socialism progressed, equality of the sexes would be guaranteed. Equality would follow on from more fundamental economic changes. Here Tereshkova was implying that equality of the sexes in the workplace was not automatic, but that special measures were needed to promote it. She went on to recommend that girls as well as boys be encouraged to take an interest in technology during their school days (*Izvestiia*, 1 February, 1987). Implicit in her suggestion was the point that girls should not be filtered away from technical subjects and that the differential treatment of the sexes in schools is an issue for concern. Although Tereshkova does not use the term 'sex discrimination', that is in fact to what she is referring.

Muslim women

Just as delegates to the Women's Conference failed explicitly to talk about sexual discrimination, so they skirted the conclusion that the 'personal is political'. This too, however, was implicit in remarks made by a Secretary of the Central Committee of Tadzhikistan, who drew attention to the marriage of under-age girls, payment of *kalym* or bride price and the restriction of the activities of Muslim women outside the home by their husbands (*Izvestiia*, 2 February, 1987). The Soviet press, too, has been elaborating upon these themes. One article has pointed out that in a district of Turkmenia an estimated 95% of marriages proceed only after the bride price has been paid, in full or in part (*Trud*, 29 April, p. 2). A bride can cost as much as 20,000 to 30,000 roubles (*Pravda*, 31 August, p. 4). Criticisms of such 'vestiges of the past' were common in the 1970s, but today more details are given. Attention has also been directed at the topic of violence against Muslim women. The story of a father who murdered his daughter because she had married without his permission was also narrated. Not only had she shamefully disobeyed her father, but she had robbed him of the bride price due to him (*Trud*, 29 April, 1987). Muslim girls often run away from home in order to marry and are then disowned by their families. The strain of the clash between Muslim traditions and Soviet culture has in some instances led Muslim women to commit suicide by burning themselves to death. Self-immolation has gone on for some time, but not been reported until recently (*Komsomol'skaia Pravda,* 8 August, 1987).

The family

Writings on the family have also become more frank. Agarkov, for example, has called for a better appreciation of the complexities of 'crisis situations' in the family, including the relevance of psychological problems and sexual difficulties (Agarkov, 1987). One popular weekly newspaper ran a round table discussion on 'What sort of family do we need?' (*Nedelia,* No. 47, 23–29 November, 1987, pp. 17–18). Various views were expressed, including the opinion that it was outmoded to award medals to mothers of large families and reward reproductive behaviour. Other women were also heroines in a range of ways. Although many questions about family life were topical in the 1970s, glasnost is keeping them alive and prompting deeper reflection. More enlightened articles about single parent families, for instance, are now appearing (Kon, 1987).

Theorizing about women

There has also been an interesting call for theoretical rejuvenation of the woman question. For half a century now Soviet ideologlsts have not admitted that theorizing about the woman question is undeveloped in the USSR. It has always been held that Soviet writings follow a scientifically correct course, inspired by Marxism–Leninism. Even though lines on women have changed in different periods, this argument has not. It was therefore bold of Tereshkova to point out the lack of research into the position of women in society and the dearth of theorizing. She called for the creative development of the woman question on the basis of Marxism–Leninism (*Izvestiia,* 1 February, 1987). It would be wrong to assume that Tereshkova wants to see an integration of feminism and Marxism, since feminism is taboo in the USSR. However, her plea registered that a theoretical gap is being felt.

Zhensovety cater to women's needs

These arguments and examples suggest that the 'woman question' is on the move in the USSR and in a positive direction. Non-topics of the past are now issues, complexities in women's lives are being addressed and more enlightened arguments are being put. In addition, at the level of practice, *zhensovety* (women's councils) have been set up in work places and residential areas to cater to women's needs. This followed Gorbachev's recommendation at the 27th Party Congress and coincided with the announcement that a Politburo meeting of October 1986 had discussed proposals to set them up (*Materialy XXVII s"ezda*, 1986; *Pravda*, 24 October, 1986, p. 1). One *zhensovet* in a textile factory visited by this author in December 1987 was particularly energetic. As soon as it was set up it sent out a questionnaire to all women workers. As one member of the *zhensovet* put it: 'We wanted to find out what women workers were happy with, what they disliked and what they wanted.' Members of the *zhensovet* saw a large part of their work as trying to meet requests put to them.

But this is not the whole story. Glasnost has prompted a range of arguments, including more conservative ones. Moreover, glasnost has not meant that all 'ideological old-faithfuls' have consistently been attacked.

Perestroika, traditional lines and new 'conservative' arguments

Alongside the more critical literature just described, there exists a more traditional one which either hesitates to challenge many of the ideological lines of the past or which champions new arguments which advocate traditional roles for women. This literature embraces topics such as the family, female employment, reproduction and domestic labour.

The family

One currently popular argument is that strengthening the family is a 'component part of perestroika'. Since the 1930s it has been held that the family grows stronger as socialism progresses. Now it is maintained that the family is in need of perestroika because of its instability. Kozlov has pointed out that sociological research shows that more than 60% of young families admit to 'persistent arguments, conflicts and longstanding disagreements' (Kozlov, 1987, p. 115). The current task of the CPSU, and one element of perestroika, is to ask why this is the case and to rectify the situation. Consistent with this, some articles in the journal *Sotsiologicheskie Issledovaniia* (*Sociological Research*) are calling for discussion on how best to make family integration a research objective (Zhvinklenie, 1987). This is also important to meet demographic needs. However according to Kozlov, the family is still not widely appreciated as 'the initial basis of demographic processes' and as the foundation of reproduction (Kozlov, 1987).

The *zhensovety* appear to be filling a gap in work with families. One of their main tasks is to participate in 'the struggle for the strengthening of the family' (*bor'ba za ukreplenie sem'i*) (Kozlov, 1987, p. 119).[3] In an interview in Moscow one member of a *zhensovet* told me that 'today we have a terrible divorce problem. Our aim is to keep the family together'. The *zhensovety* strive to do this by talking to couples with difficulties or by referring them to psychological counselling services in the factory.

Critics have noted that the party has often found difficulty in performing this work. According to Tupitsin, party primary organizations often fail to consider how to conduct work geared to strengthening the family (Tupitsin, 1987). In order to rectify this, the party in Cheliabinsk oblast held a scientific–practical conference in 1985 entitled 'Actual problems of the further perfection of family-marital relations' (Kozlov, 1987, pp. 116–17). Its main conclusion was that new criteria and approaches are needed for addressing problems of family life. However, it remains rather unclear what these are, apart from numerous meetings and round table discussions. Certainly much is being said, but actions appear uncharted. Moreover, at the levels of theory and practice, this issue is rarely linked to equality of the sexes or to female self-determination, but is frequently tied to reproduction.

Demographic goals, reproduction and female withdrawal from the labour force

Many writings continue to express concern about the small family size in Russia, the Ukraine, Estonia, Lithuania and Latvia. Rogovin, for example, has suggested that in order to resolve the 'serious contradiction' between 'work functions' and 'maternal functions', and in order to serve demographic policy, women's contribution to the workforce should be reduced (Rogovin, 1987, pp. 223–6). Part-time labour for women was advocated in the 1970s by some economists, not without support from women workers. Official party backing to part-time labour was pledged at the 26th and 27th Party Congresses. By 1987 women were entitled to a year and a half's maternity leave with pay and an option of taking further unpaid leave. Rogovin, however, ignores those who do not wish to work part-time. Rogovin's main concern is that more time at home would allow women to fulfil 'maternal functions' and 'double employment' (*dvoinaia zaniatost'*). The option for men to go on part-shifts is not mentioned.

In a similar vein, Sergeeva has argued that in those republics where the participation rate of women in the economy is high, the conditions exist for tackling demographic problems. As she puts it: 'We recommend that in these republics the level of female participation in the economy should lower a little. This would more fully answer the harmonious combination of woman's professional function and motherhood' (Sergeeva, 1987, p. 125). Going one step beyond Rogovin and Sergeeva, the economist Vladislav Kulikov at a recent conference on perestroika in Sweden contended that more women should stay at home since the economy will soon not need them. If perestroika in the economy is successful, it will result in more modern machinery, efficiency and streamlining (*Dagens Nyheter*, 11 January, 1988).[2] Whereas labour shortages in the 1960s drew the remaining housewives into the paid work force, anticipation of future unemployment is now prompting ideas that they should be withdrawn.

A reduction in the number of women in the labour force would be one solution to Gorbachev's desire 'to return completely' to women their 'truly female destiny' is most apt (Gorbachev, 1987, p. 117). In his book *Perestroika* Gorbachev maintains that socialist development overlooked women's special rights and needs. Although women were drawn into the work force they were left without enough time to perform 'everyday tasks – housework, child-rearing, and simple cosiness in the heart of the family'. This certainly enjoys a resonance among many Soviet women. Moreover according to Gorbachev, this is a paradoxical situation, which 'we have started to correct in the process of perestroika' (Gorbachev, 1987, p. 117). But it seems that the 'truly female destiny' embraces not just childbirth, but extends to housework, child-rearing and making the family cosy. Gorbachev makes no mention of the male contribution to these last three activities, presumably alien to male destiny. He added that he expected a great deal from the *zhensovety* in making the family more healthy and in increasing its role in society.

The zhensovety and female roles

Many of the newly revived *zhensovety* are preoccupied with setting up shops in the workplace or with establishing a system through which women workers can place weekly orders for food. The aim here is to reduce time spent after work in queues. Although these developments will be of immense help to women, they nevertheless define food purchase as a woman's chore. But of course women welcome it and would view such an objection as quite out of place. Faster access to food will ease working days tremendously. In fact, in responses to a questionnaire sent out by one *zhensovet,* women workers asked for a fruit and vegetable shop to opened at work, along with a shoe repair service and a hairdresser's shop. In providing these, the *zhensovety* undoubtedly meet women's needs.

Yet the criticism can be made that the *zhensovety* are relatively weak organizations, revived to carry out party policy. To a large extent, their work bolsters traditional gender roles. They try to ease the double burden rather than promote a new domestic division of labour. Moreover, they do not seem to be especially concerned about the upward mobility of women. Although Gorbachev has commented on the importance of promoting women, and despite the fact that Tereshkova has drawn attention to the poor promotion record of women, the *zhensovety* have not plugged the issue and certainly not come out in favour of preferential hiring over men or affirmative action programmes. The *zhensovety* have not yet challenged men's leadership roles. Neither have they raised questions about why women generally earn less than men. However, perhaps Western writers should beware of assuming that Soviet women should proceed in a particular way. Many women in the USSR are keen to reduce their long working hours and find the prospect of free time more attractive than the extra pressures that promotion to director would inevitably bring. Moreover it is early days yet, and once basic shopping services have been set up, women in the *zhensovety* may go on to use them for other ends.

Despite the mildness of the work of the *zhensovety* as 'helpers of the party', they have still been greeted with indifference by some party committees, trade unions and leaders in enterprises. Sometimes representatives from party committees fail to turn up when members of a new *zhensovet* in their workplace are being chosen, even when the women have invited them. Another criticism is that women themselves once on the *zhensovet* are frequently unwilling to tackle problems or do not know how to proceed (Mel'nik, 1987, p. 63).

Whatever the failings in the way in which the *zhensovety* are run and received, the theory and practice of the *zhensovety* appears to be geared to the traditional goal of preserving the family. Criticizing traditional gender roles does not appear to be their hallmark. But it would be premature to dismiss their significance out of hand given the slim literature on them to date and their recent revival. Alexandra Biriukova has aptly remarked that the solution to many problems affecting women depends upon the women themselves. In her view, women should be more active, and the *zhensovety* offer them a channel through which to be so. Much may depend on how the women wish to define initiative. But as ever, lack of time to devote to the *zhensovety* may be one serious constraint.

To conclude this second section, evidence suggests that 'conservative' arguments about female roles are integral to perestroika, just as more radical ones are. Yet it would be inappropriate to argue that one set necessarily dominates the other, although at different times since 1985 this has often felt the case. After the January Women's Conference it appeared possible that a more radical critique of male roles would follow together with analysis of sexual discrimination in the USSR. But by the end of 1987 Gorbachev was pointing out that 'the Soviet state has decisively and ruthlessly done away with every discrimination against women' (Gorbachev, 1987, p. 117). Then in November 1988 Larisa Kuznetsova boldly criticized the Soviet state for its widespread 'patriarchal habits' (Kuznetsova, 1988). Depending upon which speech has been delivered, or which article has just been read, one can be left with completely different impressions about the nature of current arguments about the 'woman question'.

Perestroika and an eclectic mix of policy recommendations

The third interpretation of the significance of perestroika for the 'woman question' is that it gives space to a range of different arguments about female roles. Indeed, from the evidence already cited above, this appears to be the case. Despite the limits to glasnost, new topics have come onto agendas and fresh arguments are being voiced alongside old ones. More radical calls for equality in the domestic division of labour coexist alongside suggestions that women should spend more time at home in order to perform women's work. Regrets that more women have not been promoted into top jobs sit alongside recommendations that to meet demographic goals, women should be encouraged to leave their jobs, or go on part-shifts.

Very practical concerns underpin some arguments. Throughout the history of the Soviet state interpretations of issues affecting women have often been inspired not by classical Marxism, but by the policy priorities of successive Soviet leaders and the economic, political and demographic pressures on them (Buckley, 1987). For instance, the practical question of who should suffer unemployment if someone is going to have to, combined with the goals of demographic policy to increase the birthrate, result in the conclusion that women rather than men should be removed from the labour force, or reduce their direct contribution to it. This conclusion is bolstered by articles which suggest that poor quality child-rearing leads to crime and that women should be better mothers. Moreover, Soviet survey data show that it would suit some women to come out of the labour force, especially if part-shifts could be more easily arranged, or if financial incentives were given for staying at home. Articles have already pointed out that more women are taking advantage of extended paid maternity leave have suggested that it should be increased to three years.

Another point to bear in mind is that the economic history of most states illustrates that when women are desperately needed in the labour force, such as wartime, the state will enthusiastically encourage them to do paid work. Similarly, when full employment does not obtain, women are likely to be the first the state calls upon to leave jobs. These trends coincide with many ideas in popular culture that men should really be the ones to work if jobs are scarce. But it clashes with the Marxlst belief that women are emancipated through participation in social production and through financial independence. Female self-determination can only blossom if women, like men, are socially creative beings. The rich many-sidedness of human nature that Marx talked of in the *German Ideology* will not develop in a limited domestic setting.

But even if practical concerns lead to a stress on women's domestic roles, there remains the theoretical constraint of classical Marxism which advocates that women should play an active part in economy and society. Whilst the content of ideology changes and can be politically constructed to suit the needs of different periods of Soviet history, and its emphases can alter, the importance for liberation of participating in social production and political life cannot be denied. It is a tenet which stands at the core of Marxism.

Thus, it seems that there are both practical and theoretical bases for arguments about female roles that pull in different directions. Indeed, the content of official party policy itself can be seen either as pulling two ways, or more charitably, as showing a flexibility to suit different categories of women, or to meet the needs of women at different stages of their lives. For example, the draft party programme released in the autumn of 1985, the finally approved party programme of 1986, Gorbachev's Political Report to the 27th Party Congress, and Gorbachev's book *Perestroika*, all carry the same policy commitments to women as political actors, workers and mothers. The draft programme announced that more politically mature individuals capable of taking initiative would be appointed to leading posts. Among their number would be women. Then Alexandra Biriukova was appointed to the Secretariat of the Central Committee of the CPSU and in Azerbaidzhan Svetlana Kasumova was given a powerful combination of seats on the Buro and Secretariat.[3] In 1988 Biriukova was further promoted to the Politburo as a candidate (non-voting) member. But these promotions are not the general pattern. Women still have a higher presence on the less powerful soviets and even here the composition shows a division of deputies into female workers by hand and male workers by brain. The majority of female deputies hold low status jobs (Buckley, 1988).[4] Nevertheless, although the number of women in top jobs remains small, the CPSU is formally committed to women's promotion.

The CPSU is also committed to creating favourable conditions for the successful combination of motherhood and work in social production. Flexibility at work, such as part-shifts, part-weeks and work to take home are supported, as well as longer paid maternity leave. Part-time labour, however, can be variously interpreted. It makes upward mobility harder, yet is desired by many Soviet women as questionnaires put out by Shishkan and others have shown. Moreover, it gives women who want it, the chance to work and be mothers more easily. It could therefore be interpreted as helping to promote the many-sided potential that Marx advocated. Indeed, a case can be made that Soviet policy is currently leading in a direction which offers women the flexibility to pursue motherhood with greater ease than hitherto without ruling out promotion for those women who want it. However, ideology tends to stress the importance of the former over the latter, and in practice promotion for women who seek it is not automatic.

How to interpret the policy to strengthen the family is more contentious. Cynically, it can be seen as a vital part of demographic policy to raise the birth rate. Divorce is criticized as a negative phenomenon by some, adversely affecting reproduction. The family should therefore be kept together and couples should marry younger in order to encourage mor births. But most Soviet women want to marry and want the state to support the institution of marriage. Kollontai's views on sexuality and family life find little open support. Although citizens may read her differently, the official line is that history proved her wrong on the future of the family.

Conclusion

The 'woman question' under Gorbachev is more open-ended than it has been for some time. Although debates in the 1970s about female roles led to an airing of many views, the range of topics under scrutiny is broader today and the space for disagreement wider. Although there are limits to glasnost which set the parameters of debate, topics which lack firm answers can be approached from a range of perspectives. Although ideological old-faithfuls, such as the importance of strengthening the family, are likely to go unchallenged, appropriate ways of running it under socialism, and various ways of running it – including single parenthood – are being discussed. Moreover, if women wish to pursue further the issue of promotion, they have the legitimacy of Gorbachev's statements to protect them. Although the *zhensovety* are not radical institutions designed to mobilize women into 'high politics' or to redefine political agendas in a feminist direction, women could attempt to harness them for issues beyond arranging shopping orders, once this basic service has been provided. Much does depend on women's initiatives. At the level of theory, however, the call for a fresh and more sophisticated analysis of the 'woman question' remains unheeded.

Notes

This was first presented as a paper at the Seminar on Women and Society in Russia and Eastern Europe, Centre for Russian and East European Studies, University of Birmingham, 3 February, 1988. I would like to thank all present for their comments and observations.

1. In official documents perestroika is described as a radical and revolutionary process of change which affects economy, politics and society. Glasnost is conceived as one of the necessary means to a successful perestroika.
2. I am grateful to Riitta Pittman for this reference.
3. Svetlana Kasumova was removed from these posts in November 1988 and made a Secretary of the Baku city party committee (*Bakinskii Rabochii*, 15 November, 1988).
4. New style elections to the soviets to be held in March 1989 may result in slightly different female profiles.

Bibliography

Argarkov, S.T. (1987), 'Disgarmonichnyi brak', *Sotsiologicheskie issledovaniia*, No. 4, pp. 81–5.

Biriukova, Aleksandra (1987), 'Oktiabrem zavoevano', *Sovetskaia zhenshchina*, No. 10, pp. 2–4.

Bozhkov, O.B. and Golofast, V.B. (1986), 'Radelenie truda v gorodskoi sem'e'. *Sotsiologicheskie issledovaniia*, No. 4, pp. 68–75.

Browning, Genia (1987), *Women and Politics in the USSR*, Sussex: Wheatsheaf; New York: St. Martin's Press.

Buckley, Mary (1986), *Soviet social scientists talking: an official debate about women*. London: Macmillan.

Buckley, Mary (1987), 'Soviet ideology and female roles'. In White, Stephen and Pravda, Alex (eds) *Ideology and Soviet Politics*. London: Macmillan.

Buckley, Mary (1988), 'Female workers by hand and male workers by brain: the occupational composition of the 1985 Azerbaizhan Supreme Soviet', research note, *Soviet Union* (forthcoming).

Dzhunus"aev, M.D. (1985), 'Rasopredelenie domashnego truda v Kazakhskoi sem'e', *Sotsiologicheskie issledovaniia*, No. 1, pp. 106–9.

Gorbachev, M. (1987), *Perestroika i novoe myshlenie dlia nashei strany i dlia vsego mira*. Moscow: Politizdat.

Gruzdeva, E.E. and Chertikhina, E.S. (1983), *Trud i byt sovetskikh zhenshchin*. Moscow: Politizdat.

Holt, Alix, (ed.) (1977), *Alexandra Kollontai: Selected Writings*. New York: Norton.

Kon, I. (1987), 'Roditeli i deti', *Nedelia*, No. 50, 14–20 December, p. 14.

Kozlov, V. (1987), 'Liniia na ukreplenie sem'i' in Slezko, P. Ia. (ed.), *Perestroika: problemy, poiski, nakhodki*. Moscow: Politizdat.

Kuznetsova, Larisa (1988), 'What every woman wants?' *Soviet Weekly*, 26 November, p. 15.

Materially XXVII s'ezda KPSS (1986), Moscow: Politizdat.

Mel'nik, A. (1987), 'Zhensovety – vazhnaia forma razvitiia trudovoi i obshchestvennoi aktivnosti zhenshchin', *Partiinaia zhizn'*, No. 2. January, pp. 59–63.

Novikova, E.E., Sidorova, T.N. and Turchaninova, S. Ia. (1984), *Sovetskie zhenshchiny i profsoiuzy*. Moscow: Profizdat.

Rogovin, V.E. (1987), 'Usilenie zaboty o sem'e, o polozhenii zhenshchinymateri'. In Mikul'skii, K.I., Rogovin, V.E. and Shatalin, S.S., *Sotsial'naia Politika KPSS*. Moscow: Politizdat, pp. 220–30.

Sergeeva, G.P. (1987), *Professionanal'naia zaniatost' zhenshchin: problemy i perspectivy*. Moscow: Economika.

Tupitsin, V. (1987), 'Sposobstvovat' ukrepleniiu sem'i, iskoreniat' p'ianstvo', *Partiinaia zhizn'*, No. 1. January, pp. 66–0.

Voronina, Ol'ga (1988), 'Muzhchiny sozdali mir dlia sebia', *Sovetskaia zhenshchina*, 11, pp. 14–15.

Zhvinklenie, A. (1987), 'Semeinaia integratsiia kak ob"ekt issledovaniia', *Sotsiologicheskie issledovaniia*, No. 1, pp. 70–3.

Index

abortion 46, 186, 202
Adams, J. 153
Adams, P. viii, 143
   on German Democratic Republic 18, 133–44
   on working class 41
Adamski, W. 81
Aganbegyan, A. 133–4
ageing *see* old people
alternatives, health care, Poland 17, 77–90
Antal, Z. 108
Arendt, H. 13
Argarkov, S. T. 217
Arnot, B. 136
autonomous articulation of human needs 3, 12–14

Bahro, R. 146, 154, 159
Bartosova, M. 203
Bauer, T. 113
Bayliss, T. A. 153
Bednarski, M. 88
Bell, D. 42, 139
Berent, J. 205
Beresford, P. 10

Besancon, A. 81, 84
Bihari, M. 113
Biriukova, A. 221, 223
Biro, D. 187
Blaha, A. 203
Bozhkov, O. B. 215
Bozoki, A. 6
Britain
   dialogue with Hungary 3–14
   dialogue with Poland 14–16
   women 41–2
Brown, A. 152
Brus, W. 10
Buckley, M. ix, 43–4
   on Soviet Union 20, 212–25
Bulgaria 1, 18, 20–22, 121–32
   practical trends in development 124–31
   theoretical concept of welfare 121–4
bureaucracy *see* state
Bush, G. 136
Büttner, T. 141

Campbell, B. 11
Castle, M., on working class 39–40, 40–41
Chalupny, E. 203
Chamberlayne, P. viii

227

on German Democratic Republic 18–19, 145–63
Chertikhina, E.S. 214
children *see* education; families and children
Childs, D. 134, 138
Churchward, L. G. 153
civil society 16, 23, 101, 172–3
   dialogue on 27–37
Comenius (Komensky) 202
contraception 46, 207
corporatist welfare 3, 4, 6
Corrin, C. viii
   on Hungary 19, 179–90
crisis 36–7
   Hungary 92, 137
   Poland 58, 66, 80
   see also Yugoslavia
Croft, S. 10
Czechoslovakia 1, 20–22, 39, 137
   women
      and ageing 19, 192–200
      education for parenthood 19–20, 201–11

David, J. 37
Deacon, B. vii, 22
   on Eastern Europe 1–26
   on working class 37
democracy 30–33
demonopolization of social policy
   Poland 59–61
   see also reform
dialogue on social policy and socialism 27–48
   Anglo-Hungarian 3–14
   Anglo-Polish 14–16
   civil society 27–37
   women's interests 41–8
   working class interests 37–41
disabled and handicapped 54, 110, 126, 167, 208–9
divorce 207
Dölling, I. 141
Doyal, L. 116
Dror, Y. 204
Durham, Bishop of 30
Dzhunus"aev, M.D. 215

Eastern Europe *see individual countries*
economy
   Bulgaria 122–3, 125, 127, 128, 130–31
   German Democratic Republic 134, 135–6, 138, 139–42
   Hungary 103–7, 180
   Poland *see* Poland, state and market and enterprise
   see also expenditure
education
   Bulgaria 125, 126, 128–9
   Czechoslovakia 19–20, 202–22
   Soviet Union 216
   Yugoslavia 166
employment *see* labour
Engels, F. 155, 214
enterprise, Poland *see* Poland, state and market and enterprise
equality problem, Yugoslavia 170–71
evaluation of social policy 23
Evers, A. 2, 171
existential security 116
expenditure on social policy
   Bulgaria 125, 128
   German Democratic Republic 133
   Hungary 95–100, 107, 109, 114–15
   Poland 53, 59, 85

Fabianism 8–9, 28
families and children
   Bulgaria 126, 128
   Czechoslovakia: education for parenthood 19–20, 202–22
   German Democratic Republic 134–5, 136, 141, 147
   Hungary 100, 109
   Poland 54, 56
   Yugoslavia 166–7
   see also health care; women
Federowicz, M. 81
Feher, F. 3, 6, 10, 11, 12–13
feminism
   in Hungary 179, 188–90
      backlash against 186–8
   see also women
Ferge, Z. viii, 2, 3, 6, 10–11, 189, 207
   on Hungary 10, 18, 21, 103–17
   on women 42–3

finance *see* expenditure on social policy
Fiser, J. 203, 207
Fourier, C. 115, 215
fourth road *see under* Hungary, future for social policy
Fracziewick-Wronka, A. 47
Francisco, R.A. 138
free market *see* market forces
Friedgut, T. H. 153
future developments in social policy 20–24
   Poland 58–62
   Yugoslavia 171–4
   see also under Hungary

Galbraith, J. K. 18, 114
George, N. 2
Geras, N. 12
German Democratic Republic 1, 20–21
   neighbourhood and tenant participation 18–19, 145–63
      and local government structures 146–52
      political meaning of 152–8
   unity of economic and social policy 18, 133–44
      and Perestroika 133–4, 136–7, 139, 142
      stability and reform 137–9
   working class 135
Gershuny, J. 164, 165
glasnost 137, 212
Glennerster 106, 111
Golofast, V. B. 215
Gorbachev, M. 29, 36, 44
   glasnost 137, 212
   see also perestroika
Gorz, A. 168
Gothe, R. 147
Gough, I. 115–16
Gouldner, A. 152
Gramsci, A. 31
Gruzdeva, E. E. 214

Halmai, G. 113
Hanak, K. 186–7
handicap *see* disabled and handicapped
Hankiss, E. 81
Harman, C. 137

Harris, N. 138
Harris, R. 3
Havel, V. 156, 164
health care
   Bulgaria 124–5, 129
   Czechoslovakia 195
   German Democratic Republic 134
   Hungary 98, 109, 110–11, 115–16, 185
   Poland 17, 54, 77–90
   Soviet Union 214
   Yugoslavia 166
Hedborg 115
Heitlinger, A. 190, 207
Heller, A. 3, 6, 12–13, 184
Helwig, G. 135
Heuer, U. J. 155
Hickey, T. 40
Higgins, J. 2
Hirsl, M. 197
Hobsbawn, E. 30
Holt, A. 213
housework
   Bulgaria 127
   Hungary 181–3
   Soviet Union 214–15
housing
   Bulgaria 124
   Czechoslovakia 193, 208
   German Democratic Republic 134–5, 140
   see also tenant participation
   Poland 66, 68–9
Hughes, Z. ix
   on Czechoslovakia 19–20, 201–11
Hungary 1, 21, 22, 137
   cooperatives 86–7
   dialogue with Britain 3–14
   future for social policy (fourth road) 10, 18, 21, 103–17
      boundary of market and non-market spheres 114–16
      economic reform 103–7
      recent reform 107–12
   radical reforms of social policy 17, 19, 91–102
      on different bases 96–101
      state redistribution 93–6

'second society' concept 81
women 19, 42–3, 45, 179–91
    anti-feminist backlash 186–8
    changes 180–83
    feminist debate re-opened 188–9
    and ideology 183–6
Huszar, T. 184
Hynie, J. 202

ideology
  and women in Hungary 183–6
  see also feminism; Marxism
industries *see* economy
inequalities, social 23–4
infant mortality in Soviet Union 213–14
inflation 66
Ivanova, S. viii
  on Bulgaria 18, 121–32
Iwanowska, A. 81, 87

Jeffries, I. 137
Johnson, N. 3, 19, 174 (*Johnston?*)
Judit, S. 187
Juhasz, P. 113

Kagarlitsky, B. 152
Kahl, A. 156
Kant, I. 13
Kasalova, H. 193
Kasumova, S. 223
Keane, J. 154
  on civil society 16, 27–33, 37
Kruschev, N. 215
Kinnock, N. 28
Kloskowska, A. 205
Kocon, W. 15
Kohl, H. 110
Kohn, R. 78
Kolakowski, L. 12
Kolarska-Bobinska, L. vii, 15
  on Poland 17, 21, 63–76
  on working class 40
Kollontai, 214, 223
Komensky, J. A. 202
Kon, I. 217
Koralewicz-Zebik, J. 72, 81
Kornai, J. 65
Korosi, S. 186

Kostov, G. 123
Kozek, W. 70
Kozlov, V. 218, 219
Krisch, H. 153, 158
Ksiezopolski, M. viii, 14
  on Poland 16–17, 21, 51–62
  on women 47
  on working class 39
Kuczynski, P. 70
Kukorelli, I. 113
Kulikov, V. 219
Kuznetsova, L. 221

labour
  Bulgaria 122, 124–7, 129–30
  Czechoslovakia 193
  domestic *see* housework
  German Democratic Republic 133, 135, 139–40, 142
  Hungary 113, 180–81, 183
  Poland 54, 57–8, 63, 65
  Soviet Union 212, 219–20
  Yugoslavia 165–6
  see also wages
Langmeier, J. 203
Lapidus, G. 189
law
  Bulgaria 127, 129
  Czechoslovakia 202, 203–6
  Hungary 99
  Poland 63–5, 66–8
learning, social 23
Lee, P. 3, 5
Lefort, C. 154
LeGrand, J. 2, 3, 4
Lehmann, H. 157
Lenin, V. I. 214, 217
  see also Marxism/Marxism-Leninism
Liska, T. 3
local government in German Democratic Republic 146–52
Lovenduski, J. 138
Lukacs, G. 22
Lukes, S. 12

McAuley, A. 2
Machova, J. 202, 203
Malenkov, G. M. 135

Malicka, L. 194–5, 196
Manchin, R. 3, 5
Manning, N. 2
Marhovnova, J. 202
market forces 3, 4, 5
   Hungary 103–9, 113–16
   Poland see Poland, state and market and enterprise
Markovits, I. 158
Markus, G. 3, 6, 11
Markus, M. 183
Markus, P. 190
Marody, M. 81
Marxism/Marxism-Leninism 22, 31, 36
   Bulgaria 121–2, 123
   Hungary 8–9
   Poland 54
   Soviet Union 215, 217, 222
   see also politics
Matejcek, Z. 203
media
   Czechoslovakia 202
   Poland 71, 88
   Soviet Union 213
Mediner 103, 115
Mel'nik, A. 221
Melvyn, P. 165
Melzer, M. 137
Michalsky, H. 134, 140
Mikhailovna, N. 213
Mishra, R. 3
mixed economy of welfare 4
   see also pluralism
models of welfare (Titmuss) 16, 51, 53, 55–7, 177
modernization see reform
Molyneux, M., on women 44–5
Morawski, W. 70
Mordel, T. 68
Moskalewicz, B. 84
movements, social 23, 39
Muslim women in Soviet Union 216–17

needs and their recognition 167–70
   see also models of welfare
neighbourhood schemes see tenant participation in German Democratic Republic

Nicaragua 45, 46
Niedbala, Z. 75
Nove, A. 12, 113, 135
Novikova, E. E. 214
Nowaki, S. 80

O'Connor, J. 139
Okrasa, W. 2, 3, 4
old people
   Bulgaria 126
   Czechoslovakia, women 19, 192–200
   German Democratic Republic 134–5, 136, 140–41
   Hungary 98, 101, 109–110
   Poland 54, 59
   Yugoslavia 167
Oyen, E. 2

Pahl, R. 165
Parsons, J. E. 138
pay see wages
pensions see old people
perestroika 41
   and Bulgaria 124
   and German Democratic Republic 133–4, 136–7, 139, 142
   and women in Soviet Union 20, 213–25
   mix of policy recommendations 221–3
   radical re-examination 213–18
   tradition and new 'conservative' arguments 218–21
planning, socialist social 3, 4–5, 6, 8, 11
pluralism, welfare 3, 5–6, 8, 9–10, 37
Plzak, M. 207
Pohl, H. 155, 157
Pokol, B. 113
Polan, A. J. 12
Poland 1, 21, 22
   dialogue with Britain 14–16
   health care alternatives 17, 77–91
      sources of 78–82
      typology of 82–8
   social policy as problem 16–17, 51–62
      future 58–62
   state and market and enterprise 17, 63–76
      social interests and changes in

231

state welfare role 70–74
welfare activities 68–70
welfare interests 65–7
women 47
working class 39, 40, 52
Polanyi, K. 104
politics
Bulgaria 121
German Democratic Republic 137, 152–8, 159–60
local 146–52
Soviet Union 212, 223
strategies 3–9
see also Marxism/Marxism-Leninism; state
Popelova, J. 202
poverty
Czechoslovakia 192–200
Hungary 94, 113
Poznanski, K. 138
prices 66, 71
private market *see* market forces
promotion of women in Soviet Union 215–16
prostitution in Soviet Union 213

Quilizsch, G. 155

Raban, C. 3, 5
radicalism
new 12–14
re-examination of women in Soviet Union 213–18
reform *see under* Hungary
recent developments in social policy 1–26
analysis of 16–20
dialogue, East–West
Anglo-Hungarian 3–14
Anglo-Polish 14–16
emergence of 2–3
future 20–24
redistribution
model of welfare 16, 51, 53, 55–7
state, Hungary 94–7
reform
German Democratic Republic 136, 137–9, 145, 159–60
see also tenant participation

Hungary 183–4
see also under Hungary
Poland *see* Poland, state and market and enterprise
Regulski, J. 15
revolution, social 3, 5, 6, 8, 11–12
Ritter, T. 158
Robertson, J. 165
Rogovin, V. E. 219
Rollova, V. 203, 207–8
Romania 20
Rose, H., on women 41–2
Rotta, L. 202
Rupnik, J. 145, 152
Rusk, R. 202
Rychard, A. vii, 73
on Poland 17, 77–90

Scharf, C. B. 136, 140
Scharlet, R. 81, 86
Schimmerlingova, V. 193, 195, 197, 203
Schmidt, P. 113
Schöneburg, K. H. 154, 155
Schönefeld, R. 155
Schulze, G. 149, 157
Schur, E. M. 203
Seldon, A. 3
Sergeeva, G. P. 219
Shishkan, 223
Sidorova, T. N. 214
Sik, E. 10, 165
Siklova, J. viii–ix
on Czechoslovakia 19, 192–200
social dividend *see* market forces
social policy *see* Bulgaria; Czechoslovakia; dialogue on social policy and socialism; German Democratic Republic; Hungary; Poland; recent developments in social policy; Soviet Union; Yugoslavia
social revolution 3, 5, 6, 8, 11–12
social welfare *see* social policy
socialism in Eastern Europe *see* social policy
socialist social planning 3, 4–5, 6, 8, 11
Sokolowska, M. vii
on Poland 17, 77–90
Solcova, M. 203

Solidarity 39
Solidarnosc 82, 84
Solyom, L. 113
Soviet Union 23, 24, 123
   comparison with German Democratic Republic 133–5, 137, 139
   women 44
      see also under perestroika
Speigner, W. 135, 141
Sracek, J. 203
Srach, J. 203
stability, German Democratic Republic 137–9
Staikov, Z. 123
Stalin, J. 36, 135
Stanizkis, J. 79, 81, 87
state
   Poland 55–7
      see also Poland, state and market and enterprise
   redistribution, Hungary 93–6
   and socialism 27–37
   statist welfare 3, 4, 6
   see also social policy
Strassburger, J. 140
strategies, political 3–9
Svetlik, I. viii, 165, 168–9
   on working class 38–9
   on Yugoslavia 19, 21, 164–75
Swinnen, H. 82, 84
Szalai, J. vii, 16, 88, 106
   on civil society 34–7
   on Hungary 17, 19, 91–102
Szelenyi, I. 3, 5
Sztachelski, J. 79

Tamas, P. 188–9
Taras, R. 12
taxation as finance *see* expenditure
Taylor-Gooby, P. 4
tenant participation in German Democratic Republic 18–19, 145–63
Tereshkova, V. 214, 215–16, 217, 220
Thatcher, M./Thatcherism 10, 30–31, 44
Thiele, F. 155
Titmuss, R. 18, 19, 167, 170, 171
   see also models of welfare

Toffler, A. 164, 165
Toneva, Z. 48
Tourraine, A. 28
trade unions
   Bulgaria 130
   Hungary 96, 185
   Poland 39
Tupitsin, V. 219
Turchaninova, S. 214

Uhlir, F. 203
Ulbricht, W. 137
unemployment
   absent in Poland 52, 54, 57, 58
   German Democratic Republic 142
   Hungary 98, 105, 180–81

Vajda, M. 22, 184
Vajna, T. 181
Velikov, N. 123, 124
Vesela, J. 208–9
Vigocka, M. 194
Vitek, K. 203, 207
voluntary work in Yugoslavia 166
Voronina, O. 214–15
Vortmann, H. 141

wages
   Bulgaria 124, 125–6
   German Democractic Republic 135, 139–40
   Hungary 101, 111, 114
   Poland 55–6, 59, 65
   see also labour
Walker, A. 3, 4, 6
welfare *see* social policy
White, L. 78
White, S. 152
Wicks, M. 3
Wilding, P. 4
Williams, F. 5, 6
Wiman 106
Wintersberger, H. 171
Wnuk-Lipinski, E. 81, 84
women
   Bulgaria 127–8
   dialogue on 41–8
   German Democratic Republic 135, 136, 141

233

see also families and children; *and also under* Czechoslovakia; Hungary; Soviet Union
Woodall, J. 138
work *see* labour
working class
   dialogue on 37–41
   German Democratic Republic 135
Wynnyczuk, V. 203, 206

Yugoslavia 19, 21, 164–75
   equality problem 170–71
   future 171–4
   needs and their recognition 167–70
   production of services 165–7
   working class 38

Zavada, P. 6
Zdravomislov, G. 124
Zebrowski, A. 137
zhensovety 217–18, 220–21
Zhvinklenie, A. 218
Zimmermann, H. 154
Zinoviev, G. 154
Zivkov, T. 15, 122, 129
Zukowski, T. 81
Zuznetsova, L. 20